REST IN PEACE
ROBBED IN PROBATE

THE STORY BEHIND A WIDOW'S $2 BILLION JURY VERDICT AGAINST JPMORGAN CHASE BANK

JO HOPPER

PAIGE TURNER PUBLISHING

Paige Turner Publishing c/o Jo Hopper at 9540 Garland Road, Suite 381-248, Dallas, Texas 75218

Email address: Jo@RIPHopper.com
Website: RIPHopper.com

Printed in the United States of America.

ISBN: 979-8-7305-0171-3

First Trade paperback edition in 2022.

Research Assistant: Lawana Glazer
Courtroom Sketch Artist (Back Cover): Christine Cornell

To all the jurors who sacrifice their days, weeks, and months for little pay to dispense justice while keeping the right to a jury trial alive.

—Jo

Contents

Explanatory Note

This is a true story. It has been reconstructed from court documents, transcripts, videotapes, and audiotapes. It has also been reconstructed from my memory. Wherever possible, I have verified my memory with documentation—lots of it. In those rare cases where it's not possible, I have endeavored to be correct, but memory is not perfect.

JPMorgan Chase Bank, N.A. is also referred to as JPMorgan, JPMorgan Chase, JPMorgan Chase Bank, and Chase Bank.

Many of the law firms in this book have long names. I have listed their full name the first time the firm is mentioned. After that, I have used the shortened versions by which they are known in the industry.

Some event sequencing, locations, and dialogue have been changed for dramatic purposes or, in some instances, to make the essence of this story easier to follow or more intelligible. The names of some real-life participants have been changed or withheld, in whole or in part, and some characters are composites.

Acknowledgments

This book could not have been written and published without the help of many people. I want to thank media attorneys, Henry R. Kaufman in New York, and Peter Kennedy in Austin, Texas. Their long and careful pre-publication review of this manuscript was invaluable.

There were many folks who helped in some way by collecting and sending me all the court-filed documents available to the public. The amount of material was staggering. Thus, I want to thank Kisha Wright with the Dallas County Clerk, Alyssa Montez at the Bexar County District Clerk in San Antonio, Samantha and Andrea with the Bexar County Clerk in San Antonio, Ana Ramon with the La Salle County Clerk in Cotulla, Maria in the 8th District Court of Appeals in El Paso, Denise in the 5th District Court of Appeals in Dallas, MacKenzie with the Johnson County District Clerk in Cleburne, Marilyn Burgess with the Harris County District Clerk in Houston, Karen Sublett Mitchell, Clerk of Court for the United States Northern District of Texas in Dallas, Robert Colwell, Chief Deputy Clerk of the U.S. Bankruptcy Court in the Northern District of Texas in Dallas, Mr. Garza with the Frio County Tax Appraiser's Office in Pearsall, attorney E.L Atkins in Arlington, and Nora Mae Tyler at the Brush Country Museum in Cotulla. To view these documents as well as a cast of characters that you can print out, please visit my website at RIPHopper.com.

Introduction

The book you are about to read is the product of tens of thousands of documents, and untold number of GBs of data, as well as extensive research from the records of my attorneys, federal and state district courts, probate courts, bankruptcy courts, appeals courts, corporate filings, property tax authorities, and governmental agencies. The documents, stacked on top of each other, reach from the ground all the way up to the top of Big Tex's hat at the State Fair in Dallas.

The thousands of dollars I spent for court and governmental records was worth it. Just getting the complete public file from the 5th District Court of Appeals in Dallas cost me $2,569.40 for the four CDs crammed full of documents. Thank God almost everything having to do with this case is in the public domain and available to you and me for research and projects like this book.

So why would I spend all this money and take precious years to write this book and tell the story of what happened to me?

To save you from what I went through.

During my litigation with JPMorgan Chase Bank, N.A., I learned that banking regulations are broken. Chinese Walls, required and designed to separate internal banking departments, fail or are often breached. Conflicts of interest are ignored or waved off. And fiduciary duties are not followed.

To stop this, I contacted the Texas Department of Banking to file a complaint. Because there was pending litigation, the Texas Department of Banking was unable to accept my complaint. Thus, to my knowledge, they did not initiate nor engage in any investigation of JPMorgan Chase Bank, N.A. My lawsuit gave the bank a free pass with their regulators.

Once I obtained a $2 billion jury verdict, I received calls from other JPMorgan Chase Bank, N.A. customers, each with detailed complaints.

I considered this a serious matter of public concern. I understood it could relate to certain governmental proceedings the bank might have now or in the future. Thus, I began my citizen journalist role. In addition to my own direct experiences, I set out to gather more news and information about possible banking abuses.

The first place I looked were in the voluminous records I mentioned above. This included court reporters' transcripts, trial exhibits, video testimony, court motions, rulings, and jury findings. Any legal case that JPMorgan Chase Bank, N.A. has been involved with, including mine, is there, on file, for anyone to read and peruse.

Why?

Because it's a *public record*, as are the depositions filed and all the witnesses who testified in open court. (Attorneys, law students, and legal scholars should study my case in depth. They could learn a lot about the banking industry, probate law, the legal system, and much-needed changes to make it all work more fairly and efficiently.)

After combing through that massive pile, I read all of JPMorgan Chase Bank, N.A.'s SEC filings, and other promotional material from 2008 to the present. I also read comments and interviews from Jamie Dimon, Chairman and CEO of JPMorgan Chase Bank, N.A. I conducted background research on him and his business philosophies. Jamie Dimon, as a public figure, has said and written a lot. It was valuable information.

Finally, I researched other lawsuits involving JPMorgan Chase Bank, N.A. This not only included actions from private individuals but governmental agencies as well. The settlement agreements of those matters, if available, are dry reading but necessary for any respectable journalist.

One case, concluded in November 2020, involved a $250 million fine against JPMorgan Chase Bank, N.A. The Office of the Comptroller of the Currency (OCC) had taken action based on JPMorgan's engaging in unsafe or unsound practices, including those relating to internal controls and internal audit of its fiduciary activities, and for violating 12 C.F.R. § 9.9 Audit of Fiduciary Activities. The OCC found that the bank's risk management practices were deficient, and it lacked a sufficient framework to avoid conflicts of interest. As you will see from reading this book, I experienced much of this wrongdoing firsthand. Here's an excerpt of the OCC's findings:

"(2) For several years, [JPMorgan Chase Bank, N.A.] maintained a weak management and control framework for its fiduciary activities and had an insufficient audit program for, and inadequate internal controls over, those activities. Among other things, [JPMorgan Chase Bank, N.A.] had deficient risk management practices and an insufficient framework for avoiding conflicts of interest.

(3) As a result of the foregoing misconduct, [JPMorgan Chase Bank, N.A.] violated 12 C.F.R. § 9.9 and engaged in unsafe or unsound practices that were part of a pattern of misconduct."

At least the OCC made Jamie Dimon, Chairman and CEO of JPMorgan Chase Bank, N.A., and each member of its Board of Directors physically sign the order.

After seeing this, I made an inquiry to the OCC for details related to this fine. The OCC's reply was "[OCC] declines to comment on any enforcement actions and anything related to a specific bank."

Interesting.

As I kept researching this, I found a violation tracker on Good-JobsFirst.org. From this, I learned that since 2000, JPMorgan Chase has been assessed over $35 billion in penalties, with over 88% being financial offenses.

After conducting all this research and in accordance with my experiences, I concluded that exposing this conduct would be of interest to you—the reader—and the public at large. Ultimately, we all form a community. If we are to live safely and freely in this country—our communities—understanding the information in this book is necessary for us to have educated discussions and debates.

As you read this book, know that Jamie Dimon, Chairman and CEO of JPMorgan Chase Bank, N.A., put into place the people who work in the Estates Department. He is also in charge of the employees involved in my litigation, including several lawyers who worked for his bank. These in-house attorneys watched over this matter and allowed it to continue, or perhaps tried to stop it and were rebuffed by executives higher up. And where was management during all this? Who was supervising these lower-level employees? After this case, at least some of those same in-house lawyers were apparently promoted by JPMorgan. As I said, this is a matter of concern to us all—the public—and JPMorgan Chase Bank, N.A.'s potential clients.

By marching forward with this project, I hope to gather and associate with a group of people, if they exist, who have been equally wronged by big banks. This will allow us to express and pursue our common interests before the banking regulators and, ultimately, Congress. Also, I have mailed a copy of this book to the Senate Banking Committee, the Financial Services Committee of the U.S. House of Representatives, the Office of the Comptroller of the Currency, and the Texas Department of Banking. Perhaps someone at one of those will be interested in JPMorgan's behavior. It only takes one!

But Chairman and CEO Jamie Dimon and JPMorgan Chase Bank, N.A., don't carry all the freight here. Our justice system needs a serious overhaul. It is too easily used by wealthy individuals and companies to flood the courts with aggressive tactics and oceans of motions. It happens in both criminal and civil venues. This conduct ultimately delays and denies justice to the poor and underfunded. And it's a crime no one is sufficiently covering.

Until now.

Here is my email: Jo@RIPHopper.com. As a journalist, I am truly interested in any information, complaint, or news you might have on JPMorgan Chase Bank, N.A., or any other bank. And don't forget: I'm also looking for any ideas on how to improve our justice system.

In summary, thank God we live in a country that affords us the right to speak freely on these vital subjects. It is my sincere wish that this journalistic work informs and engages you. But I have other wishes, too.

I wish for a full review of this matter by Congress as well as federal and state banking regulators. I also wish to motivate and mobilize the public to petition our government for action on these vital issues. But most importantly, I wish for a full discussion of these issues, not silence. We need a free exchange of ideas.

As Supreme Court Justice Louis Brandeis eloquently wrote in *Whitney v. California*, 274 U.S. 357, 377 (1927):

> "To courageous, self-reliant men, with confidence in the power of free and fearless reasoning applied through the processes of popular government, no danger flowing from speech can be deemed clear and

present unless the incidence of the evil apprehended is so imminent that it may befall before there is opportunity for full discussion. If there be time to expose through discussion the falsehood and fallacies, to avert the evil by the processes of education, the remedy to be applied is *more speech, not enforced silence*."

Thanks for joining me on this journey.

PART ONE

Death Leaves a Seed

Prologue

"Every man must do two things alone; he must do his own believing and his own dying."

—Martin Luther

Christmas Eve 2009

The thick snow had been falling for hours. Just south of Oklahoma City, it pelted the windshield of a dark gray Suburban inching its way along the interstate.

"Come on!" Max Hopper said to no one as he increased the Suburban's wiper speed, trying to see the traffic through a cloudy mix of water and snow.

A red light cut through the foggy layer on his windshield. He slammed on the brakes, gripping the wheel as his overloaded vehicle struggled to grip the pavement. Somehow, his car stopped just inches from the Toyota in front of him.

"That was too close," Max muttered, letting out a deep breath. "Much too close."

Seconds later, the Toyota moved forward, and Max followed, keeping at least a few feet between the two cars. Yet, in less than a minute, both vehicles were stopped dead.

What's going on here?

Max waited a little longer before putting the car in park and picking up his phone. When his wife didn't answer, he spoke to the voicemail. "Jo, it's me. I'm stuck on I-35 near Norman. Traffic is completely stopped. Could you pull up the news on the computer and see what's going on? Thanks, sweetheart. Love you."

He set the phone down and stared out the windshield. The wind had turned the snowflakes into white bullets. As soon as one hit the glass and melted, another appeared. Seeing no need for wipers, he turned them off and let the defroster do the heavy lifting.

Max thought about his options and picked up the phone again. "Stephen, it's Dad. I'm going to be a little late for dinner. Something has traffic stopped on I-35 just south of Norman. Call me when you get a chance. Thanks."

He sighed, pressing his forehead against the chilled window. It stung his skin for a second. The snow was so thick he could barely see the car next to him. *A man could freeze to death in weather like this*, he thought.

Glancing at his rearview mirror, he saw presents crammed up to the roof. His three grandchildren were in Oklahoma City, impatiently waiting for him so they could hurry up and have dinner and then tear open their presents. It was his absolute most favorite moment every year, seeing their eyes open wide as they clawed at the paper and ribbons. Having grown up dirt poor, Max lived through his grandchildren, capturing the excitement of Christmas he'd never experienced as a kid.

The car behind him turned off its lights. Max did the same. With nothing else to do, he turned up the volume on *He Touched Me*—Elvis Presley's gospel music album—and leaned the seat back. Then, he sang along.

A BUZZING SOUND woke Max. Blinking his eyes several times, he studied the scene. In forty-five minutes, nothing had changed. The cars around him had not moved one inch. Seeing his phone flashing, he pressed a button. "Hey, Jo. Did you get my message?"

"Hi, Max. Yes. I was at the Christmas Eve church service. Let me get home and see what I can find out."

"That would be great," he said, neglecting to mention the frozen wasteland of traffic that surrounded him. He hoped the conversation would end.

It didn't.

"Is it snowing there?" she asked.

"Yes. It just started." That was a lie.

"Well, let me get home and call you when I have more information."

"That would be great. Love you."

"Love you too."

Max breathed a sigh of relief. Usually, Jo would've started a cross-examination to unearth every detail. If she had, Max would have been forced to lie (even more) or, God forbid, tell her the truth. Neither one was a good option.

As he contemplated all this, his son called back. Max explained about the traffic to Stephen, heard his acknowledgement, and finished. Men were so easy to talk to. Solve the problem and move on. No need for touchy-feely conversation or wasted words. On and off. Max liked that. His computer background was a pattern of binary code. Zero or one. Black or white. It made life simple. Now, he faced two options: act or wait. He chose to wait.

Thirty minutes later, the phone buzzed again. "Hey, Jo, do you have anything?"

"No. I talked to the Oklahoma Highway Patrol and they don't know anything. The computer says the data is unavailable from your location. Is there an eighteen-wheeler anywhere around you?"

Max squinted through the windshield. "Yeah, two cars ahead."

"Why don't you get out and go ask him? He has a radio. They talk to their buddies and know everything."

Max swallowed hard. "I'm not going outside," he croaked.

"Why not? You're not afraid of a little snow?"

"Uhh, it's kind of blowing a little bit. I think I'll stay inside."

Silence.

Here it comes. The Jo I know and love… and dread.

"Max, did you bring a jacket?"

He drew in a deep breath. "Not a heavy one. Only the lightweight leather jacket."

Silence.

"Do you have any water?"

Max lifted his empty coffee mug and swirled it around. "No."

Jo sighed, her voice turning serious. "Okay, any food? Maybe a blanket?"

"Come on, Jo. You know I was just making a simple drive to Stephen's. I didn't plan for any of this."

More silence.

"How bad is it?" she asked sternly.

Max clenched his jaw. The stress was heating up into anger. *If she wants the brutal truth, she can have it. It'll be a relief.* "Okay, it's bad. You should see this wind. It looks like something out of a horror movie. It doesn't even look real. And I have less than half a tank. If this engine shuts off, I'm a goner. Are you happy now?"

Jo's tone didn't change. "Let me call more people. I'll get back to you."

"You do that," Max said, but she had already hung up.

IT HAD BEEN a while since he'd talked to Jo. At least he'd been cycling his engine. He'd gotten the idea from the Toyota in front when its exhaust stopped. He timed their shutdowns and followed their lead, letting his Suburban run for five minutes and then shutting it off for ten. It was the longest he could go before he got too cold. His fingers were already stiff. Whatever was going on ahead, it was probably bad.

At 6:35 p.m., his car had not moved for more than five hours. Jo's name appeared on the phone, and he answered. She cut right to the chase.

"Sweetheart, I talked with at least twenty or more people, including government officials, local police, and the highway patrol management. No one knows anything. Then I called a friend whose husband drives an eighteen-wheeler. His dispatcher told him that I-35 is shut down because of a jackknifed eighteen-wheeler in front of you with no wrecker available tonight. It'll be thirty hours until they can move it because the traffic and safety people are overwhelmed by the storm."

Max rubbed his forehead. "Well, that's bad news."

Jo's voice lowered. "It gets worse. They don't do this too often, but they've put out a blizzard warning—gusts up to sixty miles an hour and almost no visibility. *The Weather Channel* said it's actually a hurricane with snow. Max, tell me the truth. Are you okay?"

"The truth? Yes, I'm okay. But with no food or water, things are gonna get a bit dicey."

"Can you drive anywhere? The median?"

"No. The road is still melting the snow a little bit, but it's really piling up on the medians."

The phone disconnected. Max stared at it before dropping it onto the seat.

I hope that's not the last conversation I have with you.

MAX DRIFTED IN and out of sleep. It was so cold he couldn't tell the difference between dream and reality. Suddenly, a horn honked. He looked ahead and the Toyota was three hundred feet in front of him. Glancing at the dashboard clock, he realized it was a few minutes after midnight. *I might barely survive this.*

The phone buzzed.

"Yeah, Jo."

"The Highway Patrol said the wreck was cleared, so you should be moving."

"I am, thanks." He owed her more than thanks. She had called everyone in Oklahoma except the governor, and only because she couldn't get his phone number. The Highway Patrol was sick of talking to her.

"You need to take Exit 106 and cross over I-35 going west and you'll see Love's Truck Stop. I called them. They said they're open and they have gas."

"Great job, sweetheart! I can almost taste the fresh coffee."

"Now, Max, promise me you'll stay there and sleep in the car if you have to."

"I promise." What he meant was, *I promise, unless I think I can make it to Stephen's house.*

"Okay. I'm going to bed. Love you."

"Love you too." Max hung up the phone and smiled. Then he noticed his dashboard clock. It read 12:30 a.m. He had been stopped on I-35 for more than eleven hours without food or water. At least Jo hadn't asked how he'd been getting rid of the coffee he drank earlier. Some details were best left buried in the snow.

Two DAYS LATER, the dirty Suburban eased to a stop in front of a large mansion. Max opened the door to find Jo running down the steps. Before she could open her mouth, he grabbed and pulled her close, kissing her hard on the lips. "Listen here, sweetheart. If I'm ever in trouble or dying, I want you on my team. You figured out where I was and what to do. Thank you so much!"

Jo kissed him several times.

"Mrs. Hopper. Did you understand what I just said?"

It was January 24, 2010 and Jo no longer stood outside her home holding her loving husband. Instead, fluorescent lights cast an eerie pall over a hallway, the smell of antiseptic seeping from the walls and vinyl tile. "Could you repeat that?" she asked.

The emergency room doctor took a beat and steeled himself. "Your husband has suffered a hemorrhage in his brain stem. I'm sorry to say, he will not survive."

Jo blinked a few times, turning the words over in her mind, thinking about when Max had come home from Oklahoma one month earlier. Then she grabbed the doctor's arm. "Listen, you don't understand. This is Max Hopper. He can't die. He *won't* die! We need to do something. Can we transfer him to another hospital? Or get a second opinion? I'm not letting him die."

The doctor nodded nervously. "Yes. Well… we've just run some brain scans. Let me check on those, and we can talk in a little bit." He hurried away.

Jo's friend Betty lightly touched Jo's shoulder. "Jo, are you okay?"

"I'm fine, Betty." Jo's eyes were sunken and she looked terrified. "We just need to find a way to get Max fixed and back on his feet. I know for sure there is no way he's dying today. No way!"

"Okay," Betty soothed. "Let's go back to the waiting room and put our heads together."

Jo didn't move, so Betty put an arm around her and they headed back down the hallway. "Just walk with me, Jo. We'll get through this."

Chapter One

I had been dealing with stage four non-Hodgkin's lymphoma. Even though I was in remission, the doctors had warned me it might return. That's why I looked at every day as a gift—something to be cherished and enjoyed.

It was January 24, and a pleasant Sunday evening. Since Dallas had lost to the Minnesota Vikings a week earlier and were out of the playoffs, there were no football games we were interested in watching. For once, we had the entire day to ourselves. My husband Max and I relaxed in our North Dallas home after meeting my sister, Judy, and her son and grandchildren at Mi Cocina for lunch. Max was scanning his laptop and I was going over our bills. Keeping busy and working every minute of the day was how we lived; a result of our upbringing.

Max served on boards of directors and advisory boards for quite a few companies that often offered him stock or stock options as compensation for his service, which he readily accepted. His tech advice was so sought-after that it had made us wealthy, although neither of us would ever use that term. The truth was, we never thought we had enough money to feel comfortable.

I looked up from the bill in my hands, peering over my glasses at my husband. "Max, did you order another putter?"

He lowered his laptop screen and stared right at me. "I did. So?"

I liked teasing Max about his "habit." He bought rare and not-so-rare putters, storing them in our warehouse for a book he planned to write about the evolution of putters. I had no idea how many he had. Neither did he. His collection was so extensive that he commissioned a carpenter to build special wooden towers with heavy-duty rollers so he could move them around, not that there was ever a need for it. The carpenter told us he hadn't counted them but thought there were "thousands" of them. For now, those putters (some very expensive and some not at all) were doing nothing but gathering dust.

I stared at his scowl before smiling and turning back to the bills. He knew I had no cause to complain. He worked hard and traveled frequently to board meetings. I guess I teased him so much about collecting putters because he never used any of them when he played golf. Still, for some reason, those purchases made him happy, and that made me happy. So, I didn't really complain about it.

Out of the corner of my eye, I saw Max rubbing his temple for the second time. "What's the matter, sweetheart?" I asked. "Do you have a headache?"

"Yeah," he replied. "It's nagging, but I'll live."

"Do you want me to get you a Starbucks?" This was our nightly routine—one Max had started when I'd gone through chemo. As a reward for making it through the day, Max would pick up a latte for me every evening and we would share a small lemon pound cake. Over the eighteen weeks I endured chemotherapy, we sipped on our coffee and worked for several more hours before shutting down and going to bed.

"That would be great, Jo. Thanks."

I grabbed my keys and went to the garage, where my five-year-old Suburban was parked. It had survived Oklahoma's Christmas Eve Blizzard of 2009, as they now called it. I started it up, carefully backing out of the garage and down the driveway, then cruised past the guard at the main gate. I gave him a little wave.

A few minutes later, I arrived at Starbucks. As I stood in line, it hit me that Max had rubbed his temples several times. I thought about it as I sat at a table, waiting for the barista to call my name. *Maybe I should say something when I get back*, I thought.

By the time our drinks were ready, I had decided against saying anything. Instead, I called my friend and Max's assistant Betty to come over and share her thoughts.

Betty arrived at the house ten minutes later. Max was in his favorite chair in the den and hadn't yet touched his coffee. "Hi," she said to Max.

"Hi, Betty," he said as he got up and went to the bathroom. When he finished, he lightly bumped his head on a cabinet in the hall before returning to his chair.

Betty and I were sitting at the breakfast table watching him. She leaned over and said, "You're right, something's off."

Max kept rubbing his temples, ignoring his coffee. When I saw him rub his head yet again, I decided to speak up. "Do you want me to call the doctor?"

"Oh, Jo," he snapped. "Stop fussing over me. You're stressing me out."

Betty raised her eyebrows at me. I let his comment roll off my back. After twenty-eight years of marriage, I knew how Max operated. He was industrial-strength tough. Even though he was seventy-five years old, he could out-work almost anyone. He had a fire that burned all day long, or as long as the job required. He had always worked through illnesses and pain, and obviously concluded that ignoring them was the best medicine. So far, he'd been right.

Betty and I continued to study him and I wondered what I should do. His face looked strange, almost as if he'd lost control of his expression. I could see his hands running over the papers in his lap, moving slowly with no purpose. Something was definitely wrong.

I grabbed my cell phone and called his son Stephen, who is a psychiatrist. "There's something wrong with your father," I told him. "I don't know what it is. Will you call Max and talk to him? I think I need to call 9-1-1 for an ambulance and take him to the hospital, but he says nothing is wrong."

Stephen hung up and called Max's cell phone. Betty answered and held it out to him. "Max, it's your son, Stephen. He would like to talk to you."

"No," he said, shaking his head. But the word barely escaped his frozen lips. He couldn't talk.

Betty handed me the phone. "Stephen, I'm calling 9-1-1."

I could hear Stephen's answer on the other end even as my heart pounded in my ears. "Okay. I'm leaving for Dallas now."

It seemed like an eternity until the ambulance arrived. Max was still sitting in his chair, barely responding to anything. The paramedics examined him and immediately decided to rush him to the hospital. Betty and I were told we should join Max at the emergency room. As we raced to Betty's car, a strange feeling came over me, as if Max might not make it. Then I remembered he was invincible and could overcome anything.

Everything's going to be okay.

We took off from the house, leaving the ambulance behind us. We assumed the ambulance would pass us at some point but we didn't see it. I jumped out and ran inside to the emergency room, letting Betty park the car. I was a wreck. The waiting was hard.

Finally, a nurse appeared and asked me to come back. What I saw took my breath away. Max was on a gurney hooked up to a respirator. A doctor stood nearby and quickly left. I looked around the gurney and saw bottles, syringes, and trash scattered everywhere. The tables that had held the neatly arranged instruments and supplies were in disarray. I could still feel the fury and desperation as the doctors had worked frantically to save Max's life. It hung in the air over my husband. I hurried to his side and held his hand but he didn't move. My confidence in Max's invincibility was starting to waver.

I walked to the front desk and grabbed onto it to steady myself, closing my eyes and praying to God that I'd see Max again— alive and conscious. The words just slipped out of my mouth. "Please don't leave me behind. I'm supposed to go first."

A nurse touched my arm and handed me a plastic bag. "Here are your husband's clothes, Mrs. Hopper."

I nodded numbly as I took the bag but my stomach was twisting into knots. This looked extremely serious.

IT WAS MONDAY, the day after Max had been rushed to the hospital. Stephen and Laura (Max's children) stood next to me in a hospital room. Laura hopped on a flight from Kansas City and had just arrived. Stephen had driven from Oklahoma City and arrived sometime in the early morning.

We stared at Max. He had tubes coming out of every part of his body. It looked like a scene from a horror movie, except it was real.

"They're going to do another brain scan at three," I told Laura. "Then we'll know more."

"What happens next?" she asked Stephen.

"They ran a brain scan last night, so I'm fairly certain the outcome isn't going to change."

Laura put her hand to her mouth, stifling a cry. I was so emotionally overwhelmed I didn't know what to do. Then a doctor walked into the room. He introduced himself and got right to the point. "As you know, we will do another brain scan this afternoon. In the meantime, I want to discuss organ donation. Have you considered it?"

I was shocked at this because it seemed a foreshadowing of what was to come. The three of us had a brief conversation and decided Max would want to help others, so we agreed to it.

"Okay," said the doctor. "I'll have a nurse prepare the forms and get them ready *if* we need them."

The doctor left just as Max's cousin arrived. Her husband hovered behind her.

"How's he doing?" she asked.

Stephen gave her the prognosis. "He's not going to make it."

She made some small talk before telling us she planned to sell the property to her brother who lives nearby and put the proceeds into his aunt's estate.

I stared at her, stunned. Five months earlier, Max's aunt had died, leaving a house in Pollok, Texas, to Max. It was his grandparents' original home and it was very special to him. His cousin was the executor of his aunt's estate and had not yet transferred the property to him. How in the world could this woman bring up such an inappropriate subject?

Before I could speak, Stephen pulled me aside, his face twisted with anger. "Ask her to leave. Right now!"

I didn't blame him. I was just as angry as he was.

"Let's go outside and discuss this," I said, grabbing her and her husband. I wanted Max's children to have time alone with their dad.

At noon, Stephen and Laura left to get some fresh air. I took the opportunity to move closer to Max. I had read doctors were unsure if people who were brain dead could still hear and process information. I sure hoped they could.

"Do you remember the first time we went out on a date?" I whispered as I held his hand. "Twenty minutes in, you started crying right there at the table. You told me it was your wedding anniversary, but you couldn't celebrate it since you were divorced. I guess most women would have steered clear of you. But not me. I saw a loyal, sensitive, and caring man. Definitely someone who warranted another date."

I let that soak in with the beeping and glowing lights all around us. Even though I got no response, I kept talking. "I was so proud of you when the Smithsonian Institute said you were worthy of having your oral history recorded. And the Infomart Technology Hall of Fame was the icing on the cake. From nothing to everything we have, I'm so grateful someone else let you go for me to find. I'm just sorry it's not me lying here. I was supposed to die first. Remember?"

I felt tears dripping down my cheeks.

"Please wake up, sweetheart. I'm praying for a miracle."

Hours later, the doctors wheeled Max away to have his brain scanned. I held his hand as far as they allowed. Then, Stephen, Laura, and I went to the waiting room to ask God for a miracle.

It didn't come.

The doctors declared him brain dead. My brilliant, loving husband would never speak to me again. We were robbed of being able to say good-bye. We couldn't hold each other and say, "I love you." It was a bitter end to more than 28 years of marriage.

After a while, Stephen and I left the hospital. This gave Laura some time alone with her dad. Beyond distraught, I was somehow able to drive home to shower and get refreshed so I could come back and spend one last night with Max. He was on the ventilator until the next day when they would recover his organs and tissues.

Our good friends Eula and Bill had driven in from Houston and came directly to the hospital to see what they could do to help. I asked if they would go to our house and take care of Blair, our Scottie terrier, and anything else that was necessary. When I got there, I found them dealing with the crush of people coming by and asking questions. Betty was also there. She'd brought over some food.

I had no appetite and stood in the kitchen while Eula welcomed someone at the front door. Betty was taking the covers off the food she brought and mentioned something about Max's business accounts. "Do you have money to pay for the funeral?" she asked.

"Yes, assuming I can get to it."

"Why can't you get to it?"

I let out a slow breath. "Max and I saw a *60 Minutes* report. It explained that when a person dies, the bank freezes all their assets. The survivor can't even buy groceries unless they have a bank account or credit cards in their name."

"Do you have a credit card in your name?"

"Yes, but as for the money to pay the bills, if the bank finds out, I may be stuck."

"You should call a lawyer," Betty advised.

I thought for a moment. "A few years ago, I hired this attorney, Tom Cantrill, to do my will. He has an excellent reputation in Dallas. I'll call him tomorrow morning and schedule an appointment."

I RETURNED TO the hospital to spend one last night with my husband of twenty-eight years. Also, I'd learned that the ambulance had not passed us because Max's heart stopped in our driveway. The paramedics had worked feverishly to restart it. Once that was accomplished, they raced to the hospital.

The bag with Max's clothes was another horror. Each garment had been cut and sliced open. Vomit and bloodstains dotted the fabric. I left them in the bag and sealed it tight, delaying a decision on what to do with them.

In the room with Max, I stayed by his side, talking to him and God, and praying for a miracle. Once again, my prayers went unanswered.

The next morning, I left the hospital, still numb, and climbed into my car. I found Tom Cantrill's number on my phone and called him.

"Tom Cantrill speaking."

I took a deep breath. "Tom, this is Jo Hopper. I need to set up a time to visit with you. The sooner the better."

"Sure. What's the matter?"

"My husband Max has been declared brain dead. They're taking him this afternoon to recover his organs for donation."

"Oh, I'm so sorry." He paused. "Let's see… I can fit you in this Thursday at ten in the morning. How's that?"

"That's fine, Tom. Thanks."

Before I hung up, I heard him whisper, "You're not even waiting until the body is cold."

That stung me. *How could a lawyer say that to a client?*

"Thanks again," I said brusquely and hung up. I wanted Mr. Cantrill to know I'd heard his hurtful words.

I couldn't believe what had just happened. I drove home and told Betty and Eula about the conversation.

"You can't use that lawyer," Eula said.

"Yeah, she's right," Betty agreed. "Don't do it, Jo."

With very little sleep or food, I sat down at my kitchen table and thought about Tom Cantrill's comment. I rubbed my eyes and wiped new tears from them, and then I came to a decision. "We're going to do whatever we would've done if Max were alive. When this is over, we'll find an attorney to tell us what to do. If we've made mistakes, we'll fix them."

"Are you going to cancel your appointment?" Betty asked me.

"No. I will not show up for the appointment. I don't want to ever talk to that man again!"

AT THREE THAT afternoon, I stood by Max's side with my hand on his shoulder, squeezing lightly. Our final moments together. As they wheeled him into surgery, I walked along, holding his hand until we reached the elevators.

"Goodbye, sweetheart. I love you." Those were my last words to him just as the doors closed. I was now a widow with a broken heart, and no idea that a freight train of misery was heading my way.

Chapter Two

"Settling the estate won't cost you a cent."

—Kal Grant, Wealth Advisor
Private Wealth Management
JPMorgan Chase Bank, N.A.

Before Max's organ donation surgery, I had made some arrangements by phone with a local funeral home to recover his body after the surgeons were done. They urged me to come to their showroom and complete the funeral arrangements. With nothing keeping us at the hospital, I asked Stephen and Laura to go with me. I wanted their input on everything, since it was their dad we were going to bury.

Audrey, the funeral director, showed us all the options. The three of us discussed what might be appropriate. It seemed to me that every time I said I liked something, Laura didn't. If I didn't like something, she did. It was odd. The more I listened to her, the more I was certain that something other than her father's death was bothering her.

The thirty-minute process took three hours, during which Stephen was very quiet. To get everything over with, I agreed to whatever they wanted. The only matter left to discuss was the burial location. We were driven all over the cemetery and shown several good sites. Unable to decide, I suggested that we go back to the house and discuss it. They agreed.

When we returned, our home was full of guests. Eula and Bill were still there, along with Betty and some new arrivals—Chelan and Bill, and our neighbors Charles and Madelaine. They were all close friends. Of course, Stephen's wife and daughter, along with Laura's daughter, were there. If it hadn't been such a sad occasion, it could have been a Thanksgiving or Christmas Day celebration with family, food, and fun.

We sat in the den talking about our trip to the cemetery. I remarked how expensive it was. "I've never been involved in making funeral arrangements before. It caught me off-guard."

"I'm surprised you didn't consider cremation," Madelaine said. Her remark sparked another round of conversation about cremation versus burial. I think it was either Stephen or Laura who then said, "Jo, you should call the funeral home and change the arrangements. We want to cremate Dad. And let's have a Celebration of Life ceremony rather than a religious funeral."

I just nodded and pulled out my phone. When the funeral director answered, I explained the changes.

"Okay," she said. "I'll take him out of embalming and move him to cold storage."

I held the phone away from my ear, horrified by the statement. *Is it me or everyone else?*

A few minutes later, I slipped upstairs and called her back. "Can you remove a lock of Max's hair before cremation?"

"Sure," she replied. "How much do you need?"

"Just enough to put into a locket."

"No problem. I'll have it delivered to you with the ashes."

I went back and mingled with the guests. During a break, I found myself alone with Stephen. He had looked through the medical records and believed the two blood thinners Max was taking had caused him to bleed into his brain. "That explains the symptoms you and Betty saw right before the paramedics arrived."

I nodded and decided to venture onto another subject. "You know, Stephen, your father didn't have a will."

"Yes, he did," Stephen replied. "I'm sure of it."

That took me aback for a moment because I had been urging Max to draft a will for many years. The previous summer, I had pulled Stephen aside and told him Max didn't have a will. "If you have a chance to talk to your father about it, you should," I advised.

"Did you talk to him about it?" I asked now.

"Yes," he said confidently. "I talked to Dad, and he told me he'd taken care of it."

I waited for a few seconds, studying his demeanor, then said, "I think your dad lied so he wouldn't have to discuss it with you." Stephen's expression was unchanged. "But if there's a will, I'll find it," I assured him. He nodded, giving me a look that said there would definitely be a will.

WE SET THE memorial service for Saturday afternoon, four days after our discussion. It was held in the hotel ballroom at Max's golf club, which was able to hold several hundred guests.

There were nearly five hundred guests, and I found myself in the lobby greeting them. Unfortunately, I was out there too long. When someone rushed over and told me the service was starting, I dropped everything and hurried to a side door, finding a seat next to Betty.

"You should be with the children," Betty whispered. "They're sitting just across the aisle."

She was right. I got up and walked across the aisle, awkwardly looking for a seat. Unfortunately, they had not saved one for me. I found two empty seats next to Stephen's wife, Barbara, and sat down. To my surprise, no one said a word to me or acknowledged my presence.

I must pause here to explain that because I was so numb, I didn't add up all these incidents until much later. At the time, I just assumed Max's children were hurting like I was, so I brushed all of it off.

There were a lot of great speakers. One of them was Bob Crandall, the former CEO of American Airlines. As he talked fondly of Max, I remembered the time Bob had shanghaied Max in the DFW Airport. Max had left American Airlines for Bank of America. For more than a year, American Airlines had been begging Max to come back and run Sabre, the airline's reservation system but Max had refused their offers.

We were living in Millbrae just south of San Francisco, very close to the airport. On a business trip to England that connected through Dallas, Bob met Max at the Admirals Club and offered him the moon plus Mars to come back. The problem was we both loved living in California, and Max loved working for Bank of America. We had discussed this many times and decided there was no way we would return to Dallas. But this time, Bob offered a deal that Max couldn't refuse. It would allow him to retire in nine years when he was sixty. He said yes, and Bob had his man.

When Max saw me, he said in a low but firm voice, "Don't ask me any questions, but we're moving back to Dallas."

I couldn't understand what had changed Max's mind until he told me the story. I remember thinking Bob Crandall was a man who wouldn't take no for an answer. So we moved back to Dallas, bringing our extensive collection of Napa Valley wines with us. We would miss San Francisco and the surrounding areas, but Max was up to the new challenge and delivered for American Airlines.

Many other people spoke at the memorial about my dear husband—close business associates, good friends, and of course, Stephen and Laura. When it was over, there was a lovely reception where everyone mingled and shared memories. As I was leaving, the staff presented me with the bill. It was a sizable amount, but Max was worth every penny. I paid it with my credit card, thinking nothing more of it.

The next morning, Stephen and Laura said their goodbyes and left with their families. This gave me a chance to wander around the house. All I saw was a great deal of emptiness. Of course, at that moment, I had absolutely no idea what dark future lay ahead of me.

MY FIRST ORDER of business was to find a good attorney. After soliciting recommendations from friends and neighbors, I narrowed the list to four and set up appointments with each one. First on the list was Keith Brennan. I asked Betty and C.J., our CPA (whose name is Jane, but everyone calls her "Calamity Jane," thus C.J. for short.), to join me at our home on Robledo Drive, to be an extra set of eyes and ears. Since I had little experience with attorneys and was living in a fog, I didn't fully trust myself.

The meeting went smoothly until I told him that I believed my husband had died without executing a will.

"Okay," he said, eyebrows raised. "That means he has died *intestate*."

"Is that a good thing?" I asked.

"It is for Max's children. They'll inherit all of your husband's wealth."

When he saw that I was confused, he explained Texas probate law. Apparently, the state of Texas provides a default will for those who don't create and execute one. In marriages involving blended families with children who are not the progeny of the surviving spouse, everything goes to the deceased's children. However, that *everything* only includes Max's 50% share of our community property. I would retain my 50% of our community assets. It was nice to learn I wouldn't be strapped for cash.

We covered a few more items, including his $550 per hour billing rate.

After Keith left, I said, "Boy, that's a shock."

"Yeah," Betty said. "Maybe you'll find a will."

"Do you think there is one?" Calamity Jane asked.

"No, I don't. We expected me to die first. Besides, Max hated thinking about death. I'll be shocked if we find a signed one."

Betty had a thought. "Maybe another lawyer will have a different opinion. You know, like the weather. One says it will rain tomorrow and the other says it won't."

"Maybe you're right," I said. But I was pretty sure Keith knew what he was talking about.

My next stop was Mike Graham's office. Betty accompanied me for moral support. He confirmed what Keith had said, using a whiteboard to better explain everything while adding more details.

"Here's a big circle of yours and Max's assets. Let's pretend it comes to $1 million." He drew a line down the middle of the circle. "This left half is yours—$500,000. No one can take that from you. It's yours no matter what. Period."

He wrote my husband's name in the right half. "This side is Max's half of the community property—$500,000. He has total discretion to decide where it goes. And, by using the Texas default will, he decided to leave everything to his children."

"At least that will make the probate part easy," I said.

He nodded. "Jo does not receive any of Max's 50% community property. If he owned any separate property, you'll get one-third and his children the remainder."

I told Mike about the home in Pollok that his aunt had left him, leaving out the part about his cousin's attempt to sell it. (A few days after his cousin's hospital visit, she sent an email that read, "I talked to the estate's lawyer, and he says that the property will go to Max's estate.")

"That home in Pollok is separate property," Mike said. "You'll get a one-third life estate in it."

"What's that?" I asked.

"You'll have the right to occupy that house until you die. Max's children will be unable to sell it without your permission until after your death."

"What about my house, the one I live in?"

"Max owned half of it. So, his half goes to them."

A silence enveloped us. I didn't know what else to say.

Mike could see the confusion on my face. "This means that you and Max's children will be partners in your home. They will have to pay half the mortgage and insurance while you will pay all the interest on the mortgage, property taxes, and utilities. The maintenance of the house will be your responsibility. However, if some capital improvements or repairs are needed, you will pay half and Max's children will pay the other half. And, like the Pollok property, you can live there for life because it's in the state constitution."

Mike explained that someone had to be the estate's executor, and under the probate code, I was the designated person. He continued, "The executor is basically the CEO of Max's estate. He or she makes decisions on selling or distributing the assets. Trust me, you want to be the executor."

Betty and I felt comfortable with Mike Graham. He was like a law professor educating us. Then he asked me about our assets.

"We have some bank accounts and investment accounts, but Max took a lot of stock and stock options from companies," I told him. "He served on their boards of directors or advisory boards. I have no idea what all that adds up to."

"Don't worry," he said. "A team of people will comb through everything in your house and find your records, then audit them to determine an amount."

"They'll go through my house?" I asked, stunned. "Max and I are very private people. That feels like an invasion of privacy."

"Yes, it is an invasion of your privacy. However, it's the Independent Administrator's job to inventory everything. I'm sure Max's children won't waive that. What kind of relationship do you have with them?"

I didn't hesitate to respond. "It's good. I've known them since they were seventeen and twenty-three. Of course, I'm not their mother, but they won't fight me on any of this. Max always told me not to worry about not having a will. 'Stephen and Laura will always be there and stand with you,' he told me. 'You'll be a team and work together. You'll see.'"

Mike smiled. "That's the optimum scenario, and I hope it's the case. It will save all of you money and aggravation."

When we left his office, I was sure I would hire him to rewrite my will. It just felt right.

Our next appointment was with Henry Steele. He was an older man with litigation scars all over his body from decades of courtroom battles. He repeated everything we had already heard. Then he went in a different direction.

"You know the saying where there's a will, there's a way? In my business, where there's a will, there's a lawsuit."

"We don't have a will," I reminded him. "So, no worries there."

"Okay," he said, smirking. "Let me put it this way. I'm like a fortune-teller. I can see the future."

I glanced at Betty.

"A fortune-teller?" I said, confused for what seemed like the hundredth time since Max's death. "What kind of *fortune* do you see in my *future*?"

The room seemed to darken as he answered me. "You know the movie where that kid says, 'I see dead people?' Well, I see dead people who are glad they're dead and living people who wish they were dead. I see armies of lawyers and years of litigation. Everyone will have a different lawyer—brother against brother. Sister against sister. Step-mother against stepchild. Heirs against lawyers. It's going to be bad because death is the perfect time for past grievances to be aired. The probate court provides an excellent gladiatorial arena where the heirs can get in there and pull swords on each other to pay that a-hole back for all the pain they've caused them. Or 'that wrinkle cream you gave me for my birthday when I was only thirty-two' or 'sticking me with the dinner check at The French Room while you went to the restroom.' It's payback time, baby!'"

He sounded too gleeful and I felt myself tensing up. "Max's children would never do that," I assured him. "They don't want to hurt me, nor do I want to hurt them."

"I hear you, but they won't be the ones hurting you because that sword will be in their lawyer's hand. He'll be carving you up like a Thanks-giving turkey. Or, actually, he'll be carving up your assets. But the good news is that once you're broke, he'll stop. *Usually*."

I was dumbfounded listening to this nonsense. It sounded so unpro-fessional. "So, how do I avoid all that?" I asked him hesitantly, hoping to see his endgame.

"What you need is a family settlement agreement where all sides give a little. You know, fish or cut bait. Go into court with an agreement, and you'll squash any possible litigation. Believe me, you'll be better off. More than you can imagine." He rubbed an imaginary scar on his forehead. It seemed he'd been knocked around so much that I wondered if something had come loose.

Before we left, he guaranteed me that Max's children would sue me if I were the executor. "They will," he said in a booming voice. "They always do."

Back in the car, Betty and I discussed what we'd just heard.

"I don't think he knows what he's talking about," I blurted out.

"I agree," Betty said. "He's not the one for you. He's trying to scare you into a solution he just happens to provide."

I shook my head. "All that sword and gladiator stuff is ridiculous. It's lawyers like him that give the profession a bad name. Let's move on."

Still, he didn't seem like a greedy lawyer trying to take my money. He claimed he'd be helping me to save it. I wondered if he really could see the future. But on second thought, I decided he was trying to scare me, using fear as a sales tactic. So, I moved on.

We were worn out when we saw the last lawyer of the day, Ron Cresswell. He didn't add anything new, but I told him we'd seen other lawyers and their hourly rates were too high. He agreed to modify his hourly rate to $300.

"The estate can hire me and pay my fees. You can make that happen when the court appoints you executor. Then I can help you through the entire process."

That sounded great. The other lawyers were charging a minimum of $500 per hour.

Like Mike Graham, we were happy with Ron Cresswell. He was pleasant and down-to-earth, occasionally letting loose a boisterous laugh. He seemed to love his job and wanted to help people. I thought he was perfect to represent the estate and was certain Stephen and Laura would be thrilled with the lower hourly rate.

Ron made another comment that made me like him. "Wrapping up this estate will be easy. We just collect everything and divide it by two—half for you and half for the estate of Max D. Hopper. Then the estate will be divided in two to distribute to Max's children. As for the personal items like all those putters Max collected, it's even simpler. A piece of paper is generated that gives title to you and your stepchildren as joint tenants. The same thing is done for the wine, cars, everything that can't easily be divided up. Since you have no debt other than a mortgage, a couple of months in probate and it's over. Just make sure there are no signed wills because any will you find is almost guaranteed to give you more than you're getting now, which is almost zero of Max's estate. You have nowhere to go but up, so look hard for one."

I was aware of four possible wills Max had worked on. He had different attorneys drafting this and that but had never been able to sign one. Perhaps he'd wanted to leave everything to his children and thought I would be upset. Or maybe he'd wanted to leave me something and felt they would be upset. Regardless, I set my mind to finding an executed will, if one existed.

LOOKING FOR A will turned out to be a tall mountain to climb. Because I'd been sick for so long, I had two years' worth of files piled high in my office. After weeks of diligent searching, with Betty combing through everything at Max's office and me reviewing everything at home, we didn't uncover an executed will.

Calamity Jane worked with me to put together a rough dollar figure on our assets. As for the stock options, we had to guess at their value. Truthfully, they were close to worthless unless the companies either went public or were bought or merged with another company. While I was knee-deep in paperwork generating an inventory, I received a tip from Chelan and Bill about JPMorgan Chase.

"They have a Private Wealth Management Group," Bill told me. "It's kind of like a first-class concierge service for folks with a high net worth. Kal Grant is the contact person. Why don't you call her and see what they can do to help you?"

I trusted their advice and made the call. A few days later, Kal Grant arrived at my house, making a sparkling impression. She was very professional and knowledgeable, and she was a lawyer.

"It's always possible in these matters that the executor gets sued," Kal said. "That's where we can add value."

Kal explained that JPMorgan Chase Bank would stand between Max's children and me, "insulating you from any liability." And they had the expertise about the proper procedures. "We'll tell you what's legal and what's not legal. It can be very confusing, Jo. You need a professional standing beside you to be the middleman, the bad guy when tough decisions have to be made."

I liked everything Kal had to say until she explained the percentage JPMorgan Chase charged. Doing a quick calculation, I figured out it was at least $160,000.

"That's a lot of money," I said. "The kids will never go for that."

"Don't worry about the cost," she said. "You're not going to pay any of it. The estate pays the costs, and you're not part of Max's estate."

"So, your services are free to me?"

"Yes! Settling the estate won't cost you a cent. There's no reason for you not to agree to JPMorgan Chase serving as the agent to the estate."

After she had left, I glanced through the JPMorgan Chase literature and filed it away. To me, it wasn't a good option because Max was right. His children would stand by me and work this out. There would be no lawsuits or stupid haranguing over our assets.

And there was another reason. Max and I had worked too hard and saved our money to let the kids waste $160,000. That was $80,000 Laura could use to put her children through college or Stephen could use to expand his practice. With me not charging a cent to be the executor and Ron Cresswell's reduced $300 per hour fee, it was a no-brainer. I decided not to tell Stephen and Laura about the JPMorgan Chase offer.

ON MARCH 6, 2010, barely a month after Max's death, I scheduled a meeting in our home with Stephen and Laura. Ron Cresswell was there with paperwork to make me the executor. All we needed to do was explain the procedure and get the children's signatures on it. Then, in a few months, we could be done with the asset reallocation.

Stephen was 53 years old and Laura was 48. Both had good jobs and were doing well. Still, I offered to arrange and pay for tickets for them to fly in. Only Laura took me up on my offer; she flew in from Kansas City. Stephen drove down that day from Oklahoma City—at least that's what I thought.

Betty picked up Laura at Love Field and they arrived just as Stephen did. I glanced to the heavens and hoped Max would be proud of what we were all about to do.

I started the meeting by introducing attorney Ron Cresswell and explaining his role. Ron explained the probate process in Texas. Then, I told them in general about our assets.

"As you may know, I was responsible for taking care of our finances over the past twenty-eight years. With our accountant's help, we have put together a very rough and preliminary figure of our holdings." They said nothing, waiting for the figure. "It comes to roughly $14 million. That puts Max's estate at $7 million." I let them digest that amount, calculate in their minds the $3.5 million they would each be inheriting.

I continued. "We haven't found an executed will yet, so this must be handled as an intestate matter."

Uncharacteristically, Stephen said nothing. I assumed from my previous conversation that he would be shocked to learn Max had no will. Instead, his face was dark and serious.

I went on to explain how our wealth was splintered. We had a single capital hedge fund, which contained half of our assets. Some of our money was in brokerage accounts and venture capital funds. And lastly, there was plenty of stock and stock options in public and private companies.

Ron took over. "Jo negotiated a reduced rate of $300 per hour. That will save you a lot of money." He slid some papers to Stephen and Laura. "There are actions that need to be taken now. By signing this, Jo will be made the executor and we can get this matter resolved in a few months at a minimal cost. Then, you can get on with your lives and your new wealth."

Neither Stephen nor Laura touched the documents. Laura spoke first. "We want an outside person to be in charge. We don't want you to be in charge. We think it will ruin any relationship we have with you."

Before I could catch my breath, Stephen said his first words. "We want to hire an outside company to handle all this."

I couldn't believe what I was hearing, especially after learning how much a company like JPMorgan Chase charged. "Do you know what that will cost you?" I asked, dumbfounded.

Without a beat, Laura blurted out, "We don't care how much it costs! We don't want you to touch *our* money."

I blinked several times as I had an out-of-body experience. I wanted to say, "I've been touching *your* money for the last twenty-eight years."

Ron held up his hands. "Look, there are decisions that need to be made. Things are coming due. Jo, let me talk to them about all of this. Can you give us a few minutes?"

I slid back my chair and somehow made it to my office, shaking. As I replayed the last few minutes, I realized the children were already up to speed on all this. They had formulated a game plan going in, and I hadn't been included in any of it. Their refusal to sign those papers would leave me with a tough choice to make. I could oppose them and go to court where I was sure to be appointed the executor, or I could let them use an outside company. Images of them suing me as the executor flashed through my mind. I prayed we weren't headed off a cliff, because right now, it looked like the car was pointed in that direction.

When I returned to the table, Ron had finished talking. I noticed Stephen's expression had turned to anger.

"Who is paying Max's assistant, Betty Reynolds?" he asked.

"Not me," I replied. "I have no authority to pay anyone. I do know she's still working at Max's office on LBJ Freeway because I can't fire her."

Stephen shot back, "Who's paying Ron Cresswell?"

I looked at Ron. "No one," I said. "He's not under contract. He's here today to help us get started until we have an executor."

Stephen glanced at him. "I think Ron is a fine attorney... for you. We will get our own attorneys to make sure our interests are protected."

Attorneys?! I thought. *What interests?* He and Laura would receive 100% of Max's estate. What more did they want? Was it possible that attorney Henry Steele really *could* see the future?

Before I could respond, Laura cleared her throat. "Jo, we're surprised that we will receive less money than you will. I know Dad would've wanted us each to receive the same share. I think we can decide what to do on our own, regardless of what the court says. We don't have to follow the law."

I knew my mouth was hanging open, but I didn't reply to her statements. Instead, I thought about our interactions in the last month. It all added up.

Is it possible they only talked to me all these years when they needed something?

The meeting ended right then, with Stephen abruptly leaving. I called Betty, who I'd asked to watch my Scottie, Blair, so she wouldn't interrupt us, to let her know Betty could bring her home. When Betty pulled up, I took Blair inside before joining Laura in Betty's car. We headed for Love Field where Laura's return flight home awaited. I was not looking forward to this.

As the miles ticked off, I couldn't stop thinking about where this was heading.

Can I get us all on track, to a place we're all happy with the outcome?

Laura gave me an opening. "You know," she said, "it's too bad there isn't a will that provides something for the grandchildren. They're left out of all this."

"Don't worry," I said soothingly. "I'm redoing my will and putting the grandchildren in it. They'll be well taken care of."

"Jo, we don't want *your* money!"

"Okay," I managed. It was important to keep this conversation on an even keel. I drew in a breath and added, "I understand your feelings." That was a lie. I couldn't understand anything she was saying or why she was doing this. This wasn't the same person I'd known for the last twenty-eight years. It was like an alien had come down from Mars and invaded her body.

Letting Betty handle the small talk, I said nothing more during the remainder of the trip. As Laura exited the car and walked away, her back toward me, I had a thought that rocked me to my soul. *Will I ever see my grandchildren again?*

Chapter Three

"If you're stupid enough to buy it, you'll pay the price for it one day."

—Jamie Dimon, Chairman & CEO
JPMorgan Chase Bank, N.A.

Whenever a person suffers the death of a loved one, attending grief counseling should be a mandatory requirement. I know I needed it. Crying and listening to others cry in a faith-based setting helped me work some things out. I can't say I felt good after each session, but I felt something and that was the most important thing. Having feelings means you're alive. And talking about your feelings helps, even if it doesn't seem so at the time.

After I met with Max's children, I attended a session and went home to an empty bed. I missed Max so much that I genuinely wished I would've died first. Hopefully, I would start feeling better.

The meeting with Stephen and Laura kept my mind wide awake. The more I thought about it, the clearer it became: They were pulling away from me. It seemed like they didn't trust me, like they believed I was hiding something. The entire probate situation had the potential to explode. Then I received an email from Stephen.

His well-educated writings were usually thoughtful and comprehensive. This email was no different. As I read it several times, a few things stood out. First up were his feelings toward Max.

"I would have never willingly put myself in this position and I am sad and angry that Dad has created this situation for all of us."

That was the anger I'd seen seeping out of him. I thought about how hard Max had worked and how much money we had given both of them. Now, all that goodwill was worth nothing.

The next topic in Stephen's email truly shocked me. He mentioned how business and family interests rarely mixed well. Then, I reached the big news.

"The only arrangement in regard to administrating Dad's estate that satisfies this for me is the assignment of a corporate independent administrator. My preference would be to hire JPMorgan Chase."

I couldn't believe it! Of all the banks and independent companies providing services like this, he'd picked JPMorgan Chase, a bank I had just met with. It was almost too hard to believe this was a coincidence.

I sent Stephen's email to my new attorney, Mike Graham. Because of his professor-like explanations and easygoing demeanor, I felt comfortable having Mike represent my interests. He read it and pointed out several things.

First, Mike urged me to use the probate code to get appointed as Max's estate administrator instead of JPMorgan Chase. He promised it was a guaranteed thing: "JPMorgan Chase wants to get all of this money in their bank—yours and Max's children's—so they can 'invest' it. This allows them to suck 1.5% per year off you, regardless of whether or not they make money. It's a pretty sweet deal, *for them.*"

Next, he prepared me for what he claimed was the likely outcome. "The second Max's children each see $3.5 million in their bank account is the last second your contact information will be in their cell phones. You can take that to the bank—and preferably not JPMorgan Chase."

I hoped he was wrong about that.

I told him I'd consider it and moped around the house alone, totally bereft and missing Max. Then I received Laura's email. She started off nicely before cutting to the chase, saying that the situation we were in didn't seem fair. She believed *fairness* should be the solution to our future problems. Yet, she went in a different direction than her older brother.

"I am disappointed that it appears we are following the 'legal path' instead of Dad's path."

Dad's path? I thought. *What are you talking about?*

She and Stephen were getting 100% of the estate—or 99.9% if you left out the one-third life estate in which I'd get use of the grandparents' home and one-third of his separate property. Then she dropped her next concern: Max's sister was not taken care of. And if that wasn't enough, she voiced yet another "injustice":

> "With regard to the grandchildren, he loved them beyond measure. I believe he would be devastated to know that they are not being considered in the distribution of his assets. And, I'm not sure that he would be supportive of how the law currently divides assets among the three of us."

She closed the email by getting some feelings off her chest. She said Max had not spent time with her and Stephen, "… and he missed most of our childhood plays, concerts, etc." She said she wasn't a greedy person, and this wasn't about greed. She just wanted what was "fair and equitable."

Once again, I forwarded it to my attorney, Mike Graham, and asked for his opinion. He chuckled and said, "Max is taking excellent care of his sister and grandchildren by leaving everything to his two children so *they* can care for those people. She's under the impression that her children won't receive a dime from her, like new cars, college educations, expensive trips, and an inheritance from their wealthy mother. Don't forget, Laura can also give plenty of money to Max's sister."

He let me digest that before he went on. "But I'm guessing what she really means is that the $3.5 million slice Max gave her isn't big enough to feed her family. She may think it's *fairer* if you would slide your $7 million slice over to her so she could cut out a big hunk for her kids and Max's sister. Then, things would be *very* fair." He paused again. "And whenever someone says it's not about greed, well, it's always about greed. Welcome to probate law."

Mike suggested I send an email to Laura asking how she defines "fairness." I rejected the idea, hoping to deescalate the building tension. My thinking was that when the kids analyzed how much $3.5 million could buy, they'd come around.

In the meantime, I had bills to pay. Thankfully, I had a couple of accounts with the right of survivorship. Withdrawing money from those and using the one credit card in my name, I was able to get by… but only for a while. Faced with fighting Max's children for control of the estate or letting them have who they wanted, I began revisiting the JPMorgan Chase option.

In the stillness of my empty nights, I envisioned arguing to a judge that I should be the administrator while Stephen and Laura stood next to me begging the judge not to allow that. According to my lawyer, I'd win. Yet when would the lawsuits begin? Would every decision I made (albeit with my lawyer's advice) be argued and litigated? Did I want to go through all that, especially when I could hand it off to JPMorgan Chase and supposedly it wouldn't cost me a dime? The feeling that Stephen and Laura were going to hand over $160,000 of their inheritance in administration fees to JPMorgan Chase was quickly fading with each email I received from them.

I thought back to Kal Grant, the bank's representative. She had sure made a great impression. Kal was smart, smooth, and in control. Maybe I *should* let her do all the work. Max's children could complain to her if they had any problems. I started hoping that the kids would come around and like me again—at least enough to let me see my grandchildren.

After praying hard about this, I set up another appointment with Kal. She arrived with Susan Novak from the Estate Settlement Unit and Todd Baird, a banker from the Private Banking Department. I explained my concerns and Kal met them head-on. She detailed Susan's ability to work with "prickly" children and resolve any differences according to the law. "The law is our guide," Kal said. "We have a great deal of experience in dealing with disagreeable heirs."

She explained that with no will, the word "executor" changed to "administrator." The probate code allowed an administrator to be dependent or independent.

"With a dependent administrator, we'll have to run to the judge for permission every time we need to make a decision. That's very time-consuming, not to mention costly. That's why we always select an Independent Administrator, or IA, for short. The only time we see the judge is if there's a question of law or we need to file the inventory. Important stuff like that."

"But my lawyer wants *me* to be the Independent Administrator," I said.

"You can do that," Kal replied, "but you'll have to post a bond. As a corporate IA, we don't have to. And don't forget the legal liability you'll be facing. With JPMorgan Chase and our first-class staff, we stand between you and problems. And by problems, I mean *lawsuits*."

Just then the inspector for our insurance company, who had come earlier and was now upstairs, called down and interrupted our meeting. "I'm sorry," I said to the group as I explained who he was before I left them to go upstairs, "I need to speak with him. We've had roof problems and found out it's going to be very expensive to fix, so we put it off. He's going let me know how much, if any, Chubb Insurance will pay toward the new roof."

When I joined him, the inspector grinned. "I checked it all out. There are a few items of concern, but I think Chubb might pay for most of your roof, minus depreciation and your deductible. There will still be some cost to you, but nothing near what you were expecting."

I buried my face in my hands and sobbed. The stress of everything—Max's children, the probate decisions, the massive cost of replacing a roof—was too much. I stood there and cried, not thinking everyone downstairs could hear me.

Kal and Susan wanted to soothe me, but Betty asked them to leave me alone. When I came down to rejoin the group, Kal said, "Jo, the estate will pay for its share of the roof repairs since the house is now an asset of the estate. Remember, half goes to the kids."

That was the perfect thing to say at that moment. It touched the right spot.

Kal talked some more about Susan Novak's experience. Susan seemed confident and capable of administering an estate. "JPMorgan Chase will hire an attorney to advise us on the law," she explained. "Again, the estate pays his fees."

"I want Ron Cresswell," I said.

"Of course," Susan replied, writing his name down. "I'll call Mr. Cresswell right away and discuss the matter with him."

The meeting lasted almost four hours. I told them I had found no wills, signed or unsigned. I also handed them a list of our assets, including our vehicles.

"So your newest car is five years old?" one of them asked.

"Yes, the 2005 Suburban. The others are a 2003 BMW and 1986 Porsche."

Surprised, they raised their eyebrows. I guess people in our financial position drove sleek new luxury vehicles. We didn't.

Kal pointed to the list. "It says your wine collection is in the cellar here at the house. But where are the putters you mentioned?"

"In a rented warehouse about fifteen minutes away," I replied. "There are thousands of them. And we have some silver coins in a safe deposit box in San Francisco."

"Don't worry, Jo," Kal said. "We will inventory the putters and wine, and our people in San Francisco can take possession of the coins. It's no problem."

I held up some papers. "These companies are sending me letters to exercise our stock options, while others want to know where to send distributions. Plus, it's getting close to tax time. How do we handle all this?"

Kal grinned confidently. "We'll draft the papers for you to sign and send them to you. As soon as we're appointed the IA, we'll take care of everything. Just lean your seat back, pull out your tray-table, and let us lavish you with some first-class service. Trust me, we know what we're doing."

You and JPMorgan Chase are the answer to my prayers, I thought to myself.

DAYS LATER, WHILE Mike, my attorney, reviewed JPMorgan Chase's documents, I learned that tragedy had struck close friends of mine. Two of their grandchildren had been killed in a car accident in Atlanta. Just as I had finished bawling about this news, the estate administrator, Susan Novak, called to inform me that they had talked to Ron Cresswell and decided not to hire him to advise the Max Hopper Estate. Susan was looking at other attorneys.

"Do what you have to do," I told her, wiping my eyes. "I don't care."

"Are you sure?" she asked.

"Don't worry about it. I have to go."

I flew to Atlanta for the funerals. Seeing my friends in pain hurt me terribly. The two teenagers had died on the two-month anniversary of Max's death. The whole thing was excruciatingly sad.

When I returned, Susan Novak called again. "Jo, we've hired a new lawyer for the estate, and I wanted to tell you who it is."

"Okay," I said, mindlessly flipping through a stack of mail.

"It's Tom Cantrill with Hunton & Williams."

I dropped the mail and held the phone away from me as I had another out-of-body experience. "Absolutely not!" I screamed. "There is no way Tom Cantrill will have anything to do with this estate!"

"What's the matter with Tom?" Susan asked softly.

I told her what had happened when I'd called Tom the day after Max had been pronounced brain dead. I repeated his words, "You're not even waiting until the body is cold."

Poor Susan. I screamed and cried into the phone as she listened to me rant. I felt as violated as if I'd been physically attacked. When I finally stopped, she started in again.

"I hired Tom because he knows the assets. He drafted a will for Max, although he never signed it."

"No, he doesn't know any of the assets," I seethed. "That work was done in 1993. We didn't have these assets then."

She remained silent.

"Susan, this is unbelievable. I told you what happened. I can't believe, out of an entire ocean of lawyers, you found this man. It's unbelievable. No, it's impossible!"

"I'm sorry," she said sternly, "but you don't have a say in who we select as the attorney for the estate."

We spent twenty-two minutes talking. When we were finished, nothing was resolved. Without Max for advice, I turned to the only person I had available—my lawyer.

"Calm down, Jo," Mike said. "Tom Cantrill is a fine man. He has a great reputation in probate law, and he's a friend of mine. I know he didn't mean to say those things to you. Come on. You have to get over this. This is about the estate. It's not about you."

I continued to object.

"Listen to yourself," he said. "I was the one urging *you* to be the IA. Instead, you decided on JPMorgan Chase and didn't follow my advice. You need to go along with this because JPMorgan Chase is going to hire Tom, regardless of your wishes. If you throw a wrench in this, we're going to have to start over again, and it's going to take months. Don't forget, we have a lot of urgent tasks to get done."

I wasn't giving up. "But I haven't signed the bank's documents yet. I can refuse this."

"Yes, you can. But you shouldn't if Tom is your only problem. Trust me, he's a true professional."

The word "trust" was being used a lot by everyone lately. Trust and experience had been the two cornerstones of the bank's pitch to me.

I held the phone steady as Mike went on about his bromance with Tom Cantrill. By the time he was through, it sounded like Tom should win the Nobel Peace Prize. Mike urged me to sign the papers and allow Tom to be the estate's lawyer.

Later that day, as I stared at Susan Novak's email address, one point was perfectly clear: Jo Hopper would not pay anything to have Max's estate handled by JPMorgan Chase. Not one cent!

Slowly and deliberately, against my gut instinct, I sent an email to Susan and asked her to send me the documents to sign. JPMorgan Chase would be the IA for Max's estate. It would be the absolute worst decision of my sixty-two years on this earth. Nothing else would come close.

Eventually, I would come to learn that hiring Tom Cantrill was neither unbelievable nor impossible. That's because later—*much* later—I received an email explaining his selection.

Chapter Four

"We have direct relationships with… 50% of the world's wealthiest individuals and families."
—Mary Callahan Erdoes, CEO Asset & Wealth Management
JPMorgan Chase Bank, N.A.
2016 Annual Report

Going through a stressful event affects your health. It could manifest as a lack of sleep, a lowered immune system, a feeling of malaise, or even depression. Each of us feels stress differently. And I was fairly certain that stress increased the risk of cancer. That's why I felt nervous sitting in my doctor's office, waiting to be called in for my annual cancer checkup.

"Jo Hopper," the nurse called out, opening the door all the way.

I gathered up my purse and sweater and followed her back to the examination room.

"Please take a seat," she said. "I just need to take your temperature and blood pressure." While she did that, I thought about the possibility of bad news. With everything going on at home, the odds could not be in my favor.

"Okay, I'm done," she said. "Dr. Wordman will be in shortly."

"Wait a minute!" I said. "My doctor is Galvan. Is he in?"

"Dr. Galvan had a death in the family and is away for about a week. Dr. Wordman is covering for him."

I hung my head. I hated changes or unexpected events like this.

"Don't worry," the nurse said reassuringly, seeing my demeanor. "Dr. Wordman is very good. You'll like him."

I sighed as she closed the door. *Can just one thing in my life not change?*

I waited ten minutes before a tall, athletic man appeared. His big smile and bright eyes sure made a good impression. He looked to be in his early forties. I imagined the nurses lined up in the hall, hoping he'd fall for them. He was easy on the eyes.

"Jo Hopper," he said, "I see you have some history with Dr. Galvan. I understand the nurse explained the situation."

"Yes, she did. I hope everything is all right."

"It will be. He's out of town and will be back in a week, maybe two. In the meantime, I need to order some tests. But first, I'd like to understand your situation fully. Can you walk me through how the cancer was discovered, what signs you had, and how the treatment went?"

"How much time do you have?" I asked with a grin.

"All the time in the world. I don't have any more patients after you. Some of them rescheduled. I hope you'll find I'm as knowledgeable as Dr. Galvan."

"If he trusts you, so do I."

"Great. I want to know everything about your medical health as well as your family's. Why don't you start at the beginning?"

THE BEGINNING—1950. IT was so long ago. I was a shy three-year-old when my mother widened her eyes and gasped in horror. "What is that?" she cried.

I didn't know what she was talking about but soon felt her hands rubbing all over my neck. She was distraught. When Dad came home, they rushed me to the doctor. He told my parents that I had a golf ball-sized bronchial lymphatic cyst just below my jawline on both sides of my neck. The doctors decided the best course of action was radiation.

The next day, I was placed on a hard bed under massive equipment that would scare any adult, much less a three-year-old. A man dressed in white wrapped my head in lead, leaving an opening over each cyst. They rolled me under this machine and hit a button. Mom sat next to me and held my hand, which couldn't have been good for her health. I endured this nightmare for two more visits. When the doctors told my parents there had been no change, they decided to quit.

Mom and Dad were devastated as they prepared for my death. One day, in desperation, my dad decided to lance the cyst on my left side. With only a tenth-grade education, he was a simple carpenter. Despite having no medical training, Dad went forward with the procedure.

I sat very still as he pierced the cyst with an awl—one of his carpentry tools. The cyst started draining through the small hole. For the next few days, fluid continuously oozed out of my neck like maple syrup from a tree. Somehow, the cyst on my right side drained out through the hole of the first cyst. Finally, the two cysts were flat and eventually disappeared, leaving only a scar from the puncture. To this day, the cysts have never reoccurred.

My parents were Christian. To them, it was a real miracle. But our joy was short-lived because my dad got sick shortly afterward. The doctors said he had colon cancer and was going to die. Mom refused to accept the diagnosis. After all, I had made it, why couldn't he? Yet, behind the scenes, my grandmother started making funeral arrangements.

Dr. Anderson, Dad's doctor, did everything he could for him—even removing a foot of the large intestine. They didn't have chemotherapy back then, so it was a cut-it-out/wait-and-see approach.

The doctor kept Dad in the hospital for nine days. We had no money, but Dr. Anderson was "good people," as my mom explained. He said he would work with them about the financial situation when Dad recovered.

Dad eventually came home, bedridden. Mom carefully removed his dressing, cleaned the wound, and reapplied the bandages several times a day. It was a labor of love.

After a week or so, we were running low on food. We lived on a farm way out in the country and grew our own food. We had to work hard to feed two adults and three kids. Unfortunately, we didn't have any canned food, and freezers weren't for poor country folk like us. With the crops not in yet, we were even worse off.

What food we had we gave to Dad, hoping it would build up his strength. I discovered that once you get over the deep gnawing hunger on the first day, it gets easier.

Somehow, neighbors in the community and members of the Baptist church learned about our situation and brought us food. What a relief it was to see them walking down the road with bags in their hands. I could hardly wait to rip into one.

I also discovered that taking care of an adult was hard work. Dad needed a lot of fresh cool water for his wounds. I was close to four and could help pump water from the well outside our house.

I also did my older sister's chores because she was taking up the work of our older brother. He was nine and handled some of Dad's chores. What he couldn't do, Mom did. We all had to step up to fill in for our sick leader.

While we got by, Mom and the church members prayed for a miracle. God responded, and Dad lived. When he could finally go back to work, he spent years paying back Dr. Anderson. But pay him back he did. That's just how we lived.

Many years later, the medical profession discovered that patients who'd experienced radiation near their thyroid had a good chance of getting thyroid cancer. That's why each year I went in for a checkup. And each time I was clear.

But when I turned thirty-four and had another checkup, a mass showed up. I was devastated when the doctors told me I had thyroid cancer. Within a week they operated, removing half of my thyroid. I was relieved when they told me it was benign. I had dodged another bullet.

As for my mother, she had some form of bone cancer when I was born. To save her, the doctors had removed her left index finger. She also suffered various skin cancers before dying of lung cancer when I was fifty-one. In our family, it felt like cancer was an evil cousin.

In early November 2007, when I was sixty, it was my turn again. The doctors informed me that a red itchy rash I had been living with for years was cutaneous T-cell lymphoma. It's not life-threatening; however, it's a chronic disease requiring frequent ultra-violet treatments to keep it in remission.

A few weeks after this diagnosis, I attended a cancer benefit for the Richardson Medical Center. One of the items being auctioned off was an advanced body scan. This special scan creates a map of calcium deposits in your body, showing hardening of the arteries, growths, and all sorts of issues. I had already undergone several of these scans. With Dad having destructive coronary artery disease, and given all the cancer in our family, I felt like it was only wise for me to undergo some preventative testing, so I bid on and won this scan.

The Monday after Thanksgiving I had the scan performed. Later that afternoon, my internist called. "I have good news and bad news," she said. "I got your scan back, and your arterial plaque score is zero. That's the good news."

"Okay," I said. "What's the bad news?"

"It looks like there's a lymphoma the size of a beer can in your left side. You need to see an oncologist as soon as possible."

"Yeah, that sounds pretty bad," I replied, since nothing else came to mind.

I happened to have an appointment with my dermatologist that afternoon. She was treating me for skin cancer. I showed her the body scan results, and she was shocked. "Having two kinds of lymphoma which are unrelated is highly irregular." She sent me to her partner, Dr. Galvan, an oncologist at Baylor.

A few days later, Dr. Galvan looked at the records and said, "I know you want the truth, so here it is. You have stage four non-Hodgkin's lymphoma. Cancer has spread to these six organs above and below your diaphragm. We've got to start chemo right now. You don't have a second to waste."

I asked how much treatment would cost. Max and I had lost a considerable amount of money in the 2001 dot-com bust and then again in 2007, at the leading edge of the Great Recession. Most of our assets were illiquid. And we were mortgaged up to the hilt on our new home. With less than $40,000 left in American Airlines health insurance, this was a terrible time for me to get sick.

The doctor told me each treatment would cost $40,000, with one drug costing $8,000. When he said I'd need six rounds, I felt we wouldn't be able to get $240,000 together.

Through the generosity of some doctors and healthcare providers, they agreed to treat me at a dramatically lower cost. Although I was truly blessed, I wasn't out of the woods yet.

The doctor ran tests, performed a biopsy and even withdrew bone marrow from my spine. With a pathological roadmap in place, the oncologist began pumping a chemotherapy cocktail called "R-CHOP" into my body. It was made up of five different chemo drugs—Rituximab, Cyclophosphamide, Hydroxydaunomycin, Oncovin, and Prednisolone. Believe me, this stuff *chopped* you into pieces. I knew this would be a very different Christmas season.

Max and I had a real discussion about the possibility of my dying—one that prepared him to be a widower. Despite the grim outlook and futility of it all, he took excellent care of me. The doctors suggested I stay away from everyone since my immune system was compromised. Max was my gatekeeper and kept me isolated.

I took this opportunity to clean up the last of my personal details so he would have it easy. Then I waited for death.

But another miracle happened.

In April 2008, following the sixth round of R-CHOP, Dr. Galvan said, "Jo, you're cancer-free—except for the skin cancer."

It was cause to celebrate. I continued on the maintenance drug Rutiximab for two years, and by God's grace, I made it.

It was a great story to tell.

"WELL, THAT WAS certainly thorough," Dr. Wordham said. "I feel like I know you now."

"Good. Does it help you figure out which tests to run?"

"It does. I'm going to fill out several forms and give them to the nurse. She'll schedule everything and make it easy for you."

I left Dr. Wordham with a warm feeling. Hopefully, I would get good news, or at least live long enough to wrap up Max's estate. I didn't want my estate's executor to have to deal with two estates at the same time.

THE NEXT DAY, I was called to a meeting with my attorney, Mike Graham. He had a bunch of items to discuss. From cancer doctor to probate lawyer, it sure felt like a gloomy and foreboding time.

"Let's get down to business," Mike said. "The bank filed papers to be appointed the Independent Administrator. Because they are *independent* instead of *dependent*, we won't be in court much. Things should start happening fast now."

I told him I was getting more letters and emails from Max's companies. "They're repurchasing our stock, or selling the company, or reminding us that we have options to exercise. They need action. Our assets don't know Max has died."

"I know, Jo. The bank has gotten a temporary authorization to handle two stock issues. Just keep sending everything to the estate's administrator, Susan Novak. She'll take care of it."

"That sounds like a good plan on paper, but so far, she doesn't appear to be doing anything. I'm starting to get worried," I said.

"I'll tell you what. I'll contact Susan when we're done here. If she doesn't respond, I'll call Tom Cantrill and see if he can break up the logjam."

I felt like I should have been satisfied with his answer. There wasn't much I could do.

Mike continued. "Next issue: Tom looked through the notes in his file from when Max was his client. Max told Tom he had previously signed a will. Have you found one yet?"

"No, I haven't. But I still have stacks of boxes to go through at home. When I was sick for two years, I stopped filing everything. Since I was going to die, it didn't seem necessary."

"What about his office?"

"Betty is handling that. You met her when we interviewed you. Max kept the business consulting and board-related information at his office. She's carefully looking through everything and listing the assets she finds."

We covered a few more items then finished up the meeting. I drove home with a lot of issues pressing on me. One of them was searching through the remaining boxes. It was time for me to get to work.

THE WEEKS TICKED by and I still hadn't found a will. I'd carefully inspected box after box, then I'd shifted to the stacks of documents ready to be filed.

Nothing.

Returning home from Starbucks, I spotted some boxes I remembered Max bringing from our San Francisco home and storing in the garage. I carried them inside, stacking them next to the kitchen table. With my latte providing motivation, I dove right in.

After several hours, I found nothing. With one box left, I had little hope. But halfway in, I pulled out a *Fortune* magazine. As I was thumbing through it, a document dropped into my lap. Incredibly, it was Max's will.

My heart raced as I scanned it. In the first few pages, he appointed me the executor. That was great news. When I reached the bequeaths, I saw that he left me his entire half of our community property if I survived him. Nothing was left to his children. I was stunned. Carefully, I pulled back the sheets to the last page, hoping to find a signature. Racing down to the line, I saw it was blank. But at least this was something.

The next day I contacted the San Francisco attorney Max had worked with when we lived there, and he said to the best of his knowledge, Max had never signed it.

I called Mike Graham and told him what I had found. "That's good, Jo, but we need one executed. Keep looking. I hear from JPMorgan Chase that Max's children are sure there's a will, and they hope you aren't holding it back."

"Does that make sense to you?" I asked.

"No. It's like someone's pointing an unloaded gun at your face while you demand they keep searching for bullets. Either their lawyer hasn't fully explained it to them or he did and they don't believe him," he said, chuckling. "I guess they just don't trust you."

"No, I think they believe everything Max and I had was Max's, so they want it all awarded to them through probate. Anything I'll end up with would be money or property they don't want. Perhaps they think a will can make that happen."

We finished up and I sat back in my chair. High school graduations were coming up for Stephen's daughter and Laura's son. I felt so depressed at how quickly our relationship was dissolving that I wondered how I could travel to two separate cities and attend the ceremonies. I pondered all the good and bad that might happen with me being there. In the end, I decided it was better not to go. Instead, I sent a congratulations card and a gift to each child. I told them emotionally I was not up to coming, which was the truth. Attending their graduations without Max was more than I could handle.

One thing I did to take a break and console myself was visit my backyard. The day Max died, I spotted a half-eaten Texas peach wrapped up in the refrigerator. He must've been saving it for later, but later had never come. Using my farm skills, I'd dug out the pit and planted it about four inches below the topsoil in a nice sunny spot in the backyard. Then I placed a hollowed-out can around the little seed to protect it. With the sunny weather we were having, I watered it periodically.

It had been almost five months since that day. I went out to Max's spot, as I called it now, to check on the peach tree. Kneeling, I noticed a tiny shoot pushing through the soil. This gave me a boost—life from death. But the big question was: Would I be alive to see it bear fruit?

I attended more grief counseling and it helped. It also made me realize I needed more support. During one session, a woman talked about operating her husband's Facebook page as if he was still alive. The counselor explained that she needed to let it go, which was obvious to all of us. When I got home, I decided to follow the counselor's advice. I deactivated Max's Facebook account. Then, I thought about my account.

Max's children don't trust me. If I post photos about my day, going to Starbucks or the Dallas Arboretum, will they think I don't care? Or that

I'm over Max? Any post I make can be twisted and misinterpreted. One wrong move, and I'll find myself in litigation with these two.

It was sad that my mind went there, but it's often hard to tell imagination from reality when you're in the middle of a nightmare. Seeing my Facebook account sitting there, I decided to deactivate it as well.

After double-checking that the account had truly disappeared, I studied the lock of Max's hair I'd kept on my desk. I saw that Tiffany's had a beautiful sterling silver locket attached to a keyring on their website. I wanted to order one and put Max's hair in it, but instead, I felt the urge to do something different. I filled in the online information and ordered five lockets—one for Stephen, Laura, and their three children. Even though my relationship with them was cratering before my eyes, I couldn't hold onto Max's hair. They needed it more than I did. It was the least I could do.

In June 2010—five months after Max's death—the stock issues intensified. Initially I was told by JPMorgan Chase that they would collect all the community property, both mine and Max's. They said they had to create an inventory for the court and pay any debts owed at the time of death. "We must protect the creditors," they said.

When I first heard this, I was very concerned. It reminded me of that *60 Minutes* episode where some widow had all her money taken from her with the promise it would be returned down the road. In the meantime, she starved. Thankfully, I had those right-of-survivorship accounts so I was okay for now. But not forever.

When I questioned them about holding my money, Tom Cantrill, now the estate's attorney, and both Kal Grant and Susan Novak promised me that my half of the community property would be returned to me after the payment of all debts. As for Max's half of the community property, this would be held by a newly created entity called "The Estate of Max D. Hopper." The estate would be delivered to his heirs—Stephen and Laura—in equal shares when probate was closed. Max's separate property would be held by the estate, then divided as such: one-third each to Stephen and Laura, and one-third to me.

Fortunately, we had very little debt, just a handful of medical bills, credit cards, miscellaneous work done on the house, and the mortgage. That was it. After performing a cursory debt review, Tom Cantrill said the administrator would likely release my property within six months. Why would it take that long? I had no idea. Apparently, that was how these cases went.

After I signed the agreement hiring JPMorgan Chase in April and before they had been appointed temporary Independent Administrator in mid-June, I received a cash call from one of our venture capital funds. A cash call is a requirement to send in money. If we failed to make the cash call, we could lose our investment. Max had believed this venture capital investment was a winner, so I wanted to make sure we kept it.

I immediately contacted Susan to see how this should be handled. She requested I make the payment for both Max's estate and myself. After JPMorgan Chase's appointment as Independent Administrator, I could submit paperwork for a refund of Max's portion from the estate. Since I wasn't an expert like JPMorgan Chase, I followed her instructions. I barely made the deadline and was thrilled. We had saved the investment for the estate and me.

Once again, more stock issues popped up. The probate judge had temporarily appointed JPMorgan Chase to handle two companies with pressing stock needs. The first company was being purchased and needed to send the money to us. The second company needed to transfer over 37,000 shares and some cash they were holding for Max. In addition, we needed to exercise 21,000 stock options prior to their expiration date. The stock options granted us the right to purchase stock at a specific price. I called Susan and told her about this situation. Right off the bat, she told me JPMorgan Chase would recover only the estate's half. I needed to make arrangements to recover my half.

Based on earlier conversations, I was confused. After all, I'd been told that the Independent Administrator—JPMorgan Chase—was required to receive *all* the assets. Yet Susan was insistent that she would only take care of the estate's assets and that I should take care of my own.

I sent an email to both companies, giving them the wiring instructions for my investment account. Max and I had been customers with this firm since 1982, when Max had worked at Bank of America in San Francisco. My financial advisor assured me he would supervise the transfer so it would go smoothly.

A day later, alarm bells sounded. JPMorgan Chase learned from one of the companies that I had requested the transfer to an outside investment firm not named JPMorgan Chase. Without notice, I received a call telling me that an emergency conference call was happening at that very moment. On the phone was someone with JPMorgan Private Banking, another person with JPMorgan Private Investments, Kal Grant, and Susan Novak. They were not happy I had sent wiring instructions to another brokerage.

I listened to them rail on about my actions, certain I'd done something illegal. As the fog lifted from their aggressive posturing, I realized they wanted me to set up a banking and/or investment account with JPMorgan Chase and leave the money with them. They gave me the clear impression that if I didn't leave my assets at the bank, there would be a delay in releasing my assets held by the Independent Administrator.

I thought the Chinese Wall they talked about prevented issues like this?

All four of them insisted on meeting with me at my home to fully explain all that JPMorgan had to offer. I told them I'd get back to them.

Shaking, I hung up and immediately called my attorney and then my financial advisor. I detailed the conference call and asked them what I should do. They both agreed I should meet with the bank's reps.

The very next day, JPMorgan sent a grim-looking posse to my house: Kal Grant, Todd Baird with Private Banking, and David Murrell with Private Investments. To my surprise, Susan Novak wasn't with them. They launched right in, delivering their message. At one point, I said, "Do I understand you correctly that you want me to fire my financial advisor and let *you* handle my assets?"

"Absolutely!" they said in unison. They assured me David Murrell could manage my assets better than my longtime friend and financial advisor in San Francisco.

I hesitated as they waited for my response. After what seemed like an hour, I gave them my answer. "That's not going to happen. I've known him for over twenty years, and I know nothing about you. However, I will leave the assets at JPMorgan Chase. My advisor will coordinate with David on how to invest them."

They glanced at each other and were satisfied. Since the money would be parked at JPMorgan Chase, they would have the opportunity to show me how great they were. I figured as soon as it was safe, I'd move the money out. Up to this point, though, I was unimpressed. From everything I saw, they appeared to be complete amateurs. Hopefully, they'd pick up the pace and dazzle me with their brilliance.

A few hours after this meeting, I had a date at Starbucks with a friend of mine, Janie McKewen. She met me in the parking lot and we walked in together.

"How's your day going?" Janie asked.

I told her about the emergency conference call and meeting I had just experienced with JPMorgan Chase. Her face darkened. "My brother, Troy, had $200,000 in that bank. One day, he looked at the fees they were charging and decided to move his money to another bank. He went inside their nice branch in Preston Center and waited for a teller. When he told them what he wanted, she said he'd have to see a banker and directed him to a waiting area. A few minutes later, a young man in a suit escorted him to a desk and wanted to know why he was withdrawing his money. Troy was stunned. He said the fees were killing him and he wanted to move it. Next thing you know, another man in a suit stood at his side. The whole thing was very intimidating.

"They asked him questions like he was a thief and tried to bully him. He was so disturbed he agreed to leave the money there and drove to a tiny branch off Central Expressway. He waited in the parking lot for the lunch hour and went inside, catching the small office short-staffed. They didn't have anyone available to intimidate him, so they were forced to give him the money. He's never going back to JPMorgan Chase. Money goes into that bank and it doesn't come out. I wonder if their bonuses are tied to it?"

I listened carefully and filed that information away. I can say for sure I felt intimidated.

As we collected our drinks, Janie walked over and greeted a man who was sitting there pounding away on his laptop. The man had a full beard, mostly gray, and a large bald spot on top of his head, with long hair falling down around it. His thick glasses and baggy attire appeared designed to keep people away.

"Who was that?" I asked Janie outside.

"Oh, that's someone I used to know. Why?"

"He looked a little odd, like someone who wasn't looking to impress people."

"His impressing days are over," Janie explained. "He used to be one of the top litigators in Dallas. Handled all the important cases and won most of them, too. Had a big mansion, wife, kids. Then he had a breakdown. I think pills or alcohol were involved. I don't know for sure. But he lost his law license, and that was that. I see him in here from time to time. I guess he buys the cheapest drink so he can use the Wi-Fi."

"Gosh, what's his name?"

"Tarian Starr."

THAT AFTERNOON, AS I pondered the strange man in Starbucks, I pulled out a small metal box Max kept in a drawer. I had overlooked it before. But now, I was doubling my effort to find a will. Secretly, I hoped I'd find one so the kids would know I wasn't trying to cheat them. Of course, they might be shocked to find that Max reduced their current $7 million to zero. I wondered how that would go over.

As I opened the box and scanned the contents, I saw an old letter at the very bottom. It was from Max's ex-wife, Leah. After reading it, I called my attorney and told him I needed to see him immediately.

Sitting in Mike's office, I let him read the letter. When he finished, he pulled out a legal pad and grabbed a pen. "Okay, tell me why this is so important."

"It's important because it explains why I'm in big trouble with Max's children."

He hesitated. "I'm going to need more than that, Jo. Please explain."

Chapter Five

I lost my husband. He had no will.
The big bank said, there'd be no bill.
If I'd just sign, and hand things over,
I could rest, in fields of clover.

—*Without a Will* by Jack Hooper

The year was 1976. I was twenty-nine years old and working for American Airlines at their Tulsa computer center. It was really more of a help desk for travel agents who were using our reservation system and having problems booking flights or printing tickets. Computers were just coming to the travel industry and American Airlines had a great system: SABRE. Travel agents loved it.

Since I had been a reservation and tariff/ticketing agent, I could help the agents with many issues. If I discovered a problem with our program, I wrote it up and submitted it to the programmers to fix. It was an exciting time to be at the beginning of this critical expansion for American Airlines and the travel agency world.

In November, I learned I was being transferred to New York City along with several other coworkers. This was troublesome because I was dating a programmer in the Tulsa office, but he wasn't being transferred.

A few days before we left, the staff threw us a going-away party and upper management appeared. One of those higher-ups was Max Hopper. He was forty-three and had been married for twenty-two years with two kids. Max was all business, not a flirt or player. We stood in a group making idle chit-chat and that was that.

Max was also being transferred to New York to work at 633 Third Avenue, American's headquarters. He would be the Vice President of Marketing Automation.

I left for New York City and got settled in. I saw Max from time to time when he checked on the department. I was a systems analyst in marketing automation. Above me was a manager, a director, then Max.

Every Friday evening, I began seeing Max at the airport as we waited to board the only American flight to Tulsa. I was going there to see my fiancé, and he was going home to be with his wife and children.

He was habitually late arriving at La Guardia Airport. In those days, I flew on standby, only boarding the flight if there were available seats at departure time. Many a Friday night, I would be waiting to board only to see Max arrive in a hurry for the same flight. Because he had a boarding status way above me, he'd get the last seat on the flight and I'd remain in New York. Occasionally, we'd both get on the plane and end up seated next to each other. We both loved computer work—so definitive and unambiguous—and discussed ideas and possibilities with computers and our program, SABRE.

My commuting had gone on for five months when I came back to Tulsa to find my fiancé had attended a high school reunion and reconnected with his old sweetheart. He was sorry, but he had to dump me for her. I was heartbroken, but at least I stopped the Friday night flights to Tulsa.

A month or so after that, the marketing automation department was transferred to Dallas, where American Airlines was relocating its headquarters. I saw Max more frequently since we were all working in the same building. I was still an analyst.

In 1979 I was promoted to manager, with five analysts and a secretary working for me. I celebrated my thirty-second birthday alone.

A few weeks later, I met with Max about travel agency issues. When I asked about his trips to Tulsa, his eyes welled up and he said that he was going through a divorce. I told him I was sorry and left it alone.

On a Friday in June, we were all working late when Max asked if I'd like to have dinner the next evening. I thought of him as a friend, not a romantic interest, and agreed. The next evening, as we sat at a table in a seafood restaurant, he began to cry. It was startling to see someone of Max's stature tearing up in such a public place. He was becoming a legend in computer systems and reinventing the way airlines and travel agents did business. According to industry insiders, he was a game-changer. At the moment, though, he was crying over a glass of iced tea. I didn't know what to do, so I tried to talk to him. "What's the matter? Did I say something wrong?"

"No," he sobbed. "I just missed my twenty-fifth wedding anniversary."

That statement shocked me. "I thought you said you were going through a divorce!"

"I was," he said, holding back tears. "It was finalized a month ago on May twenty-third. But I didn't want the divorce. She did."

He went on to tell me his wife was interested in someone else, blaming him for always being gone. He'd been devastated. When he came to his senses, he promised her he would do better, and make it work. Basically, he'd been on his knees begging *her* to take *him* back. But she said no and filed for divorce, again laying the blame on Max. He agreed to accept the responsibility for his marriage falling apart and do what was best for his kids, Stephen and Laura. I was stunned, so instead of talking, I just listened as we finished our meal.

After that incident, we went out to dinner maybe once a month—more as friends, not as two people dating. Besides, I knew from insiders that Max was dating other women.

As time went on, we kept seeing each other, talking about our work and technology. The conversations were electric. He was excited I understood his ideas, and I loved that he was impressed with my work. When the other women he was seeing fell away, Max and I were alone, together; more leftovers than anything else.

In December 1980, Max asked me to marry him. Due to anti-nepotism work rules, I knew one of us would have to leave. I had worked twelve years at American Airlines, but of course, it was me who would give up my job. I handed in my notice in mid-May 1981 and we were married on June 6, 1981.

After we were married, I received several surprises. The first was about money. Max was in debt. He had paid for Stephen's college education and bought a new car for Leah, his ex-wife, among other things. He had also purchased a house in Arlington for himself, which came with a hefty mortgage. I carried some debt too, which meant we had to watch every penny. When Stephen went to medical school and Laura went to college, we continued to support them financially. I juggled bills each week, trying to avoid any creditor issues. It was tough.

At that time, American Airlines looked at the computer staff like mechanics—necessary but not worthy of big money. That meant I had to look for programming work to make ends meet. However, my headhunter explained that Max's reputation was so widespread that no one wanted to hire me because they were worried about their innovations ending up on Max's desk.

With no college degree to fall back on, I found part-time work at the World Trade Mart near downtown Dallas. They needed extra salespeople to show furniture and write up orders. It worked out well because I was able to purchase furniture for our home at heavily discounted prices. Yet, no matter how much we watched our money, we could not afford to fully furnish the house. The living room never had furniture. And because the house was devoid of landscaping, Betty, our good friend and later Max's assistant, along with her family, gave us a wedding gift of planting 2,000 Asian Jasmine plants around our home. One weekend, Betty, her three sisters and two brothers as well as their families, joined Max and I, as we planted them. I hoped this would help to stop the angry notices from the homeowner's association about the high weeds.

For years, each morning I hopped out of bed with one job: make sure the cash pipeline from Dallas to Tulsa ran smoothly. Stephen and Laura had everything they needed to complete their advanced educations and be successful. The fact that Stephen became a doctor and Laura ended up as mayor of a city in Kansas showed we'd made great investments in them.

After the daily inspection of the cash pipeline to Max's children was over, my next task was to check our account balance to make sure we could pay our own bills. Once that was done, I did whatever was needed to allow Max to focus on his job and not worry about our home life, including driving to my sales job and punching in. Welcome to married life.

MIKE GRAHAM REMOVED his glasses. "So, how does a letter from his ex-wife affect this probate matter?"

I sighed, rubbing my tired eyes. "When we married, Max forbade me from correcting his children or getting involved in any arguments they were having. This was frustrating, but I honored his request. Whenever they said things to Max or were insolent, I stepped out of the room, mainly because I couldn't stand to see my husband and his children fighting. I'm sure they thought I didn't care. I did care. But I cared more about honoring my husband's request.

"Now, after reading this letter his ex-wife sent, I believe she had been turning their children against Max and especially me. Throughout this letter, she uses three words five separate times: Jo, money, and power. Even though she admits in the letter *she* had found someone else, I could only conclude that she told them *I* was the cause of their breakup. Believe me, nothing could be further from the truth. Max was crying to me about missing his twenty-fifth anniversary. Despite Leah's decisions, he still wanted her back. And her words imply he tried to get back together with her after their divorce."

"Did he ever tell you he tried to get back with her?"

I thought about it for a moment. "No, but he went to Tulsa frequently on business. She mentions being at the hotel he stayed at. And she claims Max cheated her over a coin collection in the divorce. Max never mentioned anything about the coins to me. Remember, we were financially strapped. Max and a friend of his were coin dealers, buying and selling mostly American currency. Max told me he'd divided the remaining coins from the business with Leah as part of the divorce settlement. He didn't want to sell the ones he received. The first time I heard about Max allegedly cheating Leah out of anything was at the meeting with Max's children. Stephen made some remark about Max cheating on the division of the coins. I didn't understand what that was about, so I didn't pursue it."

"And you think this probate matter is their way of getting back at you, making their mother happy, and punishing the woman who ruined their lives?"

I swallowed the lump rising in my throat. "I do. This letter was sent to Max's office at American Airlines. She and Max's children bypassed me all the time. They wouldn't call him at home but at work, where I couldn't pick up or hear him speaking to them. Now that he's died, I'm afraid they're going to push JPMorgan Chase to hammer me. They seem to think I'm hiding a will." I shook my head. "I never had a chance with them. They're going to believe their mother, not me. I know I would."

Mike flipped through his notes. "That's why when Laura said in the car, 'We don't want your money,' you never asked what you had done to make her hate you. You avoid confronting them, even now that Max is dead."

"I do. Max was the bridge that connected me to Stephen and Laura. Now the bridge is gone and we're on opposite sides of a deep river. The sad truth is, my failure to die first is an inconvenient reality."

Mike sighed heavily. "Don't worry," he said, "JPMorgan Chase has a fiduciary duty to treat you properly. They must follow the law. They can't and won't go pushing Max's children's agenda off on you. Even if they wanted to, Tom Cantrill won't let them. Trust me, we'll get through this just fine."

"I sure hope so," I said, noticing I was using the word "hope" more often lately.

OVER THE NEXT few weeks, Mike continued to press me for a will. I spent many hours calling every law firm Max had known or worked with. One of them was Glast, Phillips & Murray, a law firm in North Dallas. I called and left my information with the receptionist. The next day, attorney Gary Stolbach called and said they had found two different wills Max had drafted. My heart raced in my ears as I asked him the paramount question: "Are either of them signed?"

"No," Mr. Stolbach said. "They are not."

I asked him to send the wills to Tom Cantrill. I never saw them but learned through my attorney that each one made me the executor. Unlike the first two, these left some of Max's estate to his children and employed trusts as tax savings vehicles to leave more directly to his grandchildren.

These were the last wills I uncovered. I checked with Betty and she had come up empty. All we had were four different wills from three separate attorneys, the first in 1982 and the last in 1997. None of them were signed. With no option left, it was clear Max had died intestate and would have to use the default will provided by the state of Texas. This meant Stephen and Laura would get 100% of Max's half of our community property and two-thirds of his separate property. As it stood, I would likely inherit less than $50,000 from his separate property and none of his $7 million estate. It was the law, and there was nothing I could do except push JPMorgan Chase to finish up the probate as quickly as possible and return my community property.

THE SPRING HAD turned to summer, heating up Dallas. I was also getting hot—at JPMorgan Chase. I couldn't understand what Susan Novak was doing and she never kept in touch. The two stock matters they'd been appointed to handle had not gone smoothly. I felt like I had to remind her to complete certain tasks. Even when I did, sometimes it still wasn't done. It was a pretty good business strategy for a company holding all our assets: delay, delay, delay.

As my level of frustration grew, Mike Graham gave me an out. "JPMorgan Chase has only been appointed the temporary IA. They're not permanent yet. We can still object."

"With the bungling of the two transactions and everything else, I'm thinking about it," I told him. "Why don't we have a meeting to clear the air? Then I can decide."

Since the court hearing to appoint them permanent IA was in a few days, Mike set up a meeting in his office for the following day. That night, something gnawed at the back of my mind. I picked up the phone and called Stephen.

He told me that he and Laura were also frustrated with JPMorgan Chase and Susan. We went through the problems and he agreed to see how my meeting went the next day. Then I asked him the big question: "Stephen, I need to know why you insisted on JPMorgan Chase."

"Ron Cresswell suggested JPMorgan Chase," he replied quickly.

I considered this. He and Laura had met privately with Ron when he'd come to my home, so technically it was possible. Yet, it didn't make sense. "Stephen, you hated Ron Cresswell. You wouldn't have accepted any advice from him."

"I thought it was a good idea."

I found it hard to believe him. Something was going on here. "Do you have a business relationship with JPMorgan Chase?" I asked him point-blank. "Why did you insist on JPMorgan Chase?"

"No, Jo, I don't have a business relationship with them. They're a big bank and I just thought Ron had a good idea."

I hung up the phone, still suspicious. I couldn't prove it, but one day I'd learn the truth—and it would shock me.

THE NEXT AFTERNOON, I attended the meeting at Mike Graham's office to hash things out. In my notebook, I wrote that the goal of this meeting was to receive assurance that the estate settlement would get the attention it required without undue delays. I also wanted them to act professionally, while promising that moving forward these issues would not reoccur. It seemed strange that I had to ask a bank like JPMorgan Chase to do those things.

Present from JPMorgan Chase were Susan Novak and the bank's attorney, Tom Cantrill. They sat there taking notes as I ripped through my list of questions and complaints. I pointed out that Susan didn't know how to fill out the paperwork on the stock issue. I detailed the lack of response to my emails, especially when I sent the information she requested. It seemed like they were doing nothing.

"The reason I agreed to JPMorgan Chase was the professionalism demonstrated by Kal Grant," I said. "I thought she was the caliber of person who would be handling Max's estate. It's like you folks have never handled an estate before. What are all those floors of employees doing?" I added sarcastically.

Tom Cantrill acted like the peacemaker, assuring me everything was going as planned. Susan explained how they were moving offices, and I just happened to catch them in the middle of a move between floors. "If you show up at our office tomorrow, you'll see boxes everywhere," Susan insisted. "Really, Jo, this is an anomaly. We know exactly what we're doing. I've been with JPMorgan Chase for seventeen years. I promise it won't happen again."

They continued to assert they had a handle on everything. Once they sorted out the move, the probate would proceed at lightning speed.

After listening to their pleas for grace, I decided not to object to their appointment as permanent IA. This would be the second biggest mistake of my life.

THREE DAYS AFTER the hearing to appoint JPMorgan Chase as Independent Administrator for Max's estate, I sat at my desk, poring over my latest legal bill. Everything cost money: copies, faxes, postage, long-distance phone calls, regular phone calls. I was surprised they didn't charge for toilet paper. It was overwhelming.

I pushed the bill aside and contacted my financial advisor, detailing to him the events of the last two days, including the hearing. We analyzed the numbers and some strategies to minimize my expenses. That's when I noticed an email from Tom Cantrill on my screen.

Cantrill stated that the money JPMorgan Chase had received from the two stocks in their capacity as temporary administrator might take two months for disbursement. This was outrageous. The funds were to be held to pay any debt at time of death. Since we had no debt to speak of other than the mortgage, I'd been assured my assets would be released to me without delay. After all, I had not inherited the assets; the assets were mine as community property before Max's death. Now, they were my separate property.

Right above Cantrill's email was an email from Laura to me. It read:

"I haven't heard a thing from the hearing on June 30. Have you? Do we know the outcome and next steps?? I don't feel like JPMorgan has been doing a very good job of communicating."

I couldn't believe what I was reading. She could've had me doing all this for free. We'd probably be wrapping it up right now. Instead, both she and Stephen had pushed for JPMorgan Chase. And to make matters worse, neither one had shown up in court. I stood before the judge alone, surrounded by a gaggle of attorneys—five in total. Thank goodness Betty took me to the hearing and stayed with me. She'd given me comfort.

As I left the courtroom, I prayed I'd never have to be there again. It was a game where only the lawyers knew what was going on. A place where the deceased's assets were redistributed to the attorneys through outrageous legal fees and expenses. And recently, I'd heard probate referred to by the initials IRA, meaning Involuntary Redistribution of Assets.

With all this floating around in my mind, I replied to Laura.

"I have no idea what your next steps are with JPMorgan. You should contact Susan Novak or your attorney. Susan Novak is the independent administrator of Max's assets. You and Stephen made it clear that you did not want me involved."

Needing a break, I drove to my local Starbucks for a coffee. I sat in a corner away from the cashier. I had been there ten minutes when in walked that strange man that Janie had said hi to. He sat at a table next to me, fired up his laptop, and started pounding away. I tried to remember his name but couldn't.

I sipped my coffee and studied him. All he had was the laptop and a bottle of water. And the label was faded and frayed, which told me he was refilling it. His long hair and scruffy appearance made what Janie had told me about him seem very strange.

When I finished my coffee, I got up and headed to the cashier to ask the barista a question. "Excuse me," I said, "but I thought you had to buy something here to use the Wi-Fi."

"Are you not able to log on?" she asked me.

"No. I didn't need to. Actually, I'm wondering about the man over there in the corner. He came in with a bottle of water and logged right on."

"Oh, I see. Starting July 1, we made Wi-Fi free to everyone. You don't have to buy anything."

"Okay," I nodded, pulling out my credit card. "I'd like to buy a gift card for him. Say fifty dollars."

She raised her eyebrows. "Of course. Let me ring that right up."

When she handed the gift card to me, I said, "No. You give it to him. Let it be from someone anonymous."

"All right." She stuck a note to the card, scribbling down a few words: *For Tarian*.

I walked to my car feeling like I had done something good, having no idea where that simple gift would lead me.

Chapter Six

One Year Later

The trees in the backyard swayed to and fro, the warm breeze caressing my face. I stepped off the patio and onto the grass carpet carrying a large pail full of water. The heavy load strained my right arm. At sixty-four, I should have thought about using the hose, but I didn't. The pail seemed more personal.

As I approached the spindly stick rising from the ground, I shook my head. God was incredible. Taking a pit from Max's last peach to a three-foot-tall baby tree was absolutely amazing. If I could somehow coax fruit from it one day, that would be another miracle.

I set the pail down, studying the situation. I had removed the protective can long ago and replaced it with a better support system, consisting of a collar and wires staked to the ground. This also kept Blair away from it. There was no way I'd let our dog ruin the last living connection I had with Max.

But that's not really accurate. My last living connection with Max was his children and grandchildren. Yet that connection was hanging by a thread, if not completely broken. It was its own tragedy. How I'd found myself in this position I couldn't quite pinpoint. But I had a suspect in mind.

In the past eleven months with JPMorgan Chase acting as the Independent Administrator, I'd found them to be surprisingly incompetent at collecting, dividing, and retitling the financial assets. Tom Cantrill, the estate's lawyer hired by JPMorgan, had initially informed me that my 50% of the community property would be divided out and returned to me by the end of 2010. As we neared that deadline (four and a half months after JPMorgan's appointment as IA), I discovered most of the companies had not even been contacted. They had received nothing regarding the division and retitling of assets or JPMorgan Chase's appointment as the IA for Max's estate. As a matter of fact, many were not even aware of his death!

Out of frustration, I emailed each financial asset's contact and explained that Max had died unexpectedly. I provided them the contact information for the IA and JPMorgan Chase Bank, and then went over the intestate rules listed in the Texas Probate Code. I stated that our goal was to complete the paperwork necessary to divide each asset by the end of 2010—the date Cantrill had set.

In early December, I met Susan Novak and Mike Graham for lunch. I brought with me the completed documents, with stamped and addressed envelopes, to divide our venture capital funds. All that was required was for Susan to sign them as the IA for the estate and mail them. She looked over my paperwork and said, "These documents are only for you. Where are the children's?"

I stared at this JPMorgan employee in disbelief. "Susan, that is what you do."

Due largely to my efforts, most of the financial assets were divided by the end of January 2011 and my 50% was placed in an account under my name at JPMorgan Chase Bank.

Three months after that, dejected, I sat at my desk and studied the situation. I had fronted over $200,000 for the estate and being reimbursed from JPMorgan was proving very difficult.

One example was the $38,000 I had paid for Max's memorial service and medical bills. I sent Susan emails and letters—seven different times in all—with the bills and paperwork she required. It seemed everything I sent her went down a black hole; a *Susan Novak* hole. Only in March 2011, over one year after Max's death, did the bank grudgingly reimburse me for some of the invoices I had submitted. She ignored my unpaid reimbursements, not even providing information on why they weren't being paid.

I caught a big break when several venture capital companies sent me cash distributions for both the estate and me. I discovered that Susan had not taken the time to notify those companies of JPMorgan's appointment as IA, so the account to receive cash distributions had never been changed. The estate's share was over $113,000 and was deposited to my account.

Novak and Cantrill demanded that I forward the funds immediately to the estate's account at JPMorgan. Since the estate owed me so much money, I kept it, deducting the amounts from the balance.

Trying to pry loose the additional reimbursements was next to impossible. In fact, JPMorgan waited until March 2015—*five years* after Max's death—to pay me the balance of the funeral expenses. And the March 2010 cash call that I had agreed to make for the estate at Susan Novak's request wasn't paid back until July 2015. It took multiple requests. And even then, the estate still owed me $58,000, part of which was the roof repair that Kal Grant had promised the estate would share in. If I wanted that money back, I'd need a judge or a jury to award it.

It was sad that a customer like me had to have lawyers send demands to JPMorgan for *five years* and be prepared to dive into the weeds on every piece of paper. Case in point: One day, I poured over the division of our equity in Bain Capital Fund and noticed a charge for $6,870 from Ropes & Gray. This was a law firm the fund had hired to draft the paperwork to divide the shares. Since I owned half, Susan had allocated half of the legal fees to me. But the $6,870 was so out of line compared to what the other funds charged I felt compelled to ask for a breakdown. Susan hadn't bothered.

The law firm emailed me the complete bill. As I went through it, I noticed that 93% of the bill had Laura's name on it. She had called them with extensive questions on how to receive her shares. Stephen and I only owed $255 each. When I pointed this out to Susan, she appeared to be mad at the law firm, saying, "Of course I will do the expense allocation differently based on this information. It would've been nice to have this detail in their first invoice." She blamed Ropes & Gray for her failure to question the bill. It was the same with each Hunton & Williams' invoice (Tom Cantrill's firm). It could have included a charge for a 485 Ferrari and she would've paid it. I don't think Susan ever questioned a charge or allocation they made to me.

Standing in my backyard, I took in a deep breath and thought about what they'd put me through. So far, I had spent over $45,000 in attorneys' fees, yet it felt like I had done most of the work. With no end in sight, I was stuck in legal quicksand, hemorrhaging money. Even though I liked Mike Graham, I made the difficult decision to fire him. It didn't appear that having an attorney made any difference or pushed JPMorgan to get things done any faster.

To save money, I represented myself. I was confident that operating without an attorney would bring the temperature down.

I was wrong.

By tipping the pail above the budding tree, I allowed the water to dribble into the soil. Like my bank account, I was draining it. Unlike my bank account, I was growing something of value.

With the pail empty, I spoke to the tree. "Max, I wish you were here to provide me some sound advice. This is a mess I fear I can't get out of. I sure could use some of your wisdom."

I glanced at my watch, realizing I had only a few minutes to collect my things and head out. I had an appointment I needed to get to.

Climbing into the Suburban, I shook my head. After spending thousands of dollars in attorneys' fees, I had finally managed to gain control of my own car. Because Max and I had failed to sign a section of the car title that transfers ownership to each other at death, all the vehicles had to go through probate. This meant each one had to be appraised, which led to arguments over the correct value. Since JPMorgan's management fee was based on a percentage of the total estate asset value, the cars, wine, putters, jewelry, artwork, and furnishings were valued by appraisers based on resale or auction prices.

I had been forced to purchase my Suburban from the estate at full appraised value of $19,500 by sending Susan Novak a check for the estate's half of my car. Five months later, Susan, the supposedly "highly experienced" administrator for JPMorgan, had not taken the time to transfer the title to me.

Each day, I drove that Suburban without a proper title. I legally owned half of it. Yet, no one helped with the insurance. Because of Susan's inaction, I had to pay the entire insurance bill. If I hit someone in an accident, God only knows how an insurance adjuster—or a plaintiff's attorney—would handle the situation.

As I closed the car door and hit the garage opener, I noticed the 1986 Porsche sitting there. This was another boondoggle.

The first value established for the Porsche was $9,200. Gary Matesic, a car expert, had come up with it. Because Susan had asked me about the car's options and accessories, I hired Gary to tell me what it was worth. Laura then emailed me that she wanted to buy it. I told her I'd waive my half of the car—$4,600—leaving her to pay Stephen $2,300. The car needed a $2,400 timing belt. I told her I didn't think it was safe to drive back to Kansas. Since she would receive millions from the estate, she could buy a brand-new Porsche up there.

After Laura decided against purchasing the Porsche, Susan moved to sell it. But nothing happened. Watching day after day tick by waiting for my lawyer to send me a bill, I decided to buy it so we could wrap up the estate. I made an offer and sent a check for $2,800 to purchase the estate's 50% ownership of the Porsche ($8,000 less $2,400 for the timing belt and divided by 2). I didn't ask nor expect Laura to waive her share.

And she didn't.

Now it was May 2011. For some reason, Susan hadn't cashed my check for the Porsche or even explained why, nor had she moved to sell it. Her inaction required me to continue paying the Porsche's entire insurance bill, even though I only owned half of it.

This delay was just another example of the ongoing lack of action and communication by JPMorgan. Without an attorney, I was helpless to get the bank to do anything to fix the problem.

On the other side of my Suburban was an empty space. It had held the 2003 BMW. Fortunately, the bank had authorized Gary Matesic to take possession of it. He appraised the car at $18,500, which surely pleased Susan Novak.

Gary then had the BMW towed to the local dealership where he sold it for $13,516. This bothered Laura because she had considered buying it at the appraised price. When she found out what it sold for, she was upset. After all, Susan had sold the Suburban to me at the full appraised value. Why didn't she get a chance to buy the BMW at the lower sales price or even the higher appraised value? Add in the fact that I had talked her out of purchasing the Porsche before making an offer to buy it and she seemed to think I had tricked her.

Actually, I felt the BMW was not a reliable car. Laura was lucky to have passed on it. And the bigger point was that JPMorgan had taken eleven months to get rid of that one simple car. After a deduction of $1,000 for a new battery and towing costs, the amount of cash that made it to the Max Hopper Estate account was paltry. Since Laura owned 50% of that amount, she should have been steamed, but she wasn't... yet.

I navigated the traffic easily in my Suburban, happy that rush hour was over. I was headed to an office building. I had an appointment to see Mike Graham, whom I'd recently fired. Acting as my own lawyer had lasted two whole weeks. Susan's actions made sure of that.

One afternoon, I was stopped by the guard at the front entrance to my gated community and given a letter from Susan Novak. It basically changed the rules relating to gifts I'd received from Max or anyone else. The only way I could keep my personal items was to have a signed and dated letter from Max or the giver stating the item was a gift. This was a dramatic change from Susan's and Tom Cantrill's position over the last eleven months.

Before this, Tom Cantrill had sent a letter to Laura's attorney, Lyle Pishny, in January 2011 stating:

"The Administrator thus far has accepted Jo's position on the separate property status of those cases of wine, but as we told you on December 17, 2010, if either Laura or Stephen want us to press for "clear and convincing evidence" of a gift we will do so, and if Jo cannot produce that evidence we will take the position that the wine is community property. As previously stated, the Administrator is unwilling to go beyond Jo's statement as to the separate property character of assets she claims unless there is clear evidence to the contrary, or there is a claim to the contrary from either of the children."

I remember setting the letter down in disgust. Who out there has a letter from their spouse stating, "Dear Sweetheart, I am giving you a pair of paintings for Christmas 2006. Signed, your loving husband."? This notification changing the policy meant everything was in play—my gifts from Max as well as gifts from my friends over the past twenty-eight years. It was time to lawyer up again.

I walked through the empty lobby, taking the elevator to Mike's floor. Since it was after seven, the staff had gone home. I made my way through the reception area to the conference room where I found Mike talking to another man.

"Hello," Mike said, standing up from the long table. "Let me introduce you to Jim Jennings."

A week earlier Mike had explained that he was an office lawyer, not a trial lawyer. He had handled litigation but was not a first-chair litigator. "Besides," he told me, "my office lawyer tactics have been unsuccessful in getting this simple matter resolved. You need a smart, aggressive, in-your-face litigator who commands the courtroom. Jim Jennings is the right tool for the job."

I shook Jim's hand. "I sure hope you can help me."

"I'm sure I can," he said confidently. "Mike has been getting me up to speed. Please take a seat so I can make sure I understand all this."

I pulled out a chair and faced the two men.

Jim cleared his throat. "I've gone through the entire file and think I have the lay of the land. But I want to make certain before I go popping off. The car situation is pretty self-explanatory. You need the title on your Suburban and the check cashed on the Porsche. It's the thousand bottles of wine that have me concerned, though. Are they still sitting in your cellar?"

"Yes. I can't get the bank to sell or divide them. I even provided Susan Novak with my inventory."

"Why are you inventorying everything?" he asked, leaning forward.

"Two reasons. I did the inventory mostly for myself. Like the warehouse filled with putters, I had no idea what I was turning over to JPMorgan. I wanted to create a detailed record if anyone had questions later. My goal was to separate my property from the estate as fast as possible and have it returned to me so I can stop paying attorneys' fees."

"Okay, what's the second reason?"

"It was a defensive move to protect me from accusations of stealing, damaging, or hiding assets. With the asset list and photos I've compiled, I have some solid evidence if I'm ever questioned by Stephen and Laura. I hope it doesn't come to that."

Jim Jennings frowned. "Jo, I don't understand what's going on here. This isn't Tom Cantrill's first rodeo. You're hiring people to do *their* job? It's not right."

"I hired both a car and a wine appraiser to create an inventory and appraisal for my records, to document exactly what I'm turning over to

JPMorgan. Later, JPMorgan asked if the estate could use my inventory, promising the estate would pay the invoice. But that's not the worst part," I told him. "In late January, I asked Mike to send Susan Novak an email stating I had agreed to pay the full appraised price for all the personal property: the wine, coins, putters, and furniture. It's a ridiculous offer that would cost me a lot of money, but I was desperate to get this over with. Mike sent the offer to Susan and got no response. He sent the offer again in February and again in March. Still no response."

"What about all the reimbursements owed to you for fronting money to JPMorgan and the estate?" he asked.

"In July of last year, I submitted a request for reimbursement of my expenses and received no reply. I resubmitted the expenses. Some of them I sent five times, all with supporting documentation. And still no reply. Finally, in March of this year, Susan paid a portion of the expenses. But she failed to address the ones she didn't pay. It seems like she just stonewalls me at every turn."

"Well, listen here. I'm going to schedule a meeting with JPMorgan and Tom Cantrill and demand the bank issue a title on all the personal property to you and the heirs as joint tenants. It should take Tom no more than twenty minutes. That'll remove the bank from coming between you and Max's children. Then it'll be up to you and them to figure it out on your own—sell the assets or not—without spending attorneys' fees."

"Thank you!" I said gratefully, clapping my hands. I wanted to reach across the table and hug him. "And don't forget the house."

"Right. I'll have Tom issue a title to you for one-half and Stephen and Laura for the other half. That'll take him no more than thirty minutes. Leave it to me. I'll get Tom to work for less than an hour and this debacle will be put to bed. Relax, you have the A-Team on it."

"Thanks, Jim. That makes me feel better, but I would like to ask you what I should expect in the way of attorneys' fees. Can you give me an idea of how much this will cost?"

"Good question. I'm a litigator. Litigation involves conflict. Conflict costs money. As I said, I'm going to try to get this matter resolved quickly and minimize your attorneys' fees. Tom's a seasoned professional, so I should be off your payroll fast."

I noticed he hadn't answered my question.

"And if it isn't resolved fast?" I asked in a shaky voice.

"Then we shift to the escalation game. When your opponent refuses to follow the law, you increase the legal pressure on them. They'll either fold or decide to escalate. This goes back and forth until someone dies or goes broke. But I'm sure JPMorgan, Susan Novak, and Tom Cantrill understand the law and their duties. Thankfully, the law is straightforward: divide everything by two and two again. Except for the cash, they just title everything as joint tenants. Thirty minutes of real independent administrator action and we're done. You'll never see me again."

"And what will my attorneys' fees look like if, God forbid, they refuse to follow the law?"

"It'll cost you a new car every month," he said bluntly.

My knees shook. I could see a monthly legal bill the size of a Ford Tempo. (I was relatively certain he wasn't thinking of a $65,000 Mercedes... or was he?)

I had just put my things away and was leaving when he called out to me. "Oh, and get any money you have at JPMorgan out now. If this gets nasty, the bank may seize it."

I nodded and made a mental note to move that task to the top of my list. At least JPMorgan couldn't stop me from doing that, right?

I left the meeting hopeful and feeling much better. Jim Jennings seemed to have a firm grasp on everything. No more handwringing over selling anything. Just retitle everything, distribute the cash to the heirs, and close out the estate. And he appeared ready to bare some teeth if JPMorgan stalled on anything. I figured a few thousand in fees to him and I'd be out of it.

When I arrived home, I found my Scottie, Blair, waiting for me. She wiggled her butt, begging for a walk. Since I felt so optimistic, I grabbed the leash and took off. It was like seeing the light at the end of the tunnel. For once, I could envision reaching the finish line with probate and JPMorgan Chase. What a glorious day that would be.

Chapter Seven

"We strive to treat all customers in a fair, ethical and non-discriminatory manner and work to achieve a competitive advantage through superior products and services, never through unethical or illegal business practices."

—JPMorgan Chase & Co.
2020 Code of Conduct
2.3 Ethical Business Practices

The next morning, I woke up, determined to follow Jim's advice and close out my two accounts at JPMorgan. After breakfast, I wrote a check for the balance in my JPMorgan checking account and then drove to BlueSky, my local bank. There, I deposited it into my BlueSky checking account. In a few days, that money would be drafted out of JPMorgan.

Next up was the investment account that held over $4 million. To avoid a confrontation, I contacted my financial advisor in San Francisco and asked that he transfer my assets out of JPMorgan and into my investment firm's account. I was sure this would go smoothly.

I was wrong.

For the next two weeks, he tried to move the assets but couldn't do it. Each time, JPMorgan provided him a different reason. I began to realize that what my friend Janie had told me when she recounted her brother's problem was true: money flows into JPMorgan, not out of it.

Distressed, I received a happy email from my new attorney Jim Jennings. He and Mike had visited with JPMorgan and Tom Cantrill. My attorneys felt that JPMorgan would have the property retitled by the end of the week. That sounded great.

Jim went on to explain that he'd told Susan Novak about JPMorgan's failure to transfer my money out of the bank. Susan admitted she was aware of attempts to transfer my funds out of JPMorgan. My attorney told her firmly that he wanted the account closed by the end of business that day. Sure enough, they complied.

It was a shame I had to pay a lawyer to get my own money out of JPMorgan. I imagined it was like dealing with the mob. I wondered what happened to the other widows out there who didn't have a lawyer. Was their money ever returned?

The next topic Jim said he addressed with Susan was the JPMorgan Monthly Estate Account statements. They showed all the assets JPMorgan had collected as well as all the checks they had written. The only way to verify if all my community property had been returned was to get a copy of the Master Estate Account. However, Susan had refused to provide a copy to me. She stated I was not an heir to the estate and did not have a right to see the statements. But Jim had unlocked that door. I received copies the next day.

Sitting in my study, I examined the records. As I added up the numbers, I felt sick to my stomach. The total amount in legal fees paid to Tom Cantrill's law firm, Hunton & Williams, was over $100,000! I buried my head in my hands and cried. We had worked so hard for that money. Stephen and Laura were getting screwed. This was a complete tragedy.

After analyzing the situation, I realized most of the estate left to be divided was tangible personal property like dishes, paintings, and wine—the same stuff I had previously tried to purchase at the full appraised value. Also, the home needed to be retitled. Waiting on my first legal bill from Jim Jennings and seeing no end to this legal nightmare, I sent an email directly to Stephen and Laura.

"Attached is a copy of a letter sent by my attorneys yesterday to Novak/ Cantrill. On Thursday evening I received copies of the 'master estate' account for the first time. I was shocked at the legal fees incurred. Hopefully, you are aware of them. If not, I thought you would be interested. My goal is to close the estate as quickly and efficiently as possible. I trust you share this goal."

Since neither Susan Novak, acting on behalf of Max's estate, nor Max's children were willing to let me buy the tangible personal property at full appraised price, I decided on a second option. I took the inventory and appraisals for the wine and split the individual bottles into columns marked A and B. Then, I sent Max's children another email.

"I am attempting to wrap up these matters quietly without attorney negotiations and present a unified proposal to the Independent Administrator. I continue to be overwhelmed by the amount of attorneys' fees charged to date. I just received the May statement and there is another $16,560.50 paid to Hunton & Williams. I hope we can agree on the wine. I am working on doing the same with the golf clubs. We need to work together to end this process and stop spending so much in legal fees to resolve items of relatively small value. The attorneys' fees could exceed the value of the item(s) in question."

All the heirs had to do was review the wine list and select column A or B. Then the wine could be split up. I did the same with the putters. It seemed like the simplest option since JPMorgan refused to retitle the property into our names.

Reading over the legal expenses was tough. Since the attorneys' fees came out of the estate, Stephen and Laura would take the entire loss, not me. Still, I felt heartbroken as I remembered the hard times. Max and I had paid every bill and sent money to his children before having any money for ourselves. They deserved the full benefit of the law, which meant that they should receive all of Max's estate. Yet now, JPMorgan and Hunton & Williams were going to take a considerable chunk of it. I felt like it was outright thievery. Not only was JPMorgan going to tap the estate account for more than $160,000 to cover their fees, but the fees for the lawyer they'd chosen was sucking the estate dry too.

Thinking about all this, I pounded my fist on the desk. Agreeing to JPMorgan Chase as the Independent Administrator had been a colossal mistake. Allowing them to choose Tom Cantrill as the IA's attorney had been a nuclear meltdown. This scene reminded me of one of those nature shows. JPMorgan was the lion feasting on a gazelle it had caught. When it had filled its belly, other lions and hyenas came along to feed. There would be nothing left of Max's estate to pass onto his children.

How can the legal system allow this? Am I the only one they are doing this to?

I rubbed my forehead. It was close to my usual time to get a coffee. I needed the boost to work another three hours on the burgeoning pile of mail and legal minutiae that screamed for my attention.

I drove to Starbucks, collected my latte, and found a seat in the corner. Despite the crowd, I felt isolated and totally alone.

I had been there five minutes when a barista approached me. She handed me a gift card. "This is for you."

"What did I do to deserve this?" I asked.

"It's from an anonymous source. They said you looked like you needed a lift."

I turned the card over. "How much is on it?"

"Fifty-one dollars."

I let out a snort. "Fifty-one? That's an odd number."

She shrugged her shoulders and went back to the register.

I glanced around the room, studying the faces and looking for my anonymous donor. It didn't take long to identify the culprit.

I scooted back the chair and made my way over to a table on the opposite corner. "Fifty-one," I told the man with the gray beard and long stringy hair. "That's pretty clever."

"No one out-gifts me," he said. "No one."

"Mind if I sit down... *Mr. Starr*? I believe that's your name."

"It's a free country," he replied, looking back at his computer, "last I checked."

"So, how did you know I gave you that gift card?" I asked, taking a seat.

"I'm like Kenny Rogers. I've made a life out of readin' people's faces."

"I don't buy it. I left before she gave you the gift card. There was no face to read."

"Okay, you got me. I slipped her a twenty. When reading people's faces doesn't work, paying for information does."

I chuckled. "Okay. I believe that. So, I looked pretty bad, huh?"

"I'll say. Like someone stole your puppy."

"In a way, they have. It's one of your brethren. What I thought was fair, isn't."

"*Fair.* That's a novel concept. My guess is you've been treated unfairly many times before. That's why you're so sensitive."

"What do you mean?" I asked.

"In your teens or twenties. Did someone treat you unfairly? Something that stuck in your craw?"

I sipped my latte and thought about it. Then for some unknown reason I spilled my guts to this character.

"It happened at my first job in 1968. I had just left college and was working in the auditing department of Genesco, a Nashville shoe manufacturer. It was my job to reconcile their books monthly for the retail stores and factory payrolls. I would finish my accounts every month and help other people finish theirs. Math was my major in college, so it wasn't difficult at all.

"Computers were new and the company had a computer department. One of the employees in our department who worked with the computer department to automate account reconciliation had a nervous breakdown. I guess she couldn't handle the responsibility of the job. The manager came to me and asked if I would do her job as well as my own. He promised me a nickel an hour raise in six months if I showed him I could handle the load. I agreed."

I took a deep breath, realizing I was baring my soul to this man I hardly knew.

"I loved the new assignment. I was exposed to computers and the experts in the computer department. It was heaven to me. But at the end of six months, the manager told me he wasn't going to give me the raise. He wanted to wait and make sure I was a good fit. As I stared at his face, I realized this was a good ol' boy system and that women were paid less. They probably figured I was young and wouldn't do anything about this financial abuse. Then, when my vacation came due, I made plans to visit my sister in Dallas. That's when the manager explained that because my vacation fell at the end of the month when payrolls were due, I couldn't go.

"So a few days later, I interviewed for a job at NCR, a computer company also in Nashville. Even though I thought I'd done well on the tests administered, they called saying I didn't get the job. Later, I learned they had called my company for a reference and were told I was too valuable to let go. This was back in the day when companies didn't like poaching off each other. They felt obligated to ask for permission. To me, this was incredibly unfair.

"Payday that month was on a Wednesday, so I collected my check and didn't go in the next day. I told my boss I had tickets to Dallas on

Friday for my vacation. That's when he begged me not to quit. He said if I came back in two weeks, he'd give me that nickel raise. I told him no way. I'd never move up at this company because the game was rigged. It was based on gender and I wasn't the right one. Sure enough, not only did I land in Dallas, but I landed a job with American Airlines. And the rest is history."

Tarian grinned, realizing his suspicions had been correct. "You're right, it wasn't fair. And now, you're in another situation that isn't fair. I presume some lawsuit?"

"No, it's the administration of my late husband's estate. JPMorgan does nothing but hold the money, and they've hired a lawyer who's quickly draining the estate. The work the bank is supposed to handle they have the lawyer do. This legal system is rigged. It's not fair."

"Of course it's not fair. It's not a dispute resolution forum like you nonlawyers think. It's extremely rare that we satisfactorily resolve any dispute."

"Then what is it?" I asked naively.

"It's a wealth redistribution tool. Think of it as a success tax. You and your husband were successful, so we need to redistribute some of your wealth."

"Then it's a form of socialism—for lawyers. Right?"

He closed his laptop. "I like to think of it as an opportunistic feeding by larger predators."

"Stephen and Laura have no idea what's happening to their money. They're going to lose it all."

"That's because they're simple babes in the woods. They're way down on the food chain, so their meal will be snatched from their mouths. Too bad. So sad."

I ignored his sarcasm. "And that's what you used to do," I said, a slight edge to my voice. "Snatch money from people?"

"Yes, and I was very good at it. But not now. I've turned away from the dark side. I'm writing a book on how the legal system really works—the secrets we tell no one—and how to navigate the crooked game. It'll be a bestseller."

My phone went off. It was my lawyer. I excused myself and hustled out to the Suburban.

"Hey, Jim, what's up?"

"Max's children just discovered that you were reimbursed for the funeral expenses. They thought *you* were responsible for all that—the food, drink, and facility. Now, they've learned that the estate paid for it, which really means they did."

"Oh, for crying out loud. What have I gotten myself into?"

"You've become a human piñata," said Jim. "Max's children are whacking one side and JPMorgan is bashing the other. I need to find a way to put the brakes on this before they split you open and spill your assets all over the ground."

With that, I hung up. I didn't have the courage to ask him how much longer I'd have to take a beating. I could only imagine.

Chapter Eight

"Most important, treat our clients like you would a member of your own family."

—Jamie Dimon, Chairman & CEO
JPMorgan Chase Bank, N.A.
March 5, 2013 Letter to Employees

Sitting at my desk, I removed my reading glasses and rubbed my eyes. All around my study were stacks of documents. These included bills not yet paid, letters from the companies Max had worked with, and tax statements. The volume was hard to believe. I was literally drowning in paperwork.

I picked up a document that needed filing and laughed. It was a notice of distribution to Stephen and Laura. They had complained so often and loudly (through their lawyers) that Susan Novak had finally agreed to distribute some of the estate to them. They each received $2 million in cash and stock. I was amazed it had taken so long. After all, the only reason to hold onto that money was to pay "date of death" debts. The $1.2 million mortgage was all that remained. Max's children would soon receive a title, making them responsible for half of it, and I would owe the other half. Why it had taken this long for JPMorgan to decide it had enough money to pay a debt load of zero, I had no idea.

Nothing much had happened with the estate since that point, but I still suffered mentally. Most of 2010 had been terribly rough on me. I had spent March through November working in the warehouse, creating an inventory of Max's putters. Throughout that period, my depression pushed me deeper toward the edge. I formulated a plan to commit suicide. I had selected a very high overpass in Dallas that would get the job done. I just wanted to wrap up Max's estate so that my estate's executor would have an easier time of it. Then I could join Max wherever he was. I was lost without him.

A bark drew me out of my thoughts. Blair wanted attention, so I reached down and petted her, and noticed she was standing on a document. Gently pushing her out of the way, I picked it up. It was a letter from Jamcracker, yet another debacle courtesy of JPMorgan.

Before Max died, he had told me how excited he was about Jamcracker, a company he had been affiliated with since its formation. Also, Max had served on the board of directors for another company that the founder had started. No matter what, I had planned to keep the Jamcracker stock in my portfolio.

When JPMorgan was appointed IA, I turned over all the original stock certificates in my possession, along with an asset list that I gave to Susan with contact information for each company. Like so many of the companies on the list, she had failed to contact Jamcracker to confirm Max's assets. If she had, she would've learned that Jamcracker had given Max 153,000 stock options which had an expiration date that was fast approaching. But she didn't contact them.

On January 25, 2011, while I suffered through the one-year anniversary of Max's death, unbeknownst to me I was suffering another loss: 153,000 stock options in Jamcracker. According to the bylaws, the stock options expired 365 days after the holder's death. Susan's assistant knew of the options but had somehow failed to flag them to be exercised.

In late February 2011, I sat in this same study reviewing my stocks. I followed up with Jamcracker, copying Susan on my email. Almost immediately, she slapped me back down. She reminded me that having Jamcracker receive communications from two different people would be confusing to the company and then she assured me she would keep me in the loop.

Yet, behind my back, she sent her assistant the following email:

"Perfect... Just as I said to her. She is wasting everyone's time."

The infuriating truth was that Susan wasn't keeping me informed. The last update I'd received from her had been more than three months earlier. At no time did she or her assistant let me know that any options needed exercising. She took a large butter knife, slathered her hubris over a warm piece of incompetence, and handed it to me. I would be the one eating this gigantic loss.

Life crawled along until late April. I followed up with Susan on the Jamcracker options but received no information. I considered another avenue for information: JPMorgan's Private Banking section.

Early on, when JPMorgan had made their pitch to me, Susan had explained they had a Chinese Wall between the Private Banking section and the Estate Department. This was vital because not only was it required under banking regulations, but JPMorgan wanted to assure its customers that keeping money in one part of the bank would not influence decisions made by another. The Estate section required absolute independence. They weren't supposed to know when a billionaire was in the Private Banking section. Instead, the Estate section simply needed to follow the law and make the appropriate decisions, even if it meant losing a billion-dollar whale in Private Banking.

Yeah, right.

In reality, the JPMorgan staff walked right through the Chinese Wall and often talked across it about all sorts of issues. And, like the real Great Wall of China, it was easy to penetrate when your own teammates opened the gates and let anyone through.

Even though I could get information from the Private Banking staff, it was extremely stressful to deal with them. They had used mafia-like intimidation to "convince" me to keep my money at JPMorgan. But Private Banking did have an upside. If I complained to them about Susan's lack of progress, I quickly received an email from Susan giving me a crumb of information. I imagined the local capo walking down several floors to Susan's office and "prodding" her to take care of me. It wasn't always effective, but it did move the needle.

I took a deep breath and reached out to the Private Bank staff. While I went on about how worthless Susan was, I asked about retitling the Jamcracker stock. The Private Bank staff told me Jamcracker was still waiting for the paperwork, which was still in Jamcracker's archived files. That afternoon I went to Max's office at the warehouse and looked through his files for the document. The option agreement was right there, so I faxed a copy to Jamcracker.

Nothing more happened until the morning of June 28, 2011. At 8:52 a.m., I imagine a bloodcurdling scream was heard throughout JPMorgan's Dallas office when Susan Novak realized there were stock options she had failed to exercise. She sent an email to her assistant and Jamcracker's CFO in all caps:

"...PLEASE ANSWER THESE QUESTIONS NOW: WHAT IS THE EXPIRATION DATE TO EXERCISE THE OPTIONS? AS SOON AS POSSIBLE IS NOT CLEAR BELOW. WHERE IS THE APPROPRIATE EXERCISE AGREEMENT? PLEASE SEND IT TO ME IMMEDIATELY. THANK YOU FOR YOUR IMMEDIATE ATTENTION TO THESE REQUESTS NOW."

Clearly, she was panicked.

By this time, I'd followed up with Jamcracker directly, not copying Susan on my emails. Jamcracker sent me the paperwork to exercise my 50% of the expired options and they agreed to talk to the board about extending the expiration date.

On the chance that the board granted an extension (since they had highly valued Max), I completed the paperwork and mailed it back to Jamcracker with a check to cover purchase of my portion.

Susan took a different approach. She contacted Jamcracker to find out the current market value of the stock. She didn't understand that Jamcracker was a private company with no reported value, since it was not a publicly traded stock.

Fortunately, the board of directors granted us an extension to July 15. Yet, for some unknown reason, JPMorgan waited and waited. Only when they stared at the abyss—the last full day before the deadline expired—did they pull the trigger and exercise the stock for the estate.

The person I had been communicating with at Jamcracker sent me an email saying,

"Are you kidding me—is this their first time doing this??? For goodness sake..."

Unfortunately, this would not be the only time I received emails from a company questioning JPMorgan's competency.

ONE OF MY frequent chores was to sort through invoices from my attorneys. Every time I looked at the mounting costs, I became distraught. Then, I considered Stephen and Laura. They had their own problems.

Stephen had initially hired attorney John Round before firing him in December. Laura was using Lyle Pishny, a lawyer in Kansas City whom Stephen had engaged after John Round departed. Then Stephen tried to hire another Dallas lawyer, but the attorney had a conflict. Eventually he approached Gary Stolbach with Glast, Phillips & Murray.

Mr. Stolbach worked at the same firm that Max had hired years earlier to draft a will. He was also the attorney I had talked with while searching for a signed will. Now he was about to join this feeding frenzy.

I learned about all this by mail, when a form arrived that I needed to sign to allow Mr. Stolbach to work for Stephen and Laura. Not understanding this, I called Mike Graham.

"Mike, what is this about? Why do I need to sign this?"

"Gary Stolbach is legally tainted because you spoke with him and he worked for you, even though it was a trivial act."

"What do you mean 'legally tainted'?" I asked.

"Imagine if I was the business lawyer for a man. One day, this man decides to get a divorce. His wife calls and wants to hire me as her attorney. Don't you think that would be a problem?"

"Yes. I guess you would have information about the husband that he wouldn't want his wife to know."

"That's close," Mike said. "It's because the lawyer has confidential information, communications that are protected under the attorney-client privilege. I can't work for the wife no matter what. But in some cases, the conflict of interest is so minimal, the state bar allows me to get a waiver from the protected party. In this case, that party is you."

I turned his words over in my mind. "So if I don't sign it, Stephen can't use this lawyer?"

"Correct, and from what I hear, he's struggling to find a lawyer willing to take this case. If you don't sign it, we might have more delays until he can lawyer up."

"Why? Can't Tom Cantrill just go ahead and retitle everything even though Stephen doesn't have a lawyer?"

"Sure, but so far, he hasn't."

"Okay," I said. "I'll think about it."

I sat in my study, staring out the window at the sun reflecting off a car across the street. My air conditioning kept Blair and me cool from the Texas heat. Thank God for that.

As I reread the document, I was puzzled. If Gary Stolbach was legally tainted, why wasn't Tom Cantrill? The facts seemed the same; Tom had written my will and I had a conversation with him following Max being declared brain dead. The more I thought about it, the more confused I became.

I took a break to play with Blair, I considered the never-ending delays with JPMorgan. If Tom Cantrill was unwilling to do anything so long as Stephen and Laura were unrepresented, then I'd be stuck in this Groundhog Day. I thought long and hard about it. After not nearly enough consideration, I made perhaps the third worst decision of my life and signed the waiver. I would pay dearly.

THE PHONE RANG. "Jo, we need to talk." It was Jim Jennings, my other lawyer.

"What's up?"

"In looking through the court's file, I found two motions filed by Tom Cantrill asking for a delay to file the inventory of the estate. The judge granted them. Now he wants a third delay, even though JPMorgan has been on the job for almost a year. I want your permission to object to any more delays."

"Yes!" I practically screamed into the phone. "I wholeheartedly agree. Thank you."

"Great," he replied. "I'll take care of it."

Several days later, I received a copy of the proposed inventory with a letter from Cantrill stating he would file it in two days. That meant I needed to quickly decide if I had any objections.

Spreading out the sheets of assets, I started going through it. The inventory was full of errors. Assets had been omitted, and some of the assets had incorrect valuations. I was disgusted. At no time had Cantrill or JPMorgan contacted Betty, Max's assistant, nor had they talked to our CPA. The closer I looked, the worse it got.

One particular item hurt me. It designated my precious needlepoint collection as community property. The value was set at $25,000.

I had learned this craft at the foot of my grandmother while accumulating a lifetime "needlepoint stash" and $25,000 was an outrageous valuation because no one, other than another needlepoint person, would pay a third of that. Of course, to me, it was priceless.

I remembered the nights by the fireplace as I'd needlepointed, embroidered, or crocheted. Now, I'd be forced to repurchase the estate's 50% from

Max's children for $12,500—assuming they'd sell it to me. It was a bitter pill to swallow.

The proposed inventory was a mess and Cantrill recognized this. On the motion to the court, he wrote a disclaimer:

> "So, one can still conclude that the inventory continues to be a work in progress even though it has been filed, and as filed it does represent the Administrator's best current effort to classify and value items that were on hand at Max's date of death. The time had come to file, even though there will still be some questions among all of us as to classification and value."

That was an understatement.

I sent all the errors I could find to my attorney. He forwarded them to Cantrill but learned that Cantrill had already filed the inventory with the court. In fact, he had filed it the day before the inventory was due. The irony was that for the first time in this whole nightmare, he and JPMorgan had beaten a deadline!

A week later, Jim convinced me to object to the inventory. This would take thousands of dollars in legal fees to litigate but he said it had to be done. I believed him and tossed some more chips into an ever-increasing pot.

By now, attorneys Jennings and Stolbach were discussing dividing the wine and golf clubs. It wasn't going well.

I knew from the beginning that Stephen and Laura did not want any physical property. They made it clear that they wanted me to have all the stuff and pay them their share in cash. I had already learned this when I bought back my Suburban. Yet both they and the IA had failed to accept my repeated offers to buy all of the tangible personal property at a highly inflated appraisal price.

The only property I refused to buy back was my home on Robledo Drive, mainly because I didn't have to. The Texas Constitution gave me the right to live in it for the rest of my life. The intestate laws required Max's children to pay for half the insurance and mortgage. It gave me great comfort knowing I would not be forced to leave my house or repurchase it. I was not going to allow myself to become property-rich and cash-poor.

I monitored the emails going back and forth between Jennings and Stolbach. Since we couldn't get JPMorgan to retitle the personal property, we waited on Stephen and Laura to pick which side of the wine and putters they wanted: A or B.

I had worked hard on the lists and felt I did a fair job. For many of the bottles it was easy since we had them in cases of twelve. The only tricky part was the odd-bottle groups of a particular vintage. One side would receive an extra bottle. Still, I didn't care. I just wanted them to pick a side and we'd be done with that.

The A/B list appeared to be the solution. But just when it looked like we had an agreement, Stolbach sent a document that implied I would be responsible for the quality of the wine. This was absurd. I couldn't predict which bottle was drinkable and which was spoiled. And, more importantly, I didn't have to.

When we rejected the heirs' ridiculous offer, the angry emails between Jennings and Stolbach increased. As I read each one, I envisioned tens of thousands of dollars flying out the window. Each email had to be read by the opposing lawyer at $500+ per hour. Tom Cantrill, who was usually copied in, also got to tap the estate for his hourly rate. Since I had two lawyers, they could each bill me. And I had to pay Jennings a massive fee just to write the emails. I talked to Jennings and told him to forget negotiating with the heirs. "Let's focus on getting Tom Cantrill to issue a title to the property and get the lawyers out of this mess."

This put Jennings on a vigorous campaign of visits, calls, and emails to Cantrill. He begged him and cajoled him. He instructed Cantrill to retitle the property and end this nightmare. Yet Cantrill and JPMorgan dithered. This brought forth a barrage of emails from Stolbach. His language was beyond threatening.

Stolbach stated the law allowed the IA to stick one side with all the property and give cash to the other. He claimed a comprehensive and authoritative memo was forthcoming. He made it clear that if Cantrill retitled the property, Stephen and Laura would file a breach of fiduciary duty lawsuit against JPMorgan Chase. These threats caused Cantrill to do nothing except bill more attorney's fees. I could only imagine how much money was being drained from the estate.

While this chaos raged, I took two cases of wine that were my separate property and sent them to Christie's, which auctioned them off in Hong Kong. Susan Novak found out about it and declared the cases community property, which was blatantly wrong. Max had purchased them for me as a gift. I had told Susan this when I met with her in July 2010, and she had agreed they were my separate property. But with the new sheriff in town, Gary Stolbach, policing every inch of the property, Susan must have felt intense pressure to reclassify the wine. She coldly collected the money from Christie's and applied it to the estate.

At this point, I felt the tide turning against me. The bank continually sided with the heirs. If I wasn't careful, I'd be sucked out into the swirling ocean and drown in this legal morass.

Chapter Nine

"Cross-selling is a big deal. And we do an exceptionally good job at cross-selling. We think we're among the best out there… We do as much cross-sell as a Wells Fargo."
— Jamie Dimon, Chairman & CEO
JPMorgan Chase Bank, N.A.

Sometimes, we tend to focus on our own misery, even when there's so much of it happening to other people. But the relentless and usually insignificant *Breaking News* chyron at the bottom of the TV screen slaps us back to reality.

In July 2011, there was plenty of misery to go around. Somalia was suffering through another famine. Thailand was hit with a severe flood, affecting almost 13 million people. And Chile received a massive snowfall, leaving thousands freezing in the cold. At least the TV coverage of all these events kept me focused on something other than my own problems. I felt so helpless for those people because there was nothing I could do but pray. And pray I did.

Eventually, the coverage moved onto something else, and I came back to the stacks of insanity in my study. But watching the news had given me an idea. I had noticed some reports chronologically listing the events of a tragedy. I decided to use the same tactic in my case. And I had just the right starting point.

Ever since Gary Stolbach had arrived on a mean horse, firing off nasty emails and threatening lawsuits, Tom Cantrill had been visited by the same snowfall Chile had suffered through—he was frozen. My lawyers could not get him to take ten minutes to retitle my home on Robledo Drive so we could move on.

Cantrill often promised to do so, but then Stolbach would send a threatening email (that my two lawyers had to read and bill me for), and Cantrill's hands would freeze again. It was madness.

To show how Cantrill had turned to ice, I drew up a chronological list of events for my lawyers and called it "Broken Promises."

June 21, 2011 – Cantrill letter stating: "We will be deeding the real estate assets around June 30 if there is no buy-out resolution."

June 22, 2011 – Cantrill letter stating: "We will be assigning the real estate in undivided interests in accordance with ownership."

July 15, 2011 – Cantrill letter stating: "The Administrator will, absent a request from all of you to the contrary, deed Robledo to Jo and the children just as soon as we can get the lender's consent…"

July 18, 2011 – Cantrill letter stating: "We will convey the property in undivided interests to Jo (50%), to Laura (25%) and to Stephen (25%) all subject to the existing mortgage. We are going to proceed with the conveyance of Robledo…"

July 20, 2011 – Cantrill letter stating: "We have reached the stage in the administration of Mr. Hopper's estate that the administrator desires to convey the property."

July 20, 2011 – Cantrill letter stating: "We are pursuing a path that will lead to an assignment as we have told everyone we would do."

July 25, 2011 – Cantrill letter stating: "I will be preparing an undivided interest assignment of that property."

July 26, 2011 – Cantrill letter stating: "I believe Sections 3(q), 146(a)(4), 254 and 285 of the Probate Code makes Mr. Stolbach's arguments as to Robledo untenable."

Rightfully so, Tom Cantrill and JPMorgan rejected Stolbach's absurd notion that an Independent Administrator had the power to make the surviving spouse buy out the heirs. Stolbach had also peddled the idea that somehow the IA could sell the house and land (including the surviving spouse's 50% ownership, subject to the surviving spouse living there for life), and give a clear title to the new owner over the surviving spouse's objection.

Think about that for a moment.

Our Robledo Drive home, valued at $1.9 million, would be sold to the highest bidder. How much would you pay for a large mansion that had a widow living in it until the day she died? Certainly nowhere close to $1.9 million. We had a mortgage of $1.2 million outstanding on the home. Would the buyer pay that off? Not likely.

If this ridiculous theory were allowed to become a reality, my $350,000 equity would drop to nothing. The heirs would receive the same from the sale as well. However, they would receive something valuable to them: the freedom from having to pay their share of the mortgage and insurance for the rest of my life. That would be a large number.

I talked with Jennings and asked his thoughts on the matter.

"Cantrill and JPMorgan are hesitant to go against Stolbach. They're terrified. I fear they are leaning toward Max's children."

"You think JPMorgan might go against me on this?"

Jim let out an exasperated sigh. "Cantrill acts like this is virgin territory, like this is the first time a widow has received in essence a life estate, like there has never been a case where the heirs want cash instead of the property. It's insane."

"What can I do?" I asked, afraid of the answer.

"There's an option you won't like. But before I tell you about it, let's allow the world to spin a few more times and see what happens."

That sounded good for him, but every revolution cost me more money. I needed to find some way off this expensive merry-go-round.

A COUPLE WHO lived down the street invited me out to dinner. The restaurant they selected resembled a ski lodge with good food, cozy booths, and an excellent wine list. We sat there enjoying some hot spinach dip when the husband began talking about a sports team. Before he got too far, his wife elbowed him and said, "Oh c'mon, Jo doesn't want to talk about sports, right?"

As she stared at me, I wasn't sure what to say. My best move was to grab a chip, scoop up some dip, and shove it into my mouth. Silence hung over us. The husband pursed his lips, deciding which way he wanted to go. Finally, he figured it out.

"What if I could tell you a sports story that might relate to your probate mess?"

I crunched on the chip and thought about it. Clearly, he wanted to talk about sports. Since he was picking up the tab *and* he might have some information I could use, I grinned and nodded.

"Great," he said, leaning back with a smile of satisfaction. "Here it is." He moved his wine out of the way so he could gesture appropriately. Then he spoke these words of wisdom.

"For many years, hockey was an eye-for-an-eye sport. If you ran my head into the boards, next chance I got, I'd ram your head into the boards. At some point, we'd drop the gloves and hit each other with our fists. That's why hockey is a man's sport."

"Sounds like it," I quipped.

"This payback system continued on and on, with the offender punished by the victim. Then things kind of changed because many times the victim was left twitching on the ice, slipping into a coma. No way he was coming back into the game to exact revenge when the paramedics were charging up the paddles in the ambulance. In those cases, some tough guy on the victim's team was sent onto the ice to take a stick to the head of the offender. It was considered justice.

"As time went on, that became the routine. The offender was punished by the goon on the victim's team, even if the victim was okay and still playing with all his limbs. Then smart coaches devised a third method: revenge via proxy. Are you following all this?"

"Of course," I replied. "We women can follow complex concepts— most of the time," I said sarcastically.

"Good," he nodded, clearly choosing to ignore my sarcasm. "So this third way, in my opinion, is pure genius. Let's pretend that a Dallas Stars player runs the Pittsburgh Penguins' stud player into the boards and hurts him. Let's assume the Penguins' stud comes back into the game. Well, these smart coaches now decide to change things up. The Penguins grab their nasty goon, a player on the roster for only moments like this, and send him out on the ice with specific instructions. As the goon circles the rink, everyone in the building assumes he's looking for the offender on the Dallas Stars so he can ram a stick up his ass. But then something beautiful happens. He spots the Dallas Stars' stud, a player who had done absolutely nothing wrong, and rams his elbow into the stud's throat. As the stud falls to the ice gasping for oxygen because his trachea has been crushed, a lightbulb goes off above everyone's heads. Don't punish the offender. Punish the stud on the other team. The dynamics of this brutal sport changed. It was a true paradigm shift for violence."

I swallowed some wine and set down my glass. "I fail to see how your story helps me in any way deal with my probate nightmare."

"It does," he said, eyes gleaming. "I mean, it might. Because the lesson here is when you're dealing with someone you hate, someone you want to destroy—in this case, JPMorgan wants to crush you like a bug—they don't need to punish you. Do you see?"

"Who do they punish?" I asked.

"They go after people close to you. People you care about. When you're standing there watching them stick an icepick in your good friend, you'll capitulate. Get it?"

"I see your point, but JPMorgan is so incompetent they can't formulate a plan like that. They can barely make a deadline. Sure, they seem to be against me, but that would be pretty sinister even for these folks."

He tossed his head back and laughed. "Believe me, Jo. The bank didn't get to be this big by being nice. Jamie Dimon didn't get to the top by telling his managers to kindly help a customer load up his money in a gunny sack and tote it to a competing bank across the street. No, these folks play hardball. Most billionaires do."

We finished our enjoyable meal, avoiding more sports talk. Still, the predictions of that gladiator-obsessed lawyer Henry Steele from way back at the beginning of this nightmare started rattling around in my head. Did this sports-violence-obsessed man know what he was talking about? Could his hockey story apply to me?

Two days later, I had a $1,000/hour meeting with my two lawyers to go over some new developments. Mike Graham broke it to me less than gently.

"As you know, Max's children, and thus JPMorgan, believe you are hiding assets. They're ramping up the pressure."

"In what way?" I asked, my heart rate increasing.

"They want to talk to Betty. What can you tell me about her?"

"Betty is a great person, very trustworthy. She's been a good friend to me. Between the both of us, we kept Max running."

"When did she start? What did she do?"

"Max lost his secretary in 2000, so I stepped in momentarily and helped. I typed up his speeches and such. He hired Betty a few months later and she took over, handling his general correspondence. She eventually controlled his schedule and dealt with all the travel issues. I still helped with speeches and any overflow. Max loved getting involved in projects, but he didn't like the paperwork. He was the visionary, a grand planner, the five-star general who wins you the war, not the lieutenant who leads a platoon up the hill. Between Betty and me, we kept his world running smoothly. Frankly, I don't see any reason why Betty shouldn't talk to them. The only real comment I have is what took them so long?"

"Great," Mike said. "The next person they want to talk to is Max's CPA, Calamity Jane. Right, Jim?"

Jim leaned forward with a concerned look. "That's right. It's just that with Stolbach threatening litigation, Cantrill will probably bring on a litigator at some point to deal with Stolbach."

"So?" I asked, not following his line of thought.

"Well, there's a good chance they're going to sit your CPA down and do a mini-deposition on her. Have you ever been through a deposition?"

"No."

"It's like getting a root canal."

I chuckled. "My dentist is good. A root canal's not so bad."

"It is when you don't have anesthesia."

That got my attention. "Oh!"

"Yeah, *oh!* And they'll start searching under every rock, forcing you to research the tiniest detail. They mentioned the files at the CPA's office that you said contained the last sixteen years of tax returns. Imagine that."

"But I don't have anything to hide," I told him.

"Of course you don't. But when they find a marble statue you bought in 1995 and ask what happened to it, are you going to remember? And even if you do, are you going to be able to produce a notarized receipt showing where it went?"

"They're not going to go that far, are they?"

"I'm afraid so," Jim said, folding his arms. "Litigation involves conflict. Conflict involves pain. Pain without anesthesia is—well, painful."

"But we aren't in litigation. Right?"

"Not yet, but the troops are amassing at the border. It won't take much for them to cross and create a calamity for Jane and Betty."

I listened to them tell me what my friends were in for. JPMorgan said they only wanted to meet with our CPA to discuss the cost basis of certain assets. Jennings smelled a trap.

To discern their intentions, Calamity Jane asked JPMorgan to send whatever basis questions they had in writing. JPMorgan refused, giving more credibility to my lawyers' theory. After all, how hard is it to send an email listing the assets with a blank for their cost basis?

Jim suggested he be allowed to be present when they questioned her because she was my CPA too. He wanted to protect my private financial information and social security number from falling into the wrong hands.

Tom Cantrill refused.

The only arrangement Cantrill would agree to was putting Susan Novak and Calamity Jane in a room by themselves. Our CPA responded that she was happy to disclose Max's information, but I was her client too. She couldn't release privileged information without my permission. She said she'd meet with Susan if Jim Jennings was present to protect my private information.

Cantrill again rejected that, then mused that she was hiding information. He sent an email stating they needed access to Max's records to ensure they had recovered all the property. This expanded the initial "cost basis" reason and exposed their subterfuge.

Cantrill asked Calamity Jane if she had her own lawyer because he wanted to talk to that person. This disturbed her.

"Am I going to get dragged into a lawsuit, Jo?" she cried on the phone.

There it was—hockey's new strategy of hurting those close to you. I'd already heard from Betty. She was worried about ripping through her life savings to hire a lawyer. I understood that feeling.

"I don't know what these people are doing," I told Calamity Jane.

All this drama added fuel to the Stolbach conspiracy theory. *What is Jo hiding? There must be assets still missing.*

At a standstill, Cantrill filed a Motion to Compel Delivery of Papers. He asserted that our CPA and I were withholding documents. It was preposterous.

Calamity Jane read the motion and found herself in a dilemma. JPMorgan also wanted my information to date, which included everything after Max died. To comply, she'd have to release my private information, accounts, balances, and tax returns. I refused that because I had no idea what some angry person on the other side of this nightmare might do. I could be dealing with identity theft problems for the rest of my life. Plus, they weren't entitled to my information post-death.

Calamity Jane contacted the Ethics Division of the Texas State Board of Public Accountancy for guidance. She gave notice to Cantrill that she would wait for a ruling. That wasn't acceptable to him. For the first time, it seemed Mr. Cantrill was in a hurry.

Stolbach, reading all this correspondence, added some of his own. His email, copied to Calamity Jane while excluding my attorneys, ended with this:

> "Finally, depending upon how this is handled by [the CPA], **we will begin a grievance with her professional licensing association immediately** [emphasis added]. If there is something we don't understand that mitigates what appears to be an unreasonable delay by the Bank in collecting important estate information and a failure, by [the CPA] to provide a client's representative with documentation to which the client is entitled, [I] invite the Bank and/or [the CPA] to inform me."

Calamity Jane sent me Stolbach's email. There it was—the hockey stick to the throat. Like those hockey players, I had not seen this coming.

Cantrill soon filed a suit against Calamity Jane. Initially, it appeared the estate would pay for her attorneys' fees. Later, that disappeared underneath an avalanche of claims that she was unwilling to cooperate. That left me to step in to pay the tab. Just another stack of cash to add to the slag heap.

At one point, Calamity Jane's attorney held a meeting at his office where any of the parties could come and review the files in question. Despite their desperation to see the files, my attorney, Jim Jennings, was the only person who showed up. This pretty much told us that the fuss over her records was a sham.

On the day of Calamity Jane's hearing, the bank's attorneys showed up to say they were pulling the case from the docket because a confidentiality agreement had been worked out. That was the end of that.

I WOKE UP every morning in a lovely mansion, situated in a neighborhood of Dallas's movers and shakers, all behind a gated community. A security guard monitored our safety 24/7. I had money in the bank and food in the pantry. With all this abundance, I should have felt safe and secure. Yet I was far from it.

I watched the money drain from my account like beer at a fraternity keg party. I dreaded getting emails, which were often full of legal filings or attorneys' bills. And I feared seeing new emails pop up from my attorneys.

I told a friend that I felt like Han Solo, Chewbacca, Luke Skywalker, and Princess Leia when they were trapped in a garbage masher on the Death Star's detention level. The walls were slowly closing in.

If I thought life would get better, I was sorely mistaken. Like Jim Jennings had predicted, Tom Cantrill brought on a litigation attorney to face off with Gary Stolbach. I called Jim to discuss it.

"What do you know about this new attorney?" I asked him.

"His name is John Eichman, and he's a top litigator. If Stolbach is a flamethrower, Eichman is a nuclear bomb."

"Is he more than a yeller and screamer?"

"Definitely! JPMorgan only hires top legal talent."

"Will Tom Cantrill get along with Eichman?"

"Of course. They're partners. They work at the same firm."

I was confused. "Isn't that some kind of conflict? After all, it seems like Stolbach will sue Cantrill and his firm Hunton & Williams. How can they have a lawyer from the same firm represent them when they're a party to a potential lawsuit?"

"Stolbach hasn't sued yet, so let's wait until that happens. And Hunton & Williams is a big firm. They have over seven hundred attorneys with experts in every aspect of law. They're not about to make a simple ethical mistake and subject themselves to a malpractice lawsuit from JPMorgan. That would be career suicide."

Jim put me on hold. A few minutes later, he came back. "Hey, Jo, sorry about that. My secretary handed me something fresh off the wire. Cantrill says there's not enough money left in the estate to pay for the projected legal fees to defend Stolbach's impending lawsuit. As such, he's freezing all the assets of the estate."

"This is getting worse," I moaned.

"Yeah, it gets worse," he said, not understanding my comment. "They're freezing any money you have at the bank too."

"Oh, for crying out loud, Jim! This is ridiculous."

"At least his letter says you aren't responsible for JPMorgan's IA commission."

That one comment was the spark that started another fire with Max's children. Their attorneys claimed that I had a secret agreement with JPMorgan and thus JPMorgan was protecting me. I did not have a different deal than they had. We all signed the same contract produced by the bank. It read:

"JPMorgan's Estate Settlement Services are priced on the market value of all assets included on the federal estate tax return. These fees are not annual charges. Rather, they apply to the entire estate settlement period."

JPMorgan Chase's salesperson, Kal Grant, had explained that the deceased's estate pays for the settlement of his/her estate, not the surviving spouse. Once the heirs received a copy of the letter and found out I wasn't paying half the bank's commission for settling the estate, a massive explosion occurred. They would not let this stand. Yet the agreement we all signed stated fees were paid by the estate. With this new revelation, Stolbach felt JPMorgan had stuck them with the full dinner tab. And it appeared the bill would be a 72-ounce steak at the Big Texan. Good luck swallowing that.

After digesting all this, it still appeared Stephen and Laura thought I was paying half the estate's attorneys' fees. Amazingly, likely due to Stolbach's constant threats, the bank and their attorneys decided I did indeed have to pay a portion of the estate's attorneys' fees. The troops were about to cross the border.

Both Jim and Mike believed all these threats and activities were a brazen attempt by JPMorgan to bully both the heirs and me into a family settlement agreement.

"Cantrill seems to believe that the IA's role is first a mediator, then an arbitrator," Jim explained. "Instead of simply retitling the assets, the bank is determined to impose a settlement on us, like it or not."

The fireworks continued.

Stolbach peppered Cantrill with information about how the IA needed to partition my house right out from under me. At first, Cantrill held firm, telling Stolbach to get bent. Then Stolbach played his trump card. He threatened to sue JPMorgan for breach of fiduciary duty. I asked Jim about this.

"A fiduciary duty is a sacred one," he told me. "If your brother is taking care of your sick mother, wouldn't you be distraught if he spent some of her money at strip clubs? People with fiduciary duties are like a mother holding her baby. If necessary, she's going to protect that child with her life. JPMorgan, if they breach their fiduciary duty to care for your money and investments, might as well shut down. No lawyer or financial advisor would ever send their clients to the bank. It'd be like recommending a patient to a doctor who chopped off the wrong leg or took out the wrong lung. You'd be sued for the recommendation if anything went wrong. A finding that the bank breached its fiduciary duty will make JPMorgan damaged goods."

"Am I going to end up in a lawsuit?" I asked him directly.

Jim paused. "Either Gary Stolbach is a big bag of hot air, a toothless tiger, or he means business. My guess is the latter."

"What can I do?"

"If you think you'll be sued, it's always best to be the plaintiff. You get to tell your story first, like when you were a kid and ran to tell on your brother. The first story usually wins."

I paused. "Are you saying I should sue JPMorgan first?"

"We'd also have to sue the heirs since they will inherit Max's estate. Trust me, you don't want to be a defendant. The word just sounds bad."

I hung up from Jim and took Blair to the backyard. While she took care of business, I saw Max's peach tree, now four feet high. I wondered morosely how tall that tree would be when I was done dealing with JPMorgan.

Walking back inside, my cell phone dinged. I had more emails from attorneys. They were all legal bills.

I took out a calculator and added up what I had spent in the last 75 days—$128,000! It was stunning.

And technically, I wasn't even in a lawsuit—yet.

My figure almost matched the $150,000 Tom Cantrill had charged the estate.

Realizing I needed to get out of the house, I went to my favorite Starbucks, hoping for some kind of a good feeling. And who did I see but my favorite burned-out lawyer.

By now, I'd learned that my friend Janie McKewen had been wrong. Tarian Starr had never been disbarred or even suspended. He had gone through some type of detox program for lawyers to get sober. Thankfully, he was still a licensed attorney.

"Tarian," I said, sitting down. "How are you doing?"

"Better than you," he replied, looking up over his screen.

"Does it show?"

"Remember, I made a living out of readin' people's faces."

"You mean paying for information."

"Oh yeah," he chuckled. "I forgot."

I picked up my coffee from the barista, sat back down, and told him about my current situation. He listened carefully before imparting his thoughts.

"The reason why they always have someone from private banking hounding you is the Great Recession."

"I don't understand what one has to do with the other," I said, sipping my coffee.

"New regulations and relentless government auditing mean banks like JPMorgan must pass stress tests. They're required to have a large amount of money on hand to lend to customers and stay in business. They're aggressive at making sure every dollar brought into JPMorgan stays at JPMorgan."

"But I've pulled my money out," I reminded him.

"Then they're gonna be on your bad side very soon. For now, at least, you're still a potential customer."

"Why would they be interested in me as a potential customer?"

"Every potential customer means possible bank fees. Banks make a ton of money on bank fees."

"I can see that," I said.

"And if they invest your money for you, they can tap 1 to 1.5% off your pile of cash for investment fees, whether or not they make you money. Pretty sweet deal. Basically, it's cross-selling. Remember when they pressured you to open up a financial account? JPMorgan bought Bear Sterns, so they need to grab all the investment business they can. What better way than to have the Estate Department coerce their existing clients to gamble on stocks with them? The easiest customer to hustle is an existing one."

I processed all that before speaking. "Do you bank at JPMorgan?"

"No, they're too highbrow for me. I bank with the street thugs at Wells Fargo."

He knew I'd ask him to explain that comment, and I did.

"I had some oil wells that started producing money. I needed a special checking account to put the money into so I went to Wells Fargo. The bank manager explained they'd have to charge me a hefty bank fee every month. But if I opened up a savings account, they'd waive that fee. I just needed to put $600 in there, and everything would be good.

"Oh, and I'd have to transfer money back and forth between the accounts each month to make it look normal. The manager explained he could set that up automatically. I wouldn't have to do a thing. I told him I didn't need a savings account, and he asked me if I needed bank fees more. I signed the paperwork and suddenly had two accounts when I only needed one.

"A few days later, I received a debit card for the checking account. I didn't need that either, so I shredded it. The next day, I received a debit card for the savings account, and I shredded that too. A week later, the bank manager called to say that I had failed to activate the debit cards, so I would now be charged bank fees. I told him I had shredded them. He said he'd send two more, which I received and activated.

"Two months later, I was setting up an LLC and needed another checking account. I went through the same routine. It was crazy.

"I talked to a neighbor and told him about this. He explained how Wells Fargo tells investors that each customer averages six to eight products with the bank. That level is unheard of in banking. I counted everything up and have about fifteen myself. A thick rubber band keeps all my debit cards in one place. My neighbor said he was shorting Wells Fargo stock because what they are doing is blatant fraud. They're coercing people with the threat of fees to make their quotas and selling it to Wall Street that we all love this bank so much we can't wait to have dozens of accounts and debit cards. He's sure they're doing even more sinister things than that."

"What does that have to do with me?" I asked, feeling like I was back listening to hockey stories.

"Like I said, Wells Fargo are street thugs. They're way too obvious. It's like walking in and robbing a 7-Eleven and pulling out a gun. Everyone can plainly see the crime. But JPMorgan is like Bernie Madoff. On the outside, they appear legitimate, with stamps of approval from the SEC. But on the inside, there's a different story. The world is just waiting for some CPA or investigative journalist to talk to its former employees. I'm guessing they have some incentive or bonus plan for employees to intimidate customers into leaving their money in the bank. Maybe some smart guy will set up a website and aggregate every lawsuit, complaint, and fine against them. Only when you do that will you see a pattern. It could be honest behavior. Or it could be outright fraud like Wells Fargo is committing."

I drained my coffee. "Even though I love talking to you, I usually feel worse when we're done."

"My first and third wives said that exact same thing," he joked.

"What about the second wife?"

"She didn't love anything about me."

I held up my coffee cup and tapped it against his. "Maybe the fourth time's the charm."

"It wasn't," he muttered as I stood to leave.

I left it there.

Chapter Ten

"Capricious and Wasteful Litigation System: Our litigation system now costs 1.6% of GDP. 1% more than what it costs in the average OECD nation."

—Jamie Dimon, Chairman & CEO
JPMorgan Chase Bank, N.A.
Letter to the Shareholders 2018 Annual Report

August 2011

A s I drove down the streets of Dallas, I watched parents picking up their children from school. A few blocks away, I noticed workers enjoying a quick meal at a fast-food restaurant. Pulling into my gated community, I waved at the guard. All these people seemed so carefree. I wondered if they had any legal problems in their lives. Of course, I know everyone has them, and some are likely worse than mine.

With each passing day, the echo chamber of rhetoric ratcheted up another notch. I felt like a frog in an ice bath with someone turning up the flame. It was maddening.

Gary Stolbach continued to write blistering emails to both the IA—Susan Novak and JPMorgan Chase—and their lawyer, Tom Cantrill. They were the decision-makers. They had the power to snap their fingers and grant Stolbach's wishes.

In mid-August of 2011, Stolbach demanded a meeting with Susan's boss, Wendy Bessette. Part of Stolbach's demand was that Tom Cantrill be excluded. The meeting was scheduled for early September. JPMorgan replied that Cantrill would be present but would not utter a word. How ridiculous was that?

Bessette flew in from Phoenix, where she officed. It made sense to assume she had flown in the night before the meeting and rented a car. After parking herself in a hotel for the night, she showed up the next morning at JPMorgan's Dallas office, ready for this crucial meeting. Stolbach notified them that since Cantrill would be present, he would not be showing up. It didn't make sense since JPMorgan had previously notified Stolbach that Cantrill would be present but remain silent. So, no meeting was held.

And this is what grown-ups do?

Stolbach continued throwing fastballs. He demanded a "neutral" third-party attorney review Cantrill's work and give an unbiased opinion about how banks charged clients for handling estates. Stolbach appeared to cling to the belief that I had a "secret" deal with JPMorgan. (Keep in mind that the property just needed to be retitled, not divided—forty minutes of work.) Cantrill and "top litigator" John Eichman agreed to this demand and began looking for an outside attorney to fill that role. This surprised me, since it seemed the law was already quite clear on everything that needed to be done.

And now, Stolbach was complaining about the unfairness of the agreement with JPMorgan Chase, most significantly that the IA was not charging me any of the settlement commission. He claimed this was unusual and out of line.

Cantrill studied this request and decided to call five other estate settlement firms to verify how they charged estate clients. Each one said they handled it precisely the way JPMorgan Chase had handled it: all settlement fees went to the estate. Of course, Cantrill was able to bill all this research to the estate's account since Susan didn't do it.

By the end of August, Cantrill wanted to compel a settlement. He suggested one big meeting—a get-together of only the attorneys—so they could resolve my house and partition issue. This would allow everyone to bill their clients.

To force everyone to the table, Cantrill stated he would only release the property if there was an agreement between all parties, and each party signed a release for JPMorgan. Seeing this, I'd had enough.

I fired off an email to Stephen and Laura. And I put some emotion into it.

"Below is an email that my attorneys received yesterday from Tom Cantrill. I thought you should be aware of what is going on here with the Independent Administrator. Susan is about to abdicate her position and close out the estate. In other words, she is taking her money and leaving us with a fistful of attorneys and legal action in court. The ONLY thing that created this situation is—MAX DIED! He would be as horrified at this scenario as I am. We worked hard, paid our taxes, and invested our disposable income to make money which we did not spend. Our goal was to have enough funds to take care of ourselves in old age—not to fund an army of lawyers over nothing. The attorneys are only too happy to feed your emotions with nonsense, such as dividing the land under our home and your being able to sell it! What foolishness. Do you think your father would be happy if he saw what you are doing? Max loved all of us. He told me not to worry about the lack of a will because you would always be there to support and stand with me. He was wrong. Stephen, you asked for the appointment of an Independent Administrator and specified JPMorgan. Laura, you stated your desire for an outside person so that it would not interfere with our relationship. I agreed to the administrator because I thought it would take some of the emotion out of dividing the community property. As I count, you have four attorneys, the estate has two attorneys and I have two. They have one objective: to continue to escalate the tension and to bill fees. They did not know your father and don't give a hoot whether you win or lose. They just want to draw this out as long as possible and bill as much as possible."

I went on, complaining about their inability to select list A or B with the wine and putters. (I had also created an A/B list for the putters.) I lamented about how they had gone after Calamity Jane and other actions they had taken. I emptied the cupboards and threw in the kitchen sink. I knew we were headed into war; the troops were waiting for the order to march. It was all so sad.

After reading my email, Stephen fired one back.

"Jo, shame on you. Your attempt to present yourself as a victim here would be laughable, if not for the tragedy. I approached Dad a few months before his death, at your request, to urge him to finish an estate plan. Remember? His response was that estate planning had proved impossible because of you. Out of kindness, I will spare you his other comments. I feel that you have taken every opportunity to control, manipulate, hide and reclassify assets while shifting as much cost to the estate as possible. I ask you to please stop this. I believe the real cost of this mess is due to the complete incompetence of JPMorgan and your own maneuverings. We have just scratched the surface of attorney costs, so how about a reality check? How much is self-righteousness worth? It looks as if we have one last chance before the courts intervene to finish this nonsense in some fair and equitable fashion. Given the great costs you are incurring to prevent the administrator from having the accounting records they are entitled to, we obviously need complete assurance that all assets have been classified. Once that has been ascertained, I believe we can come to a reasonable division of the assets and the costs between us. This would not include any joint ownership, so again, please stop these maneuverings. Additionally, perhaps we could join each other in obtaining relief from the expenses, fees and attorney costs due to the complete mismanagement of JPMorgan. If you have an interest in presenting a fair and balanced settlement offer that encompasses all of the outstanding assets and expenses, I assure you Laura and I will give it our due and fair consideration. Let's get on with our lives..."

This was a challenging moment. The law required the assets to be retitled so we would be joint tenants. Yet, he stated, "This would not include any joint ownership..." I heard his message loud and clear, and it was hollow. Except for my home, I had previously made repeated offers to buy them out at highly inflated prices. Instead of a "YES!" I had received nothing but crickets.

A few weeks later, Tom Cantrill sent an email to my attorneys saying that he and the IA were revisiting the issue of asset distribution. He wanted a white paper from my attorneys explaining and supporting their position. Stolbach had already provided him with one.

I could see the writing on the wall. The fog was fading away, giving form to the real objectives: selling my Robledo home out from under me and sticking me with the over-appraised personal property while the heirs received a pallet of cash. Stephen and Laura repeatedly stated that they did not want the house or personal property except for a few items. They wanted cash and, in my mind, they wanted to be totally free of me.

I met with my attorneys and discussed the options. They agreed with me about the IA's future actions. If I objected, the IA or Max's children would sue me. Being a defendant was bad news; Jim Jennings had already told me that. And I believed him. If I wasn't careful, I'd find them sticking me with the estate's commission and attorneys' fees, too. Kal Grant's "You won't pay a cent!" appeared to be a load of crap.

The more I studied the huge advantages a plaintiff had at trial, the more convinced I was that I needed a first-strike strategy. Jennings had a great saying: "If you're walking into a fight with a bully, pop him in the mouth first. At least you'll get one shot in."

I hung my head and thought hard about this. After deliberating about it, I let out a heavy sigh and nodded. "File the suit."

The date was September 21, 2011. The war had just begun. I assumed it would be painful. Naively, I had no idea just how devastating and hurtful it would be.

THE NICE SURPRISE with filing suit was how calm things became. Now that it was on, much of the back-and-forth vitriol stopped. I had the clear impression that Stephen and Laura had been itching for a fight. And I believed they were being pushed by their mother, with JPMorgan Chase more than willing to set up the circumstances that pushed things along. I was going to suffer no matter what I did. So, filing suit made sense to me.

As for Cantrill and Eichman, they could fully open the tap to the estate and drain the money as fast as Susan Novak approved their massive invoices. At least they didn't have to waste any more time with the outside attorney they had hired to review everything. My lawsuit made that irrelevant.

My original petition stated that JPMorgan Chase was the cause of this mess. They were my focus. I wanted them to pay dearly for the harm they had caused.

Unfortunately, in Texas litigation, there is Rule 39:

"A person... shall be joined as a party in the action if in his absence complete relief cannot be accorded among those already parties."

This rule meant that for me to take a piece of lumber to JPMorgan Chase, I'd have to bring Stephen and Laura along for the ride. They were necessary parties. To obtain a ruling against the administration of the estate, I needed the two of them.

Even with all they'd been doing to me, I did not feel good about suing Max's children. They were inexperienced in matters like this. Max had been a lawnmower dad, racing ahead of them, clearing away any anticipated problems. When they did get into a jam, he would fly in and erase the problem, usually with cash.

What burned me most was that my emails had given them every chance to move forward. They could have picked side A or B on the wine and putter lists. They could have accepted my offer to give them cash for the personal property. However, I was not going to stand by and let them take my home. Not if I still had one shallow breath in this battered body.

It was time to get to work.

Litigation not only involves conflict, but also paperwork—massive quantities of it. Each day, documents stacked up in my study, waiting for me and my faithful fur-kid, Blair, to take up residence and sort through it.

Because I stayed up late reviewing all this paperwork, I made evening trips to Starbucks. I usually saw Tarian there. I soon realized he had lots of valuable information about the legal system.

I loved sitting down and chatting with him. But due to the nature of Starbuck's seating, we had very little privacy. When he suggested we move our clandestine meetings to a nearby Vietnamese restaurant, Pho Bidden, I agreed. He knew the owners, which led to first-class service in the almost empty restaurant.

"I've been trying to advise them," he whispered to me, "but they don't get it."

"Don't get what?" I asked.

"Look around. It's always like this. They're never full. I think it's because of the name. It sounds like an Asian spa or some adult bookstore. And to think they were going to call the place Pho Play."

I laughed hard. "You've got to be joking."

"No, I'm not," he said seriously. "They struggle with the language. It's a shame, too, because the food is excellent. And they have great Wi-Fi."

We ordered some items from the menu and continued our discussion. I brought him up to speed.

When he heard I'd filed suit, he appeared genuinely distraught. "I wish I could introduce you to my good friend Voltaire. He's a bigtime free speech advocate."

"And?" I asked, curious as to where this was going.

"We were sitting in a café in France when he told me, 'Tarian, I was never ruined but twice: once when I lost a lawsuit, and once when I won one.'"

"That's what you get for listening to a Frenchie."

"I admit I'm an unabashed Francophile, especially when it comes to their wines. But I digress. You see, now they've got you in the trap. That's what they want, all of you twisting and turning in the spider's web. With you immobilized, they can eat you piece by piece."

"Maybe," I said, setting my jaw. "But they aren't going to take my house."

"What is it with you and this property? You're telling me you can't buy another house?"

My eyes glistened. "I'm not letting a bunch of men do this to me. I've already told you how they mistreated me before with that nonexistent nickel raise. What I didn't tell you is what they did to my parents."

"It seems I've pressed another sore spot," he said apologetically.

"No. They did it, not you."

"Tell Uncle Tarian all about it," he said sympathetically, fastening a napkin under his chaotic beard as the food arrived. "I'm a great listener so long as I can shovel food down my piehole at the same time."

I smirked as I took a sip of hot tea and began. "I was sixteen in 1963 when the Tennessee Valley Authority announced they were building the Percy Priest Dam. Our family home was upstream of the proposed site. I remember my father wondering what that meant for us. We didn't know what would happen.

"Soon after the announcement, two men in suits drove up to our five acres. They told Dad that the plans showed our place would be eight to ten feet underwater. We'd have to move.

"Well, we didn't have any money to move. We were barely getting by. To fix this, the men said they'd send another man to give us some money. When they left, Dad paced around the house and didn't know what to do.

"Years earlier, he had purchased two one-hundred-year-old log cabins and combined them, building this special place I'd grown up in.

I couldn't imagine living anywhere else. We were all terribly stressed over this.

"Dad had only a 10th grade education but wasn't stupid. He got hold of the plans and saw that another ten acres we owned across the street would not be touching the water. We'd have a house on the lake's edge, looking out every morning to the sun glistening off the blue water. Everything would be just fine.

"The fellow finally showed up and told him what they deemed our place was worth. Dad looked it over and was happy inside because it was a very fair price for our five acres. When the man casually mentioned that it also included our nearby ten acres, Dad's jaw dropped. He asked why. The man explained that the lake would have a buffer around it, and no houses could be built near the water. Buyers would have to be satisfied with living farther up the slope, assured they'd have an unobstructed view of the lake. So the offer was for all fifteen acres we owned.

"It was a devasting blow. With little education or money to hire a lawyer, Dad had no choice. He was forced to take the government's paltry offer and give up our land. Dad bought some land a few miles away and built a stone house. That's where we moved in May 1965."

Tarian pointed a half-eaten spring roll at me. "So, that log cabin is underwater now?"

"No," I replied. "Dad retained ownership of our log house and found a man who bought and moved it to another location. That was the only good news out of this entire fleecing.

"Too bad. You could've owned prime property on the lake."

"Yeah," I said. "And guess what? Years later, after they had sold every square inch of land around the lake to all those wealthy people who enjoyed their unobstructed view, they decided to sell the land all the way down to the water's edge—the very land they'd taken from us. What a dastardly deed. I tried to repurchase the land, but Max and I had nothing but debt. We couldn't afford it. So, our old land was sold on the courthouse steps to the highest bidder. A sad ending to a tragic tale."

"I'm sorry that happened to you," Tarian said, wiping his mouth. "I hate hearing stories like that. It's like I'm a gunslinger riding into town as some thug shoves a kid's face in the mud. Makes me want to draw my gun and pop a round in his noggin."

"We sure could've used a guy like you."

"Yeah, but the way I was back then, I would've legally beaten those men to a pulp before taking your land for myself."

"I don't believe that," I said honestly.

He grinned. "You don't know me. In fact, you really know nothing, Jo Hopper. Do you have any idea why those men took your land at rock-bottom prices?"

"No."

"Because they could. And do you know why JPMorgan Chase is doing this to you?"

"Because they can!" I cried.

"Now you're learning. I'll make a fake lawyer out of you yet."

I could only hope.

Chapter Eleven

I'll go lawyer shopping, find one to agree,
That all his wealth, should pass to me.
I'll pour boiling water, she'll soon lose her hold.
Lawyers all know that widows will fold.
But this one gets stronger, the more I do.
Instead of folding, the reverse is true.
                    —*Thought It Was Mine* by Jack Hooper

I f I thought filing suit would quell the anger coming from JPMorgan, Susan Novak, and Tom Cantrill, I was wrong. Rather than doing their jobs, they continued making it hard on me. Look no further than the Flying Needles.

When the dot-com bubble burst in 2000 and a huge chunk of our assets vanished, Max and I found ourselves in financial peril. We were cash strapped. At times, I thought we would lose the Robledo house we'd purchased in 1997. I felt like I needed to make some money to help pay our bills.

I set up a small business, called Flying Needles, that manufactured and distributed specialty tools for needlepoint and beading retailers. This brought in $25,000 to $35,000 each year. It wasn't a lot of money, but it helped cover some of our bills.

After Max's death, I realized that keeping my business running was not only good for my mental health, but it brought in money too. In order to keep it going, I had to write another check to the IA for the estate's half of my business. I shook my head in disgust, sealed the envelope, and sent the check to Susan.

For a year and a half, I'd been making the payments on the lease, utilities, and insurance for the warehouse holding Max's golf clubs and my business, Flying Needles. Finally, I'd had enough. It was time for me to move my business out of our leased warehouse space.

After another expensive exchange of unnecessary emails, I was allowed to move my inventory and supplies, as well as the furniture and fixtures for both businesses. This included the filing cabinets from Max's business, Hopper Associates, which I'd purchased from the estate in February 2011.

This created an unexpected problem.

The filing cabinets contained all the files and documents from Max's business. Concerned these would be lost, I packed and moved them with the furnishings. When the bank and Gary Stolbach learned that potentially critical estate documents were in my hands, they went through the roof.

I immediately received demands to return everything. This set my lawyers back into the email squirrel cage. Gary Stolbach's unusually long emails ripped a gaping hole through the estate's cash (the heirs' lawyers sent their monthly bills to Susan and were paid under instructions from the heirs as if it wasn't anyone's money). I had no idea how Stephen and Laura were putting up with this.

As for Max's files, I boxed them up, knowing full well that we'd need them for determining the cost basis of various assets for the IRS. There was no way I wanted to lose those documents. Yet Gary Stolbach and the heirs appeared concerned I was up to no good. Instead of blaming Susan for not getting out there and taking possession of the documents, they pointed fingers at me. Sadly, I was becoming used to it.

Joining in on this outrage, and without even calling my attorney, Cantrill followed Stolbach with a scathing accusatory letter that included this line: "The IA has learned that Mrs. Hopper has caused several items of property not purchased by Mrs. Hopper in which the Estate owns an interest to be removed from the warehouse on TI Blvd. without the Administrator's consent." Reading their emails to my lawyers made my blood boil.

The only good to come out of this incident was that I realized had I not filed suit first, I'd now be a defendant. No doubt about it, they would've sued me first.

To counter the theft accusation, I provided my lawyers with copies of the inventory listing and cancelled checks that had been cashed by the estate for the purchase of the inventory and fixtures in question. After studying all this, I received a feeble letter of apology from Cantrill's office for their mistake. However, Cantrill made it clear he could not withdraw the court filing that contained the bank's theft allegation against me. This meant I'd have to spend more money fighting that claim.

Another boondoggle was the Porsche that used to sit in my garage. For whatever reason, Susan would not simply retitle it to the heirs and me. After refusing my offer to purchase it for an effective price of $5,600, she had a friend who picked up the car and tried to sell it. He said he would charge $500 if the vehicle sold. This was nineteen-plus months after Max died. At least Susan now had time to deal with it. I guess $160,000 in bank fees only gets you so far.

Her friend worked hard, selling the Porsche for $6,500 while earning himself a nice $1,000 commission instead of his previously quoted $500. Susan must have realized that this meant she had sold it for less than I had offered, because she told her friend that he would have to take a $100 cut from his commission, which he agreed to do. Once the dust settled, the estate and I each received a check for $2,800—the same amount I had offered the estate months earlier—the only difference being that Susan's friend made $900.

You just can't make this stuff up.

IN RESPONSE TO my lawsuit, JPMorgan filed various defenses and claims. Among the fancy legal wording I saw was that they wanted the court to allow them to give me full title to the house while taking my cash and giving it to the heirs. The bank admitted that no matter what, they couldn't eliminate my right to live on the property for the rest of my life—my *homestead right*. They also admitted that the mortgage would stay in place too. They just wanted the right to stick me with the entire amount. And they wanted the court, if necessary, to force me to return the money they'd already released to me so they could give it to the heirs.

Another request in the lawsuit hearkened back to Stolbach's earlier memo: They wanted to sell my home's structure and the land below it, leaving me there under my homestead right. I could only imagine how much that would bring at auction. Surely not enough to even pay the mortgage. Then, at the very end of the pleading, they asked for attorneys' fees for all this litigation. I assumed it would be a massive number.

While JPMorgan was busy trying to find ways to stick it to me, Stephen and Laura weren't standing still. Their next move was a good one. They hired Stanley Johanson as an expert witness. His job was to tell the court that my lawyers and I were wrong. The IA could sell my house or partition the personal property and home in order to stick me with all of it. The bank's lawyers readily agreed with Mr. Johanson's legal opinions.

The problem was that Mr. Johanson was professor emeritus of probate law at the University of Texas Law School. He'd been there since 1963. Most of the lawyers and judges in Texas had either learned probate law directly from him or been taught from his textbook *Wills, Trusts and Estates*—the authoritative word on probate law. This book is so valued, it's used at more than 120 American law schools.

Having a brilliant mind like this in their corner stung me. If I were the judge and had Professor Johanson standing before me saying that Jo Hopper's attorneys are wrong, it would be hard to go against *the* probate expert in the state (if not the entire country!). It wasn't looking good for me.

My lawyers swallowed hard and hired the next best thing: Gerry Beyer, a professor at the Texas Tech Law School. However, the heirs' attorney objected. There was some conflict with Professor Beyer. This confused me. They claimed to have contacted Professor Beyer regarding representing the heirs before hiring Professor Johanson. They spoke with him for less than five minutes, and because of that call, they said he was tainted and could not represent me.

Ethical conflicts didn't seem to affect anyone but me. If asked, I signed a waiver. But when I wanted Professor Beyer for my case, no one was willing to sign a waiver. Cooperation in litigation was for fools.

Lesson learned.

To replace Beyer, my attorneys turned to Thomas Featherston. He had attended law school at Baylor University with Mike Graham and had worked extensively with Mike on trust and estate-related legislative matters throughout his career. At this time, Mr. Featherston was a law school professor at Baylor. Hopefully, he could counterbalance Johanson.

One of the first things I learned about lawsuits was that everyone gets paid. Mr. Johanson received approximately $22,000 to write an expert witness paper and appear twice in court as the heirs' attorney. If you want an expert witness acting as a lawyer to tell a judge or jury that you should win, be prepared to write a hefty check.

While all this was happening, I learned another fun fact about lawsuits: discovery. You put questions in writing along with items you want the other side to produce, like *all emails composed, sent, or received during the last ten years.* Or *all financial records for the previous twenty years.*

Broad discovery requests allow lawyers to file expensive countermotions and go to court, where they'll argue that the requests be narrowed. After tens of thousands of dollars in legal bills, the judge might limit the emails to the last four years and the financial records to ten. Then comes the next round of pain.

A litigant gathers up all those documents, both paper and electronic, and hands them over to their lawyer, who goes through and carefully reads each page. As he holds the document in his hands, he must study it and contemplate its meaning and context. Only then can he decide if there's any reason to object to producing it.

For objectionable documents, another round of court hearings and legal bills is on tap. This goes on and on. Whenever a lawyer needs some money, they can fire up their laser printer and crank out more discovery requests. This will surely bring more objections and court appearances. It's like they have a printing press for money in their office. All they need is enough toner.

Truly, it's a brilliant system of wealth transfer. And the litigant is told failure to object or fight could be the death blow to the case. "If you want to win, we must fight on every point, even if it means spending every last dollar you have." (Okay, the last part isn't said aloud, just implied.)

One day in November 2011, my attorneys received 28,000 pages of discovery documents from JPMorgan Chase as the administrator.

Twenty-eight thousand!

Instead of delivery trucks loaded down with boxes (as in the olden days), they were all on a disk. I had them printed out—all 28,000. Then I read and sorted them in date order. Finally, I categorized each one.

With paper everywhere, I set up an Excel spreadsheet and got to work indexing each document by date, time, and subject matter. As an added bonus, I typed every email verbatim into the spreadsheet. If I wanted to win this case, I had to know these documents better than the lawyers on the other side. I convinced myself that my financial life depended on it.

And I put aside my grieving. This is what I've always done: focus on work to keep from examining my emotions or feelings and kick the can down the road. Max did that, too. I learned that people who grew up poor often followed this pattern because it's too scary to stop and examine one's grief.

With my emotions suppressed and my determination stoked, I grabbed some Starbucks and dove right in. It didn't take long to strike gold.

Holding several emails at once, I read how Max's children complained about the funeral costs. I knew they had blown a gasket when they learned the estate had to pay the funeral expenses. But reading emails they had written to the IA was beyond sobering.

This was their primary complaint: "That was Jo's party, it was not Dad's memorial service." Obviously, we had different memories.

The next discovery was a slap in the face. Stephen had sent an email to the IA wondering if there wasn't a missing executed will.

"What do you make of the will by Alan Jones? As he is the attorney my dad last worked with, why was Mike [Graham] given first look at a file that was apparently not copied before being sent to them? What do you make of the sudden discovery of an unsigned last will and testament? Where is the unsigned last will and testament that Alan Jones prepared? I will emphasize to you again that the reason my dad gave me for a lack of estate planning was that Jo wanted her half and control over his."

I was amused at Stephen's apparent ignorance of the law. Every unexecuted will we had found made me the executor, or executrix as females are called. Any executed will would likely appoint me to make decisions over *their* money all day long.

As I had said before, he and Laura would get exactly what they had now or worse. They could not possibly get more than 99.3% of Max's estate, which they were bound by law to receive.

Then came the next slap to the face.

"Jo is the reason that 'a man so bright and capable' didn't have a will."

That hurt. But the hits just kept on coming.

"Before we wrap up any of Dad's investments, I would make sure that stock and options were not his only assets. My dad made direct venture capital investments in some of these companies and a very large investment was coming back to him around the time of his death. I would love to believe that there would be no attempts to manipulate this process by Jo, but this is not my almost 30-year history with her. For me, it is not a question of if but how. Perhaps I am also jaded by my profession, as I don't tend to see the best of humanity. In any case, I would appreciate your vigilance."

After reading this, I hoped he was happy with Susan's vigilance. I know I wasn't. Of course, I had absolutely no idea what his "30-year history with her" comment referred to.

For hours, I sifted through hundreds of documents that had limited relevance. Reading one particular packet had me chuckling.

JPMorgan employees discussed in emails how the fees allowed in the probate code were 5% of all assets they took in and 5% of all assets distributed. But there was a cap of 5% of the entire estate and many exceptions. One of the exceptions was our largest asset—a venture capital fund. It would be excluded. This meant that if JPMorgan followed the probate code, they would've received much less than the $230,000 fee they charged the estate. (Initially, the bank's fee was projected to be $160,000.)

I smiled, knowing they had misled us when they implied we were getting a special deal. The contract's payment terms were not the cheapest estate fees and they knew it. I guess JPMorgan had used the cheaper probate code payment section before on other estates and realized it wasn't enough money to feed their organization. That's why they had a different fee structure, one that paid much more than the probate code allowed. Thank God the estate was paying the entire fee and not me. That was one bullet I'd dodged.

Next up, I found a series of emails from Stephen's first lawyer, John Round. He met with Stephen the day before I'd met with Stephen, Laura, and Ron Cresswell at my house to float the idea of me being the IA. Round took credit in the emails for sending all this business to JPMorgan, where his wife, Debra Round, just happened to work in JPMorgan's trust department as a senior trust officer. If that wasn't a conflict, I didn't know what was. This email appeared to confirm for me that Stephen had not been open with me about how he'd selected JPMorgan Chase.

Reading emails that I was never meant to see felt like voyeurism, but it was hard to turn away as I read how JPMorgan employees virtually high-fived each other over landing a whale—Max's estate. I made a note for my attorneys to use at trial.

The next goodie was again from John Round. He'd sent an email taking credit for getting Tom Cantrill selected as the IA's counsel. This was a total contradiction to what Susan had told me on the phone when I cried and screamed about bringing him on. Her words to me were, "I hired Tom because he knows the assets and drafted a will for Max."

Sure.

This email told the real story. Round, acting as Stephen's lawyer, and whose wife worked in the trust department at JPMorgan, had gotten Cantrill the job. A fiduciary's responsibility is to put their client's interest before their own interest. Weren't these relevant facts JPMorgan, as my fiduciary, should have disclosed to me?

Getting an inside peek at this dirty system was both illuminating and frightening. I couldn't imagine how a weaker person could survive it.

After I'd spent three hours reading only a fraction of the scattered mess, Blair wiggled her butt and pawed through the papers demanding attention. I took a break and cuddled with her. It was nice to hold and love something that wasn't trying to stab me in the back.

I hooked up Blair's collar and took her for a walk around the neighborhood. The fresh air was good for both of us. Blair loved checking her pee-mail. By the length of her sniffs, it was apparent a few boy dogs had left her some enticing messages. She squatted near one particular note and left her reply.

Once we were back home and she had some water and a treat, I fixed myself some hot tea and returned to the stack of 28,000 documents.

EARLY ONE MORNING, I drove through my neighborhood, awash in Christmas lights and decorations. Our neighbors always went big. Of course, there were a lot of wealthy folks living around me. I had heard rumors about the various lawsuits some of them had been in and shuddered. Now I was in one.

As I pulled away from the main gate, I knew that wouldn't be the last depressing thought I had for the next twelve hours. I was on my way to see my two lawyers and go over all the documents we'd received in discovery. It would be another grueling day in litigation.

"Jo," Jim Jennings said, "I see you have your Starbucks. Mike and I have our office-made brew, so we're all awake. Let's begin with some interesting finds we have here."

The first one he picked was from Laura. She had revealed in an email to Tom Cantrill that she was pleased he was representing the estate. She found it "… comforting that you knew my dad and that he discussed his business dealings and personal wishes with you—I just wish he had finished what he started!!!"

It still amazed me that Stephen and Laura, two college-educated professionals, would continue banging around for a will that could not possibly give them more and might take some of their money. When would they ever learn?

Jim thrust a sheet of paper at me. "This is an email Laura sent to Cantrill and the IA complaining about you."

"Although specific amounts of assets were not disclosed, you will see that my father did have shares of United Airlines Stock, American Airlines Stock and Retirement Accounts, and personal banking accounts in both Tulsa and in Dallas at the time of their divorce and before he and Jo married. My mother told me that my dad deposited ALL of his bonuses into his Dallas account. Her estimation is that his Dallas account and his American Airlines stock/savings accounts were significant, as he was an officer of the company at that time, and she did not receive any of those assets. I thought this would be helpful information to share and hope that a thorough investigation will be done to discover the status of these assets. (divorce decree attached)"

"This is what you were telling us," Jim said. "There it is in writing. Besides fighting JPMorgan, Gary Stolbach, and Max's children, we're apparently doing battle with Max's ex-wife, Leah. Man, some grudges last a lifetime."

I nodded, feeling sick.

"Here's a good one," Mike Graham said, handing me an email.

"I saw that one and flagged it," I told him. "Did you know Gary Stolbach is currently representing JPMorgan in another estate?"

"No, I didn't," Jim said.

"Me neither," Mike added.

"I think that's why they're bending toward his crazy idea of taking money from me for the house or selling it out from under me," I said. "All these lawyers and IAs seem to be in bed with each other. What a corrupt system. How do you two deal with it?"

"Alcohol, mostly," Jim quipped.

I had no doubt he was right. I'd been spending a lot of time with Tarian Starr and he looked weathered, to say the least. But at this point, I was thinking about popping the corks on a few bottles in my wine cellar myself. And maybe a day or two off would do me some good.

Chapter Twelve

"One in five Chase households is affluent, and roughly 50% of all U. S. affluent households are located within two miles of a Chase branch."
—Gordon Smith, CEO Consumer & Community Banking
JPMorgan Chase Bank, N.A.
2012 Annual Report

When I spent time with close friends, I could tell there was something they wanted to ask me; one burning question they couldn't get off their minds. They never asked it, though, so I decided to at least consider it myself: Are you angry at Max for failing to execute a will?

My lawyers asked me that question, in a roundabout way. I answered them in my usual straightforward manner, perhaps giving them too much information. Here's what I said.

When you lose your spouse, the loneliness and loss are overwhelming. In my case, added to that was the personal disappointment that Max had failed to execute a will. He'd left his children and me without any guidance regarding his assets.

Yes, Max and I were aware that no one in Texas dies without a will. The state provides one—a default will. However, I had no idea that I'd receive almost nothing from Max's estate. I was reasonably sure he didn't know that either. So, yes. I truly wished he had executed a will.

But once you get into the legal system, you learn that people who execute wills end up in court all the time anyway. The probate courts are swollen with unhappy heirs who contest wills and file lawsuits.

Why?

Because there's money to be had. It's just sitting there, waiting for a disappointed heir to come and claim it. I call it the "last bite of the apple." It's their final opportunity to receive property and/or cash from their deceased loved one.

Even if Max had executed a will, there was a decent chance that he could have accidentally left me property that wasn't his or left someone else property that belonged to me. For example, if he had left the entire wine collection, believing he fully owned it, to his children, I could have contested that bequest because, due to Texas community property rights, the wine was half mine. He couldn't possibly leave my half of community property to anyone. When these circumstances occur, the surviving spouse must make a choice called the "widow's election" *before* probating the will. The decision is tough.

One option is to accept the terms of the will being probated and waive contesting the community half of the property. This option would give away something the deceased had no right to bequeath in the first place.

The second option is for the survivor to refuse to probate the executed will and instead elect to accept the property given by the Texas default will—the intestate statute. In my case, 99.3% of Max's estate would go to his children.

If this was the situation, any rational person would let the wine go. But what if the community property was a large piece of property? Or a valuable painting?

Lawyers who draft wills make mistakes. Their clients make them by misclassifying property. Many of these "mistakes" end up bleeding the estate and litigants dry. I understood that.

The terrible part of my situation was that JPMorgan Chase was essentially trying to force me to make an election I did not have to make: accept my house entirely and assume 100% of the mortgage while the heirs receive an undisclosed amount of cash, or fight. Since Max didn't have a will that forced the widow's election on me, the bank could not force it on me after his death. I had no choice but to fight it out in court.

It was bad enough not receiving anything under Max's default will. But having JPMorgan Chase put a gun to my head?

So the short answer to that question is that my anger, which should have gone toward Max, was redirected to JPMorgan Chase and Max's children. I made my election, and it was litigation—just what all the lawyers wanted.

By now, the legal bills were mounting. Twenty months after Max's death, I had paid Mike Graham a total of $265,527.58 and Jim Jennings $308,000. It was a race to see who would go broke first: JPMorgan Chase or me. I hoped my willingness to outwork the other side made up for the lack of funds. Only time would tell.

I know this is obvious to anyone reading this, but going through 28,000 documents takes time. If a person reads twenty documents each hour (which is unlikely given the length and importance of some of them), you're looking at 1,400 hours. At 10 hours per day, that's 140 days. But I was also logging each one into a spreadsheet, making them searchable by date and subject. This meant closer to 3,000 hours. How many hours I actually spent, I have no idea, but I know I spent endless weeks and months reading and categorizing the documents.

I was trying to piece together the story. Once I'd finished the first stage of entering them, I went back and typed them verbatim into the spreadsheet. This included my opponents' legal bills by date of entry. The retyping of the documents helped burn them into my brain.

By the time I was done, the spreadsheet was immense—35 cells wide and 17,844 cells down. It took up a great deal of memory on my computer. Yet when I hit the sort-by-date button, I realized all the hard work had been worth it. I could see a clear story as to what had happened (or not) each day. And if I could see it, so could my lawyers. This spreadsheet was a litigation gamechanger. I had typed so much data in to create the spreadsheet, I wore out my laptop's trackpad. Rather than send my laptop to a repair shop, I purchased a wireless trackpad and continued entering data.

My attorneys relied on me to do the bulk of the sorting and categorizing. Jim told me my work had saved at least $500,000 in attorneys' fees. I guess a most people would just have to walk away from what JPMorgan Chase was doing.

By digging deep into the documents, I occasionally stumbled across a piece of gold that reminded me why I was doing all this. One such nugget was an email from JPMorgan's salesperson, Kal Grant, to someone at the bank. She stated that it looked like the bank was going to land the Max Hopper Estate administration. Then she mentioned "Jo Hopper and her (apparently contentious) stepchildren." Another email between the manager of the bank's Estate Department and Susan Novak repeated the same shocking phrase.

I set the documents down and wondered about these statements. I had never said that the estate administration involving Max's children and me would be contentious. Had Stephen, Laura, or their attorney told JPMorgan that we would be hard to deal with? If so, what did that mean for my case?

I decided it was time for another visit to my wise old oracle.

"Happy New Year. 2012 is here!" I said, removing my thick jacket and sliding into a booth at Pho Bidden.

"Same to you," Tarian replied, "although I find it odd meeting on New Year's Day."

"Why?"

"In the past, I would've been hungover for days. But I guess this is a new year for me. I plan on being a new man—a *sober* man."

"That's great," I said with a smile, picking up a menu. "Order what you want because the meal is on me."

"It was always going to be on you," he said with a wry expression.

"Aren't you sharp as a tack."

The owner took our order and we relaxed in the empty restaurant.

"I'm sure glad they're open today," I said. "I don't know where we would've met."

"They're on a different calendar than ours. To them, even though this is Sunday, it's just another workday." He glanced back toward the kitchen. "I think they might sleep in this place. I don't know for sure."

I hadn't considered that, but he was probably right. When you're going through something stressful and challenging, it's easy to lose sight of other people who have their own problems. Sometimes theirs are more serious than yours.

"So, what's on your mind?" he asked, stirring two Sweet'N Lows into his tea.

I handed him the emails containing the "contentious" language. "Why would they say that?" I asked him.

"I'm guessing they hope the gig turns into more than the usual fee."

"I don't understand."

"It's the beginning of the gaslighting."

"I still don't understand."

He pushed back his hair. "Gaslighting. You don't understand that word?"

"No. I've never heard of it," I said honestly. "What does it mean?"

"Oh my, you are a babe in the woods." He rolled his eyes. "Okay, let me explain it to you. There was this play in the 1930s called *Gas Light*. It was set in London in the 1880s. A husband and wife were living in a downstairs apartment while the upstairs had been sealed off because a woman had been murdered there. Each evening, the husband left the apartment and his wife had no idea where he was going or why. We eventually discover that he is going to the upstairs apartment, turning on the gas lights, and searching for the valuable jewels that belonged to the woman, who it turns out he'd murdered." He stopped and waited for my reaction.

"Okay, and? How does this apply to me?"

He held up his hand to imply he wasn't finished. "After months of watching him leaving the apartment every night, his wife started to become suspicious. She was also confused by the banging and scraping noises she'd been hearing upstairs, since as far as she knew, no one lived there.

"But what really bothered her were the gas lights. Back then, there was only one major gas supply line for all apartments in a building. When one tenant turned up the lights, it dimmed the lights in the other apartments. Each time the husband left, the wife heard noises in the apartment above, and the gas lights dimmed. She finally decided to confront her husband. That's when he realized she might expose his criminal behavior and he could be hung as a murderer, so he devised a plan to convince her she was imagining all of it.

"He repeatedly dimmed the lights of their apartment while he was there. When she noticed the change in lighting, he told her she was imagining it. He even pretended to read the newspaper by this light, to convince his wife that it was all in her head.

"Of course, she began to believe she was going crazy, which is exactly what her husband wanted. Thus, the term gaslighting. When one person wants to psychologically manipulate and disorient another by causing them to question reality, or what they truly believe."

"Okay, Tarian, but please tell me how all that relates to my situation," I pleaded, more confused than when he'd started.

"Jo, the gaslighter wants control over the victim, to make them do whatever they want."

"And?"

"JPMorgan is gaslighting you and Max's children. Don't you see?"

I shook my head and frowned as I tried to understand what he was telling me.

"They start by seeding their staff that this estate will be contentious. To make sure they have that outcome, they suggest to Max's children that you are hard to deal with; you're manipulating them, maybe even hiding assets, a will, whatever. The bank then withholds information from you, such as that Max's children don't trust you or that they think you're hiding assets or a will. It's like in high school when two boys have a disagreement. Before long, a crowd gathers around them. Neither boy wants to fight until someone in the crowd pushes one into the other and boom! The fight is on. That's what lawyers do. If we do our job right, it's your idea to run up our fees and make us rich."

I listened to his words and processed everything he'd said. "So you think there are traces of this gaslighting in these emails. Well, now that I understand the concept, I'll look for more. But there's a huge hole in your logic."

Tarian shook his head. "My logic is impenetrable."

I chuckled. "You mean impeccable?"

"No, impenetrable. I chose a word and I'm sticking with it. I'm not a disloyal wordsmith like some people I know."

"Okay," I said, ignoring his irreverent (or irrelevant) comment. "But the hole is this: How does JPMorgan benefit from increased legal fees? They aren't a law firm. As far as I understand, they can't make money off legal fees."

"Right you are," he agreed. "But what does a bank want most?"

"Money."

"How do you get that money?"

"From depositors and borrowers," I answered. "But I guess it all starts with depositors."

"Right again, and how do you get depositors, especially filthy rich and slobbering fat ones?"

"Advertising? Reputation?"

"And referrals," Tarian said, grinning. "Estate lawyers refer their clients to the bank. Yet, the bank can't give them a commission. It's highly illegal. What the bank *can* do is appoint that lawyer to advise them on an estate. And the lawyer doesn't bill JPMorgan. They bill the estate. Essentially, the bank lets its clients pay the commission fee they aren't legally allowed to pay. Of course, this could all be eliminated if the law required disclosure of this behavior. Or, better yet, if local authorities established a rotating wheel of lawyers qualified to advise any bank. They would be automatically selected. But that's not going to happen because there's too much money involved."

"It sounds like some big conspiracy," I said skeptically.

"Nah. Nobody convened a meeting and organized this. They didn't have to. It's just understood. The way business is done. Make a million-dollar campaign contribution to any politician and believe me, they understand."

Tarian was starting to make sense.

"I hate to say it," I said, "but I learned that Gary Stolbach is representing JPMorgan on another estate. Now that the bank has sided with him, we're at war."

"Of course you are. Every lawyer thanks you from the bottom of their wallet. Let the good times and legal fees roll."

I left Tarian feeling sick to my stomach. Every time I talked with him, it was like opening up another closet from which another monster popped out. But at least I had someone like him to tell me not only where the closets were but what was behind the doors, especially JPMorgan's doors.

JANUARY WAS FREEZING, which is fairly common for Dallas. With the new year upon us, it was time to deal with a lingering matter.

Several months earlier, my lawyers had reviewed the documents I was accused of stealing, as well as the ones from my home files. Half of them were household items and the other half related to Hopper Associates, Max's business. After a thorough review, my lawyers decided to produce all of them—all thirty-four boxes. Then, the next issue arrived.

The boxes were at my house. I was not comfortable turning them over to my attorneys and moving them out of my home. My lawyers and I discussed the issue and decided the best course of action was to produce them in my three-car garage. The IA and the heirs could view them there.

We scheduled a disclosure meeting for January 3, 2012. I knew the lawyers and their staff couldn't endure a frigid garage, so I ran heaters around the clock beginning the day before. This somewhat negated the harsh temperatures outside.

I set up tables and chairs to help make the process go smoothly. With that, I went shopping and purchased water bottles, soft drinks, and pastries. It wasn't the luxury of a law firm, but it was tolerable.

"Jo, we've got a problem," Jim said.

"What's that?" I asked.

"Bathrooms. They'll be here all day. They're going to need to take a break."

"Oh," I said. "That means having them traipse through my home."

"Exactly. They might get a peek at something you bought recently and claim you failed to disclose it. Also, they can and will take photos of your home. If they find something, they can use it. They'll send it to me as part of discovery."

I let out a deep breath. "So, I can't let them in my home. Right?"

"I wouldn't advise it," he replied, eyebrows raised.

"What are they going to do? Pee in a bucket?"

"Well..."

"Come on, you're joking, right?"

"Let's send them to the restroom at the nearby 7-Eleven. They're usually clean."

I couldn't believe it, but I knew he was right. Any painting, bottle of wine, needlepoint work, anything I had recently purchased was fair game. Don't give your enemy any advantage. I'd already learned the foolishness of granting conflict waivers.

After kicking it around with Mike Graham, Jim decided the 7-Eleven was good enough. He also stationed a paralegal in the garage to make sure none of the documents disappeared. I locked everything up tight and left. There was no need for me to be around while they went through everything.

At the appointed time, Stephen and Laura appeared along with their attorneys and paralegals. Cantrill and the bank also had a team of people at my home. I did a quick calculation. Between everyone there, it had to cost over $5,000 an hour.

The lawyers carefully studied every page in all thirty-four boxes, placing special tags on documents they wanted copied. After two full days of grinding through box after box, it was over. A service arrived and picked up the designated boxes. After copies were made, the boxes were returned to me.

By January 5, I had my home back. Happy New Year to me.

Chapter Thirteen

"The homestead shall not be partitioned among the heirs of the deceased during the lifetime of the surviving spouse or so long as the survivor elects to use or occupy the same as a homestead..."

—Texas Probate Code Section 285

As I neared the second anniversary of Max's death in late January, I faced a new challenge. Up to this point, my lawsuit had been mostly theoretical. We had exchanged documents in discovery and argued about a wide range of issues.

Instead of JPMorgan acting like the judge and making decisions according to the law, they had decided to blaze a different path, one I thought was contrary to the law. I kept hoping the bank and the heirs would come to their senses and this mess would be over. But now we were about to attend a hearing and face a real judge. I was sure he'd set my opponents straight.

One of the most important issues in the lawsuit dealt with my home on Robledo Drive. Stephen and Laura appeared to be very upset, because even though they owned one-half of the house, they couldn't effectively sell it. Who would pay anything for their half, especially with me allowed to live in it until I died?

They also couldn't rent out their half. Nor could they show up and sleep in one of the rooms (not that they wanted to). From my point of view, the biggest burn was the fact that each month, they would have to send me money for the mortgage and insurance. If I made capital improvements, they'd have to pay their share. It was a tough pill to swallow.

Because of the intensity of Gary Stolbach's arguments, voluminous emails, and threats of filing a breach of fiduciary duty lawsuit, JPMorgan and their attorneys bought into his new and creative approach to probate law. He and JPMorgan claimed that when Max died, all our community assets—cash, stocks, real property, wine, golf clubs, vehicles—were placed in a grab bag called a community estate. No one owned anything, just a percentage of what was in the bag.

Under this wacky theory, JPMorgan, as the IA, could reach in and dole out whatever they wanted to whomever they wanted, so long as each of us received the proper overall percentages. It was an insane idea, not supported by the probate code or decades of court decisions, but that didn't stop them.

From day one, my lawyers had explained that Texas was a community property state. They said that while Max was alive, we had each owned 50% of everything we had. I had full use of his car, and he could sit at my desk and work. I could spend every last dollar in our bank account without talking to him, and he could do the same. That was how community property worked.

At the *instant* of Max's death, that "community" dissolved. My 50% became my separate property, and Max's 50% became the property of the Estate of Max Hopper. Since Texas is an "item" state, I owned half of each and every property item, whether a bottle of wine, a golf club, or a stock.

To stop their crazy "grab bag" idea, my lawyers filed a motion for summary judgment. This essentially said that since the facts weren't in dispute, the judge could decide which party was right under the law. My lawyers explained it like this: A law says all vehicles must not travel over 60 mph. That law is very clear and straightforward. *All* vehicles must obey the law. But if an ambulance has to race a patient to the hospital, the ticketed ambulance driver can ask for an exception because the facts are not in dispute. In other words, both sides admit he was speeding. The judge can rule for or against the driver.

And that's what we asked the judge to do: tell JPMorgan and the heirs they were wrong.

We filed a document chock-full of statutory law citations, case law (previous decisions from courts around Texas), and affidavits from me and my lawyer. This elicited responses from JPMorgan and the heirs. The stack of paperwork was staggering. All told, for this one event, there was probably a total of $300,000 in legal bills, including expert fees paid by all sides to get this issue before a judge.

We went to court and presented our argument. The heirs trotted out their prized expert: Stanley Johanson. He spoke with authority, his hands pinned to the lapels of his jacket like a scholar. The more I listened to him, the more it seemed like he was lecturing the lawyers and the judge on probate law. It made me very nervous as I couldn't believe this might go against me.

To cleverly confuse this issue, both JPMorgan and the heirs used the wine and golf clubs as the major issue. This obscured the bigger prize—my home on Robledo.

They told the judge that it was easier to give the wine to me and cash to the heirs. If they could convince the judge to declare that the bank had the authority to partition the property, giving all the wine or clubs to me, they could use the same ruling to force me to purchase everything else, including the heirs' half of the home. It was a sneaky move.

We all knew that whoever was stuck with all the golf clubs and wine would come out the loser. The inflated appraisals meant someone would be holding a bottle of wine *valued* at $500 while the other received $500 cash. The person holding the bottle would then have to spend time and money finding someone to purchase it for at least $500. Good luck with that.

The bank's lawyers made solid arguments. That's why they get paid so much. They're highly skilled and know how to pound the life out of an opponent.

When they finished, my lawyers spoke again. Jim Jennings argued that if this new scheme was allowed, every widow or widower would have to borrow money and go into debt to pay their spouse's children simply because they didn't like the laws of intestate. He also argued that the court's ruling would have to be implemented in every probate case, not just mine. Every litigant would march into his court and demand all the cash. It was a powerful argument.

Jim also pointed out that what Stanley Johanson had just said in court was the opposite of what he had written in his book *Texas Probate Code Annotated*. Jennings had blown up posters from Johanson's book for the court to read. Each one contradicted Johanson's oral argument.

The judge, bamboozled by all this, asked questions. When Jim finished speaking, the judge said he'd have to decide which authority was right: Johanson or Johanson.

I sat in the first row, urging my attorneys through mental telepathy to point out that Johanson's probate book was written *before* he was paid $22,000. But I was unsuccessful.

We waited three weeks for a ruling. Finally, on Valentine's Day, my lawyers received the judge's order. The heirs and JPMorgan had won. Not only could the bank stick me with all the property, including my home, but I'd have to pay an undisclosed amount set by the IA for stuff I didn't want. I was sunk.

On the phone, Jim Jennings explained more details. "Everything you owned at Max's death is now being called the 'community estate' and can be transferred to the heirs. And the bank can claw back money they've already distributed to you so they can give it to the heirs. It's a total loss."

I started to cry. My community property rights meant nothing.

Stanley Johanson had done a masterful job. He was worth the $22,000 they had paid him. I just wish we had gotten to him first.

IT TOOK DAYS before I could get back to work. Rummaging through all the court filings, I discovered that the heirs and JPMorgan now valued the entire community estate at $25 million. That was news to me. Of course, the higher the value, the more JPMorgan received in administration fees. And it also meant the heirs would get more of my cash once they stuck me with the personal property. It was another brilliant move. Then, my phone rang.

"Jo," Jim Jennings said, "we may not be dead yet."

"What do you mean?"

"The judge's order has an inconsistency. He found for you on item seven and in the next paragraph he found against you on item seven."

"Okay, what do we do with that?"

"I'm going to file another motion and point it out. Ask him to reconsider."

More filings. More hearings. More time. It all meant more money.

"Okay," I said reluctantly. "You're my lawyer. Do your best."

EVER SO SLOWLY, February and March drifted by. In April, the judge reviewed his order and brought the lawyers in again. From listening to his statements, it was clear the judge realized he had made a mistake on item seven. The issue now was how to correct it.

My lawyers argued he had to issue a new order. My opponents told him he just had to make a *correction* on the order.

Mike Graham argued that the judge should uphold the Texas Probate Code related to partition. As I watched Mike, it felt like Superman had just stepped from his business suit and donned a cape. He was fantastic! I could see my team was trying hard to pull a victory out of certain defeat.

Attorney John Eichman argued for JPMorgan. He said, "Judge, we're here to tell the Court that the Court has ruled wisely, so we'll sit down." It was a clever move, quit while you're ahead.

Gary Stolbach argued for the heirs. He explained that the heirs would lose big time if they had to pay money to me for property they couldn't use. It just wasn't fair.

Mike Graham told the judge the heirs would have to be happy getting 100% of Max's estate. And because the Texas Probate Code was the legal authority, the heirs would just have to tough it out and pay me for their half of Robledo's mortgage and home insurance.

At one point during the hearing, the judge said to JPMorgan, "It sounds to me like the bank doesn't really want to be an Independent Administrator. You want to be the dependent administrator, right?"

Wow! The judge had hit the nail on the head. JPMorgan, Cantrill, and Susan Novak wanted the cozy compensation but not the responsibility to make a decision. They all knew that with responsibility comes liability. It was safer and financially beneficial to run to court and let the judge screw up. Try suing him.

After the hearing was over, I went home. I sat in my study and played with Blair, thinking over the whole situation. I was spending more money and nothing was happening. Litigation is slow, costly, and painful. No wonder people who are innocent settle cases.

IT TOOK A month, but we finally received the new order. As I read it, I realized a miracle had happened. Now, I was the winner and the bank and the heirs were losers. Justice had prevailed.

I couldn't believe this reversal of fortune. "What happens now?" I excitedly asked Jim Jennings.

"Gary Stolbach said the heirs will appeal. I assume JPMorgan will too."

"How does that work?" I asked worriedly.

"We wait thirty days for this judgment to become final. Then, the record of the proceedings is typed up by the court reporter. When that's sent to the appellate court along with the court's file, Stolbach will file his brief. We'll have to file a response. The bank will also file a brief."

"Then what?"

"We wait until the appellate court decides to set a date for oral argument. Once that happens, we go in and argue the matter and wait for their ruling."

"Should I ask how long all that will take?"

There was a long pause. "Probably not."

I've never been to prison, but I imagine time crawls by, much as it does in litigation. I couldn't see an end to this nightmare. So long as JPMorgan and the children wanted to go against the law and delay this probate proceeding, I had no choice but to continue.

It was late May 2012 when I happened to be in Houston, visiting my good friends Eula and Bill. As I was headed back to Dallas, I decided on a whim to veer east and drive by the old home in Pollok; Max's grandparents' house, the one that had been left to him by his aunt.

I was surprised to see the yard mowed and the house secured. Susan Novak had at least done something right.

I walked around and noticed a huge tree next to the house. Max had told me of his fond memories of the house and that tree. I imagined him taking a nap under the large limbs, letting the deep shade cool him on a hot summer day. Unfortunately, it was clear the tree, like Max, was now dead. Suddenly, I remembered Max's idea for the tree.

When I returned home, I sent an email to Stephen and Laura. I asked for their permission to cut down Max's special tree and have a woodworker make plaques from it. I would have each plaque inscribed with words about the house, its history, and relation to the Hopper kin. I wanted to give one to every descendant of William Waller and Sarah Hopper, Max's grandparents, so they might have a piece of their heritage. It was what Max had planned to do prior to his death. Now, it was my job to complete his unfinished business.

I ended my email with, "Hope all is well with you and the kids and you have wonderful plans for the summer. Jo."

It took eleven long days before I received a response. Stephen had the honors.

"I have spent the week trying to decide how to reply to your email and, given my prior communications with you, do so with considerable trepidation. I must say I have always found you a bit confusing. As I have tried to communicate, I have never wished conflict with you and do not wish this now. I have not wanted to hurt you, nor to be hurt by you. I would love a give-and-take relationship of fairness and mutual care and respect. Perhaps the current problem between us is the definition each of us has regarding the word 'fairness.' In a fair world do you feel the Texas probate laws to be unfair? Do you feel that your's and Dad's sacrifices over all those years preclude an inheritance to his children? As you might wish for me to put myself in your shoes, do you try to put yourself in mine? Perhaps you could just give me your idea of fairness. I might accept your point of view regardless of my own."

I was halfway finished with the email when I looked away from the screen. He and Laura were inheriting *all* of Max's estate. How much fairer could it get?

I turned back and continued to read.

"I would like a chance to grieve for my dad. Part of that grief might lead to decisions regarding a dead tree. As to Judge Miller's decision, I suppose I must now decide whether to take it to the Supreme Court. Though I did not attend the hearings, I too, like you, are capable of understanding the different views. Not really that complicated... to spend... what... a couple of million dollars on? Let's see if I can summarize all the lawyers' rhetoric. You certainly win and we even agree on the points that when Dad died intestate he left undivided interests, including Robledo, and that one cannot partition the homestead. However, we could win on appeal, given our view that the statutes support the principle that once undivided interests enter independent administration, fair treatment must be given to their partition. As we have seen with Judge Miller, it could go either way, depending on the day. I use the word 'win.' As I told you, the reason we have spent this kind of money was to further our complaints against JP. Your 'win' has dramatically weakened our case. What are your true reasons for this fight? Please let me know what you need from me in order to feel you were treated fairly. Steve."

His thought process and reasoning stunned me. I wanted to shout at him, "Max had a will! It was provided by the state of Texas. You and Laura get everything! Sorry you two own half of our home and the wine and golf clubs. Max would be disgusted with you. Get over it!"

I withdrew my request to preserve the legendary tree and cried. Later, Susan paid some workers to chop down the tree and billed it to the estate, thus taking more money from Stephen and Laura. I would have gladly saved the heirs some money and paid that fee to have a piece of something Max had cherished. But it was not to be.

In late June, Cantrill filed an amended inventory. It was full of errors. I couldn't understand how a bank as large as JPMorgan and a lawyer as experienced as Tom Cantrill could not get this simple instrument right.

As usual, my attorney urged me to object. I took his advice and spent another wad of cash attempting to show them the correct numbers. The heirs spent money, too. I could see Tom Cantrill happily billing the estate for his fees. It was a neat little process, at least for the attorneys.

Simultaneously, following the judge's order, JPMorgan deeded our home—50% to me and 25% each to Stephen and Laura. I could not imagine it taking more than thirty minutes to an hour to fill out a stock form. Yet it took close to two years, along with hundreds of thousands of dollars in legal fees, to make it happen. It was absolutely shameful.

Of course, Gary Stolbach and the heirs were livid. Now, the heirs owed me $6,384 for their share of the homeowner's insurance since Max's death. Stephen cleverly sent me a check for only $600. He computed it from the date Robledo was transferred to him and Laura. I returned the check and demanded the $6,384, half of two years of homeowners' insurance. The IA and heirs refused to reimburse me the back insurance payments even though the IA had committed to this each year. So, on August 6, 2012, we attended another hearing before Judge Miller, this one regarding the insurance payments.

Stolbach had brought another lawyer from his firm, Glast Phillips, named Mark Enoch. Mr. Enoch was upset that I would not add Stephen and Laura to the policy until I was reimbursed for the back payments. Judge Miller heard the arguments and ruled nine days later that the estate had to pay the back insurance premiums. After tens of thousands in legal fees, JPMorgan finally paid me the balance. The absurdity of all this was mind-blowing.

Because the house mortgage was interest-only, the heirs didn't have to make any back mortgage payments. But the principal payments were about to kick in. Then they would have to start sending half of that amount to me on a monthly basis. This turn of events surely left a stain. (To avoid sending me any money, they ultimately sent their insurance payments directly to Chubb and their mortgage payments into a special account at my bank. Apparently, they didn't want me physically touching their money.)

One interesting aspect of all this was the discovery we had received from JPMorgan. By reading each page, I learned that Susan Novak had not contacted the mortgage company during all of 2010. It wasn't until after I'd filed suit in September 2011 that she finally reached out to them. More than a year after JPMorgan had been appointed IA, she finally got around to it. Her incompetence, or at least sheer negligence, continued to stun me.

Susan had also spent time thinking about the golf clubs and memorabilia. Even though the appraiser had stated it was worth over $300,000, she mused in an email to the heirs and me that we should consider donating the whole lot to First Tee. Why Susan thought it was her job to dispose of the clubs, I had no idea. All she had to do was retitle them into our names and it would no longer be her concern.

I responded harshly by attaching a section of the probate code and asked her why she thought she had any say in what I did with my property. She abandoned the idea but would not retitle it. Thus, JPMorgan still controlled the personal property.

Still, I was steamed. JPMorgan Chase would rather I agree to give away my property than return it to me. It felt like this was JPMorgan's first intestate estate. Their behavior was hard to believe… unless it was all intentional?

THE HEIRS FILED their notice of appeal in August 2012, triggering Jim to file a "Notice of Appearance" for Michael Yanof with Thompson, Coe, Cousins & Iron, LLP. Michael was an appellate lawyer that had been working with Jim on and off. But now, he'd be needed to ensure

Jim did everything right, since the appellate rules were different from the trial rules.

In early November, we received notice the appeal was being transferred to El Paso. I didn't fully understand the ramifications of this until almost a year later.

Also in November, we learned that Gary Stolbach had been fired by Stephen and Laura, who were considering suing him and his firm Glast Phillips. I guess for a lawyer, it's part of doing business and why attorneys carry malpractice insurance. Live by the sword, die by the sword.

The heirs filed their appellate brief listing all the reasons why the trial court's ruling should be reversed. Then I received a gift. It was Christmas Eve, a Monday, when the mail arrived. Blair followed me to the door, then watched as I sorted through the coupons, catalogs, and other junk mail. Amidst all this, I saw an envelope addressed to Jo Hopper and Quagmire, LLC. What an ironic name, I thought. I studied it more closely and realized it was from the Dallas County Appraisal District. Curious, I took it to the kitchen table, sat down, and opened it.

It was a letter telling me the amount of property taxes due on my home. But Stephen and Laura should have been listed as co-owners. They weren't.

By now, I had become an expert in researching anything. I hopped on the computer and learned that Quagmire, LLC was a limited liability company in Oklahoma. It had been created a few months earlier by a lawyer with an address very close to Stephen's office. I made some hot tea and pondered this. Then, I called Jim Jennings.

"What do you think about this?" I asked after filling him in.

"Hmm," he said. "I'm thinking."

I let his brain work. "You know, Jo, this just might be the kill shot."

"What do you mean?"

"I mean, Stephen and Laura might have screwed themselves. They don't have standing."

"Standing? What are you talking about?"

"I sell my Lincoln Continental to you. You now own it. Later, I learn that those specific Lincoln Continentals were made with defective steering wheels. I decide to sue the manufacturer for selling me a defective car. But they tell the judge that since I don't own it anymore, I lack standing. The person who should be suing them is you, Jo, since you own the car. Get it?"

I smiled. "So Quagmire, LLC should have filed the appeal brief, not Stephen and Laura?"

"Exactly. I'm going to file a brief and ask the court of appeals to dismiss their appeal."

My shoulders sagged. "Will Quagmire then file an appeal? Aren't we just wasting time?"

"No," he said, laughing. "Quagmire can't. Their time has expired. This will make the judge's order final. Game over, we win!"

"Oh, Jim," I cried, "what a wonderful Christmas present!"

"Well, don't unwrap it just yet. I still have to file the motion and win it. They'll put up a big fight. And as you've seen in court, anything can happen."

He was right about that. Still, I was happier than I had been in a long time. Quagmire LLC might just turn my legal swamp into a prime piece of real estate. Suddenly, I planned to have a great Christmas.

Chapter Fourteen

"An important strategy is, we have to execute to win."
—JPMorgan Chase Bank, N.A.
Our Business Principles website

In January, Jim Jennings filed a motion to dismiss the heirs' appeal for lack of standing and then filed our appellate brief. JPMorgan filed a motion to strike my brief, claiming an email we had used in our brief, one from Tom Cantrill to Susan Novak, wasn't part of the record. Jim Jennings read the motion and remembered that Judge Miller had over-ruled everything not included in his final ruling. And the email had been attached to a JPMorgan motion claiming it was attorney-client-privileged and had been accidentally released.

This "attorney-client privileged" argument made no sense to me. After all, Tom Cantrill represented the Estate of Max Hopper. Susan Novak was the IA for the same estate and thus Cantrill's client. Suppos-edly, the beneficiaries of the estate, Max's two children and me, were not allowed to see anything Cantrill and Susan discussed. Yet both Cantrill and Susan were being paid by the estate! That meant Stephen and Laura were paying their bills and couldn't see what they discussed. It was crazy. If Susan and Cantrill talked about misdeeds and wrongdoing, they were protected by the attorney-client privilege. And this is a microcosm of the legal system: The very people the estate looks to serve can be legally kept in the dark about what is actually going on. It's not right.

Here is the privileged email dated August 23, 2010 that Tom Cantrill wrote to Susan Novak a few months after JPMorgan had been hired and more than a year before I sued them:

I had no doubt that you had told Jo the answers to her questions. I do hope you keep some kind of calendar where you can pinpoint days that you have given her responses that are oral – we will have the emails. Jo once told me she was a note taker, but she continues to raise these issues. Strange. But keep some kind of record so that you can respond to her when she raises issues like this one.

On the home, it was community, so her direct share is 50% plus home-stead right. In a dependent administration, once the inventory is filed the homestead is to be set aside to the surviving spouse. So, I would think once the inventory is prepared and filed you should deed the property to Jo – her community one-half (to release the administrator's right to manage it) and the other half to the children subject to Jo's homestead right. She then carries on paying the expenses as they mature, and I guess Mike and John Round can try to figure out what to do with capital repairs. If Jo wants to buy the children's interest, then shouldn't Mike and John work that out? Let's discuss before I reply to Jo's email.

Cantrill said right here what should be done with my home. I win! Too bad JPMorgan didn't do it. But the most interesting part for me was Cantrill and Susan worrying about documenting their correspondence and behavior. Except for that one initial phone call as Max lay in the hospital brain dead, I had not talked to Cantrill in over a decade. Yet somehow he remembered I was a good notetaker. Strange indeed.

It took more money and lots of hard work by Jim Jennings, but the court of appeals denied JPMorgan's motion to strike my brief and considered this devastating email in evaluating the appeal. They also refused to dismiss the heirs' appeal based on Quagmire, LLC but left the door open to consider their lack of standing in the final ruling. Then another miracle happened.

Jim Jennings was researching cases for our final appellate reply brief and found a case out of the Fort Worth appellate court that was spot on. *George v. Taylor*. The facts were very similar to my situation. A man and woman were married, and each had children from other marriages. They had no children with each other.

The man died first without a will. Four years later, his wife died. The only property of value was a house in Wichita Falls. The husband's children were suing the wife's children because the wife's children were trying to force half of the bills for the wife's debt and funeral to be paid out of the proceeds from the sale of the home.

The court sold the house and put the money in a special account before deciding who got what. In their ruling, the court of appeals corrected the misunderstanding of community property that so many lawyers have. Community property only exists when someone is still married and both spouses are alive. Once the spouse of a blended family dies without a will, the surviving spouse becomes a tenant in common with the children of the deceased spouse. That surviving spouse's 50% share becomes separate property the instant the spouse dies. I was very excited. To me and Jim, the case was another kill shot to our opponents' arguments.

Just before Thanksgiving 2012, I was in Mike Graham's office as we waited for an oral argument date to be set. Suddenly, I spotted Stanley Johanson's *Texas Probate Code Annotated* sitting on a desk. I picked it up and started reading. After a few minutes, I knew I had to read all of it so I told Mike to add the book to my tab.

With Johanson's law book in hand, I went home and spent the four-day Thanksgiving holiday reading it from cover to cover. By the time I'd finished, it was filled with yellow highlighting and dog-eared pages. And I had discovered that brilliant Stanley Johanson was clear: My attorneys were right.

Johanson's book was utterly illuminating. I could see the importance of the state constitution in probate law and how Texas was set up to make probate easy and simple, not long and complicated.

With my new knowledge, I felt more confident questioning my lawyers on specific points. I was also armed with a strategy as I went through the discovery documents that trickled in. JPMorgan might have been the largest bank in the world, but I was determined to give them a fight they would remember for a very long time.

As I went through the long briefs filed by JPMorgan and the heirs, I read one claim that disturbed me. They argued to the court that I was now responsible for one-half of the attorneys' fees run up by Cantrill and Eichman. This was a considerable sum. I immediately called my attorney.

"Jim, how can they do this? They told me I won't have to pay a cent. Have they lost their minds?"

"Don't worry," he said. "We have your written agreement with the bank stating that you don't have to pay any money. Plus, we found a case that says your half of the community property is not part of the estate nor subject to administration after the debts are paid. It's just being returned to you."

I started breathing again. "And I'm not part of the estate, right?"

"Well, you are an heir because you're inheriting a tiny sliver of Max's separate property. But that shouldn't supersede the agreement or make your community property subject to the estate's attorneys' fees."

"So, they're just trying to put pressure on me to negotiate a settlement, right?"

"Probably," he replied. "And JPMorgan knows the estate may run out of money to pay their lawyers. They need to find another pocket to reach into. Don't forget the heirs most certainly blew a gasket when they learned you weren't responsible for half of the estate's expenses, including attorneys' fees."

He was right about that. My lawsuit was upsetting everyone's idea of how this whole estate thing should have gone down. Laura had made that clear.

JULY ROLLED AROUND. It was 2013, three years after JPMorgan had been appointed IA. Like the annual migration of the red crabs on Christmas Island, Tom Cantrill filed another amended inventory filled with errors. And following suit, my lawyers suggested I spend money to object.

I did.

Tom Cantrill was a puzzle to me. Last year around this time, he had found a few minutes to fill out a simple form that retitled the house. Now, one year later, he'd found a few minutes to retitle the golf clubs and wine. In a burst of activity, Cantrill had also retitled the home in Pollok, Texas, that Max had inherited from his aunt. It was still incredible to me that it had taken three full years to do all this. But it had.

Susan Novak still had not retitled the furnishings, artwork, or Max's jewelry. I guessed she or Cantrill would get around to it, maybe next year, assuming they needed to hold onto the property in order to keep billing the estate. But more importantly, it seemed like the bank had been determined from the very beginning to bring every asset into the bank or under their control, including my half of the community property. Once they collected all my money and possessions, they could hold onto them for as long as they deemed proper. This had the effect of pressuring me to make a deal with the heirs, even though I wasn't required to do so, or to drain what separate property I had left to fight them. You see this tactic in divorces: one side controls the money, perhaps withholding it from the other spouse, while trying to negotiate custody. Negotiation through strength. Believe me, I felt the pressure, and it was immense.

IN AUGUST, I received another accusation of theft. This time the amount was $2,515. Cantrill believed I had received a check in that amount from one of the investment companies and failed to tender it to JPMorgan so they could cash it and presumably seize my half to pay legal bills.

After reading the accusation, I contacted the company and asked them about it. They explained they had made a direct deposit of $1,009 into the account Max and I had originally specified to receive distributions. I don't know where Cantrill got the $2,515 number because it wasn't correct.

I looked back through my bank statements and found the deposit. Because it wasn't identified with the party that had sent the funds, I had placed a question mark beside the payee. I explained all this to Jim, who spent way more than $1,009 to resolve this latest theft accusation.

As I played with Blair, I realized that Susan had not contacted that same company to give them a change of address or any transfer information. It was easier to let someone else do it—like me.

A week after the theft accusation was resolved, my lawyers negotiated a settlement with Stephen and Laura over the wine and golf clubs. Finally!

With Stolbach gone, their new lawyer, Chris McNeill from Block, Garden & McNeill, was much more reasonable. Still, I was steamed that the heirs wanted access to the golf clubs to show to charitable organizations. It's not that I had anything against charities receiving the clubs. I just couldn't believe after all this time that the children didn't want to keep the golf clubs as something Max had loved and valued. Instead, they were willing to give them away for a possible tax deduction.

The worst part of all this was the underlying cost. I had spent $104,000 in storage space over fifty-two months. And that didn't include the other storage costs. This money would come from the estate, which meant the heirs had to pay it. Again, the madness of it all!

As with this entire case, nothing was ever easy or final. Three days after our lawyers signed the settlement agreement on the wine and golf clubs, Chris McNeill notified us that his clients had done a complete reversal on him. He claimed he did not have the authority to sign a deal.

I called Jennings and asked how this was possible. He explained that when lawyers in Texas reach small agreements on matters in lawsuits, they execute a Rule 11 agreement. So long as it's in writing and signed by the lawyers, the parties—*their clients*—are bound.

We immediately filed a new lawsuit for breach of contract, suing Stephen and Laura again. We also filed to partition the property, since reaching an agreement with these two would clearly be impossible.

As I looked through all the emails where McNeill represented the heirs, I became confused. How could he be their lawyer on Monday but not have any authority on Tuesday? Wasn't that fraud?

Jennings pointed all this out to McNeill, including that a state bar complaint was being filed against him. To counter this, McNeill filed an affidavit stating that he did indeed have the authority to make that agreement. His affidavit alone meant we would win the lawsuit. Of course, all this took a lot of money. Why Stephen and Laura were backing out of an agreement their lawyer claimed they had approved, I had no idea. Wouldn't they need to sue Chris McNeill and Block, Garden & McNeill now?

In late October, oral arguments before the Court of Appeals finally took place. I was both excited and afraid. Whoever lost here would have to appeal to the Texas Supreme Court, which wasn't required to take the case. Instead, the loser would have to beg them to take it. This put more pressure on my team.

The case had been transferred from Dallas to El Paso, and I now discovered what that meant for me financially. From Dallas, El Paso is over nine hours by car if you drive without stopping. I couldn't afford to pay lawyers by the hour to ride in a car. We all took a plane out there the night before and stayed in a nice hotel. Meals, plane fares, transportation, and hotel bills went on my tab. In for a penny, in for a mound—of cash.

On the morning of oral arguments, we had a hearty breakfast and shuttled over to the appellate court. Just outside the courtroom, a flag caught my attention. It displayed a coiled-up snake with the words "Don't Tread

On Me." That was my entire attitude about this case. I had been trodden on by so many people, I'd reached my limit. It was time to bite someone.

I stood in the hall waiting for our time to present the case. Mark Enoch, the heirs' appellate attorney, stood twenty feet away passionately arguing to a wall. He was working on his speech, oblivious to my presence. Seeing him and the flag just made this entire trip surreal, like some Netflix or HBO series.

Finally, it was time. I walked inside to find a mini-amphitheater. The spectators sat behind the lawyers, who sat at two large tables facing a female three-judge panel. There was a podium between the tables that each attorney used when presenting his oral argument. If I had been a lawyer, I sure would've been intimidated.

From the two heirs, only Stephen attended. He sat in the last row by the door to enter or exit on the left side. My attorneys told me to sit on the third row back on the far right side. This arrangement seemed to show the chasm between us.

Before the heirs' attorney started his oral argument, the Chief Justice interrupted him. "Let me tell you all for the benefit of your information, as far as your arguments are concerned, the panel today is composed of a former probate judge and two family law specialists. So, we are a bit familiar with community property laws and descent and distribution."

I felt good about that. Having experts in this field gave me a better chance of winning.

During the heirs' allotted time a justice asked Mark Enoch, "What is your definition of estate?"

Enoch told her that the estate was valued at $26 million, with the house comprising about $2 million of it.

The justice came back with, "I disagree with you… the estate before he died, half of which became… Mrs. Hopper's separate property the minute he died. Correct?"

The justice was right on. The estate was only $13 million. Johanson's law book and *George v. Taylor* made it clear that the second Max had died, the marriage was dissolved. Community property only exists in a marriage. So, my 50% community property instantly became my separate property, and there was nothing the heirs or JPMorgan could do about it.

As the argument went back and forth, my brain clicked with the new estate valuation of $26 million. Again, it had been ridiculously inflated by JPMorgan. Like the peach tree in my backyard, this number kept growing with me hardly lifting a finger. If this case dragged on long enough, I might be a billionaire—on paper, at least.

One of the justices leaned forward. "Counsel, could you please explain to the court how you may have standing as to the Robledo property?"

Enoch cleared his throat and took a swing, stammering through some of his response. "Yes, ma'am. Addressing motion to dismiss, is that the issue? Yeah, the… the Robledo, if… if I understand your… your question correctly, Mr. Jennings' client, Ms. Hopper, has claimed that since there was a deed of the Robledo property to Quagmire, an LLC one hundred percent owned by Dr… uh… Dr. Hopper…."

"I thought it was fifty percent to each," the justice fired back.

"I think that's right," Enoch replied. "Yeah, I'm sorry."

I guess the wall he'd been arguing to was more forgiving than an appellate justice.

Jim Jennings followed Enoch and had an answer for everything. He was prepared, confident, and brilliant. It was some of Jim's finest work.

Even though we had won several issues in Judge Miller's probate court, there were still some issues we needed the court of appeals to rule on. Again, Jennings gave coherent explanations for everything we wanted. The body language of the three female justices told me he had a receptive audience. When he sat down, I smiled at him.

Good job, Jim, I thought to myself.

John Eichman, JPMorgan's attorney, stood up and, like Enoch, attacked our case. I felt like a slice of ham between two pieces of bread: the heirs and JPMorgan. Experiencing this two-against-one was tough. And Eichman had a different approach than Enoch. Eichman asked the court to undo the cases we had won and affirm the cases the bank had won. His clear thinking and even clearer answers to the justices' questions wiped the smile off my face.

Jim followed up on rebuttal and repeated his flawless performance. When the entire event was over, I felt great. The body language of the justices seemed incredulous that this case had gone like this. I got the feeling one of them wanted to come down and choke the lawyers for JPMorgan and the heirs. Of course, it could have been my imagination. I'd been wrong about Judge Miller. Perhaps I was wrong again.

DECEMBER 2013, ANOTHER Christmas season.

I sat at my desk poring over the legal bills. In thirty months, I had spent $2.7 million. I couldn't believe it, yet there it was.

Cantrill and Eichman had run up $2 million in legal fees. I assumed the heirs had spent at least the same. By now they had gone through eleven attorneys. Stephen and Laura's latest attorneys were operating under a contingency fee agreement, which meant the attorneys wouldn't be paid unless they won. They hoped to tag JPMorgan for a big number.

I somewhat envied them. For the time being, Max's children had stopped the bleeding. Of course, they still had to pay JPMorgan's legal bills, either directly or through the estate. I hoped not to be around when that happened. And this led me to another thought. JPMorgan was not only taking my money, but they had stolen my grief. Yes, I had suppressed it to work on discovery and the lawsuit, but should I even be going through this ordeal? Isn't probate supposed to go smoother? Shouldn't I have been allowed to grieve while JPMorgan professionally and legally handled the estate? I chalked it up as yet another thing JPMorgan had taken from me.

While waiting for the court of appeals to rule, I put the new breach of contract and partition suit against the heirs on hold. Hopefully, if I could pull out an El Paso victory, Stephen and Laura would fold. Then, we could take on JPMorgan for what they had been doing to us. I was sure JPMorgan was gaslighting the three of us.

Speaking of gaslighting, it was time for another visit with my good buddy, Tarian. Somehow, Pho Bidden was still open.

Seeing Tarian sitting in the booth was refreshing. He seemed to be happier as time went on. Staying sober and not practicing law was turning him around. He might become a respectable person after all.

"No ruling from the court yet?" he asked.

"No. I keep checking every night after midnight. That's when they post the new rulings. It's always a tense moment."

Tarian smirked. "Yeah, I understand. When I play the Ten Commandments scratch-off game, I'll get four golden calves and need one more. It gets tense. I'm so close it makes me want to buy more tickets."

"I'll have to take your word for it," I replied. "To me, it's closer to when I get a legal bill from my attorney, and I check the last page to see the figure. *That* is a tense moment."

"I've never thought about it like that. I was the one sending those bills. To me, it was always tense until the client *paid* the bill. After all, Lamborghinis don't pay for themselves," he winked.

I told him how much I had paid in legal fees. He didn't flinch.

"It's discovery. It allows lawyers to run up the bill under the guise of exposing the truth from the other side. All good lawyers send way more requests to the other side for production and interrogatories than they should. And we get to go to court and argue over everything. This runs up the tab for everyone."

"So you did that too?"

He nodded and leaned back. "Of course. That's how we get rich. And there are all sorts of tricks. One time, I had my staff photocopy a phone-book. I included the eight hundred pages in a massive discovery packet to the other side. Then, I buried some key documents that hurt our case between pages six hundred seventy-five and six hundred seventy-six. They never found it, so I chalked up another win. At least my opponent racked up $100,000 in legal fees reviewing all that discovery. I met him at a bar conference, and we laughed for hours about that one. Oh, what good fun!"

"How do you see this ending up?" I asked, ignoring the sting of these horrific revelations about the legal world.

"Like *Bleak House*," he said bluntly.

"What does that even mean?"

"Remember the log cabin and the land those TVA men stole from your father to make a lake? This is the same thing, only it involves Charles Dickens."

"This sounds like another long story" I sighed.

"It is. Can we order first?"

The owner came over and took our order. When we'd meet here, I'd order one of their delicious soups. They warmed me up, especially on cold days like this. The hint of coconut milk topped by chopped mint, cilantro, bamboo shoots, and a squeeze of lime just made me happy.

With our hot tea steaming in front of us, I urged him to continue.

"*Bleak House* is a novel Dickens wrote in the 1800s. It's about the outrageous probate court system in England. The story revolves around a man who died with several conflicting wills. Litigation between a plethora of potential heirs had kept the case in court for decades. Some of the heirs died, which brought *their* heirs into court. Everyone had different lawyers who submitted their bills to the court. Once the judge rubber-stamped them, the bills were paid from the pending estate.

"There are several plot lines and dozens of characters. There are good heirs, bad heirs, and evil heirs. After following these characters around for many years, we finally arrive at the last chapter. It seems a new will has been found. This one is very clear.

"Because it's the latest will, the judge calls for a big hearing. It's like the Super Bowl of court cases. When the special day arrives, the court is packed with lawyers and clerks. It's exciting because this case has created a mini-industry of lawyers and clerks who do nothing but work on this case. Since everything was written by hand in those days, clerks spent days writing copies of the motions constantly being filed. And the name of the case—*Jarndyce and Jarndyce*—is known throughout England. It's fictional, of course, but it's much like the *Exxon Valdez* case here, which lasted twenty years. Or the *Myra Clark Gaines* litigation in New Orleans, which took over fifty years! Just mentioning *Jarndyce and Jarndyce* brings smiles to lawyers faces because it represents how they're able to support their families and educate their children in the style to which they become accustomed.

"So anyway, the hearing comes. The bad heirs, evil heirs, and good heirs are standing in the front row, leaning forward to see who the winner will be. The judge takes his time but finally rules the good heirs win. They almost pass out. The judge asks for the lawyers' final bills. He studies the detailed invoices for less than a second before ordering the clerk to pay them. Then, the judge asks the clerk for the size of the estate.

"Everyone holds their breath as the clerk calculates the new sum the heirs will receive. He hands the paper to the judge, who says, 'It appears the costs of litigation have consumed the entire estate. I'm sorry, but there is no money for you. Case closed. Next!'

"The clerks and lawyers gleefully tear up papers and toss them in the air like confetti to celebrate the end of the case. The heirs all leave heartbroken while the lawyers head to the pub to both celebrate and lament the end of an era. Kinda brings a tear to my eye, since I had a case like *Jarndyce and Jarndyce*. I was planning on leaving it to my grandchildren. So sad when a massive moneymaker ends."

I told Tarian his story didn't comfort me, which of course he knew.

Later that night, I went to the computer and read more about *Bleak House*. It was definitely depressing. I prayed my Ro-*Bleak*-do house would have a better outcome.

LIKE EVERY DAY since oral arguments, I checked the appellate court's website. Nothing.

I pulled out an old file looking for a document. Another file was stuck to it. I noticed the label said "Henry Steele."

I thumbed through the file, remembering that old lawyer's words: "I see armies of lawyers and years of litigation. Everyone will have a different lawyer—brother against brother. Sister against sister. Stepmother against stepchild. Heirs against lawyers."

I shook my head in disgust. Steele had been right. His 2010 predictions had all come true. I had made so many mistakes.

I could have refused JPMorgan Chase. I could have rejected Cantrill. I could have denied Stolbach from entering the lawsuit. I could have done a lot of things differently but I hadn't. Instead, I'd fallen into the bottomless pit created by the bank and the attorneys.

All the long-winded emails putting each other down. The ridiculous demands. It was so outrageous.

And then there were the massive sums that had gone into fighting over the wine and golf clubs. We could have planted vines and grown our own grapes. Or bought some land and built a golf course. What a waste.

Yet at the end of the day, this was a complete failure by JPMorgan. They were the experts. They were the ones who got paid to make this easy and smooth. Not only had they not done their job, they shoved the heirs into me so a rumble could start, and it did.

What they didn't realize was that they had pushed me to do the only thing I knew: work hard. I had to make sure JPMorgan was exposed and held accountable before I died. It would be my magnum opus, something I could leave for all the surviving spouses who come after me. My life was going to count for something.

IT WAS DECEMBER 3, 2014, and cold again, not like what Max had gone through in Oklahoma in 2009, but still cold and dreary.

I held *Bleak House*, the Dickens novel. It was one full year after I'd met with Tarian and he'd told me the story. It was so similar to my case that it was a tough read.

Not much more had happened on my case except a letter we received from the trial judge asking for money. He was running for reelection and needed cash for his campaign. I was stunned. A judge asking litigants for money? I assumed my lawyers and I would go directly to the FBI and show them the letter so they could set up a sting operation. Maybe I could wear a wire. That's when I learned the judge's request was not only normal, but perfectly legal.

FOMO—Fear of Missing Out—is a real concept. FOMO is used by salespeople to convince buyers to sign right now before someone else buys it. FOND is also a real concept. It means "Fear of Not Donating." We discussed how my donation might affect the rulings in my case. And we certainly didn't want to be outbid by JPMorgan or their lawyers. I assumed we would at least beat the heirs. It all felt so sleazy.

After running the numbers and kicking it around, my lawyers donated some money. I never saw a line item on my legal bill but assumed they squeezed it in there somewhere, maybe calling it "4.3 hours to research *Jarndyce and Jarndyce.*"

I took a break and went to Max's tree. During the summer, I had collected a couple of lovely peaches from it, the first time since planting the pit from his half-eaten peach. I cried when I'd eaten the first one.

Yet tonight, the backyard was cold and dark. Blair sniffed around and took care of her business. After she was done, she decided to lie down in the dead grass. Since I was bundled up, I stayed with her. I had nothing more important to do.

I tried to take my mind off the lawsuit but couldn't. At a recent meal with Tarian, he had told me about an old gypsy curse he'd learned from an Irish Traveller. "May you have a lawsuit where you're in the right."

I chuckled now, although I hadn't at the time.

Another significant development was the inventory. It was still wrong. Hunton & Williams should've charged one fee to compile the first inventory for the estate. Subsequent corrections to the document should've been free. Otherwise, there was no incentive for the correct information to ever be filed. Of course, I guess JPMorgan should've filled out the inventory and subsequent changes. Wasn't that *their* job?

Their agreement had said they would be doing the inventory. But instead of Susan Novak compiling it, she'd farmed it out to Cantrill. This led to the draining of untold sums of money from the estate for three error-riddled inventories. It was a complete joke. Since I wasn't ever going to pay the estate's legal fees, though, I didn't care. It had been a costly error for me to keep fighting that. I gained nothing. The inventory didn't affect me. It only affected the heirs.

A cross breeze shook a nearby bush, bringing me back to the present. Watching Blair lie there on her stomach, her legs splayed, I envied her. She had no concept of what I was going through or the world's problems, for that matter.

Like every year, the world had been busy in 2014. Ebola had broken out in West Africa and spread to Dallas. Then a Malaysian jet took off and was never seen again. Some new terror group called ISIS appeared. The Russians invaded Ukraine and shot down another Malaysian plane.

Robin Williams and Joan Rivers died. Bill Cosby now had twenty women claiming he had raped them. NASA landed on a comet. Michael Brown was killed and riots broke out, burning parts of Ferguson, Missouri. A video of NFL running back Ray Rice beating his wife surfaced. I guess other folks were having problems too.

I moved closer to Blair and sighed. She was such a great companion. During the long hours consumed by my legal issues she had forced me to take a break. Otherwise, I might have died at my desk. I just loved this dog. I'm so glad Max and I rescued her.

Scooting closer, I leaned against a stone wall and rubbed her ears. She smiled, which soothed me. After a few minutes of petting her, she turned around and licked my hand.

"I love you so much, Mommy. You have made my life a dream."

I stared at my dog. She was talking and I understood her. It was a miracle!

"I want you to be happy," she said, "even though I'm not here with you."

I jolted upright off the stone wall. Blinking several times, I reached for Blair but she wasn't there. I used both hands to try to find her in the darkness, waving over the grass.

Nothing.

I called for her. "Blair! Come, now."

She didn't come.

I rubbed my eyes, inhaling deeply. Then it hit me. She had died of a stroke eight days earlier, on the eve of Thanksgiving. I had buried her at Tooth Acres Pet Cemetery in Parker County. All our rescue dogs were buried there.

I must have been dozing in front of Max's tree and dreamed about her. I missed her so much.

Then I remembered Patty, my next-door neighbor. She had died two days earlier. So much tragedy in such a short time.

In the dead of night, I wrapped my coat tighter around me and stood. Wiping the tears away, I trudged back to the house.

After putting away my coat, I ambled to my office. It had been 406 days since oral arguments. How much longer would this go on?

I looked at the clock: 12:18 a.m.

I said a prayer, asking God for a sign. I was so alone I didn't know where to turn except to God.

When I was done, I pulled up the appellate website and typed in the case number. The page appeared. I scrolled down to the bottom. Suddenly, my heart stopped.

There it was.

The court's opinion.

I couldn't believe it. I started sobbing and shaking, letting four years of pain and misery out. Truthfully, I thought I was having a stroke. Then, I wondered if this was like seeing Blair. Was I dreaming again?

No, despite my shaking hands, I could see this was real. The ruling had finally come. This was the day of reckoning for someone.

.

Chapter Fifteen

"Our strategy is simple. When we are right, we will fight mightily to ensure a just outcome. When we are not, we will say so."

—Jamie Dimon, Chairman & CEO
JPMorgan Chase Bank, N.A.
Letter to the Shareholders 2010 Annual Report

My hands were still shaking as I tried to open up the ruling but my fingers couldn't type anything. I leaned back in my chair and tried to focus on breathing. That didn't work.

I thought getting down on the floor would help. I could lay back, relax, and stroke Blair. My loving dog always knew how to calm me down. But Blair wasn't here anymore.

I picked up my cell phone and managed to call Betty, Max's personal assistant and my friend.

"What's the matter, Jo?" she said groggily.

"I-I think I'm having a stroke," I stammered. "Can you c-come over?"

"Right away!"

While I waited for Betty, I was able to dial Jim Jennings' phone number.

"Hullo?" a sleepy voice said.

"J-Jim, this is Jo. The ruling just came in, but my hands are shaking so much I c-can't open the file and print it off."

"Hang on." I heard a light click. "Let me find my glasses," he mumbled, then let out a big sigh. "Okay. Let me get dressed and come over. I'll be right there, and we'll read it together. And you'd better have some coffee ready."

"Thank you, Jim," I said, feeling a little bit better.

Betty arrived quickly. "I came as fast as I could," she said, grabbing me. "Let me check you out."

I sat in the same chair Max had been in when Betty and I had hovered over him, looking for signs of distress, only this time, Betty was inspecting me. It was eerie.

"You're just having a panic attack," she declared with some relief. "You've been keeping all this inside." She put her hand under my arm. "Come on, get up. Let's go see if I can pull the case up."

She helped me to my office. Sitting at my desk, she was able to open the file. "How do you feel now?" she asked me.

"Better, I guess. Jim Jennings is coming over. I called him after I talked to you. Let's go put on some coffee."

Jim arrived just as the coffee was ready. I showed him the opinion on my laptop's screen. "I can't read it," I said. "I'm too nervous."

"Okay," he said. "Let's sit down at the kitchen table and I'll take a look at it."

Betty placed a steaming cup of coffee next to him and left. I sat across from my lawyer, watching his facial expressions, looking for a sign. But I couldn't read his poker face. He gave up nothing.

"Okay, Jo, I need to go through all of this with you, so you fully understand it. Scoot around here so I can show you the opinion."

I moved my chair next to his. He sipped on some coffee as he gathered his thoughts.

"Read this part," he directed.

"JPMorgan Chase Bank, N.A. was appointed to serve as independent administrator of the estate. At the time of Max's death, the community estate approached $26,000,000. We caution here that the community 'estate' is not the same thing as the decedent's 'estate,' which would be half of that amount, or $13,000,000. While the issues presented are voluminous, the dispute may be drilled down to whether the heirs can force their stepmother to 'buy out' their interest in Robledo to avoid being 'unfairly burdened' by Jo's constitutional homestead. As she suggests in her brief, this was a perfect storm."

"Often, justices give away their ruling when reciting the facts of the case. Here, I see the word 'force' and I like it. Then notice how they put 'unfairly burdened' in quotes. These are good signs."

I took off my glasses. "Okay, if you say so."

"Now, read what they wrote about our argument that the heirs lacked standing."

"It is undisputed that the heirs' undivided interests in Robledo are now owned by Quagmire, LLC, a non-interested party. As such, there is no real controversy between the heirs and their stepmother that will actually be determined by judicial declarations... Because the heirs lack standing regarding all matters involving Robledo, we sustain Jo's first issue, grant her motion to dismiss in part, and dismiss the heirs' first issue."

"Does that mean we won?" I asked, barely able to contain my excitement.

"On that issue," Jim said. "There's more to go. The heirs' second issue had to do with a probate code section and partitioning the entire community property as it existed before Max died. Read this."

"In the argument portion of their brief, the heirs have failed to direct us to the portion of the record wherein these prior distributions are enumerated... As such, the issue is improperly briefed."

"Did they screw up?" I asked.

"Not really, because they had no evidence to make an argument. Keep reading."

"Finally, having determined that the heirs are without standing to urge any matters regarding Robledo, we do not address them in relation to these issues. We overrule Issues Two and Three."

"Those are winners!" I cried.

"Yes, they are," Jim said, smiling. "But we're not done. In this issue, we argued to the court that your homestead right to live in this home until you die vests in you the second Max died. Thus, neither the heirs nor JPMorgan Chase could sell it out from under you. However, if you recall, the trial court ruled against us on this issue. Now, the appellate court has something to say about it. Read this."

"Article 16, Section 52 of the Texas Constitution and Texas Probate Code Section 37 provides for the immediate vesting of an intestate decedent's estate in his heirs at law... Pursuant to these provisions, the trial court clearly erred in denying her second summary judgment issue."

"That's another winner!" I yelled. "Right?"

"You are correct, ma'am. First four rounds to Jo Hopper. And notice they mention the Texas Constitution. We tried to tell the trial judge that's kinda important."

"I'm feeling better all of a sudden."

Jim chuckled. "Winning often cures a whole host of health issues. But let's keep going. Our next complaint said that the trial court messed up by refusing to tell the heirs they could not use your home or force a partition of it. Read what the court said about that."

"Article 16, Section 52 of the Texas Constitution and Section 283 of the Texas Probate Code provide that upon the death of the husband or wife, leaving a spouse surviving, the homestead shall descend and vest in like manner as other real property of the deceased and shall be governed by the same laws of descent and distribution, and Section 284 prohibits the partitioning of the homestead among the heirs of the deceased during the lifetime of the surviving spouse, or so long as the survivor elects to use or occupy the same as a homestead... Under these provisions, the trial court clearly erred in denying Jo's third summary judgment issue."

"Oh my!" I exclaimed. "Round five's a winner too."

"We're on a roll," Jim said with a lopsided grin. "You only need to read these two sentences to see who wins round six."

"... Jo sought a declaration that the constitutional homestead is not subject to administration, and no party may be granted a partition thereof as long as she maintains it as her homestead... The trial court clearly erred in denying her fourth summary judgment issue."

"This is almost too much to take," I said, unable to keep the relief out of my voice.

"Do you want me to stop?" Jim asked sarcastically.

"I can't stop while I'm winning. Isn't that what gamblers say?"

"It is. For our next two issues, we had asked the trial court to rule that JPMorgan could not make you pay cash to the heirs for your homestead right, nor could they partition the homestead. Read the justices' opinion on that."

"The Texas Constitution and Probate Code 284 prohibit the partitioning of the constitutional homestead among the heirs during Jo's lifetime, for so long as she elects to occupy it as a constitutional homestead... Because Jo's fifth and eighth requested declarations are supported by law, the trial court erred in denying them."

"Another winner!" I yelled.

Jim kept going. He pointed out that I won the next two issues before I lost one. But it wasn't a big deal because the court said I could litigate that issue at trial. They just didn't want to give me that victory now.

For my final issues, I claimed the trial court erred in ruling that JPMorgan could clawback money from me. After showing the court the mistakes JPMorgan had made in failing to file a motion for summary judgment, Jim pointed to a few lines in the opinion.

"We agree... Jo presents well-reasoned complaints and again correctly challenges as erroneous the trial court's second and third declarations regarding Chase's ability to 'clawback' prior distributions..."

Two more winners!

"Jo," Jim said, staring at me with that same expressionless face. "This is as complete a victory as possible. The court saw through all the bullshit and shut down both the heirs and JPMorgan. Congratulations," he said, his face finally beaming.

We hugged.

"Now what?" I asked.

"The heirs can appeal to the Texas Supreme Court. But I'm sure their lawyers will talk them out of that unless they want to blow a lot more money. It would be tremendously stupid."

"Okay. Assume they don't appeal."

He set his mug down. "The battle shifts back to the trial court. Now, it's time to pursue your claims against the heirs and especially JPMorgan. What they've done to you is a complete travesty."

"But will I get back all the money I've spent on this nightmare?"

"We'll see," he said, rubbing his jaw. "Right now, I could use some single malt scotch."

"I'm sorry, I gave you my last bottle for Christmas. I'm all out."

Jim grinned. "I guess I'll survive."

I let Jim go home. Then, later that morning, I made an appointment to visit a friend.

"I've already read the opinion," Tarian said, holding his hands up. "Let's order first. I'm hungry."

We ordered. With the food on its way, I refocused him. "So, what do you think about it?"

"I think JPMorgan and the heirs are going to have a bad Christmas. Not only did Stolbach get slapped down, but Eichman and Cantrill were hammered as well. They'll likely be embarrassed because they failed to file a motion for summary judgment. Truthfully, though, they still might have lost the clawback issue. But to me, that was a big boo-boo."

I shifted the discussion. "What's my next move? I want to be made whole, so how do I make that happen?"

Tarian puffed out his cheeks and exhaled loudly. "As you know by now, being in litigation is a losing game. If you win, you lose. If you lose, you lose big time. Only the lawyers get rich. Are you fighting ancient battles against a different enemy or are you here in the present?"

"Wow, that's heavy," I said. "You sound like a shrink."

"I am an attorney *and* counselor. But if you're thinking of using this victory as leverage to settle, forget it. It won't happen."

"Why not?"

"Come on, Jo. Think about it. I've trained you better than that. You're claiming JPMorgan has done you wrong. They're being advised by Tom Cantrill of Hunton & Williams. He's being defended by John Eichman of Hunton & Williams. What are the odds that Eichman is going to recommend to JPMorgan that they settle? Do you think Eichman will say, 'Look, my partner and I have made some serious errors. You need to pay Jo Hopper millions to make her whole.' Do you think that's gonna happen?"

"Probably not," I said despondently.

"Try *no fucking way!*" he yelled, drawing a few stares. "They'll tell JPMorgan that they're right and to pursue Plan Bleed. That's when lawyers litigate you dry of money. If that doesn't work, they'll try Plan C."

"What's that?" I asked, afraid to hear the answer.

"Plan Cancer. They know you're sixty-seven years old. They'll stitch together a voodoo doll and stick pins in it until your stage four cancer comes back. If you die, they'll get to deal with an estate lawyer—a fellow brother or sister. He or she will bleed your estate dry fighting JPMorgan while Hunton & Williams rakes in more fees. When the estate is almost dry, the lawyers will all settle and celebrate at a local watering hole, buying beer for their horses and whiskey for their men. Remember *Bleak House*?"

"I hadn't thought about it like that," I said quietly.

"Wake up, Jo! You're in a knife fight to the death and your left arm is tied to your enemy's left arm. You'd better start stabbing or you're gonna be dead."

The food arrived and we talked about other things, like sports. The Dallas Cowboys were 9-4 and angling toward the playoffs. We also covered politics. The Republicans had just cleaned up during the midterm elections. They now controlled the Senate and the House of Representatives. President Obama was going to have a tough time getting anything done.

After the dishes were cleared away, Tarian had more words of wisdom. "I see that expression on your face. Are you thinking about changing lawyers?"

"I don't know," I replied. "Do you think I should?"

"Jennings has racked up a ton of victories for you. Staying with a pitcher who's still getting outs is a great strategy. But you should still go home and make a list. Write down all the stuff you like about Jennings and all the stuff you don't. That list will help you come up with an answer."

I paid the bill and said goodbye. I had a lot of thinking to do. If I made a change now, it could be disastrous, not to mention expensive. If I stayed with Jim, would he be the best advocate for my case in front of a Dallas jury? It was a tough decision. One screwup now and my financial situation would be rocked hard.

This would be one of the most important decisions of my life. And after allowing JPMorgan Chase Bank, Tom Cantrill, and Gary Stolbach into my life, I was batting zero on important decisions. I had to hit this one out of the park.

PART TWO

The Fruit Arrives

Chapter Sixteen

"In the United States, our share of the ultra-high net-worth ($10 million or greater) is 8%."

—Jamie Dimon, Chairman & CEO
JPMorgan Chase Bank, N.A.
Letter to the Shareholders 2017 Annual Report

I was still coming down from my high when a friend sent me a *New York Times* article with this note: "Don't feel so bad. James Brown has it worse."

James Brown, the legendary entertainer known as the Godfather of Soul, died in 2006. It was now 2014. For the past eight years, despite clearly written instructions and an audiotape of how Mr. Brown's property was to be distributed, armies of lawyers and heirs had been fighting over his estate.

In a bold move, the state government ignored Mr. Brown's instructions and seized his estate. The article said that the South Carolina Supreme Court overruled this asset grab, calling it "...an unprecedented overstepping of authority that threatened to undermine public confidence in the probate process."

Unprecedented overstepping of authority.

That sounded like JPMorgan's blatant disregard of the Texas Constitution and Probate Code.

That threatened to undermine public confidence in the probate process.

Yep! My confidence was pretty much undermined.

The article, superbly written by Larry Rohter and Steve Knopper, detailed the piles of legal bills paid by the estate, the many court hearings, and the endless litigation. Three executors Mr. Brown had appointed to handle his estate had resigned. The court had appointed two more executors. When the new executors found themselves on opposite sides of the heirs, they were removed. Another executor replaced them and so far, is still on the job.

Through the years, Mr. Brown's estate had undergone valuations ranging from $6.5 million to $86 million. One side accused the other of inflating the number to make more money administering it. From everything I read, it seemed like an earlier version of my case and *Bleak House*.

One quote in the article sent chills down my spine:

"This thing could go on for an eternity," said Alan Leeds, a former tour manager for Mr. Brown.

When I was done with the article, I saw similarities between James Brown and Max Hopper. They both had been raised dirt poor. Their children were unhappy with what they had been left. And the probate system allowed the lawyers to drain the estate. It was all so ridiculous.

I sat at my desk, pondering my situation and how 2015 was almost upon us. The fifth anniversary of Max's death was less than a month away. Even with James Brown's estate entering its eighth year, I knew without a doubt my case would be over before we hit the eight-year mark. I was even more determined to make sure it ended with a victory.

My opponents had been busy. After losing in the court of appeals, JPMorgan filed a motion for rehearing. The bank wanted the justices on the El Paso Court of Appeals to clarify their opinion and eliminate some misimpressions. Yet six months after the motion was filed, the appellate court denied it. Rack up another loss for JPMorgan, though they did drain more time and money from me. In all, I spent three long years in the appellate court.

Stephen and Laura had been busy, too. They didn't file for a rehearing and let the judgment stand. Instead, they fired their appellate attorney Mark Enoch of Glast Phillips, Gary Stolbach's law firm. That essentially eliminated Glast Phillips from my case. Good riddance.

I knew with the appellate ruling finalized, the discovery process would ratchet back up. That meant it was time for me to get things going. To do so, I needed a work boost. I drove to Starbucks and ordered a latte with a double shot. As I sipped the warm jet fuel, I rubbed my hands together and dove right in. I needed to get this case moving.

WHEN YOU GO through a lawsuit, other parts of your life are left behind. My email account was one of them. It was chock-full of unopened messages. Many of them were from Gerry Beyer, the probate expert I had hired in 2011 who was then disqualified because he had spoken with someone on the other side for five minutes. Gerry has a blog, *Wills, Trusts, and Estates Prof Blog*, that publishes daily articles about probate cases. I had neglected it for a while and decided to get caught up.

As I read through the articles, I found one detailing a lawsuit involving JPMorgan and Hunton & Williams. I carefully studied the article, which had originated in the *Houston Chronicle*, and learned that Hunton & Williams was representing JPMorgan. John Eichman was one of the attorneys on the case. I decided to study this case closer.

The lawsuit against JPMorgan had been filed in San Antonio by some of the beneficiaries of the South Texas Syndicate Trust. The trust owned mineral rights on thousands of acres in South Texas.

The lawsuit claimed JPMorgan sold oil leases at very low rates to two of its commercial oil clients. These were called "sweetheart deals." The plaintiffs alleged the companies then resold their rights in those leases for a profit to other companies, who then resold them again for as much as ten times the original price. The lawsuit claimed damages in excess of $600 million.

Some of the trust's beneficiaries were represented by Jim Flegle with Loewinsohn Flegle and Deary. Mr. Flegle was able to track the sales and calculate the alleged damages. It had been a tremendous amount of work.

Eventually, the case made it to a jury trial. On the second day, JPMorgan and the plaintiffs reached an out-of-court settlement. The terms were confidential due to a non-disclosure agreement (NDA) signed by all the parties, but a newspaper reported the plaintiffs had received $40 million in total.

I assumed Jim Flegle was based out of San Antonio. He wasn't. His firm was in Dallas… and it was close to my Robledo home. I read everything on his law firm's website. Then I prayed and thought about whether to contact Mr. Flegle. I knew if I contacted him and Jim Jennings found out, he would quit. I would be in big trouble if that happened. I tabled the matter for months but kept praying about it.

IN MARCH 2015, JPMorgan found the time to retitle and release from administration the furnishings and artwork in "undivided interests." All this time I'd lived with hundreds of yellow sticky notes pasted on everything in my house. Some had an A and others had a B. The idea was to sort choices for the heirs and show my separate property versus community property like I had done with the wine and golf clubs. For years, visitors had asked what all this was about. It had been very embarrassing.

At the same time as the retitling of my furnishings and artwork, JPMorgan retitled Max's jewelry and 5,000 shares of stock in another company. This was more than four-and-a-half years after being appointed Independent Administrator.

Wow!

And life kept getting better when Max's tree produced a bountiful harvest of peaches. I enjoyed many of them, freezing the rest for when I needed an emotional boost.

SITTING AT MY computer, I received a notice that Gerry Beyer had published a paper titled *"Morals from the Courthouse: A Study of Recent Texas Cases Impacting the Wills, Probate, and Trust Practice."* (Again, Mr. Beyer was the probate expert I had wanted to hire in the beginning but couldn't due to a conflict of interest that wasn't waived.) This time, attorney Beyer included a summary of my appellate victory. As I read it, I smiled. He wrote:

> "Morals: A party who wants to make claims with respect to inherited property must own that property when making a claim. Persons inheriting property subject to a homestead right must wait patiently for the homestead claimant to die or abandon the homestead before they can use or occupy it; they cannot force a premature partition."

Well said.

After going through my emails, I continued thinking and praying about changing lawyers. As Tarian had advised, I'd made a list of the positive and negative attributes of Jim Jennings. On the positive side were his many victories. He had also overturned one huge loss in the trial court. He had a sharp legal mind and could think on his feet and tangle with the best of them. Jim had also become a good friend, exchanging gifts with me at Christmas. We had spent a lot of time together battling JPMorgan and the heirs. He'd even invited me to his daughter's wedding in Greece, where he'd been born.

Then there were the negatives.

First, Jim's invoices arrived intermittently. Sometimes it took three or four months. Without a monthly bill, I had no way of knowing how much money I was burning through (the "burn rate").

I brought this up several times, and he promised to try to put a bill together and send it out, but he wouldn't commit to monthly billings. My other attorneys routinely billed monthly. On this issue Jim was unmovable, which left me holding my breath each time I received an invoice, scared to look at the balance owed. It was maddening as I looked at how much it was costing me.

I shifted tactics and tried to get him to work within a monthly budget, but again he refused. As a last-ditch effort, I asked him to switch to working on a contingency basis. I hit the trifecta when he flatly refused, though he did have an excellent explanation for why he didn't do contingency work. The whole process left me helpless with no control over the money being spent.

This led me to the second negative, which bothered me a lot. Jim would occasionally ask me how much money I had left. I felt like he was making sure I could still pay his multi-month invoice. Once, he suggested I get out of all this when my funds fell below a specific dollar level. This warning made no sense. I couldn't walk away from this lawsuit. I was "pot committed," a term Tarian had explained to me. It meant when a poker player has more money committed to the pot than he has in reserve. Even if I tried, neither the heirs nor JPMorgan would let me out.

The last negative was the issue of suing for attorneys' fees. One day in January 2015, Jim had mentioned something about *recoverable* attorneys' fees. The word "recoverable" had stunned me. It implied some of my attorneys' fees weren't recoverable, but I had always assumed that they were all recoverable.

When I questioned him about it, he said he had the other attorney in his office researching the issue (and, of course, billing me by the hour). I learned he was going through his billings and segregating recoverable versus non-recoverable. I was surprised and felt blindsided. I asked why I was just now hearing about recoverable vs. non-recoverable fees after three years of litigation. Why weren't these attorneys' fees placed on a spreadsheet and categorized as I was billed? It seemed obvious to me.

The issue of recoverable versus non-recoverable fees drove me deeper into despair. Why would my litigation lawyer not spell it out in writing, or at least tell me all the money I was spending might not be recoverable? I certainly had the impression someone down the road would reimburse each dollar I had been forced to spend. Now it sounded like that wasn't a sure thing. And the worst part was, I'd have to pay more attorneys' fees to find out how much was recoverable. Paying attorneys to divide recoverable versus non-recoverable fees felt like paying Tom Cantrill to produce an incorrect estate inventory, then paying him again to file another error-riddled inventory. Corrections to work already paid for should be free, as should any work done to show me which fees were not recoverable.

Still not able to come to a decision, I contacted Henry Steele in late July. Henry was the 2010 attorney who had predicted armies of lawyers and millions of dollars in legal fees. I went to his office carrying several boxes of humble pie.

Henry was very gracious as I explained my predicament.

"Mr. Steele," I said, "if I could turn back the hands of time, I would've hired you. I'd still have a relationship with my grandchildren."

"Nah," he said, waving his hand in the air. "This was headed for the gladiatorial arena from the beginning."

I mentioned the *South Texas Syndicate Trust vs. JPMorgan* case and the settlement. I explained that I'd been praying about whether to contact Jim Flegle. I thought Mr. Flegle might take the case on a contingency basis rather than an hourly rate. When I told Henry I'd spent over $2.7 million so far, he said, "You need to contain or curtail the monthly burn rate for attorneys' fees." He took some documents to look over and said he'd get back to me if he had any suggestions.

After the meeting, I drove home and was caught in a massive traffic jam. Despite winning in the appellate court, this case felt like my car: going nowhere. I was determined to do something.

In early August, I met with Henry Steele again. He went over my pros and cons. He suggested I had nothing to lose by calling Jim Flegle to discuss the case and his experiences with JPMorgan Chase Bank.

I remembered that Henry had not sent a bill for our previous meeting. When I asked about it, he said, "You've been charged enough. I'm not going to bill you." He's an amazing attorney with such empathy and insight and I was grateful for his gesture.

I took Henry's advice but had to be careful Jim didn't catch wind of it. On August 12, 2015, I went to Mr. Flegle's website and completed a Contact Us form. It asked me to provide a brief description of my problem. I did so, requesting an opportunity to meet with him in person to discuss my situation.

Two days later, I received an email from his office setting up an appointment for Friday, August 21. I was elated. There was a lot I loved about Jim Jennings, but maybe changing pitchers was the right thing to do.

WALKING INTO THE lobby of Loewinsohn Flegle and Deary, I could tell it was different. The firm had the entire ninth floor of the office building. It had more lawyers than Jennings's or Graham's offices combined. For some reason, I liked the atmosphere. It just felt comfortable.

I was shown to a large conference room. Jim Flegle soon appeared along with his partner, Alan Loewinsohn. They sat across the table from me with legal pads, taking notes.

Mr. Flegle explained that he was involved in another case and not fully available to help me, so Alan would be doing the heavy lifting. Alan was a litigator and had some exposure to probate matters.

Before we got too deep in the weeds, I handed them a list of parties and attorneys involved and asked if they had any conflict. I had learned early on not to spill the beans about my case until the person I was talking to was conflict-free. If this firm had represented Stephen, Laura, or JPMorgan Chase, I couldn't use them unless I obtained a waiver from those parties, which would be unlikely.

The two lawyers went through the list and said they would check deeper later but were almost certain they didn't have a conflict representing me.

I handed them the second document I had prepared, a bullet-point list of the key issues in my case. They read it and seemed impressed. They should've been. I'd spent over $3 million to get my "law degree."

The two attorneys asked questions and I responded. The entire meeting lasted one hour. I learned they didn't work under contingency agreements. And Alan's hourly rate was $650, higher than Jim's. This would certainly be something for me to chew on.

We concluded the meeting with the understanding that they would complete their conflicts check. They also agreed to review some documents and give me a second opinion based on their experience. We agreed to meet the following Friday to discuss their conclusions. I needed their insight to make sure switching pitchers was the best move. This decision was too important to rush.

IN THE FALL of the previous year, 2014, I had met with another Dallas attorney who specialized in fiduciary litigation and worked on a contingency basis. In the past, he had been a law partner of Mike Graham's. I hoped he would represent me on a contingency basis. We also had met for an hour. When we finished, he said he would talk with his financial partner and get back to me. That was the last I'd heard from him. I assumed this case and/or the players had gained a reputation in legal circles around town, and was becoming toxic to some.

I sat under Max's peach tree, praying about this decision. If I wanted to be 'made whole' and get every penny back, I felt a jury trial was the only avenue. Otherwise, JPMorgan would get away with its behavior and do it again to other unsuspecting and vulnerable widows.

On the appointed Friday, I was back at Loewinsohn Flegle and Deary, meeting with Jim and Alan. I opened the meeting by asking them if I should withdraw my case and quit. "I've spent over $3 million. I've won at the probate court and the court of appeals. But there's no end in sight. At least, if I walk away now, I stop draining my cash. It's all I have to live on for the remainder of my life."

They both responded that withdrawing was not a good option. "It's better to be the plaintiff in a lawsuit than a defendant," Jim Flegle repeated the words Jim Jennings had said to me in 2011.

The two lawyers agreed that no matter what, I'd end up in court either as a plaintiff or a defendant. And they reminded me that neither JPMorgan Chase Bank nor Max's children would dismiss their case and let me walk away. They both would sue me for legal and administrative fees.

Jim and Alan said I should remain the plaintiff and pursue my case against JPMorgan Chase. After about an hour of discussion, I asked them to send me their agreement for review.

At home, in the comfort of my study, I looked over the agreement. It seemed fair. But before I signed it, I wanted to learn more about the South Texas Syndicate Trust case and the subsequent settlement. I needed to see if there were similarities to my case or if this law firm had won by some fluke. I decided to get as much documentation on that case as possible and do a microscopic analysis. What I found shocked me.

Chapter Seventeen

"They have seven mineral managers. They have 12,000 accounts.
They manage 200,000 assets. How can they manage your asset?"
Pattie Schultz-Ormond, former Mineral Manager
with JPMorgan Chase Bank speaking to beneficiaries
of the STS Trust about JPMorgan Chase Bank

The public file containing the South Texas Syndicate (STS) Trust was hefty. As I started looking through it, I noticed that JPMorgan had been acting as a trustee. In my case, the bank was the Independent Administrator. To me, a trustee works in a similar manner as an Independent Administrator. They both owe a fiduciary duty to the beneficiaries. They both act like CEOs of the entity. They both have a set of rules to govern their conduct—the Texas Probate Code for estates and the terms of the trust for the trustee. But perhaps the biggest similarity, and problem, is that both the IA and trustee are unsupervised. They have no boss. Only a lawsuit, which most of civilization can't afford, is a possible remedy when things go wrong.

As I studied the STS Trust case, I wondered about my own will. After Max's death, I'd rewritten it and set up trusts for my beneficiaries. At least this research would give me insight as to how a trust works in the real world. My discoveries forever changed my opinion.

THE TRUST STARTED in South Texas. Down there, large tracts of land with little development and no inhabitants idly sit, waiting for someone to figure out a way to make money off of it. One such tract belonged to the South Texas Syndicate Trust, or STS Trust. It held 132,000 acres of mineral and water rights for more than 200 beneficiaries.

Created by five men from Minnesota in the early 1900s, JPMorgan Chase Bank eventually became the trustee due to bank mergers. In 2005, JPMorgan hired Pattie Schultz-Ormond, an oil and gas specialist, and placed her in San Antonio. Pattie reviewed the STS Trust land and decided to commission an analysis of recent seismic studies in the area. After carefully examining all the data, she concluded the land had tremendous potential for oil and gas. She then publicized the land as being available for leasing.

In 2008, Petrohawk Energy Corporation negotiated a lease and drilled a discovery well. The results showed great promise. This turned out to be the very beginning of the Eagle Ford Shale bonanza that would soon sweep South Texas with rivers of black gold.

Drilling activity exploded overnight. Crews and rigs were in short supply but the STS Trust land was in production and doing fine. This led to increased distributions to the beneficiaries.

In November 2009, JPMorgan downsized the San Antonio office and Pattie was laid off. Her responsibilities were handed off to H.L. Tompkins, a JPMorgan oil and gas specialist in Houston.

Out of work, Pattie started an oil and gas consulting business and met with the STS Trust beneficiaries, presumably to get some work from them. To my surprise, she released some inside information about her former employer, JPMorgan Chase Bank. Because there were beneficiaries who could not attend the meeting, Pattie's presentation was recorded and transcribed. Here are some of the claims Pattie made:

- JPMorgan had only seven mineral managers to handle 12,000 accounts and 200,000 assets.
- She questioned why JPMorgan leased out 640 acres when they could've leased the minimum acreage around a well bore to get a permit.
- The bank income reports sent to the beneficiaries did not include barrels of gas condensate. This prevented the beneficiaries from knowing the true value of their wells.
- JPMorgan was not on top of what was happening in the market and not keeping pace with what the landowners in proximity to the STS Trust land were generally doing.

■ She alleged JPMorgan was paid handsomely the previous year to handle the STS Trust assets and would be paid handsomely from now on.

As I read the documents, it was both educational and sad to see how JPMorgan appeared to handle trusts. Pattie even shared her opinion about JPMorgan's expertise, or lack thereof.

> I think JPMorgan [should] get out of the mineral business. I like H. L. Tompkins. Do I think he's a good Mineral Manager? No, I don't. I think he's a terrible Mineral Manager. I think he's a great banker. Banks are corporate trustees. They are not groomed to be Mineral Managers. They don't market. They're not proactive. They want to sit back and take care of your money. That's—that's their core perspective. That's how they're geared. That's what is drummed into them—to preserve the asset, not to develop the asset...

There were many other issues Pattie detailed about JPMorgan's handling of the trust assets. One such example she described involved Pioneer Natural Resources (PNR), who had signed a lease to drill on STS Trust property many years before the Petrohawk discovery well. Oil and gas leases allow the exploration company time to drill. This period can be three years or any other timeframe that's in the contract. If the company fails to drill the well at the end of the time period, the lease expires and the minerals revert back to the landowner. Yet PNR had not drilled on STS Trust property and JPMorgan had not terminated the lease. This gave PNR a free ride, tying up the minerals and preventing the re-leasing of the minerals to another exploration company and the receipt by STS Trust beneficiaries of upfront bonus payments from the new company. Pattie didn't like that.

> "Well, the lease should have been released, and the bank should have sought release of the lease. And they did. They just didn't do it force-fully. They lacked guts. They didn't pursue it because they're bankers. You know what I mean? They're bankers. They got sold—they got sold by these exploration—I read the notes. I read all the files. And what would happen is the bank would make noise about—gee, there's no development, and the oil company at the time would parade in three or four people. They had big pow wows, and they promised to do better

and the bank would go—oh good, they're gonna do better. And they waited two years, and nothing would change. And the banks would get tired. And the bank wouldn't do anything... They're trustees. They're not managers. That's the problem. They're not managers."

Eventually, one of the beneficiaries got tired of all this and sued JPMorgan. The lawsuit alleged that the bank had failed to sue Pioneer and another company, Enron Oil & Gas (EOG, which became independent from infamous Enron Corporation in 1999), and had a cozy business relationship with Pioneer, creating a conflict of interest with JPMorgan's fiduciary duty to the beneficiaries.

The lawsuit also alleged that:

- JPMorgan charged the STS Trust unreasonably high, excessive, and unauthorized fees for managing the trust
- JPMorgan breached their fiduciary duties
- JPMorgan committed fraud, and
- JPMorgan needed to be removed as trustee

Soon, more beneficiaries filed suit and joined this litigation. Yet for some reason, not all the STS Trust beneficiaries joined the lawsuit.

I read through public document after public document. Debra Round, who I remembered was the wife of Stephen's first attorney, John Round, was listed as a person with knowledge about this case since she was the Executive Director of JPMorgan's trust department in Dallas. When I saw that John Eichman with Hunton & Williams had joined the litigation, it sounded all too familiar.

The case lined up with mine. I saw a document JPMorgan had produced that mentioned Chinese Walls and conflicts of interest. And when more than 51% of beneficiaries voted to remove JPMorgan as trustee, the bank responded with a threat to liquidate the trust by selling the mineral and water rights, much like when JPMorgan asked the judge for the right to sell my home. But the judge in the STS Trust case ordered JPMorgan to resign before they found a buyer for the mineral/water rights.

The *Houston Chronicle* had mentioned the so-called sweetheart deals so I reviewed the documents about those. Reading the actual pleadings, the plaintiffs alleged that when Petrohawk struck oil on STS Trust land and started the Eagle Ford Shale Rush, JPMorgan allowed Petrohawk to keep the results secret. This allowed Petrohawk to lease additional acreage fast (80,000 acres in total) using the original contract terms, while the beneficiaries were unaware of what they now had. And this hurt the STS Trust because by publicizing the find, bonus and lease payments would have escalated and brought STS Trust better deals and more money when their minerals were leased.

I didn't understand why JPMorgan would help Petrohawk, but it didn't take long to find out. Court filings showed that Petrohawk had a $1.1 billion credit line with JPMorgan Chase Bank.

Petrohawk was both commercial client and trust vendor to JPMorgan. This created a potential conflict of interest for JPMorgan: protect Petrohawk to ensure they paid back their loans or protect their beneficiaries to whom they owed a fiduciary duty. It was explosive stuff.

But perhaps the best part of all this was when Pattie Schultz-Ormond asked a simple question:

> Where is all this money? I mean—you know, today—the Pipers, Bill Piper has asked for data to allow him to obtain an estate tax valuation and because of that, we made a request to JPMorgan for detailed production and income information, and today at that meeting JPMorgan told us we could get that information. You never get that information. That information is provided to every other trust beneficiary on a routine basis by that bank, but not STS. You never can get that. I don't know if you have asked, but they've never given it to you. I think JPMorgan should give it to you. I think when you ask for accounting, they should give it to you. When you ask for information on production, they shouldn't sidetrack you because you're not as sophisticated about oil and gas exploration matters and they can. That they should say, yes, we have that data on our system. Here, we have it in digital form. Let me email it to you.

On November 12, 2014, the case went to trial, and on the second day settled with all parties signing a Settlement and Mutual Release Agreement and a nondisclosure agreement (NDA). Later, newspapers reported that JPMorgan had written a check for $40 million to the STS Trust. If true, then Jim Flegle and several other law firms had made the bank pay dearly. However, other documents showed that from this amount more than $19 million was paid out in attorneys' fees.

As I pored through the massive file, the STS Trust plaintiffs mentioned two other cases involving trusts, breach of fiduciary duties, and JPMorgan. One was the Patricia Burns Clark Dailey Trust and the other was some company called MOSH. I put that information aside and made a note to check it out later. Right now, I had a law firm to hire.

AFTER SIGNING MY new law firm's fee agreement, I called to make an appointment. This time, I met with Alan Loewinsohn alone. Jim Flegle would be second on the case and make some appearances, but Alan would be the lead. Alan cut a smooth line through the air as he made his way to his seat in the conference room. He was tall and slender, exuding a healthy, if not athletic, appearance. His Italian suits were tailored perfectly, as were his shirts—buttoned sleeves, no cufflinks. A golden tan set off his white hair. Confidence and a quick mind were my instant impressions.

"Welcome to our firm, Jo," he said, shaking my hand. "I'm so glad you retained us."

"I feel comfortable. And I like your firm's motto: We are in business for the same reason as you—to win."

"That's our goal. But JPMorgan won't roll over and play dead. They'll put up a tremendous fight so they can keep doing this to others. JPMorgan may be the largest bank in the world, but they get shrunk down in a courtroom. That's where they sit at the same-sized table as I do. They stand at the same podium. They wear the same suits. And they speak the same language. In front of a jury, we all look the same."

"So what makes you different from them?" I asked, very interested in his answer.

"The evidence. It's a powerful weapon in the hands of a lawyer who knows how to wield it."

I nodded and suppressed a smile. That was a great answer.

"I want to be honest with you," Alan said. "By no means am I an expert in probate law. I'm a litigator. That's what I excel at. After all, the word litigator is derived from the Latin phrase 'alligator.'" He smiled broadly. "My job is to clamp these jaws onto an opponent and crush the life out of them. However, I do know a few things about probate."

I made notes as he talked.

"In Texas, the probate system has been designed to be simple and fast. No one wants to spend money on attorneys when their loved one has just died."

I agreed whole-heartedly with that.

"The second thing I know is that after paying the debts, an Independent Administrator should quickly retitle the assets and send the parties on their merry way. If the parties don't like the hand they've been dealt, they can move to partition the assets in a separate action, but at least they're done with the Independent Administrator and probate court."

"Well, that hasn't happened here," I said. "But listen, Alan, I want you to promise me one thing."

"What's that?"

"Don't ever ask me how much money I have left."

Alan nodded. "It's none of my business." There was an awkward pause before he started up again. "Besides this case, have you ever had dealings with a will or probate?"

"Yes, I have," I replied, stunned he'd asked.

"Tell me about it."

Boy, like Tarian years earlier, he had just hit a deep nerve. I had a lot to tell him, but I wasn't sure I could get through it without crying. I decided to try.

"My Aunt Nell, whom I'm named after, never had children, so she treated me like her own. She promised me and my mother that when she died, I would inherit her jewelry.

"When she died, she left everything—financial and personal—to my mother. Then, Mom fell and broke her back, which caused her to be in constant pain for over a year. Mom tried praying the pain away, and miraculously, it worked. But she was suddenly confined to a wheelchair, which was awful for her.

"I watched as she dealt with this new reality. The loving mother I had as a child was gone, replaced by an angry and vengeful person. She seemed to realize she was old and disabled, and didn't like it one bit.

"I visited her often, hoping the mother I had grown up with would return but she never did. During one visit, she glared at me and said, 'The only reason you've come to see me is because I've got something you want.' I remember my response like it was yesterday. I said, 'Mom, there is nothing you have that I want. The reason I come to see you is that I love you. It's not because of anything you've got.'

"During one of my later visits, I stumbled on a sheaf of papers. It turned out to be her will. I read that she'd left everything to my sister. Mom had cut out both my brother and me. She was punishing her only son for an incident that had occurred when she had wanted to go live in Tennessee to be near him. At the time, she lived in a retirement community in Irving, Texas. According to Mom, he'd told her, 'I've got enough to deal with. I don't need you staying here.'. I guessed that was why Mom wrote him out of the will. But who really knows?

"I told my brother about Mom's will, and that both he and I were not mentioned. He absorbed the news, saying very little. Several months later, he went to see her. But Mom had just received a devastating diagnosis of lung cancer. The doctors said there was nothing they could do. I told him not to say a word to Mother about the will. I said 'You had plenty of opportunities before she got sick, so you're not going to say anything now.' He didn't bring it up and returned to Tennessee, but never saw her again.

"When Mom died, her will was probated. Everything my aunt had given her went to my sister including my aunt's jewelry. I had to admit being cut out of Mom's will hurt a great deal. Obviously, the money wasn't the issue. It was not being acknowledged as one of her children. Her will made it seem like she had given birth to one child—my sister.

"During the process, I learned Mom's estate came to $300,000. As Mom had requested, it all went to my sister. My brother, upset he had been cut out, looked for someone to blame, and eventually landed on me. He threatened to sue Max and me for turning Mom against him. There was no evidence of us doing that, but it didn't matter. He was still angry. He never filed suit, but it did motivate me to hire Tom Cantrill to execute my will. I wanted to leave Max everything if he survived me and wanted to ensure my brother could not tie up my estate when I died. Of course, hiring Cantrill led me down this current path."

When I finished, I wasn't crying, but I was emotional.

Mr. Loewinsohn took a good thirty seconds to ponder everything I'd told him. "When you told your mother you didn't need anything from her, she cut you out of her will. Then, years later, when Laura said she didn't want your money for her children, she inadvertently brought up those buried feelings." During our initial interview, I had told Alan about Laura and our trip to Love Field. "Did you cut those grandchildren out of your new will?"

"As she requested, I did."

"And your husband left you only a one-third share of his separate property. When his coin collection sold and it netted $40,000, you only received $13,333.33. That's painful too."

"It is," I admitted.

He pursed his lips. "And JPMorgan took all that emotion and started gaslighting you against the heirs. The fact that this nightmare is in year five is all I need to show a jury. If you have discovery documents adding more wrongdoing by JPMorgan, this will be a massive case."

I could tell we were going to get along just fine. I went home and released Mike Graham, Jim Jennings, and my appellate attorney, Mike Yanof, from representing me. They had gotten me a big victory, but it was time to cut the main booster and shift to the second stage rocket. I hoped my new lawyer, Alan Loewinsohn, would be that powerful. At least he had the word "win" in his last name.

Chapter Eighteen

*"Don't do anything stupid, and don't waste money. Let
everybody else waste money and do stupid things. Then
we'll buy them."*

—Jamie Dimon, Chairman & CEO
JPMorgan Chase Bank, N.A.

Septembers in Dallas are transition months. The heat is still with us,
but relief is on the way. Sometimes, you can feel the cool air coming.

The case was also undergoing a transition. My new attorneys
reviewed everything with a fresh eye, looking for any strategy to get me
out of JPMorgan's mousetrap.

It was a Tuesday afternoon. As I carried in some groceries, trying
to negotiate the door, Alan called. I set the bags down and answered
the phone.

"We've been ordered to attend a mediation," he said. "I'd like to
discuss this with you."

I took the bags to the counter and went to my easy chair. "Oh, Alan,
this is going to be another waste of time. We need to object to it. They'll
just waste your time and my money."

"Jo, please. Objecting will be a waste of time. We'll spend money
fighting it and probably lose. Obviously, you had a bad experience. Will
you at least take a day to consider it?"

"Okay," I said reluctantly.

I put the groceries away and made some hibiscus tea. Then I dredged
up all the mediation memories in my mind. They weren't pretty.

It was September 2011—four long years ago—and I had just filed the
lawsuit. A hearing was held. I showed up in court to watch the lawyers
argue back and forth. At one point, the judge brought up mediation. He

told us to agree on a mediation date or he would order it to take place by January 15, 2012.

The heirs' lawyers immediately objected. They informed the judge they needed more time to conduct discovery. The continuing message to me was clear: Jo Hopper has hidden assets and we need time to find them.

I guess if the shoe were on the other foot, I'd be taking the same position. Most people would. You can't negotiate a deal until you know all the facts.

After the court hearing, the Independent Administrator, JPMorgan, sent an email about mediation. Their big idea was to get everyone together in one room and decide how to divide the property. It appeared to me that they believed that once Stephen and Laura and I settled our differences, the lawsuit against them would disappear. I didn't think that was a possibility.

I had heard the word "mediation" before, but never in the context of litigation. Of course, I'd never been in litigation before, so everything was new to me.

Like always, I did some homework on the internet and ordered a mediation book from Amazon. I learned that mediation was an effective tool in resolving litigation. On paper, here is how it's supposed to work:

Both sides select a mediator from a long list of available attorneys and former judges. Many times, the folks on this list are professional mediators, so this is all they do.

After selecting a mediator, the date and time are worked out. Usually, the mediation is held in the mediator's office, since it's a neutral location expressly set up for mediation.

At the appointed time, both sides show up and are escorted into a large conference room, where they sit on opposite sides of the table. The parties and their lawyers exchange pleasantries and make small talk until the mediator appears. The mediator takes their seat and explains the ground rules.

- All offers and discussions will remain confidential and cannot be used in court.
- A solution must be found that works for everyone.
- Each of us will have an open mind and work in good faith.

- A break will be taken at lunch. The mediator will provide the food (usually "settlement sandwiches" from a local deli).
- The entire day is devoted to settling this matter. Quitting time is around 4:30 p.m.

When the mediator stops talking, both sides can make an opening statement. Occasionally, the attorneys don't say anything to avoid inflaming the situation. But most lawyers have a hard time remaining silent.

Opening statements are made. According to the book, both sides wear big smiles on their faces and still have "that lovin' feeling" as they head to separate waiting areas to await next steps. These places are smaller conference rooms stocked with soft drinks, snacks, and sugary comfort food to keep the litigants happy. There are also putters with a sleeve of golf balls and other stress-relieving toys such as Rubik's Cubes, Chinese meditation balls, and desktop cornhole. In the middle of the table are plenty of outlets for your lawyer to plug in their laptop and work remotely. Occasionally, your lawyer will look up and see if you made the putt.

With the parties separated, the mediator will come into the plaintiff's room and politely discuss the case. They will ask the plaintiff to make an offer to settle and then go into the defendant's room. There, the mediator will relay the offer and obtain a counteroffer. After several rounds, the parties sign an agreement and settle the matter. On the way out, they hug each other, apologizing for getting into this mess, and become lifelong friends. If they're related, they'll promise to start bringing the grandkids over again. The mediator reports the settlement to the court, and the district clerk sends another file to archives.

After finishing the mediation book, I was heartily on board. I told my lawyers to get a quick date and see if we could settle this nightmare.

We floated some dates, but the heirs' lawyer, Gary Stolbach, had shot the entire mediation down. Again, Stolbach said he needed more time.

As the days and weeks trudged by, the parties engaged in discovery disputes. The heirs wanted certain depositions and written discovery. We wanted our discovery answered, too. In the midst of all this, the mediation idea was pushed aside.

In early November 2011, two months after the first suggestion of mediation, Tom Cantrill brought it up again. He proposed Nikki

DeShazo, a former probate court judge, as the mediator. She had 20 years on the bench. I liked this choice because I was sure she would tell Stephen and Laura they were wrong about the law. Fortunately, no one objected.

Cantrill focused on late January 2012 for the mediation. But apparently Stephen and Laura weren't available, and Judge DeShazo wasn't available the week after.

The other hurdle was JPMorgan's proposed plan: a two-day mediation. They suggested the heirs and I settle the home and property issues the first day. Then, we'd come back the following day and meet with JPMorgan and settle with them. With no prior experience in mediation, it seemed okay to me.

Jim Jennings, who had much more experience in mediations, was against a two-day event. "It's a waste of time," he said. He laid out his objections, and I changed my mind. I felt Jim knew what he was talking about.

The two-day mediation idea took another hit when John Eichman, Cantrill's partner, said he wouldn't allow me and the heirs to mediate alone. Instead, he wanted JPMorgan to be present at all negotiations so the bank could watch what happened between us.

This didn't go over well. Added to the continuing discovery disputes, the mythical mediation slipped from everyone's consciousness and disappeared under a blizzard of papers.

Then in the middle of January 2012 the idea resurfaced. Stephen and Laura's lawyers floated some new dates. Jennings talked with the opposing lawyers and explained how it would be a waste of money. JPMorgan disagreed and wanted a mediation. With no choice, Jennings filed a motion to postpone the mediation and the heirs' lawyers filed a similar motion.

For whatever reason, those motions seemed to jolt the lawyers into action. A few days later, a mediation was scheduled for February 13, 2012. Then Eichman wanted some changes.

First, he wanted the date changed to February 23, 2012. Then, he requested the heirs make a substantive offer to resolve the Robledo issue. This was before my victory in the appeals court and way before Tom Cantrill found a few minutes to sit at his desk and retitle Robledo.

The next problem was Judge DeShazo. She wasn't available until March 5.

Despite being happy with the February 13 date, Stephen and Laura renewed their objection regarding the timing. I'm sure they were still searching for the lost Treasure of the Sierra Madre. They wanted more discovery completed before they could make a reasonable offer.

From a layman's point of view, the biggest hurdle appeared to be the heirs and their attorneys coming to terms with the fact that there was no hidden treasure. No amount of time or investigation would ever scratch that itch. Once you consider someone a thief, you never change your opinion. And if you never find the stash you're looking for, you assume they simply hid it too well.

The back and forth continued. Eichman didn't want to spend money taking my deposition and instead wanted the heirs to make a reasonable offer to resolve the Robledo deadlock. But Stephen and Laura wanted to wait until all the depositions and discovery had been completed. With no experience, I wasn't sure what to do.

Out of desperation, JPMorgan filed a Motion to Enforce *Meditation* (Their spelling error, not mine.). In other words, they asked the judge to force us to sit in a room and make offers. We weren't being ordered to settle. All we had to do was go through the *motions* (no legal pun intended).

The mediation date was eventually set for April 17, 2012. Finally, after tens of thousands of dollars spent in telephone calls, emails, and court hearings, I would get my first taste of mediation.

A day before our sit-down, Eichman told Stolbach his legal invoices to the estate were on hold. This troubled the heirs. Each month, Stolbach sent a copy of his invoice to the heirs and JPMorgan before receiving payment directly from the estate's bank account.

To pound his point home, Eichman wrote an extremely sobering letter to Stephen and Laura. He told Stolbach that the IA was reviewing whether the estate would have enough cash to keep paying his invoices.

Gulp!

The message seemed clear to me: JPMorgan Chase may have to drain the estate to pay legal fees to JPMorgan's lawyers to fight this ridiculous lawsuit. So basically, Stephen and Laura were looking at an inheritance of zero dollars.

It was strategies like this that landed the Eichmans of the world the important cases and the big bucks. Unfortunately, there was nothing the heirs could do to stop this legal-fee Drano except settle.

Good luck with that!

April 17, 2012 finally arrived. The mediation was held at Hunton & Williams' office in downtown Dallas. The last time I had been there was in 1999 when Tom Cantrill helped me execute my will. At the time, Tom's firm was called Jenkens & Gilchrist. I remember Tom had made my trip easy by having the witnesses lined up. Back then, my trip to Tom's office had been productive... but not this time.

Jim Jennings was excited because he planned to make an opening statement to Stephen and Laura to tell them the truth about how the division of property should work. His goal was to inform, not inflame. I hoped it would work. But as it turned out, they were too dug in, confident of their legal positions.

As the mediation ended and we were leaving, I passed Laura. It was the first time I had seen her in over two years. She reached a hand out to me, and I grabbed it, pulling her close. We hugged. I told her I loved her and that she needed to hear my story. She needed to know what was going on in Dallas with her attorneys and the bank. I let her go and left with my attorneys.

Bitterly disappointed, I went home to reflect on the day. I took my sweet fur-kid Blair for a long walk. Her excitement and happiness improved my mood. And her kisses didn't hurt either.

The following morning, I was awakened from a deep sleep when my phone rang. It was Stephen. I glanced at the clock: 5 a.m. I was sure someone had died or had been in an accident. I couldn't imagine any good news at this time of the morning. Besides, I hadn't talked with him in almost eighteen months, and that included the mediation.

I stared at the ringing phone and his name on the screen. I had read the discovery emails and knew his true feelings. He'd accused me of theft and said that Max didn't love me. His words were especially painful because I thought we had developed a bond. I thought he'd be there for me if something happened to Max. Because of all this, I let the call go to voicemail.

After a few minutes, I sat up in bed and listened to his message. He wanted to meet at the house or Starbucks. I was afraid to be alone at home with him, yet I didn't want to let this opportunity to talk to him one-on-one slip away. I pondered all this.

I decided to call Stephen back. There was too much at stake to let an opportunity like this pass us by.

When he answered, he said he was about to leave for his drive home to Oklahoma City. After being so disappointed with his first mediation, he again said he wanted to meet me at my home or Starbucks. Since Starbucks was a public place, I agreed to meet him there.

I quickly dressed and made the short drive to the coffee shop. Because it was 5:30 a.m., we had the place to ourselves. Venti latte in hand, I joined Stephen at a table.

He asked me not to record our conversation, and I agreed. We talked for almost an hour. I reiterated what Jim Jennings had said about the law. I told him it appeared to me his attorneys were not telling him everything. I asked if he had seen the discovery containing 28,000 pages of documents from JPMorgan. He said no, and I believed him. After all, he was a doctor with a busy practice.

I suggested he get those documents and read them. I also said that he and Laura needed to be in the courtroom to see, unfiltered, what was happening. I told Stephen I would send him some documents on the law to read and make up his own mind, not just blindly take my attorneys' word.

As we sat there, I remembered his and Laura's worries about me hiding assets. I decided to say something about it.

"Stephen, I know your attorneys are concerned that I have not reported all the assets. Have you considered hiring a forensic accountant to go through all the records and see if that's true?"

He said he'd never heard the term "forensic accountant" before but agreed to discuss it with his lawyers. I urged him to consider it so we could get that issue behind us. Then, he changed the subject. He asked me if I thought his attorneys were lying to him. I knew he might be recording me, so I refused to go down that path.

"You know, Stephen," I said, holding up a Tiffany bag to redirect the conversation, "after Max died, I had the funeral home take a lock of Max's hair." I showed him one of the tiny boxes I had brought with me to our meeting, perfectly gift-wrapped. "I ordered heart-shaped silver locket keychains for you, Laura, and each of your children. I put Max's hair on the left side and a picture of Max on the right. It's a wonderful photo of Max, a big bright smile from the Smithsonian award ceremony in Washington, D.C. Will you make sure everyone gets one?"

"Of course," he said, taking the bag from me. Shortly after that, we ended the meeting pleasantly, and I returned home.

After fully waking up, I sent both Stephen and Laura some documents. When Stephen again asked if I would state in writing that his attorneys had not been providing him with full disclosure of communications, I stopped all emails. The last thing I needed was to be drawn into a lawsuit with Gary Stolbach.

Now, AS I considered trying another mediation with Alan, I remembered Tarian's advice about lawyers. "You hire and pay a pitcher to win games. When you bring him into the game, he's not there to intentionally walk batters. Let him pitch to the batters. Tell him to let 'er rip."

He was right. I needed to let Alan implement his legal strategy. After all, Alan's firm had already thumped JPMorgan in the South Texas Syndicate Trust case. I had to *trust* (again, no legal pun intended) that he knew what he was doing. Besides, he convinced me I'd spend $20,000 fighting a mediation that would cost me $10,000 to attend.

After calling Alan and telling him to go forward with setting another mediation, I decided to take Blair for a walk. I started to call for her, but then I remembered she'd died last year. That's litigation. It takes so much out of you.

I settled into my easy chair with another cup of hibiscus tea. The house was quiet and still. I could feel Max's imprint on each room fading with each passing day. By the time this was all over, I wondered if I would have anything left to remind me of my husband, other than his peach tree.

Chapter Nineteen

My baby's a fighter, not easy to bluff.
They tried to take her, but they ain't got enough.
Can't break her spirit. Can't beat her down.
Too bad for them, she's back for another round.
—My Baby by Jack Hooper

The mediation was set for November 9, 2015. To my surprise, I learned from Alan that it had been court-ordered since August 2013 and put on hold through the appeals process. Now, with my new lawyer, it was finally happening.

The weekend before the mediation, Alan invited me to his office to prepare for it. I called Tarian and discussed mediations with him. As usual, he had a lot to say.

"You must have a strategy for mediation," he told me. "And there are several to choose from. First, there is the Standard Strategy. You decide on the lowest number you'll take and start way above that. Let them Baptist you down. That's the term my Jewish partner used," he winked.

"How about *whittle me down*?" I offered.

"That works too, so long as they're coming to your number faster than you're going to theirs. Just make sure that you're polite throughout the initial joint meeting. Smile. Relax. Send lots of love their way."

"In this case, that sounds tough. So what's the next strategy?"

"The Walkaway. You do everything in the Standard Strategy, except when JPMorgan makes their first lowball offer, and believe me, it'll be lower than a turd in an outhouse, you pack up your stuff fast and walk out of the mediator's office in a huff."

"What does that accomplish?"

"Often, settlements occur not in the mediation but *because* of the mediation. Posturing now can give you leverage down the road to settle."

"Okay," I nodded. "What else?"

"The Determined Litigator Strategy. This starts at the initial joint meeting. Your lawyer gives a serious speech to the other side, pointing out the problems and exposure they face. But he's not a turd. Instead, he exudes confidence, toughness, and the ability to take an industrial-sized paddle to their ass. This strategy will not only scare the litigants but give ammunition to their lawyers to push them to settle."

"I like that one. Anything else?"

"The I Beg You Strategy. That's where you start crying as you beg Stephen, Laura, and JPMorgan to settle this mess. You keep crying until you reach your assigned room. Then you can stop. If you don't settle, start crying again on the way out."

"Okay, what else?"

"The Crazy Strategy. Your lawyer acts crazy, deranged. You can act crazy, too. The other side will realize that you're an irrational actor—you can't be reasoned with. Unless they pay big money, you're too crazy to stop litigating. Their best-case scenario is to write you a check."

"Anything else?"

"The last one is the Wild Wild West Strategy—my favorite. So right as the other side's lawyer is slandering and defaming your case, you stand up and pop that fucker in the face."

"Oh Tarian, you must be kidding!" I exclaimed.

"You don't have to do it. Just bring in another lawyer to do it."

"Who would do such a thing? Wouldn't a lawyer lose his license?"

"Not if he's not licensed. You plead ignorance, say you thought he was a lawyer. I like to bring in guys from Detroit. For $2,500 and a new suit, those cats will do a two-year probation with no problem."

"That's insane," I told him.

He chuckled. "Not as crazy as some of the stuff I've seen in mediation. Guns being pulled. Litigants assaulting litigants. Sometimes, they beat up the mediator. Anything goes. I once had a mediation that started at 9 a.m. Since we were the plaintiff, the mediator met with us for ten minutes and went to the other side. Two hours later, she returned for ten minutes before going to the other side again. Three hours later, she returned and repeated this process. Over ten hours of sitting in this room with my client, and she spent three ten-minute sessions with us. We finally left."

"What's so strange about that? Wasn't she with the other side, beating them down?"

"No. After the case ended, I ran into the opposing lawyer at a conference in the Woodlands. As he staggered up to the bar, he wanted to know what had been going on in my room during that mediation. I told him I had the same question for him. As we talked, we realized the mediator had spent the same amount of time with them. I guess she left the building for the rest of that ten hours."

"You're kidding! Did you ever find out where she went?"

"No idea. Maybe she had another mediation. Maybe she had a client to deal with. Or maybe she was catching a movie and a massage," he shrugged. "We never found out."

"Didn't you tell your clients?"

"Hell, no! We'd been paid ten hours to be there, so we weren't going to refund that money. We just never used that mediator again. Which reminds me, tell your lawyer to insist that your mediator is either in your room, their room, or the can. He shouldn't be working on other stuff or sweet-talking his lover on the phone."

"I'll tell Alan. Any other advice?"

"Yeah, it takes two for peace, one for war. If they don't want to settle, it's not going to happen no matter how prepared you are."

"Okay, thanks, Tarian." I hung up and carefully reviewed my notes. Hopefully, Alan had a solid and sane plan.

THE SATURDAY TRIP to Alan's office was easy. I took a seat and sipped on my latte. "Okay, how are we going to handle this?" I asked.

Alan was dressed in blue jeans and a crisp Sea Island cotton shirt. Even casually, he looked like something out of *GQ Magazine*.

"I've prepared a speech for the joint session. We want to be determined, confident, and firm."

Yep. It sounded exactly like Tarian's Determined Litigator Strategy. "Let me hear it," I said.

Alan took a sip from a Fiji water bottle and cleared his throat. "Good morning. There are three reasons I don't intend to discuss all the claims and evidence or give a rousing jury speech on behalf of Mrs. Hopper, although it would be easy in this case. First, by this point in this many-year saga, I think the parties and their lawyers are pretty familiar with the facts and the issues. Second, it's not my practice at mediation to tell the other side in detail how I am going to prove my case and cross-examine their witnesses. Third, today is supposed to be about resolution, not confrontation. Having said that, I do want to discuss some of the issues and some of the evidence because I have found over the years it is helpful to at least understand where the other side is coming from in negotiations—whether you agree with them or not.

"The bank took a very simple task of dividing assets and turned it into a five-year legal battle, one that has cost millions. This will be a common theme throughout our case.

"On the Robledo homestead issue, Mrs. Hopper has had to incur over $2.5 million in attorneys' fees to date. A significant portion of those fees was spent litigating the Robledo partition issue, an issue she should never have had to fight. But she had to fight the issue because, in breach of its fiduciary duty, the bank refused to timely distribute the individual interests in Robledo. And she had to fight the issue because the heirs and the bank decided to take various indefensible legal positions in the litigation."

I sat back and watched Alan as he stood perfectly still. Occasionally, he gestured with his arms for emphasis. So far, I liked what I saw.

He even had a PowerPoint ready on a large screen. He pulled up the Court of Appeals ruling and explained how it had been a complete victory for me. He hammered that fact home by asking the imaginary opponents why they thought the trial would be different.

Next, he showed the actual statute that allowed me to collect attorneys' fees. I could only imagine the looks on the faces of Stephen, Laura, and Susan Novak.

Once that was done, Alan tried to unite me with the heirs by showing how much we had spent dealing with JPMorgan. Again, this all felt like a home run.

Then it came time for the heirs to take some medicine. Alan showed an email Laura had sent to her attorney Gary Stolbach. Laura made it clear she thought they were right on the Robledo homestead issue. Alan said he didn't think the heirs would be able to distance themselves from their now-fired lawyer's strategy because, under the law, he was their attorney-of-record. Besides, we had emails that tied their approval to that strategy.

Next, Alan shot down JPMorgan's assertion that the bank was caught between two warring sides. He discussed documents showing the bank taking sides with the heirs. No way they were neutral.

My mental anguish was next. He described the torment I had gone through in not only dealing with the death of my husband but having to face a behemoth bank intent on breaking me financially and emotionally. "Who knows how much a jury will award for that?" Alan mused.

The last issue he covered was more defensive. He made it clear that if the bank or the heirs thought they would stick me with the administration fees and attorneys' fees for handling my community property, they were sadly mistaken.

He then laid out my agreement with JPMorgan and an email from Cantrill, which said,

> "The administrator made a commitment to Mrs. Hopper, which is consistent with its general practice when administering community property, that it would not charge Mrs. Hopper any portion of its commission for administering her community property."

It was a powerful blow to the bank's argument.

Finally, Alan wrapped up his presentation. "Now, I want to return to where I started. Mrs. Hopper is here in good faith to see if we can resolve the remaining issues in dispute. However, everyone needs to understand that she has both the economic means and the emotional resolve to see this through to a conclusion, just as she did on the Robledo house issue, if a fair result cannot be obtained today. Thank you for your patience."

I pushed back the chair and got to my feet, clapping loudly. "Very good, Alan! This is excellent."

"Do you think it'll make a dent?"

"Yes," I said confidently. "I believe there's a chance Stephen and Laura will fold, and JPMorgan will write a large check." Suddenly, I couldn't wait for mediation. This would be it!

A BLUSTERY COLD wind whipped through the parking garage. It was 11 p.m. on the nose. We'd been holed up for 14 hours in Ross Stoddard's office after each party paid him $1,250 for mediation.

Alan had been there with me, along with his partner, Jim Flegle, and associate Kerry Schonwald. JPMorgan had shelled out for four lawyers—Wendy Bessette, the JPMorgan Chase designated corporate representative and supervisor of estate administration; Susan Kravik, in-house legal counsel for JPMorgan Chase; Tom Cantrill, representing JPMorgan Chase; and his partner, John Eichman.

Stephen had shown up with his wife, Barbara. He was represented by Lenny Vitullo with Fee, Smith, Sharp & Vitullo, and Chris McNeill of Block, Garden & McNeill. Fee, Smith et al was his new lead law firm since Stolbach and company had been fired. Laura mistakenly thought she didn't have to appear and instead monitored events by phone from Kansas until the mediation ended.

I ground my teeth as Alan drove me to my car in the dark. There had been so much energy wasted today that it was disgusting.

As the striped concrete passed underneath Alan's Hyundai, I briefly calculated my legal bill for the day: $8,750 for three lawyers, with Flegle leaving at noon. Add in the $1,250 I'd paid to the mediator, and it was another *Chase* down the drain.* I just couldn't get away from this bank.

Finally, we reached my car. "You know," he said, "I never asked if you received a thank you card from Stephen and Laura for the silver lockets with Max's hair."

"No. To this day, I don't know if Laura or any of the grandkids got theirs."

"Okay," he said.

We arrived, and he parked next to me, leaving the engine running so he could get out and make sure I safely got into mine. As we stood there, he said, "We gave it our best shot, Jo."

"We did," I replied. "Only a jury verdict is going to end this ordeal."

He nodded. "Thank you for giving me an opportunity at mediation. Now it's time to make them pay. Are you ready?"

"Yes," I said with determination. "I'm ready. Let's win this."

Then I drove home and collapsed.

---

* A "Chase" is a ten-thousand-dollar bill. The face of Salmon P. Chase is on the front. He was the U.S. Treasury Secretary and a Supreme Court Justice. The bank I was suing had been named in his honor.

Chapter Twenty

"The banker is a member of a profession practiced since the Middle Ages."

—J. P. Morgan, Jr., 1933
JPMorgan Chase Bank, N. A.
2011 Annual Report

In real wars, when last-ditch efforts to resolve disputes fail, the diplomats go back to their superiors and tell them to prepare for battle. The leaders then pass the word down to the generals to go to war. The generals organize their troops and attack. It's the same in litigation.

After our unsuccessful mediation, the parties took the gloves off and started preparing for war, otherwise known as the trial. But, first, there were a few belated Christmas gifts to open.

Judge Miller, our trial judge, had lost his reelection to Margaret Jones-Johnson. At the first hearing, Judge Jones-Johnson looked out over her bench and saw six attorneys standing before her. She pulled up the case on her computer and began scrolling through the hearings, motions, and rulings. As the computer pages flew by without end, her eyes opened wider and wider. When Alan started by saying Max had worked at American Airlines, she stopped him and said she might have a conflict. Shortly afterward, she recused herself. This placed the case in limbo as it waited to be assigned to a new judge. I hoped our September 2016 trial date was still good.

Next up was JPMorgan. We learned that they had hired Mark Sales, an expert on attorneys' fees. Presumably, it was his job to testify that JPMorgan's attorneys' fees were reasonable and necessary, and mine were not. The only interesting aspect about his hire was that it had occurred in January 2012. It was now December 28, 2015, three years later. We were just learning about it.

Stephen and Laura hadn't been sitting idle either. Before we had rung in the New Year, they added James Bell to their long list of attorneys. Mr. Bell wasn't on a contingency fee arrangement. Instead, he was being paid a $200,000 flat fee for the sole job of defending Stephen and Laura against JPMorgan's and my claims.

Mr. Bell was young and had his own firm. He had won some big cases. I assumed he was highly talented, brilliant, or both. Just looking at the photo on his website scared me. I imagined he'd been a middle linebacker in high school, busting the ribs and collarbones of quarterbacks. There was no doubt he was foaming at the mouth, ready to take JPMorgan and me to the ground.

With Mr. Bell pounding on my claims and Lenny Vitullo trying to take the rest of my money, I faced formidable opponents, as if a stud lawyer like JPMorgan's John Eichman wasn't enough.

To wrap up 2015, I received an email from Jim Jennings dated December 23. I thought it was nice that even though I had terminated his services on September 1, 2015, he had taken the time to write to me almost four months later.

I sat at my desk and sipped some coffee, interested to see what my former attorney had to say. Maybe he wanted to wish me good luck on my case.

I quickly realized it wasn't a letter but a nine-page invoice for $20,655 covering all the legal work Jim had been doing for me. The last entry was on November 25, 2015. Most of the entries were for coordination with Alan on the turnover and answering questions.

I reread the invoice, still confused and a bit shocked. That usually meant it was time for a visit with my favorite legal oracle, Tarian Starr.

Eschewing our regular Vietnamese restaurant for Dickey's Barbecue, I watched as Tarian attacked a relatively large pork rib.

"You ask me why lawyers send bills months and months after they've been terminated or the case is over?" he said. "I can't speak to Jennings' motives, but for other lawyers I know, the answer is simple: it's a hard habit to break. It's like the firemen in steam locomotives. They were responsible for shoveling coal into the furnace. But when we switched from steam to diesel, the firemen were allowed to keep their jobs even though there was no need for their services. It was a hard habit to break. And a hard union, too."

"Are they still on the trains, holding their shovels, ready to toss in some coal?" I asked sarcastically.

"No. Twenty-six years after we made the switch to diesel, President Reagan got rid of them. So what does that have to do with lawyers, you ask? You must understand that there's a small village underneath us. We have wives who need lots of stuff. Girlfriends who demand even more stuff. Kids in private schools. Nannies. Tutors. Summer homes. Ritalin prescriptions. It takes a lot of cash to keep us running. Trust me, it's very stressful.

"I knew a high-net-worth couple getting divorced. The wife's lawyer managed to keep that case alive for over five years. She was even able to leave her law firm and start her own firm, the monthly invoices to her client of $30,000 paying for her overhead. As a lawyer, you never want the case to be over. Period."

"So, what do I do, Tarian? I knew Jim was working with Alan during the transition, but receiving this bill now really took me by surprise." I was getting frustrated with his longwinded answers. "Spell it out for me."

"Pay it," he said bluntly. "He did do transitional work for you that your lawyer needed and asked for, and he did win in both the trial and appellate courts."

I hung my head. "Then I guess that's the end of a chapter."

We sat there chatting about nothing. I was about to leave when he added this bit of wisdom.

"I must confess something. Jo, a rich person like you is a cash cow. Every lawyer is continually on the lookout for a client to milk. My first one was a businessman. I was a young lawyer. I handled a matter for him, and he liked my service. As his business grew into a mammoth enterprise, so did his problems. I was so thankful that he possessed a quick temper.

"The first time I used his temper to my advantage was when he had a contract dispute with a vendor. I met with the opposing attorney and returned to my client to report my conversation. He was in a meeting with his executives and invited me in. I can't recall everything I said, but I added a little spice to his life by saying, 'I get the impression that your opponent is planning on teaching you a lesson. They said there's a paddle for every ass.'

"'What?!' he said, his neck and face turning red.

"'Yeah, it's essential that your opponent hang another skin on the wall to show his employees how tough he is, especially with big game like you. He's sure you don't have the stomach for battle. And he's positive you'll fold at the first sign of trouble.'

"Well, that did it. My client ordered me to fire the phasers, photon torpedoes, and even load up the shuttlecraft with explosives and send them over there to explode. It was glorious. I used that trick on him for the next fifteen years. It started and maintained many lawsuits. Words like, 'You're showing your enemies how tough you are. People respect you now.' If that didn't work, I'd say, 'You're not going to let these guys bitch-slap you, are you? And in front of your employees? Come on. Get your fists up.'"

"And that worked?" I asked, incredulous.

"Every time. Challenge a fellow's manhood, and he'll do all sorts of stupid stuff. Thank God women don't run the world. We'd be *screwed*. No pun intended."

"What does this have to do with me?" I said, ignoring his non-pun.

"I spoke with some former colleagues. While they're always looking for an explosive businessman with money, they've recently discovered another cash cow. And this one rarely needs prodding."

"So what is it?"

Tarian grinned. "Blended families. When dear old Dad divorces Mom, the kids are upset to find a new woman in the picture. Once Dad dies, the kids are ready to put some whoop-ass on the interloper. All they need is an experienced lawyer whispering in their ear, 'Your mother would want you to get her money back. Besides, he earned all of it. Not his new wife. She didn't do a thing except her nails.'

"These kids, who have generally been given wads of cash over the years, have no experience when it comes to litigation. And they don't care. All that matters is destroying the second wife. Truthfully, I think blended families could feed, clothe, and house generations of lawyers. My colleagues are excited about the arrival of this new cow. It almost makes me want to go back to the dark side and milk a few tanker trucks' worth."

Although it wasn't always pleasant, I gained a great deal of insight listening to Tarian. Each session taught me more and more about our legal system. But the lessons came with a cost: depression. The mess I found myself in was terrible. With each movement, I sank deeper and deeper. There was no end in sight, except maybe bankruptcy.

ONE OF THE first things I learned about litigation is that a new lawyer loves making a splash. They must throw their weight around and let the client know they're earning their retainer. Because when the retainer is used up, the lawyer needs the client to cough up another one. Nothing makes a client happier than seeing their lawyer walk up to their opponent and pop them right in the face.

That's why when 2016 was rung in, I wasn't surprised that James Bell employed the best-defense-is-a-good-offense approach and filed an Anti-SLAPP motion against me. Throughout my brief legal career, I'd never heard of such a thing. I was quickly brought up to speed by my attorney. SLAPP stands for Strategic Lawsuits Against Public Participation.

The idea behind an Anti-SLAPP statute is good. Before it was created, some poor reporter might publish an exposé on a nasty bank ripping off its customers. But then the bank would SLAPP a lawsuit on the journalist. This was followed by mountains of discovery. Most journalists and local TV stations couldn't stand the strain of millions in attorneys' fees.

States around the country realized that our First Amendment was in jeopardy. Big bullies used the legal system to hide their corrupt conduct while financially breaking their opponents. To solve that problem, Anti-SLAPP statutes arrived.

Under the authority of such a statute, a journalist who is hit with a lawsuit (SLAPPed) can now file an Anti-SLAPP motion in court and instantly stop the entire case. The burden shifts to the plaintiff (the big ugly corporation) to prove their lawsuit has a reasonable probability of winning. If they can't do this, the case goes away with minimal cost to the journalist, who can recover their fees from the plaintiff. It's a good law, one that keeps the First Amendment's right to free speech alive in this country.

After reading James Bell's Anti-SLAPP motion, I learned that I was the big ugly corporation, and the heirs were the poor journalists. I had questions for my attorney, so I picked up the phone.

"What exactly are they saying I did?" I asked Alan.

"That you violated their First Amendment right to free speech, freedom of association, and their right to petition the government."

"And when did I do that?" I was dumbfounded.

"When you filed a claim against Stephen and Laura, alleging they tortiously interfered with the contract between you and JPMorgan."

"So that makes me guilty?"

"Of course not," Alan replied. "But now we must *prove* to the court that we have a likelihood of prevailing at trial, which we do."

I sighed. "More money wasted."

"For sure. But the big kicker is a complete stop of discovery."

"What?" I said, clutching my chest.

"Yes. Until the court rules on this motion, all discovery stops. That means we can't complete it before trial."

"What happens then?" *Please don't say the trial will be delayed.*

"The trial will be delayed."

Aaaiiiieeee! I screamed inside. "You've got to be kidding!"

"No, Jo, I'm not. But we can drop that claim and make Bell's motion moot."

"Should we do that?"

"Despite the issues you've had with the heirs, the real damage in the case was done by JPMorgan. They were the adults in the room. It was their responsibility to make everything smooth and calm. They are the cause of all this madness. And this particular claim is not our strongest. We have plenty more to hit them with."

We talked more about it. For me, a delay in discovery meant twelve to twenty-four months of additional legal bills. And now I knew that even after the case was over, I could receive legal bills for several months. At some point, there was the likelihood I'd just run out of money.

I realized the real evil in the justice system is never getting to trial. That's why so many people settle when they've done nothing wrong. The judge and the lawyers say, "We know you're thirsty, but the oasis is just over the next dune. Keep walking and spending money." At some point, they find your bleached bones in the sand, yet another victim of the United States judicial system.

"Let's drop this claim," I said to my lawyer. I had no choice.

After I hung up, I thought about James Bell. He'd been on the case less than a month, and already I was dropping claims against his clients. Man, this guy was tough!

It took me several days to recover from the beating Mr. Bell had given me. Once I could see straight, I had another surprise. Lenny Vitullo stepped into the ring and popped me a few times in the face.

We had sent requests to Laura for the production of documents. This required them to produce certain emails and documents. Instead, they sent back a filing so loaded with objections, it would take a court two to three days to go through it.

For example, we made a simple request for some documents and they lodged fifteen separate legal objections. And this didn't include the pages of objections to the defining terms listed at the beginning. I could see my lawyers charging tens of thousands of dollars to prepare responses and attend court hearings. Once there, they would argue over each item for hours. It was such a waste.

The Lenny Vitullo and James Bell team also sent some bullets JPMorgan's way. They filed a motion to stop JPMorgan from draining the last $800,000 in the estate's bank account to pay Hunton & Williams's attorneys' fees. I assumed that Vitullo, being on a contingency fee agreement, needed to tap some cash to pay his bills. Seeing the $800,000 there was too tempting.

After a court hearing, the judge ruled in favor of JPMorgan. This meant that Hunton & Williams had $800,000 waiting for them. All they had to do was bill for it. What happened when JPMorgan ran out of someone else's money to spend on lawyers, I had no idea.

In February, we had depositions in the separate partition case. Even though JPMorgan had retitled the personal property to the heirs and me, we were still fighting over the division of it. Actually, we had settled quickly with a Rule 11 agreement, but Stephen and Laura claimed that the agreement signed by their lawyer, Chris McNeill, was invalid since he didn't have any authority to negotiate it. With their lawyer's affidavit in our hand saying he *did* have authority, it seemed like an easy win for me. All I needed to do was cough up more money for the pot. And depositions are the absolute best way to spend lots of money fast.

On the day of the first deposition, we went to a conference room in Lenny's office. The scene was quite ominous.

At the end of a long table was a chair. This was the spot for the victim (person giving their deposition). A videographer stood opposite the victim, aiming a glaring camera over the table. To the victim's right was their lawyer. To the victim's left sat a court reporter. Next to her sat the lawyer taking the deposition. It was very crowded and quite intimidating.

The depositions of the heirs lasted two long days. Stephen testified that from the beginning, he and Laura wanted an Independent Administration to partition the estate before distribution. They thought an IA could do that.

Laura testified that instead of dividing it up, she wanted the court to sell the stuff. She didn't want to mess with it.

We did receive a nice nugget from Laura. She had sent an email to Stephen about Max's separate property in 2012 when we were still battling over my home. The last sentence was perfect:

"Not sure how this can be true with separate property but her lawyers always appear to be right so we need to better understand this one."

Immediately after the heirs' depositions, JPMorgan filed a response to our motion to compel production. We had asked JPMorgan for certain records as part of discovery. After refusing to produce them, JPMorgan's filing stated that complying with my requests would cost at least $500,000 and several months to complete. JPMorgan wanted *me* to pay *them* $500,000 before producing the records. This sounded so familiar.

By now, I had been digging into the Burns Clark Dailey Trust lawsuit. Like the STS Trust, the Burns Clark Dailey Trust involved thousands of acres in South Texas. The Burns Ranch happened to be one of the largest contiguous tracts of unleased minerals in the newly discovered Eagle Ford Shale formation, and it sat right in the heart of this magnificent find. Mr. Burns' descendants would be well taken care of. However, JPMorgan Chase was the trustee.

The Burns Clark Dailey Trust allegations were very similar to the STS Trust litigation, with the plaintiffs alleging now-familiar claims like breach of fiduciary duty, fraud, failure to disclose material facts, charging unreasonable fees, and signing undervalued leases, thus cheating the beneficiaries ($125/acre vs. $3,000/acre). The plaintiffs also requested removal of JPMorgan as trustee. The alleged damages were over $40 million and the case eventually settled with NDAs keeping it secret.

During my research of the Burns Clark Dailey Trust lawsuit, I remembered an affidavit signed by Michael Varzally, executive director of eDiscovery Group of JPMorgan in New York. Varzally stated the discovery requested by the Burns Clark Dailey Trust plaintiffs required the review of 862,800 documents. JPMorgan would have to spend

$138,500 to restore the emails from taped backups and an additional cost of $115,000 to post the emails to a special platform so each one could be painstakingly reviewed. The first pass review performed by offshore attorneys would cost $690,000. The second pass review would cost $1 million. To comply with the plaintiff's discovery requests, the total drive-out price would be $2,669,308 for domestic attorneys or $1.5 million for offshore attorneys. The judge denied JPMorgan's motion and made the bank pay for it.

I thought to myself, *This is a neat trick. Scare your opponent to back down from their discovery requests, or at least shrink them.* Then a lightbulb went off in my head. Wasn't this the same trick JPMorgan pulled in the STS Trust litigation?

I dug through the files and found the affidavit. This one from JPMorgan stated it would take 12 to 15 months to produce the discovery requested by the STS Trust plaintiffs and over $8 million to make it happen. Of course, JPMorgan wanted the STS Trust plaintiffs to pay them $8 million and then wait 15 months. When the judge denied JPMorgan's motion, he had this to say:

Judge: Don't you think—Mr. Williams, don't you think this is just delay, delay, delay?

Mr. Williams: No, sir.

Judge: Somebody who's not involved, being me, I'm telling you I get a different impression, all right? And this is 32 years of doing this job... But I'm telling you, reading between the lines indirectly, that I get the impression it's stall, stall, stall.

All this was sickening. To get my judge to do the same at the Burns Clark Dailey Trust and STS Trust litigants would cost more money. Either way, JPMorgan won.

BUT IT WASN'T all bad news. We learned that the probate case had been randomly assigned to Judge Brenda Hull Thompson. She was known to be fair and clearheaded. And she had a lot of experience as a lawyer in the probate courts. Hopefully, we would get some justice in her court.

Judge Thompson soon sent out a letter moving the trial date from September to October. I was grateful it was just one month. The only way out of this madness was to have a trial and get it over with.

I took a piece of paper and, with a magic marker, wrote OCTOBER in big letters, pinning it to the wall. All I needed to do was focus on October, just eight months away.

As I read through her orders, my heart sank. She had ordered another mediation—our third. I was reminded of something Tom Cantrill had told the judge regarding the possibility of the first mediation: "This group can't agree that the sun rises in the east."

Sad, but true.

To comply with this new order, the lawyers began working on the details. Some wanted the first mediator. Others wanted the second mediator. And a few wanted a new one. To me, it was another waste of time.

I called Tarian and told him about this development. He gave me another perspective.

"Judges order so many mediations because they work. Litigants settle because they see their bank accounts draining as fast as a smartphone's battery. And their lawyers often encourage the parties to settle because they need to cool the mark."

"What does 'cool the mark' mean?"

"All good lawyers know that once we've squeezed a great big pile of money out of our client, we need to convince them that paying us was proper, but settling is now the best path forward. You see, when we started the litigation, we talked bravely. We explained how we'd wipe the floor with these assholes. Now that the fun is over and we've made a killing, we need the client—*the mark*—to walk away, not realizing they've been scammed. We need to *cool* them down. Otherwise, we might lose the case and get sued or have a grievance filed against our law license. Cooling the mark is an essential part of being a lawyer."

That made sense. Still, I was certain Alan wasn't like that. And if I refused to settle, I could never be cooled. I pounded my fist in my hand. Someone else would have to be the mark in this case because it wasn't going to be me.

In late February, I attended a hearing in front of a district court judge in charge of the upcoming partition trial. As the judge asked questions about the case, she made demeaning and insensitive comments about the property Max and I cared for deeply. When she laughed about the situation, tears started to well up in my eyes and then run down my cheeks. I quickly realized my crying would become too powerful to hold back.

Unable to control myself, I cried out and ran from the courtroom. I found a corner of the hallway and curled up in a fetal position. My wails could be heard throughout the floor.

Alan ran out and found me there.

"I don't want to do this anymore," I sobbed. "I want it to stop."

Alan crouched down. "Jo, I know you're distraught, but the opposing lawyer Chris McNeill is right over there listening."

"I don't care," I wailed. "I just want to quit all these lawsuits."

McNeill edged closer, seeing me ready to give up a winning hand.

Unable to stop me, Alan helped me up and we left the building. I had reached the end of my capacity to care. I was going broke. I worked all the time. The lawyers on the other side spent their time obstructing my case, which cost me more money.

I needed to find a way to drop all my lawsuits and end this nasty litigation. It was time for me to get on with my life while I still had a few dollars left.

Chapter Twenty-One

"Personally, I guess I'd like to be remembered as someone who liked other people and other people liked me—my family, my kids, my grandkids, my wives. That would be, to me, a great legacy if you could have that."

—Max Hopper

After my meltdown, Alan whisked me back to his office. There, he plied me with water and snacks until I fully recovered. I could tell he was thinking about whether he should let me drive myself home. He knew I'd considered jumping off the High Five Interchange. So, to make sure I was okay, he decided to make lemonade out of lemons.

"I need to know more about your late husband. Max Hopper will be a big part of this trial. My job requires me to paint a clear picture of the man for the jury. I need all the details you can give me: his childhood, career, how he made it at American Airlines. Can you give that to me?"

This caught me off guard and redirected my thoughts off me and onto Max. I had to think for a moment before answering. "Max had a very contradictory life. He was a visionary, brilliant in technology and entrepreneurial concepts but not in estate planning. He hated conflict in his personal life, preferring to absorb the blame or pain if it meant keeping the peace. Yet at American Airlines, he was lovingly referred to as 'Max the Ax' or 'Hopper the Chopper' due to budgetary issues."

"That's interesting," Alan said, grabbing a pad and scribbling some notes. "What about his early years?"

"Okay," I said. "Max was born in Pollok, Texas, on November 4, 1934 in the south room of a small log cabin built by his grandfather in 1906. His parents, Norma and Irving Hopper, were poor. This was an era where people used an outhouse, made their own soap, and chopped down trees for firewood to heat their home. There was no running water in their home. During his childhood, one thing was always constant: work. Everyone worked, whether they were hauling in water, tending to crops, shucking corn for hominy, or making quilts to sell when there were no crops. You only stopped working when you died.

"Max's father wasn't always around. After Max was born, a brother and two sisters followed. His youngest sister, Joann, died the day Pearl Harbor was bombed. She was almost two. Max was seven and never forgot his sister's death. He also witnessed a cousin being killed crossing the highway at his grandmother's house.

"When World War II started, his family moved to Texas City, near Houston. Oil refineries were in full production, cranking out fuel for the war effort. Max was only nine and should have been in third grade, but the school administrators had moved him up to fifth grade due to his aptitude.

"Before he was ten, his parents divorced. It forced him to become the man of the family. His mother, Norma, a nurse's aide at a local hospital, relied on him to keep tabs on his siblings."

Alan interrupted me. "Do you know what kind of student Max was?"

"Brilliant," I replied. "When Max was in the sixth grade, he entered two bank-sponsored contests. One tested English skills and the other tested math. They gave out the awards at a high school graduation because they assumed a high school student would win. Instead, Max won. Everyone was stunned. School officials had to make sure he was there so they could give it to him. The $25 prize for each contest put food on the table for his family. In both junior high and high school, he won the contests again, picking up even more prize money. Learning came so easily to him that he graduated from Texas City High School at sixteen."

"Wow!" Alan remarked. "I knew he was smart but that's something else. What about college?"

"Max took tests with Rice University and the Navy, hoping to snag a scholarship. He felt he did well on the tests, but they didn't want him because he was only sixteen. He got into the University of Texas in Austin, where costs were lower, but he still needed more money than he had saved from working various jobs."

"Did his parents help out?"

"His mother did, a little bit, and the Kiwanis Club of Texas City provided some loans that Max would have to repay. He also found jobs he could work between classes, and the boarding house he lived in let him clean, cook, and do handyman chores. On the lighter side, the landlady there taught Max how to play bridge. It was a game he continued to play throughout his life. He even earned master points in tournaments. Add in the chemical engineering major he'd selected, and Max had his hands full in college, even more so for a sixteen-year-old.

"But after two years in college, he was flat broke. His mother gave birth to another son and stopped sending him money. With nothing up his sleeve or in his pocket, he was forced to drop out and go back to Houston, where his mother lived."

"Did he get a job or just live with her?" Alan asked.

"He worked. He learned about an open job for a lab technician at Shell Oil. They gave him a test and were shocked by his score. It was one of the highest they'd ever seen. A young Ph.D. engineer looked over Max's application and just so happened to know Max's chemistry professor at UT. With his high school accomplishments, two-year college record and that connection, he got the job for the princely sum of $330 per month. That would cover forty minutes of your time, right?"

Alan grinned. "I suppose. Keep going."

"This amount completely floored Max because it was almost what his father was making after climbing up through the ranks of a local union for the last ten years. To further motivate him, he got a $13 raise the day he started because Shell started giving a general raise across the board to keep their employees. In 1953, this was too good to be true."

"What about the women in his life?"

"Max was not like his father. Being younger than the girls in his high school kept him from dating. At UT, he struggled socially since he was still two or three years younger than other freshmen. But he met a girl, Leah, and started dating her while also carrying a full class load and working at least one job. Once he had some money in pocket from Shell, he bought his first car, a 1949 Ford, and drove to Austin, where Leah was still attending school. He was just eighteen but was able to keep her interested enough until they married when he was nineteen."

"How long was he with Shell?" Alan asked.

"Only a couple of years because Max joined the Army in 1955. The VA bill for free college was ending and he wanted to earn a degree. The bill was his best shot. Incredibly, Shell had a policy where they paid one-half of Max's current salary to cover the gap in his Army pay which made the decision easy."

"Okay, good," Alan said. "Give me a brief overview of his military service."

"After testing Max, the Army moved him to a secret branch called the Army Security Agency. Max completed the training and was made a Morse code intercept operator. The Army sent him to the Vint Hill Farms Station, a high-tech listening post just west of Washington, D.C. During his assignment, Max listened in on the French and other allies. He intercepted messages involving the Suez Canal crisis, Venezuelan rebels, and Cuba. Later, he was given even more sophisticated equipment to intercept telemetry transmissions from Russia's Sputnik. Cryptographers cracked the Russian code, and the assignment was a huge success. During his tour of duty, Max won 'Soldier of the Month' and was discharged as Specialist 2nd Class."

"Wow!" Alan said. "This guy's incredible and he's still in twenties. What happened next?"

"While in the service, Max attended the University of Virginia part-time. Isn't that where you went to law school?"

"Right you are," Alan replied. "It's a great school."

"Max enjoyed it there, too. He took plenty of business courses, including accounting, economics, and business law. His accounting professor was with the CIA and begged Max to work for him. Then, the NSA jumped in and tried to recruit Max because he had Q clearance—a level above Top Secret. Even though the offers were tempting, he turned them down. He had a baby boy now, Stephen, and wanted to return to Houston and his job at Shell Oil. With his honorable discharge in hand, he packed up his small family and left for Texas."

"Did he finally get his college degree?"

"Yes. He took advantage of the VA educational bill and attended the University of Houston, earning his undergraduate degree in mathematics. He spent another four years studying operations research, which was like modern-day industrial engineering. He didn't get his master's degree because his thesis adviser left academia to work in Cleveland and Max didn't want to start over with another adviser."

"How did he get into computers?" Alan asked.

"Max wandered into a group that was starting a business and saw their Burroughs Elecom 101. The idea was to use this computer, which was essentially a giant calculator, to crunch numbers for clients. Then at Shell, he was introduced to the IBM 650. Being in a lab, he wasn't allowed to mess with them, but later, he applied for an opening in the exploration and research division and was accepted.

"He saw the potential for computers, so he went back to school and got a degree in programming, which was a brand-new area, and started working on the IBM 650. But his boss had him selling time on their new computer, the IBM 7070, to other Shell divisions instead of programming all day. He sold as much time as they had and then went back to programming, where he could apply the skills he learned in college.

"Pretty soon, he had three or four programmers, including the first female programmer that anyone had ever heard of, designing economic analyses of the price of oil and gas-producing properties. This work alone saved Shell millions of dollars, more than paying for his staff and the computers."

"I'm ready to give him a Nobel Prize for Economics," Alan joked. "What else?"

"By now, Laura had arrived. This made four Hoppers. Shell moved them to New Jersey, where Max worked with Bell Labs and MIT to study Project Mac and SABRE. Then EDS, Electronic Data Systems, in Dallas, came knocking on his door."

"Is Ross Perot involved in this story?"

"He is," I replied. "In 1967, EDS wanted Max to join them in New York. At the same time, Shell tried to send him to the Hague, where Shell's parent company, Royal Dutch, was headquartered. Both Max and his wife, Leah, hated the idea of living overseas, so he turned down the move, as well as EDS's offer, and stayed with Shell in the U.S. Later that summer, Ross Perot, EDS's founder, called. Ross wanted Max to move to Dallas and work for him. After Ross wooed Max with the full-court press, Max made the move, leaving Shell after thirteen years. At EDS, he worked with Mort Meyerson to design systems for Texas Blue Cross. With his management experience, he rose through the ranks fairly quickly."

"When did he get to the airline industry?" Alan asked.

"When he was at EDS, he was assigned to work on a project for United Airlines. But when it was ready to be installed, United management told EDS the software would now be installed in Chicago, where all their reservations were made. On top of that, they no longer needed EDS's help. Of course, they failed. United Airlines called EDS, begging them to work on a cost-plus basis, but EDS refused. United wouldn't give up and they approached Max to take over the project. To do that, he needed Ross to let him out of his contract. Surprisingly, Ross agreed. He told Max he was welcome to come back anytime.

"At United Airlines, Max worked on the reservations side of the business, bringing a lot of computer systems online. Then, an upper management change left him with no executive support, so he started looking for another job. When American Airlines decided to migrate their SABRE from an old to a new system, they needed someone to head it up. Max had experience with SABRE at Shell *and* he had the airline experience. He was a natural hire for them."

"Do you want to take a break?" Alan asked me.

I took a long sip of water. "No, I'm good."

"Okay. Tell me about Max and American Airlines."

"Max dove into his new job with everything he had. Almost immediately, he pushed the technological envelope with computers on ticketing, reservations, and pricing. Bob Crandall was hired as the CFO and he brought on Jim O'Neill. Max had worked with Jim at United. Max was promoted to run all the data processing for American Airlines, in what would be the IT director in today's world.

"American Airlines moved all the computing from Briarcliff, New York, to Tulsa, Oklahoma, sending Max and his family there. He set up the systems that let airport ticket agents print tickets onsite. This was followed by the boarding passes that everyone takes for granted today.

"Max chaired an industry-wide initiative called JICRS that was going to create one system for all travel agents so they could book any flight on any airline from their desktop. The American Airlines executives agreed to invest money with United Airlines and the other carriers to develop a joint open system, but when Max ran into Bob Crandall on a street corner in New York, he asked him, 'Do you want someone coming between us and one of our principal distribution channels?' They sat down and discussed the situation. If an industry-wide standard was created, American Airlines would not only lose their current advantage but they'd be on the same level as any other start-up airline. Bob got it, and if he did, so would the other airlines.

"Bob told Max to prepare for when United Airlines would withdraw from the joint initiative so United could offer their own system to travel agents, effectively tricking American. Max crunched some numbers and asked for $20 million to create American Airlines' own system. This was 1975. The economy was in the tank and money was short. But with Bob pushing the board, Max got his money."

"Did they pull out?"

I nodded. "In January 1976, United Airlines backed out of the joint initiative and announced they had a system to install in every travel agent's office. Before this, the agent had to call each airline, learn the price and availability, then have the ticket mailed to them or the client. Now, United Airlines gave the agents the power to do it all from a terminal in their office. And printing tickets? No problem. The printer United Airlines provided did all that. The industry was stunned. Several attempts were made to automate travel agents during the last decade, but this was the first bold step. United Airlines said they'd start the first installs in September on a first come, first served basis. This news was a death blow to American Airlines because United's flights would now pop up first to travel agents, increasing their market share immensely. And that assumed other airlines would even *appear* on United's terminals. The world suddenly looked grim to United's competitors.

"A few hours after this announcement, Bob called Max and asked for an update on their own computer systems. The next day, American Airlines announced that they had a reservation system, but it was different from United's. First, it wasn't an airline system; it was a travel system. It would have access to rental cars, hotels, cruises, and almost everything a travel agent needed. It would be a system very similar to the initiative that had been abandoned. Also, travel agents wouldn't have to wait until September because American would begin installation in March. But it wouldn't be on a first come, first served basis. American Airlines would decide who received it, most likely its biggest and best travel agents. On that very day, the travel industry was revolutionized."

"Keep going," Alan urged. "This is getting good."

"Max's group began installing the units, but of course, each one had a screen preference for American Airlines. With SABRE sweeping through the country and landing in the most prestigious travel agencies six months before United could even install their first one, American

Airlines was suddenly in the forefront of the industry. This screen preference advantage lasted *four* years, until the government ordered it to be screen-neutral. But American Airlines had already grown their business exponentially during that time. They were a behemoth when other airlines like Eastern and TWA bit the dust.

"There was another interesting facet of this airline computer war. United Airlines' system was fundamentally different from SABRE and it had to do with FOMO—Fear of Missing Out. If a travel agent looked at a flight on United's system, it showed whether a seat was available or not. Yes or no. That was it. On American's system, the exact seat count availability was displayed. United wanted the agents to fear missing out on the seat so they would book it right away. But American wanted the agents to have the best information available. Max's ability to understand the customer's desires and not withhold information from the customer made it so American's SABRE system excelled. It also explains why Max is known in the industry as 'the Father of Travel Agency Automation.' None of this would have been possible without the support of high-level executives like Bob Crandall, Al Casey, or Jim O'Neill, and the money that was appropriated for Max to spend on his ideas. American also didn't micromanage Max, which would've chased him away. It was a productive arrangement.

"When did he retire?" Alan asked.

"In 1995. That's when he opened his consulting business, Max Hopper & Associates. He provided limited consulting services, mainly serving on advisory boards or boards of directors for different companies. A lot of these firms were start-ups and welcomed his mentoring."

"I've looked on the web and saw all his awards," Alan said. "Even the Smithsonian Institute interviewed him in their Oral History Project. I'm convinced Max was a brilliant man."

"Yes, and he made a huge difference in commerce and travel. He also wanted to be liked. It's too bad this probate disaster will be a part of his legacy."

Alan set down his pen. "We'll just have to do what Max would've done and change JPMorgan for the better. A large jury verdict might just do it."

"And it might not," I said, looking at my hands. "That bank will probably never change. We're all just bits of data to them, a percentage point added to a dollar."

We talked for a few more minutes and I left, my meltdown in court a distant memory. But with this litigation still going, I was pretty sure it wouldn't be the last time I cratered.

Chapter Twenty-Two

*"JPMorgan Chase may have fiduciary obligations to our
clients to act in their best interests."*

—JPMorgan Chase & Co.
2019 Code of Conduct

After my breakdown in court, I thought my opponents would be circling my soon-to-be-dead carcass. Instead, something momentous occurred. On March 11, 2016, more than six years after Max died and three years after JPMorgan retitled the personal property, the heirs and I reached an agreement on how to divide up the furnishings, artwork, wine, and, of course, the putters!

The only reason this happened was that a trial for the partition case was on the horizon. And, even though we had reached a Rule 11 agreement on August 20, 2013, I had been forced to keep litigating because the heirs denied that they had authorized their lawyer to make a deal.

With so much distrust on both sides, the final agreement and release documents were ninety-seven pages long. Our lawyers probably spent $100,000 in combined attorneys' fees working it out. And I had to give up a lot to reach this deal, mainly my lifetime collection of needlepoint supplies and other sentimental keepsakes which JPMorgan had designated as community property. Sure, it was just stuff. But to me, it was a warm connection to past. The whole ordeal was another painful probate experience.

Fortunately, this settlement did not eliminate my chance of recovery from Stephen and Laura for their conduct in the probate matter. I was counting on getting most, if not all, of my attorneys' fees back from them and/or JPMorgan. Unfortunately, they could still recover against me for their attorneys' fees. We'd have to see what a jury said.

Once I had my half of the wine, golf clubs, and other personal property, I could do with it what I wanted. For me, I needed to turn the wine, putters, antiques, and artwork into cash so I could continue feeding money into my lawyer's meter.

JPMorgan had valued my share of the wine at $70,000, but I found no auction houses willing to sell it. I scoured the world for interested buyers but found none. With no choice left, my share remained in my cellar until I sold it for $32,000.

At least I had high hopes with the collection of putters and golf clubs. They had been appraised at $300,000, so my share should have been worth $150,000. I looked high and low, contacting every buyer of golf clubs I could find. Eventually, I took the best deal I could find: $15,000. Knowing now how JPMorgan and the legal system works, I should've given the heirs everything plus a check for $50,000. I'd be millions ahead.

After disposing of everything, I estimated we had spent $1 million in combined attorneys' fees arguing over the wine, clubs, and furnishings. This figure included the mediations, thousands of angry emails, endless motions and hearings, and the partition lawsuit. Over $100,000 had been spent on warehouse storage for the clubs.

With the settlement done, I offered Stephen and Laura some of Max's property. This included a desk he made in high school shop, family quilts, a photo album, several sentimental putters, and personal memorabilia. They gladly took it.

And never said thank you.

And never offered to sell me my needlepoint.

Life moved on.

We raced through March, as I kept my focus on October—just seven months away. Finally, I could see the light at the end of the tunnel. And believe me, it looked marvelous.

At the first hearing in front of the new judge, John Eichman asked if it would be appropriate to send her a letter about the case. She agreed, and I received a copy of his letter as well. One of the points Eichman made in the letter was that the Max Hopper Estate was complicated.

He was wrong.

The estate had some financial assets: public/private stock and stock options, venture capital funds, and an investment in a hedge fund. As far as property, the estate consisted of one home, a separate inherited house, and tangible personal property. In half a day, it could've all been retitled as joint tenants, and the estate closed out.

Eichman next trotted out the contentious relationship between the heirs and me. That should've had no effect on JPMorgan Chase's performance. He also emphasized the lack of common ground between the parties. But he had to know that, too, was irrelevant. JPMorgan wasn't a mediator. They were the administrator. All they had to do was retitle the property, return mine, and distribute the heirs' property according to the law, and we would have been finished. For that, JPMorgan Chase would've received 3% of the first $2 million and 2% of the remaining amount. How hard could that be?

Eichman cleverly minimized the massive volume of information I'd turned over to the IA. He said I provided some information, "…but the information in many instances was incomplete." Well, guess what? It was JPMorgan's duty to collect the information, not mine. We'd soon see what a jury thought about their performance versus mine.

Alan read Eichman's letter and sent in our response. He addressed Eichman's points and emphasized the fact that I had achieved a clean sweep in the appellate court. This was an important point because we had recently seen how JPMorgan was trying desperately to distance itself from its failed legal analysis.

Alan told the judge that while JPMorgan was now blaming the heirs for selling them a counterfeit legal argument, only JPMorgan had filed for a rehearing in the appellate court. This had delayed the case and cost more money. JPMorgan didn't appear to care. Their fingerprints were all over the murder weapon. They weren't worried about the body count.

APRIL ARRIVED, AND so did the start of a deposition marathon. We had so many people being deposed over so many days that Alan prepared me for getting used to these characters.

"You'll be seeing them so much they'll become like family. But don't treat them as such. They're the enemy."

I nodded.

"And while you're at the depositions, don't speak to anyone other than Kerry and me. Don't say anything to Stephen, Laura, or anyone else." Kerry Schonwald, a litigation attorney, was an associate at Alan's firm.

"Don't worry," I told Alan, "I can follow instructions."

Alan provided me with a stack of notecards. If I wanted to make a point and have him ask a question, he told me to write it on a notecard and hand it to Kerry. She would be sitting between us. Kerry would read it and pass it to Alan if she thought it needed to be raised. He also encouraged me to take plenty of notes. I would be like a paralegal. And I could talk to him during the breaks, if necessary.

Wendy Bessette, JPMorgan's designated corporate rep, was first on the firing line. She seemed intelligent and capable, which made me wonder how this mess had gotten to this point. If JPMorgan's employees were all stupid, I could understand how this might have happened. But they weren't. Wendy even testified that she was a licensed attorney in Arizona. You had to be smart to get through law school and even smarter to pass the bar exam. Stupidity was unlikely to be the reason JPMorgan had done all this to Stephen, Laura, and me.

Ms. Bessette's deposition appeared very contentious to me. Eichman objected over and over again. He claimed Alan was badgering the witness. However, Alan kept his cool and asked all the questions he had. As a result, we obtained some solid evidence.

Even though Ms. Bessette was a lawyer, she testified she'd never practiced law, and had instead been in estate management most of her career. So plenty of smarts *and* estate experience. She said JPMorgan takes difficult matters all the time. "We are used to families in conflict," she claimed. "It's why we're brought in."

Ms. Bessette explained that JPMorgan promotes their ability to handle those types of situations. And she admitted JPMorgan knew there was a contentious relationship before they took the matter but added that she believed she could manage the issues.

Alan had her detail the vast array of JPMorgan departments: Estate Administration, Investments, Private Bank, Tax, Fiduciary, Legal, Accounting Team, Closely Held, Operations, and Real Estate. As I listened to her lay this out, I was amazed they had so many experts and still couldn't get the job done.

Alan then probed about JPMorgan's desire to cross-sell other services to probate clients. Ms. Bessette admitted JPMorgan tries to move probate clients into other services they may need. But she said it's because the client may not want to deal with or may not even be able to handle vast amounts of wealth. To her, it was about being useful and providing a service to the client.

Ms. Bessette explained Susan Novak had been selected to administer this estate because Susan was the most senior Texas person and had successfully handled intestate estates. The impression I got from her testimony was that Susan was the cream of JPMorgan's crop.

The best part of the deposition came when Alan asked Ms. Bessette if JPMorgan owed a fiduciary duty to me. A fiduciary duty is a heightened responsibility to take extraordinary care of your client and put your client's interests before the bank's interests. If JPMorgan had an ordinary duty to deal with me, I would have a tougher time winning in court. This was a big question.

When Alan asked Ms. Bessette this question, she sat there for a good minute, thinking, making faces, and squirming in her chair. At times, it seemed like she was thinking, "Is this a trick question?"

Alan sat there quietly, refusing to help her in any way as the seconds ticked by. Finally, she admitted JPMorgan *did* owe me a fiduciary duty. The crazy thing is that Bessette worked in JPMorgan's Fiduciary Department! I saw Alan write a note to himself that read, "Play this for the jury!"

When Alan had finished with Bessette, he passed her to Lenny. For Ms. Bessette, it had to be like going from one predator to another. As Lenny slicked back the pomade on his California-length black hair and studied his notes, I could only imagine what it would be like when I had to go through this gauntlet.

Lenny spent a lot of time on the emails I had sent to Stephen and Laura. He was especially interested in the ones where I complained about JPMorgan and begged Stephen and Laura to pressure Susan Novak to do something. Lenny did a great job racking up the points. By the time he was done with that line of questioning, I wondered what Ms. Bessette thought of Susan Novak.

Lenny pushed her to discuss how much money was left. Ms. Bessette testified JPMorgan owed me $64,000 but was keeping it to cover my share of estate administration fees, the same ones both Kal Grant and the agreement had told me I wouldn't have to pay. I shook my head. This truly exposed the dishonest soul of JPMorgan.

Ms. Bessette also said they held me responsible for another $400,000 in attorneys' fees to cover the same estate administration. Again, Kal

Grant's words, "You won't pay a cent," echoed in my mind. Had Kal flat-out lied to me?

Finally, Lenny wanted to know how much of the $800,000 in the estate account was left. When Ms. Bessette testified she had just paid Hunton & Williams $200,000, he appeared to blow a gasket. I hoped the heirs weren't counting on receiving more money from the estate.

Once again, my mind drifted back to the STS Trust litigation. In that case, the plaintiffs asked a judge to order JPMorgan to pay the bank's attorneys out of its own pocket. Sure enough, the plaintiffs won that motion and JPMorgan could no longer drain the STS Trust of money. I wondered if Lenny would do that in this case?

After two long days, Bessette's deposition finally ended. I was exhausted. I couldn't imagine how the lawyers, and especially Ms. Bessette, felt.

That night I went home and climbed straight into bed. The next morning, I had the day off. Ms. Bessette's deposition had been on Tuesday and Wednesday. Stephen's deposition didn't start until Friday. It was scheduled to run through Saturday. Before I entered another two intense days, I needed a break.

I'm not a huge movie-goer, but the escapism of movies was something that appealed to me just then. I looked up the latest movies and set out for the nearest theater. I planned to watch a Leonardo DiCaprio film that had been released over Christmas and was still in the dollar theaters in April. I bought a ticket and found a seat, then waited for the movie to begin. But before the lights dimmed, there were the display advertisements on the screen showing other movies still playing in this theater. One of them was the latest *Star Wars* installment, *The Force Awakens*. That's when I realized I was in a *Star Wars* movie. All the characters were there. Lenny was Han Solo, the swashbuckler. I could picture him firing his laser machine gun into the forest, hoping to hit something. In another life, Lenny's hair might even have been long enough for a ponytail. As it was now, it looked just like Han Solo's mop, except it was black.

James Bell, Lenny's co-counsel, was Luke Skywalker. No longer the young apprentice, he knew how to use a lightsaber.

Then there was my attorney, Alan Loewinsohn. He was Obi-Wan Kenobi—the thinker, the planner, the strategist. He could hide in a cave or lie in a tree and wait for the perfect shot. Alan would always be two steps ahead of his opponent.

Finally, there was John Eichman. He was Darth Vader on steroids. Eichman used brute force to get the job done. He was highly capable of guiding the Death Star to the rebels' hidden base on Yavin 4. Once there, he would be more than willing to press the button to destroy it. That's why he was in such demand.

All of them had wildly different personalities and methods of grinding your porcelain body into dust. Lucky me! I had them all present in one case. As Tarian said, "Big money brings out the apex predators."

Leo's flick was good, and I wasn't surprised that he'd won an Academy Award for the role. With my movie fix satisfied, I sat back down at my desk and prepared for my former stepson's deposition. On the wall in front of me was the word "October." Our jury trial was barely six months away. I just had to hang on.

I woke Friday morning feeling queasy. After Wendy Bessette's deposition, I *felt* the litigation. Before, I had always known I was in a terrible situation. But now, the strain on my heart and the burning in my gut was intense. It felt like a laser was trying to bore a hole from the inside out.

The day didn't get any better.

I watched Stephen take the hot seat. I had known him ever since he was just twenty-two years old and going off to medical school. Now, his job was to testify against me. It was the worst feeling.

Alan opened the deposition with his brilliant tactics. First, he probed for friendly information, the low-hanging fruit. He had Stephen say that he believed JPMorgan was mismanaging the estate in 2010. I agreed.

Stephen admitted under oath that Max and I had a loving relationship. But he did reveal Max had difficulty with intimacy that Stephen had tried to bridge. There was always a distance between them.

Stephen said he was very close to his mother. And he was able to get in a dig by saying he wasn't sure when the relationship between Max and I had begun, whether *before* or after his parents' divorce. I knew Stephen was just answering the questions, but it still hurt.

We learned that Stephen had met early on with Cantrill, three days after JPMorgan had been hired. During their meeting, Cantrill had written a note saying that Stephen believed Max might have hidden $2 million from his ex-wife during the divorce. I knew that was ludicrous. From the moment Max and I had married, we lived in debt. Anyone who knew us during that time would have laughed out loud at that accusation.

When Alan moved on to Stephen's first lawyer, John Round, Stephen admitted that Round had recommended JPMorgan and that I told him how expensive it would be. I knew Ron Cresswell, the lawyer at that first meeting at my house, had not recommended JPMorgan.

Stephen said he knew John Round was related to Debra Round, who worked for JPMorgan in Trust Administration. He assumed JPMorgan or Cantrill had told me. I didn't learn that fact until November 2011, and he didn't tell his sister Laura either.

Interesting.

Staying on the theme of conflicts, Stephen said JPMorgan had a conflict of interest because I had a relationship with JPMorgan before they were hired to handle Max's estate. Stephen believed he should have been told that information before hiring JPMorgan. If it was true, he was right, but unfortunately for him, I had no prior relationship with JPMorgan.

Sure, JPMorgan pursued my money once we hired them. And yes, I set up an investment account solely to prevent them from keeping my assets. But all that happened *after* he and I had signed on the dotted line. That's why it was interesting to discover Stephen had failed to tell us about *his* prior relationship with JPMorgan.

He had obtained a mortgage from JPMorgan to buy a house. And he had a credit card with JPMorgan. All of this was *before* he had told me he wanted JPMorgan to handle the estate. I knew none of that until his deposition.

Stephen went on to say that JPMorgan never asked him to provide information about the location of estate assets. This was incredible to hear. I was being accused of hiding assets and JPMorgan never asked my accusers where they might be? It was hard to believe.

Stephen testified that he had been duped by JPMorgan when it came to the fees. Stephen had thought he and Laura were getting a preferred fee schedule. They were not. They were paying more than the probate code would have charged them. It was a slick move by JPMorgan.

Stephen admitted he was under the disastrous impression that I was paying half the estate's admin and legal fees while he and Laura covered one-fourth each. Obviously, he didn't read the contract he'd signed with JPMorgan.

As the questions went on and on, I grew more and more tired. I was thankful when we finally took a break.

Wanting to follow my lawyer's advice, I tried to ensure I had no contact with the other side. This meant timing my bathroom breaks when the other women had finished theirs. Seeing the coast clear, I made a beeline for the women's restroom. I found an empty stall and took care of business. When I came out and closed the stall door, I was shocked to see Stephen's wife, Barbara, directly in my path. Before I could move, she started screaming at me.

"Why are you doing this to us?! You are driving Stephen crazy. You are trying to bankrupt us. What did we do to you?!"

Barbara was not only in my face, but she had lost all control.

"Would Max understand what you're doing?!" she hollered. It was ear-piercing.

I held up my hands, signaling I wanted no part of her. But she didn't back down.

I blinked several times, realizing that the twists and turns in this litigation were like a roller coaster. Most folks wouldn't believe all that I had been through. I'm not sure I would.

Yet now, at Stephen Hopper's deposition, a fifty-something-year-old woman wanted to brawl with a stage-four cancer survivor one month away from turning seventy. If I was going to win this lawsuit, I would first have to survive this bathroom ambush.

Chapter Twenty-Three

You really think you can take what's mine?
I'll tackle you one day at a time.
So go on bud, and give it a whirl.
Just remember, though, I fight like a girl.

—*Fight Like a Girl* by Jack Hooper

My heart pounded in my ears as I stood toe-to-toe with Barbara Chappell. Somehow, I remembered my attorneys' instructions: "Don't say a word to anyone on the other side." I assumed that also ruled out fighting.

Suddenly, I had flashbacks of how Max loved to watch reruns of those big fights like *The Thrilla in Manila* and *The Rumble in the Jungle*. During interviews after the bouts, the fighters wore sunglasses because their eyes were so puffy. I looked terrible after a long cry. I could only imagine what the mirror would reveal if I had a *Brawl in the Stalls*. Or even a *Scrapper in the Crapper*. Was it possible that cancer wouldn't kill me but a fist to the face followed by a porcelain toilet cracking my skull open would?

I decided that "peace" would be the operative word here. I continued standing there with my hands raised, showing Barbara that I wanted no trouble. At least I was ready to attempt a block of her right cross.

As my heart beat fast enough to explode, I saw a tiny opening to escape. Squeezing through it, I managed to sidestep her to the sink while she continued screaming at me. I turned on the water to wash my hands when I heard a sound to my right. It was another stall door opening. If this was a cohort of Barbara's, I was done for.

Scared to look over, I waited for the mystery person to approach. When I got a glimpse of her, I realized it was Susan Kravik, JPMorgan's in-house legal counsel. A wave of relief swept over me. After all, she was a lawyer with a law license that could be revoked. Surely, *she* wasn't into fisticuffs.

I glanced at Ms. Kravik's eyes, which were wide open as she stood there dead still, saying nothing as Barbara tore me a new one.

Drying my hands quickly, I left the restroom and a screaming Barbara behind. I could still hear her curse as the door closed automatically and I walked down the hall. I was visibly shaken but relieved.

I found Alan and pulled him into an adjoining conference room, telling him what had happened. His jaw tightened as he left me and found Lenny. Alan got close to Lenny, leaning into him when Ms. Kravik walked in and gave her side of the story. As she spoke, Lenny's shoulders drooped and his face darkened.

In the meantime, I retook my seat in the deposition. A few minutes went by when Barbara reappeared and sat down next to me, fresh as a daisy as if nothing had happened. And she looked happy.

Barbara turned to face me and said, "How's Jack Hooper? Is he doing well?"

My stomach sunk at hearing his name. I decided to ignore the comment and the obvious smirk on her face.

"Barbara, can I talk to you—*please*?" It was Lenny sticking his head in the doorway.

Ten minutes ticked off before Alan reappeared. He leaned over and whispered in my ear. "You won't be seeing Barbara again. We'll talk later."

Stephen's deposition resumed, but his demeanor seemed to have changed. His answers had a rough edge. He let me have it. First, he painted me in a different light—at times, mean, uncaring, distant, responsible for hiding assets and destroying evidence. I was mercurial and unpredictable, he claimed. My behavior created an air of caution, anxiety, and discomfort.

He claimed I'd failed to disclose many items and was still hiding assets. He said I'd told him that I knew how to shred, the implication being that I had done so to documents that were part of this litigation. Of course, I did have a shredder. When Max worked for Bank of America, he and I had some security training and we were instructed to shred every document that contained our name and/or address before placing it in the trash. We did that when Max was alive and I continued to do so after his death. But I never destroyed anything relevant to the estate or my lawsuit.

That would be ludicrous. I had a good case as to what JPMorgan had done to me. I wasn't about to accidentally shred key evidence.

Seeing me take some body blows, Alan switched subjects to Gary Stolbach and his firm Glast Phillips. Stephen testified that he'd fired them because he'd realized they had given him the wrong advice on Robledo, and they'd overcharged him. He said he and Laura had paid Glast Phillips $750,000. When I heard that amount, I thought it was a bargain.

Stephen said Glast Phillips was still chasing him for $350,000 in unpaid bills. Alan didn't ask if he was going to pay them.

Stephen continued, saying he'd retained Mark Enoch for only $30,000 to handle the court of appeals, but Mr. Enoch had found reasons to charge more. Wrapping up this line of questioning, Stephen admitted different law firms had represented him at various times. What a quagmire.

Yes, that's a lead-in to Alan's next question, which was about the name "Quagmire," the one he'd used for his new limited liability company to hold his property interest in Robledo. He said the term meant a situation in which a person couldn't get out of, an expression of his frustration that he had joint ownership of a house and personal property with me.

Alan finished up and passed Stephen to Eichman, who promptly earned his hourly rate. Eichman went over an email I had sent Stephen explaining how probate was a lengthy process that might last two years or more. Eichman's point was that Stephen shouldn't have been surprised at how long everything took. I also got a glimpse of the beating Eichman would be giving me in my upcoming deposition.

Eichman worked hard on Stephen to show that he and Laura could have worked things out with me, and thus it wasn't JPMorgan's fault. Anyone could tell Eichman was racking up the points. This would certainly help his case at trial.

Eichman managed to extract from Stephen that Stolbach had *guaranteed* he and Laura would win on Robledo and be reimbursed with attorneys' fees from JPMorgan and Hunton & Williams. But Stephen admitted Stolbach was wrong. He also admitted that I told him Stolbach was wrong, sending Stephen statutes and writings of Stanley Johanson that all proved my point. Yet Stephen had ignored them.

Eichman was doing an excellent job laying the blame at Stephen and Laura's feet. But, of course, JPMorgan had access to the same statutes and Johanson's writings. So why didn't they read them carefully? Hopefully, Alan would explore that at trial.

Eichman finally delved into a subject near and dear to my heart: Stanley Johanson.

> Eichman: Have you had any communications with Professor Johanson about his responsibility for any harm that you might have suffered as a result of the opinions given here?
>
> Stephen: No.
>
> Eichman: Do you intend to do so?
>
> Stephen: No.

I guess Stephen and Laura were giving Mr. Johanson a free pass. Maybe the $22,000 he had earned for his work was pocket change compared to the millions we were all spending.

Alan questioned Stephen one more time after Eichman finished. This exchange gave me a huge lift.

> Alan: If you had known what you know now about the law regarding the Robledo house back in 2011, would you have still fought the Robledo house issue?
>
> Stephen: No.
>
> Alan: If you had known what you know now about the law regarding the Robledo house issue, would you have agreed to Mrs. Hopper's position, assuming that was her position, that the house should be deeded in undivided interests and not partitioned?
>
> Stephen: I would not have wanted that to happen, but I would have accepted that as the law.

Alan obtained one final gem from Stephen. He testified that not once had anyone told him that he would be responsible for attorneys' fees if he lost the Robledo issue. It was a hard lesson for Stephen to learn, and Max wasn't around to set things right, so I was going to make sure he paid the bill for it.

When the deposition wrapped up, Alan held back the participants in the room so I could get away first. After every deposition from that point forward, Alan ensured that I left before anyone else to guarantee

I made it to my car without being accosted. Making the hurried walk each time was very stressful. Checking the back seat before starting the car became my routine. It was a terrible way to exist.

LITIGATION CHANGES YOUR life forever, and not in a good way. An example of this is the cell phone. Like everyone else, I type in the person's name with the number I'm storing on the phone. That way, I know who's calling me when the phone rings. When Max was alive and his name popped up, I'd smile. He was my husband and the love of my life. I knew who I'd be talking to.

When you're in litigation and your lawyer's name appears on your phone, the bottom of your stomach drops out and your blood pressure skyrockets.

Why?

Because you know that, usually, it's horrible news. Something like, "You're not going to believe what just happened!" or "We just got served with some new claims. We need to go over them." When you hang up the phone, even if it's good news, you just spent another $200—*if* you're lucky.

In litigation, the ring or vibration of your phone becomes a new source of anxiety and paranoia. Some people even slip into depression and fail to answer it. Sleeping or taking a shower was blissful because I couldn't receive bad news no matter what. The longer I slept or took a shower, the longer I could avoid reality. I had the same feeling when I received an email from my attorney. It was terrifying to open. Apparently, that's just the nature of litigation. Hearing from your lawyer scares the living daylights out of you.

It was Sunday. I had sat through two brutal days of Wendy Bessette's deposition and another two days of Stephen's deposition. I was utterly exhausted. But Alan was anything but. He called me from the office, where he was preparing for Laura's deposition the following day. Hers would be another two-day affair. And we had at least seven more people to depose. I could barely focus.

"Jo, we need to talk," Alan said. "Can you come to the office?"

I sighed. "Sure. I'll be there in thirty minutes."

Walking into his deserted office, I found Alan at his desk.

"You want something to drink?" he asked.

"No, I'm good. What's up?"

"After Wendy Bessette's deposition, Lenny heard some things that have driven him to file additional claims against you. Here they are."

That hollow feeling in my stomach returned. "Okay," I said, trying to keep it together. "Tell me what I need to know."

Alan explained it plainly. Lenny had added a claim against me for secretly conspiring with JPMorgan to pay no fees in Max's estate administration while shifting all the costs to Stephen and Laura. According to his lawsuit, this secret agreement gave me "exclusive access to and control over critical Estate records and assets for months after they were appointed."

To make this fairy tale work, Lenny claimed that JPMorgan had come to their senses and eventually sided with the heirs, thus dissolving our conspiracy. Lenny also stated that because I asked for the removal of JPMorgan as the IA, I had depleted $2 million in the estate account. But he didn't stop there. He claimed that I rigged the appraisals for a lowered amount to buy out the heirs for pennies on the dollar.

"What do you think?" I asked Alan.

"Let's look at these claims," he said, holding up the document. "This one, where you rigged the appraisals to be low. First, you sold everything for ten percent of the appraised value, so that claim doesn't fly. Next, a low appraisal only benefits the heirs because they pay a percentage to JPMorgan based on the property's appraised value. You *saved* them money. Finally, JPMorgan is the one responsible for the appraisal. They are to blame here."

"What about their claim of me trying to remove the IA and costing them $2 million?" I asked.

"You did try to remove the IA, but we have emails and a tape recording of them agreeing that JPMorgan was terrible and needed to go. If $2 million was spent on anything, it was the wine and golf clubs, not removing the IA."

Hearing Alan's calm voice made me feel a little better. "And the conspiracy claim?"

"I think JPMorgan will fight that. And taking your side? They were on the heirs' side from the beginning. I mean, come on, Jo. The heirs' lawyer's wife worked for JPMorgan. They'll have to explain how the conspiracy worked with all that."

"What about Ms. Bessette's testimony that when I called all the stock companies, I was trying to do an end-around on the IA and get everything for myself?"

"This is the way our system works. We take facts, such as you calling those stock companies, and attach a bad motive to them, hoping the jury makes the same attachment."

He was right. Lenny was able to take facts I couldn't refute and attach evil, greedy motives to them. Under the standard of proof in a civil action, all Lenny had to do was convince the jury there was a 50.1% chance I had done wrong.

I didn't have to ask what all these new claims meant. I allocated another $250,000 in attorneys' fees to handle them. And it would probably add months, if not years, of more discovery. I wanted to throw up. Unfortunately, I was sure there would be more moments like this.

"What else do we need to discuss?" I asked Alan. I wanted to leave.

"One more thing, Jo. Let's discuss what Barbara said to you: Jack Hooper."

"Jack Hooper," I said, staring out the window at the bright sunny day. "He's my companion. What do you want to know?"

"I need to talk to him," Alan said.

"Why? I don't want to drag him into this quagmire."

"Because you've claimed severe mental anguish. Have you suffered that?"

"Yes! You know full well I have. What JPMorgan has done and is doing to me is debilitating."

"Eichman will try to show the jury that because you have a boyfriend, you've moved on with your life. You're feeling good. Will Jack talk to us?"

I sighed. "Yes, of course. I'll bring him in."

"Good. Now, go home and relax," Alan ordered as if that were even possible. "We have another deposition tomorrow. And that means we're getting closer to yours."

"Thanks for the reminder," I quipped, feeling my stomach drop.

I went home with a heavy heart and spoke to Jack. He agreed to meet with Alan so we set a date. Before I knew it, we were sitting in front of Alan's desk.

"Thanks for coming in, Jack," Alan said as he grabbed a legal pad. "Let's start with your background and how you know Jo."

"Okay," Jack said, shifting uncomfortably in the chair. "I grew up in Antioch, Tennessee, just outside of Nashville. I was sixteen the first time I remember seeing Jo. She was walking down the hall of Antioch High

School without a care in the world. I got to know her and started going over to visit her. I loved to hear her father talk. He made $50 a week and told me how he saved three out of four paychecks so the family lived on $50 a month. If they didn't have the money for something, they didn't buy it. If someone in the family wanted something, they had to grow it or save up for it. They raised crops, chickens, and other animals, so they didn't need to buy much food at the grocery store.

"I remember Jo's log house, which her dad built in the forties. It had an outhouse in the back and a well for water. In the fifties, the home was updated with running water and a bathroom.

"When we graduated high school, Jo and I attended the same college, David Lipscomb in Nashville. I found out she was going to be kicked out because she was late a lot to her 8 a.m. English class. She didn't have a driver's license, so she paid a classmate to give her a ride. He wasn't very dependable. Her entire life revolved around getting an education and leaving the farm because it was a really hard life.

"Jo lived in books. She got excited by reading and wanted to experience more of the world. I wanted to do something to help her, so one day I asked her if she needed a ride to school. She did. In exchange for that, she tutored me because I was getting failing grades. She worked hard to help me improve my grades so I wouldn't be drafted and possibly go to Vietnam if I couldn't stay in school. I was desperate, and she saved my life.

"Unfortunately, I got very sick and had to leave college. That made me eligible for the draft. When they held the lottery, my birthdate came up, so I knew I'd have to go. Since I enlisted before being drafted, I got to choose the branch I wanted, which was the Air Force. I served three and a half years and made it out alive. By the time I got back to Antioch, Jo was gone. She moved to Dallas and started her career at American Airlines."

"When did you see her next?" Alan asked.

"In 1975 at our high school's ten-year reunion. I decided to go. Jo's best friend Joan was coordinating it and apparently, Jo called her to find out if I'd be there. I had no idea Jo had had a crush on me in college, but I guess when she found out I'd be at the reunion, she decided to come.

"As I was waiting in line for my nametag, I saw her come bouncing over. She was always bubbly, but this time she seemed different, like she was extra happy to see me. She screamed, 'Jack, is it really you?!'

"Being a smart aleck, I pulled out my wallet and looked at my driver's license and said, 'Yeah, it's me.' She asked me if I was married and I told her no. Then she asked if I was engaged. I told her yes just to mess with her.

"She looked deflated and demanded to know who it was. She had her hands on her hips. I told her, 'After ten years, you're ten minutes too late.' I tried not to smile. Then I pointed at Joan, who was standing behind the desk giving out nametags. The truth was, I barely knew Joan.

"Jo squinted at Joan, who looked confused. They were best friends so Jo knew that Joan would have told her if she was engaged. Then she realized I was teasing her and she was her bubbly self again.

"After the reunion, I took Jo home. She told me she was going back to Dallas in the morning and I knew I might not see her again. We had a few hours together and then she was gone."

Alan wrote furiously. "Did you fly down to Dallas to see her?"

"No," Jack said, sighing. "I actually started dating Joan because she still lived there and was loads of fun and really nice. The next thing I knew, we were married for 33 years. We had a great marriage and the best life together. I had my own business in Nashville, so I was doing well. Joan was diagnosed with kidney cancer and I lost the love of my life on September 1, 2009. She was just sixty-two."

"I'm sorry to hear that," Alan said. "You must have been devastated."

"Yeah. I was. I became extremely depressed and hit the bottle hard. I even considered killing myself. I didn't think I could go on. Just making it to the first anniversary of her death was a miracle. Then, out of the blue, on October 14, 2010, I got an email from Jo. She told me that she lost her husband in January and apologized for not making it to the last reunion. She said her dog was diagnosed with cancer and they had to start chemotherapy."

"During your marriage, were Jo and Joan close?" Alan asked.

"No. They lost touch right after that first reunion, so Jo only heard about Joan's death from a class notice. I decided to call her. I wanted to talk to her about Joan and how lonely and depressed I was. I even confided in her that I was thinking about killing myself. She admitted she was going through the same thing. She planned on wrapping up Max's estate and then killing herself.

"But then we talked a few more times and I started to wonder if there was a way that life could be worth living again."

Chapter Twenty-Four

"Make new friends but keep the old. One is silver, and the other is gold."

—Girl Scouts saying

A lan handed Jack a box of tissue. "Do you need to take a break?"

"No," Jack said, dabbing at his eyes.

"Okay, so what happened next?"

"Jo and I talked about her situation with JPMorgan. She was torn up about her deteriorating relationship with Max's children and she was very frustrated that the Independent Administrator wasn't making any progress. We cried on each other's shoulders. I started thinking about asking if she wanted to meet me somewhere but she beat me to it. Out of the blue, she said Hawaii. I asked her when. I was excited for the first time since Joan's death.

"She suggested Christmas. It was a month away. I knew that meant she wanted to lose some weight first but actually I did too. Between the booze and pills, I wasn't looking much like a human being. Having this to look forward to was the motivation I needed.

"She sent me a first-class plane ticket to Hawaii. When I balked at the cost, she said, 'Don't worry, I get points every time I use my credit card and I have enough points for this trip.' Then she hesitated and told me I didn't even know what she looked like. She asked me if I was sure that I'd show up.

"I told her I didn't care what she looked like. I was going to Hawaii! She thought that was cute and she took everything in the right spirit. Maybe we would both pull out of this after all.

"We emailed and texted each other almost every day, like pen pals. We got closer. We talked about nothing and everything. Honestly, there's no friend like an old friend. We had so much history.

"By the time our Hawaii trip rolled around, I was already in love, and I think Jo was too. It didn't matter what either of us looked like. We had bonded so much and we were both relieved to know we weren't going to die from loneliness. There was a light at the end of the tunnel because we had companionship. I felt happy again."

"So once Jo reconnected with you in late 2010, she was happy again, too?" Alan asked.

Jack shook his head. "Unfortunately, no. She couldn't shake her depression because JPMorgan wouldn't finish up with the estate. Everything she tried to resolve the situation failed. But the invoices from her attorneys kept coming, that's for sure. *That* never stopped. I think for her, there was no light at the end of her tunnel."

Alan set down his pen. "But she did have some good times when you were together?"

"Jo's life was a roller coaster, so there were a lot of times when it was hard being with her. She'd get a court ruling in her favor, then the other side would do something to erase her good mood. She even drove me to the High Five in Dallas and showed me where she planned to commit suicide. So, yeah, there were occasional ups, but there were far too many downs. Even now she's down."

"Did you move in with her?"

"Near the very end of 2014 I did," Jack replied. "Her Scottie, Blair, had had a stroke and died the day before Thanksgiving. Her neighbor and dear friend died four days later. Even though she had just won a big victory in the appeals court and had an up moment, it was all too brief. She fell back down and felt isolated and afraid and alone in a big, empty house. So, I threw caution to the wind and left Nashville, leaving my business to be run by a colleague. I moved to Dallas to be with Jo. It was exciting."

"So you live there full-time?" Alan asked.

"No. When I say moved to Dallas, it's not like I shipped down my furniture and stuff. It means I have a toothbrush by the sink and some clothes hanging in a closet. My business and family are in Tennessee so I'm up there a lot. I need to check up on the business and deal with any family issues. I haven't always been there for Jo in the way I would've liked to. She's been alone and is still alone most of the year, and it's tough on her. Yet here she is in 2016, six years after Max died, and they're no closer to resolving this estate. It's a tragedy."

Alan asked some questions before letting us go. I truly hated getting Jack involved in this mess but there was no choice. To make the case for my mental anguish, the other side was entitled to discover if I'd ever smiled or laughed since Max's death. If so, that up moment could diminish my recovery.

I'm not sure, but I think Barbara googled "9 Robledo Drive" and found that Jack had given my address as a mail forward. I had also posted a couple of photos of us online that she might have discovered. The images made their way to the other side and were passed up the food chain to JPMorgan Chase's lawyers, and now the lawyers wanted each and every photo of Jack and me. They were determined to make sure that every good time I had would lower the amount of damages I was entitled to. Every hour that helped take my mind off the torture they were putting me through would be used to claim that my damages should decrease. Helping yourself harms your case. It's a cruel irony.

I went through my photos—cell phone, social media accounts, and computer—and produced what I had. Alan warned me I'd be hearing more about this subject. Sure enough, whenever he could during court hearings, John Eichman loudly proclaimed, "Your Honor, she's got a *boooyyy*friend!" He'd spit the word out like a bully on a playground. It was a clever move on his part, one that caused me great personal embarrassment and additional mental anguish. I hoped one day I could make Mr. Eichman pay for the pain he was causing me.

Six days earlier, I had begun a deposition-fest with Wendy Bessette. Now Monday was here, and Laura was on deck. Three depositions in seven days. What a grind!

As I settled in for Laura's deposition, I assumed her answers would be all over the place. Where Stephen was the controlled thinker, Laura was the emotional talker. She had a difficult time holding back her feelings. As such, I expected fireworks. What I got was something much different.

Yes, her answers were long, with many drawing objections of being nonresponsive. But to my surprise, she hit on the heart of JPMorgan's misconduct. And I needed her to hit hard if we were going to prevail against this giant.

First, Alan grabbed some low-hanging fruit. Laura said before Max's death, there was nothing about me that would lead her to believe I would steal property or money. I was happy to hear this. She admitted that I had not caused her parents' divorce. Again, great news. She admitted to writing an email that said it seemed Jo Hopper's lawyers were always right. And she acknowledged I was on top of estate matters, but she would have been happier if JPMorgan was on top of them instead.

She thanked me for getting the Jamcracker options reinstated after JPMorgan had allowed them to expire.

Alan: To your knowledge, did Mrs. Hopper play any role in getting the expired Jamcracker options reinstated?

Laura: Yes.

Alan: Were you glad she did?

Laura: Yes.

Alan: Did you object to her doing so?

Laura: No.

Alan: Why not?

Laura: It appeared at that time that we needed Jo's help to do that because the Independent Administrator was not doing that.

She was asked if I'd said why I wanted to be the administrator from the beginning. The answer she gave was this: "I think she was concerned about the cost."

Bingo!

I bet she wished we could turn back the hands of time. I sure did.

Once Alan gathered the easy fruit, he moved into rougher waters. Laura bluntly denied saying she didn't want me touching her money. And she admitted that she and Stephen wanted me to buy them out of the house so they could get their share of the equity, about $400,000. When I'd refused and her attorney said it could absolutely be partitioned, she and Stephen had gone to the bank for its opinion. The bank agreed with them. Thus, JPMorgan could have stopped this by following the Probate Code, but they didn't. As a result, $1.2 million was drained from the estate's account—their money.

Laura eventually took some jabs at me. She couldn't understand how someone...

"... who had just inherited over $13 million was not willing to exchange assets or pay the appraised value that—the share of the appraised value to my brother and I, and instead would go down this legal path. That did not seem reasonable to me."

Again, she seemed to think I'd inherited something. I'd inherited almost nothing from the estate, only $13,333 from the sale of Max's coin collection. I received one-third interest in Max's separate property only. They'd inherited everything else. *Everything*. I merely had my half of our previous community property returned to me.

It was probably my failure to make Laura see that Max and I had a partnership. It was called "marriage." If I won the lottery or made a lot of money by inventing something, half of it was his. If he made a lot of money, half of it was mine. We were 50-50 partners. All marriages in Texas are set up that way. Yet many heirs attribute all the money to the person who earns it, not the partnership agreement or marital status.

The other mistake Laura (and most of the lawyers in this case) made was misunderstanding community property and death. All they had to do was read Stanley Johanson's book.

The instant Max died, the marriage dissolved. Without a marriage, there was no community property. Period! If all we had was $100,000 in the bank, $50,000 instantly became my separate property, and $50,000 went to the Estate of Max Hopper. My separate property was *returned* to me, not distributed. Yet, so many lawyers wanted to apply cases and laws that touched on *distribution* and *community estate* to my separate property. They didn't understand or, more accurately, accept this concept. Maybe they still don't.

When pressed on these issues, Laura admitted she had thought Max's estate (community property before Max's death) was the entire wealth between Max and me. Her attorneys kept referring to it as a "community estate." By now, that wasn't a surprise. Every move they'd made signaled their misapplication of the probate law.

Laura testified that the reason they'd hired JPMorgan was to broker deals with me and divide everything up. If they had felt comfortable dealing with me directly, they wouldn't have needed JPMorgan. It was crazy. They had seldom had problems dealing with me when Max was alive.

Laura admitted hiring Gary Stolbach was a monstrous mistake. That was obvious.

She also admitted she had called me vindictive, spiteful, and greedy. Part of this stemmed from the deep hurt she claimed I'd caused her, which in turn caused mistrust. The best example of this was the fact that I'd kept a valuable stock while the bank sold her stock. After the sale, the stock went up. This meant she missed a lot of the upside from that stock—$3 million, to be exact. She thought it was unfair for me to make all that extra money while the bank denied her that financial gain. As she said, I was greedy.

Unfortunately, she was wrong. The discovery we had provided her lawyers showed my stock was sold at the same time. I had missed out on the $3 million gain too. Yet she thought that I had committed this dastardly deed.

Where had she gotten this idea? From the gaslighter herself—Susan Novak. Laura said she had received an email from Susan telling her what I had done. During the deposition, this was quite a revelation. To open her eyes to this untruth, Alan dropped the bomb like this:

Alan: So, as you're sitting here today, it would come as a great shock to you to learn, if it were true, that Mrs. Hopper's stock was also sold at the same time as yours because that's contrary to what you've believed for years, right?

Laura: Yes.

Alan: Okay.

LENNY: Is that true, Alan?

Alan: Yes, sir.

EICHMAN: It is.

Alan: It's absolutely true, and it's been true since day one.

LENNY: Are you stipulating that?

Alan: Am I stipulating? I don't know how you stipulate it. I've got proof of it.

They had believed this despicable lie for years. Now, the foundations of their hatred were crumbling. This meant their case against me was less solid. For me, the look on Lenny's face was priceless—about $4 million in legal costs so far.

As I said before, Laura surprised me. It was when she began bashing on JPMorgan that she did some of her best work.

When asked about Susan Novak, she testified, "… I believe the estate was grossly mismanaged, so, yes, I would believe to this day that she was incompetent."

Again, Laura confirmed my gaslighting beliefs when she said Susan had given her signals that I was interested in buying her share of Robledo. I was never interested in buying their share of the house. I didn't have to because the Texas Constitution said I didn't.

Laura nailed the crux of this case when Eichman asked her what information JPMorgan should have given her before signing the bank's Independent Administrator agreement.

Laura: Well, what I didn't know when I was signing the Estate Settlement Services agreement was that, in addition to paying the 3% estate administration fee, I was going to have to pay Hunton & Williams over a million dollars or close to a million dollars to manage the estate. I didn't know that. I didn't know at the time I signed it that Hunton & Williams actually represented JPMorgan's best interests and not mine. I didn't realize that Jo Hopper and JPMorgan had already entered into a wealth management banking agreement or that Jo Hopper wasn't going to be responsible for paying any part of the estate administration services. I didn't realize that JPMorgan could use another million dollars—more than a million dollars of my money if we had any grievances with JPMorgan, or that if Jo Hopper wanted to remove—remove JPMorgan as the Independent Administrator because of things JPMorgan was not doing well. I did not know that they could use my money to defend those claims, so, no, there were a lot of things when I signed this agreement that I didn't understand.

Yet Eichman was tenacious. He worked on her, scoring some vital points. He did get her to admit she had made a mistake in hiring Gary Stolbach. But then she fired back by explaining her distrust of JPMorgan. "Why has JPMorgan taken $3 million of my money, and my assets were still not divided?"

Good point!

Regarding the eminent Professor Stanley Johanson, Laura was asked if I had shown her his writings, which proved he contradicted himself. She admitted I had, but her attorneys "…kept telling us that she [Jo] was wrong and they were right."

Finally, Laura said she had never made an offer to purchase my half of the house. However, she did make an offer to sell her interest to me but couldn't remember the dollar amount. When pressed on this, she said the proposal had gone through Susan Novak. Yet, I had never received an offer. So far, it appeared all roads led right to Susan.

When the last lawyer asked the final question, I rubbed my eyes and realized it was Tuesday afternoon. Laura had endured eight hours on Monday and five hours today. I could only imagine how long my deposition would run.

SEVERAL WEEKS HAD disappeared down a sinkhole of nonstop work. Every day, something happened in the case. Regardless of whether Jack was in town or not, I worked on the case all day long and into the night. My friends asked if I was working forty-hour weeks. I told them I was working forty-hour days!

To make it through the tens of thousands of documents, I continued my runs to Starbucks. I could've owned my own coffee shop with the money I had paid them.

During the drive there, I ruminated about the latest rumblings. Alan wasn't sure the October trial date would hold. The judge had said the courtroom was scheduled to be remodeled, and thus, jury trials would not be held. And the list of depositions continued to grow. When experts were designated months from now, more depositions would be on the menu.

As for all the arguing in the depositions between lawyers, nothing ever happened. It was either posturing between lawyers or a waste of money, since the clients paid for the time and pages to be typed up.

A lot of this stuck in my craw. That's why I was happy when I saw Tarian leaving Starbucks just as I arrived.

"How's your case going?" he asked, his beard in need of a trim.

"It's all so ridiculous," I replied, standing on the patio. "The lawyers argue about who's breaking the rules in a deposition, and nothing's ever resolved. And it's like the judges in every court don't care if we ever get to trial. They won't do anything to push the case and the lawyers along. This gives the lawyers the freedom to waste time and money while filing frivolous motions with no penalties or consequences!"

He scratched his jaw. "I hear you. During my career, I've seen only two judges who moved their dockets fast and hard. One was Judge Vic

Cunningham over in the Crowley Criminal Courts Building. That guy worked all the time. I think two years into his first term, he had his entire backlog of cases whittled down to nothing. I remember a lawyer coming in on a Monday and aggressively demanding a jury trial. Judge Cunningham said, 'Okay. We'll set it for Thursday.' The lawyer asked what month. The judge said, 'This one. Actually, *this week*. See you in three days.' The lawyer was upset because there was no way he could be ready by then. He didn't believe it was true, but it was."

"So when he had no cases, did Judge Cunningham even bother showing up for work?"

"Oh, yes. He went to the court next door and asked if he could peel off some of their cases. Sure thing, he tried cases for that court, whittling down their backlog. Judge Cunningham would be picking a jury while another one was deliberating. The guy was a master."

"What happened to him?" I asked.

"He ran for Dallas County District Attorney and lost."

I nodded. "Well, my case is civil anyway, not criminal."

"I know," Tarian said. "That brings me to the curious case of Judge John H. McBryde. Like Judge Cunningham, Judge McBryde didn't have a backlog because he ran his courtroom like a maniac. Cases moved—fast! It seemed like every week, he found witnesses and lawyers in contempt of court for wasting the court's time. Lawyers who asked the same questions over and over were quickly shut down and returned to their chairs. And discovery abuses like you've been enduring? This judge was Batman, Superman, and Captain Marvel all rolled into one. He spanked lawyer after lawyer for ridiculous objections. He lowered the boom on someone every day, at least until lawyers understood not to mess around in his court.

"If a trial lasted four weeks in another court, it lasted two in his. For litigants, that kept the costs down while getting to court fast. Judge McBryde is the poster boy for the smooth, efficient operation of a courtroom."

"So you liked going before him?" I asked.

"Hell no!" Tarian blurted out. "I hated it. Just finding out I drew him as a judge on a case caused me to drink more. When I was in his court, all the tricks up my sleeve were worthless. It was a total nightmare. If all the judges were like him, lawyers would be earning the same pay as teachers. And that's not what the framers of the Constitution wanted," he joked.

"Judge McBryde must have won a bunch of awards."

"Awards! Him? No way. There were so many complaints about Judge McBryde—his demeanor, his harsh methods—that the court system took away all his cases for one year. Because a federal judge is appointed for life, that meant he showed up and did nothing except whatever few cases were on his docket at the time."

I couldn't believe what I was hearing. "So, a judge like that was punished?"

"Yep," Tarian replied. "And some defendant even hired a man to kill him."

"What?"

"Yeah, luckily, it was an FBI agent posing as a hitman, so they caught the guy."

"Sum this up for me," I said. "I'm craving a double shot of caffeine so I can stay up until 3 a.m. working on my lawsuit."

"Judges hold the key to everything. If they enforced the statutes and rules covering sanctions and frivolous lawsuits, lawyers would be in big trouble. But, fortunately, they don't. Why? Because all the judges come from the same womb as lawyers. They are us—of the body, of Landru—the brotherhood. We helped them obtain that position, so they're not about to shit on us. After all, we brought them into this world and we can take them out."

I shook my head in dismay. "Just what I figured. You're all working together to make sure the rest of us get screwed. What a shame."

"Yeah, what a shame," he said, laughing. "Makes me almost want to write a book about it. Oh! That's right. I am."

I waved off Tarian and went in to get my coffee. I didn't need to hear chapter twelve from him when I was trying to avoid chapter thirteen.

Chapter Twenty-Five

"Picking the right executor—and the right team of supporting professionals—can make a meaningful difference in how easily and efficiently your loved ones will receive their inheritance. And how well your plans are carried out."

—U. S. Estate Services
JPMorgan Private Bank website

M ay 5, 2016. My cell phone displayed the dreaded date. Try as I may, I could not wish away my deposition. It had arrived.

I awoke at 5 a.m., my heart pounding from the moment my feet hit the floor. First, I went through my morning routine, dressing in comfortable slacks, a loose-fitting top, and a soft jacket. Then, I made my way to the garage, where my bright yellow 2008 Volkswagen Beetle awaited.

In 2012, I'd spent months searching for this car. After looking around on the internet, I'd found a used one on a dealer's lot in Houston. It had a five-speed manual transmission with 30,000 miles. The daisy wheels and daisy-covered taillights sold me. I paid $12,000, and the dealer even shipped it to me. When it arrived, I gave the well-worn Suburban to a relative, who needed a vehicle. Once I had my Beetle to drive around Dallas, I was content.

As I pulled away from my house, I felt the lure of Starbucks. Even though I didn't need it, I grabbed a coffee and headed to Alan's North Dallas office. I arrived before everyone else and headed to a conference room. When Alan appeared, he took me back to his office to wait it out. With nothing to do but relax, I tried to chill out. It was difficult.

Despite being scheduled for 9 a.m., we didn't start until 9:40.

All the usual cast of characters was there. Alan, of course, and Kerry Schonwald, his colleague who was helping with the case. Even the elusive Jim Flegle sat in this time.

JPMorgan had John Eichman, who was bravely going solo. Surprisingly, Lenny Vitullo was not there. Instead, another lawyer, Jon Azano, had the honors.

Stephen and Laura were present as spectators. In addition, JPMorgan's in-house legal counsel, Susan Kravik, who had witnessed the *Big Scream in the Ladies' Latrine* with Barbara, was there. But I also recalled seeing her name mentioned in the STS Trust and the Burns Clark Dailey Trust lawsuits. I figured she had to be seeing every tactic JPMorgan was pulling. I wondered what her role was in these lawsuits. Did she care about the beneficiaries who were forced to sue JPMorgan Chase?

Rounding out the spectators was Susan Novak herself. Add the videographer and stenographer, and we had twelve people crammed into one conference room.

Much like the bullfights in Spain, the crowd expected a spectacle. The well-dressed matadors shifted from side to side, eagerly awaiting the bugle call from the videographer. In front of them were several Mont Blanc and Gold Cross *banderillas*—sharp barbed sticks—they would use to pry information from me. I would have to concentrate and endure this for two days. They would be disappointed if I collapsed and died too quickly. They were so looking forward to the final *estocada*.

Eichman was first. He started with the usual platitudes. If you don't understand a question, please let me know. And please let me finish my questions. Are you on any drugs that might affect your testimony or memory? It was the same opening drivel from lawyer to lawyer and deposition to deposition.

After the easy stuff was out of the way, Eichman went straight for the mental anguish damages. He asked if I had seen a psychologist after Max's death. The fireworks started.

Alan objected to medical questions that covered my entire life. He instructed me not to answer various questions. Surprisingly, Eichman didn't argue with him.

When allowed to answer, I explained how I had received grief counseling. Eichman listened, nodded his head, and moved on.

Eichman asked about any medication I'd taken to minimize my grief and depression. I could tell he was trying to pin my emotions on the loss of my husband and not on the beating I'd been receiving from JPMorgan. It was a good move.

Once he'd gleaned everything about my mental state, he shifted to my past lawyers. He wanted to show that all my problems were the result of hiring multiple lawyers who couldn't get the job done. It was very effective.

He detailed the $620,000 I'd paid to my probate lawyer, Mike Graham. Then, he went over the $2,032,000 I'd paid my litigation attorney, Jim Jennings. Next, he listed the sum of $220,000 I'd paid to my appellate attorney, Michael Yanof. Finally, he discussed the fees I'd paid Alan's firm. In total, I'd paid him almost $1 million.

So far.

Eichman scored heavily when he induced me to say that I was seeking attorneys' fees as damages. I learned later that I should have said I was seeking to *recover* them instead. This would potentially hurt my case down the road.

During the previous depositions, I had seen how skillful Eichman was. Now that he was carving me up, it felt different, like being put in a car with no brakes and pushed down a hill. The cliff was coming, and I had no way to stop.

Thankfully, I kept my wits about me. He tried to get me to admit that Gary Stolbach and his firm, Glast Philips, were the cause of all my mental and financial suffering, but I dodged the punch.

By the time we reached our first break at 10:30 a.m., I was mentally exhausted. And I still had the rest of the day and all of tomorrow to go. I tried not to think about it, instead focusing on one question at a time.

After the break, events just melted together. Eichman tried to show my foolishness in spending $4+ million in attorneys' fees fighting over my $400,000 share of equity in the house. He painted his partner, Tom Cantrill, as a problem-solver who tried to get the parties to agree instead of wasting all this time and money.

Eichman handed me a document that showed Susan Novak had asked me for more information, and another one that showed her doing her job. Then, he handed me documents that proved an answer I'd just given was wrong. I was drowning in my chair.

He painted my relationship with Max's children as the root of the problem. Stephen and Laura just sat there, staring at me.

He pointed out a trip I took to New York where JPMorgan paid for my dinner and a play, *The Phantom of the Opera*. He made it sound like I had taken advantage of the bank to get some free goodies.

Nothing went untouched. Eichman recounted an argument Max and I'd had where I'd left the house and threw my wedding ring at Stephen when he answered the door. Stephen and Barbara had witnessed it and told JPMorgan. It was embarrassing to be going over that moment again, but I had no choice. It was the truth.

With each question, Eichman zeroed in on the information in my brain. His words were like fingernails, intrusively examining my arms and legs, looking for any sores or cuts. When he found one, he scratched it hard until it started bleeding. That was what this ordeal felt like. And it just went on for-*ever*!

By the end of the two days, I was sure my case was lost. Why Alan wasn't lifting his head to the heavens and screaming aloud in disgust, I had no idea. I had just undergone a complete and thorough gutting.

"You did fine," Alan soothed.

"How can you say that?" I asked. "They drilled me for shredding documents at Max's business. And when they went over how Max died, it was like they were somehow blaming me for his death! I'm sorry I cried so much."

"That's perfectly fine. It's a painful moment you had to relive. Who wouldn't cry?"

"It was so painful," I agreed, holding back more tears.

Alan put his arm around me. "That's their job. To discover facts about the case."

"And to cause pain. It seems like that's all this litigation is. How we can win our case after my deposition, I have no idea."

"Look," Alan said gently, "a deposition is like a basketball game. Each team scores points. At the end of the game, one team wins—even if the score was 118 to 117. The winning team gave up 117 points. Yet they won. All it takes for victory is one extra point."

I hung my head. "But they scored lots of points today."

"Sure. But we've been scoring points ourselves. And the good news is that when they were scoring points, you didn't foul and give them an extra free throw. You let them have their points and no more."

I shook my head. "I don't know, Alan."

He chuckled. "I do. And that's all that matters. Wait and see how the rest of the depositions go. You'll feel better."

I sat in his office for a while, decompressing. When I finally left, it was 5 p.m. on Friday. We had started Thursday morning. Where the time had gone, I had no idea. I didn't even remember going home Thursday evening.

As I drove on the streets of Dallas in my yellow Beetle, I saw cars speeding off to happy hours and restaurants. Their workweek was over. Mine still had two more days to go.

When I arrived home, I had planned on reviewing documents all night, but my brain was mush. Instead, I opened one of the expensive bottles of wine we had fought over. Sitting in my easy chair, I swirled the wine around in my glass, waiting to relax. When I took a sip, it was bitter. The wine was ruined. So was another bottle. And another. No wonder it hadn't sold. It was a fitting end to a brutal week.

AFTER SUCH A bruising experience, on Saturday I would've liked to have been relaxing by a pool with a frozen drink and a good book. Instead, the anger inside burned too much to allow such indulgences. So, like always, I turned on the computer and rolled up my sleeves. Work was my elixir.

I decided to look into another lawsuit against JPMorgan that had been mentioned in the STS Trust litigation. The records were mainly in Houston, and the Harris County District Clerk had already helped me download them online. I spent day and night reading everything before coming up with a basic understanding of the case. Here's what I learned.

T. Boone Pickens founded and operated a company called Mesa Petroleum. Eventually, Mesa grew into one of the world's largest independently owned oil companies. In 1982, Mesa was making a ton of money from overriding royalty interests in producing wells located in Texas and Louisiana. In these leases, the "overriding royalty interests" were the money the mineral owner received from the driller after deducting all the production expenses. Texans usually call this money "the royalty check" they receive each quarter.

To raise capital for more exploration, Mesa carved out some of these oil and gas leases and put them in a trust. Shares in the trust were issued to Mesa shareholders and traded on the Over-The-Counter

Bulletin Board, a place for small and volatile stocks, under the ticker symbol of MOSH.

In 1996, Mesa was in financial trouble and Pickens sold it. A year later, it was merged into Pioneer Natural Resources, the same Pioneer that was sued in the STS Trust case. In 2003, JPMorgan Chase was installed as the trustee of MOSH and the plot thickened.

By 2005, MOSH had over 12,000 unit holders (shares in a trust are called "units"). At some point, the unit holders learned that JPMorgan had provided a $1 billion credit line to Pioneer. (Sounds familiar.) When the unit holders looked at the records of JPMorgan's activities as trustee, they filed a lawsuit. And the story they told was a doozy. Based on the documents I read, this is what the plaintiffs alleged:

Due to the Mesa merger, Pioneer now controlled the mineral leases in the trust. Per the lease agreements, Pioneer could drill more wells or not. If they drilled a well and it produced oil or gas, Pioneer had to pay an overriding royalty to MOSH. Drilling wells is costly, especially if they're offshore, so on one well, Pioneer cut a deal with another company, Woodside Energy, to allow Woodside to drill it. Having one driller contract with another driller is called a "farmout" in the oil industry. Woodside spent its own money to drill the well and paid Pioneer an overriding royalty when the well produced. Pioneer, in turn, paid MOSH its cut, although it was much smaller now since Pioneer was a middleman instead of the driller. The plaintiffs claimed this deal hurt them financially.

Then the story took an interesting turn. The plaintiffs claimed Pioneer did drill the well, since Woodside was too small to handle it. Essentially, the farmout was a sham—something on paper—allowing Pioneer to cheat MOSH. And they alleged Pioneer manipulated the accounting records to hide the income from the well. My impression from reading these documents was that the overall goal was to choke off the money flowing to MOSH so the mineral leases would be worthless and thus trigger the trust's termination. Since Pioneer now owned Mesa, it would receive the mineral leases back from the trust and be free of paying MOSH.

But a hero was standing in Pioneer's way. This hero's job was to watch over all these mineral leases, study the accounting records, and prevent these shenanigans from happening in the first place. This hero was JPMorgan Chase. They were the trustee of MOSH and thus *had a fiduciary duty to protect the beneficiaries.*

When the dust cleared, the plaintiffs claimed JPMorgan had done nothing to prevent any of this. Instead, it appeared the bank realized they had a conflict of interest (because Pioneer was borrowing $1 billion from it) and agreed to resign as trustee.

Of course, JPMorgan, Pioneer, and Woodside claimed that none of this was true and that all the deals benefitted MOSH. They even produced experts who stated these deals were perfectly fine. Visions of Stanley Johanson danced in my head.

In their 2005 lawsuit, the plaintiffs listed all the usual claims like fraud and breach of fiduciary duty. They also claimed JPMorgan had failed to sue Pioneer (also JPMorgan's client) for this sham farmout. (Remember in the STS Trust litigation, JPMorgan was accused of failing to sue Pioneer to terminate its lease on STS Trust property.) Due to this scheme, MOSH stated it had lost at least $1.2 billion.

Seven months after being served with this lawsuit, JPMorgan announced they intended to resign as trustee, effective January 31, 2006. But then they claimed that not a single qualified person or entity could be found to replace them so they had no choice but to stay on as trustee to the bitter end.

In reviewing the documents, I spotted one of JPMorgan's previous litigation tricks from the STS Trust litigation, as well as my Robledo home issue. Both JPMorgan and Pioneer were trying to shut down the trust and sell the assets for a low value. This was during 2009 when the world economy was in a tailspin. JPMorgan even held a public auction but received no bids, likely due to the ongoing legal action. This no-bid result would undoubtedly set a lower cap for any damages at trial. After all, how have you been harmed when your assets are worthless?

I found one document where the MOSH plaintiffs stated that JPMorgan had agreed that the sham farmout to Woodside claim had merit. Then I read another where JPMorgan stated they had done nothing wrong, but if they had, they had relied on experts in good faith. I wondered what a jury would think about that.

The litigation had taken four long years. Hurricane Katrina even made an appearance, damaging production and delaying new drilling. Finally, in 2009, the parties settled, with the results made public, since MOSH was a publicly traded company.

The final settlement ordered JPMorgan to pay the trust $5 million and forgive a $5 million loan it had made to the trust to pay expenses.

(This tactic of borrowing money from itself and taking money from the trust to pay for the loan was something I'd see later on in my case.) Pioneer had to pay the trust $13 million and another $700,000 after selling some mineral interests, and Woodside was ordered to pay the trust $1 million. Oh, and JPMorgan and Pioneer got the court to approve shutting down MOSH and the trust. Upon the first liquidating distribution, each beneficiary received 11.6 cents per unit. If you were an investor and held 100,000 units, you received a check for $11,600. So who really won here?

Sadly, another JPMorgan trustee job had been consumed by the flames of litigation.

ALL TOO QUICKLY, Tuesday morning arrived. By now, I was calloused and hardened. Five years of litigation, dozens of court hearings, and seven depositions meant that I was ready for anything. Susan Novak, the one carrying the flag for JPMorgan, now sat in the hot seat.

Strangely, it felt like a year since my deposition had taken place, though it had only been four days. That's how jampacked this schedule was.

Lenny Vitullo was here, as were Eichman and Alan. I was glad. I wanted the A-Team to put Susan through everything I had experienced and more.

As usual, Alan started with the easy stuff. Susan had first been with Bank of America, where she attended the American Bankers Association Trust School. It was a three-year program in Chicago, and she graduated with honors. She was no rookie, but someone who had been trained to do this work.

Susan explained that she had been working for over seventeen years in this industry, handling 150 to 200 estates. However, she had never dealt with stock options before this estate. That was hard to believe.

The first big shock came when we learned that she had been handling twenty-five to thirty estates when she began work on the Max Hopper Estate! To me, that seemed like an overwhelming workload. Then, she testified that she was the only estate person in Dallas for JPMorgan. There was another one in Fort Worth, but that was it. She said she could've stayed after 5 p.m. every day to work more but chose not to. For the world's largest bank, her workload seemed like a horrendous management failure. But then I remembered my favorite case, STS Trust. Discovery in that case had produced an email from Pattie Schultz-Ormond when she had worked for JPMorgan. Pattie stated she was managing 140 oil and gas trusts and struggling to find time to do the job properly. She wrote her boss:

> "I am underwater and do not have the staff I need to address the many leases and drilling initiatives... for which I am responsible. I am trying to get the help but am in a position at this point of simply trying to put out fires."

JPMorgan laid off Pattie in 2009 as they downsized her office. Did that make any business sense? Was this part of CEO Jamie Dimon's management plan—to keep labor costs chopped to the bone to prop up the stock price? It seemed to me that instead of paying all these lawsuit settlements and governmental fines, a CEO would simply peel off $100 million and staff up to provide first class service. After all, JPMorgan is always claiming they do the right thing, *and* that they provide first class service. Why not write a check and live up to those claims? But then, I wasn't CEO of the country's largest bank.

And speaking of management failures, Susan Novak laid some of the blame at Wendy Bessette's feet. She testified that because it was escalating into a threat of litigation, Bessette was more responsible for monitoring the legal positions of the bank's lawyers. I wondered how any manager could allow a matter like this to get so out of hand.

As Alan probed into more sensitive areas, Susan said, "I don't recall" or "I don't remember" several times. I began making a mark every time she said that. I was interested to see what the total would be at the end of the deposition.

Susan said she had worked two intestate estates like Max's, maybe more, but she couldn't recall. Alan asked more about these particular estates, and Susan's answers were surprising.

Alan: In the mid-'90s, while at Bank of America, was the estate in Texas?

Susan: I don't remember the details of that estate.

Alan: Okay. So you don't remember whether it was in Texas?

Susan: I don't remember.

Alan: Okay. What was -- Do you remember the size of the estate, approximately?

Susan: No.

Alan: Do you remember whether it was a male or a female?

Susan: No.

Alan: Do you remember whether there were any heirs?

Susan: I don't remember.

Alan: Do you remember whether there was a surviving spouse?

Susan: I don't remember.

Alan: Do you remember whether there was a residence?

Susan: No.

Alan: Do you remember the nature of the assets?

Susan: No.

Alan: Do you remember whether any property was partitioned?

Susan: No.

Alan: Do you remember whether there were any disputes between the heirs?

Susan: No.

Alan: Do you remember anything about that estate?

Susan: Not at this time.

Alan: Is there some reason you have no recollection regarding that estate?

Susan: Years.

Alan: Other than that?

Susan: No.

Susan said the fact that I'd inventoried everything was helpful, but admitted she couldn't provide proof that she ever wrote to Laura and told her how much I was helping her. She also didn't recall ever passing along the negative things Stephen and Laura were saying about me. All of this was a big part of the gaslighting that Tarian had warned me about.

Susan said she had plenty of experience dealing with heirs who were at odds or contentious, and if the bank had to do it over again, it would still take the Max Hopper Estate. This statement would come in handy later on.

She told us Kal Grant was responsible for bringing in the business, not managing it. That was too bad. A sharp lawyer like Kal could have only helped. Susan also explained that there was a banker assigned to every estate. And she admitted it was possible Todd Baird, who was with Private Banking, had been there to reel in other business from me. This went to the bundling claims and pressure they put on people like me to stay with JPMorgan.

On the issue of selling my house, Susan claimed that without Gary Stolbach's intervention and threats, the bank would have distributed the house in undivided interests. But then she admitted the Hunton & Williams lawyers merely made their recommendations to the bank, and the bank approved the legal position. With the bank's in-house lawyers studying each move and thus approving everything, it appeared to me that it would be much tougher for JPMorgan to claim that the Hunton & Williams' law firm was to blame.

Eichman made the usual objections and, at times, appeared to instruct the witness. Alan called him out on it. When Vitullo asked questions, Alan said he saw Eichman shaking his head in an apparent signal to the witness. Eichman denied it. Unfortunately, it was not on camera. Big-time lawyers like Eichman and Alan knew where the razor's edge of the rules was located. And after what Tarian had told me, I knew nothing would come from this.

Susan admitted she owed me a fiduciary duty, and it included an obligation to disclose material facts, as well as operate in good faith, and with honesty. Alan reminded her of the duty to put my interests ahead of the bank's interests, and this caused her problems when he discussed the Rounds.

Susan had apparently known John Round was representing Stephen *before* I signed the agreement but hadn't told me. Nor did she tell me that John was married to her co-worker, Debra, because it had nothing to do with the estate as far as she was concerned. Yet, she admitted I had the right to decide what was important before I signed the agreement. To me, the fact that John Round's wife worked in the trust department of JPMorgan was critical information I should have been told. It was a conflict as far as I was concerned.

Alan then dove into the hiring of Tom Cantrill. Susan said it was her decision as estate administrator to hire the lawyer, and she had no hesitation in hiring Cantrill. But then Alan showed her an email she had written expressing hesitation in hiring him. Susan had no explanation as to why at 4:04 p.m. she had problems with Cantrill, but at 4:56 p.m. of the same day, she no longer had a problem. Something had happened during those fifty-two minutes that had changed my life.

Susan then claimed she didn't remember any specifics of the twenty-two-minute phone call she and I had, where I screamed and cried for her not to use Cantrill. In fact, she didn't remember a lot of things.

Alan plowed ahead, getting her to flat-out admit to key pieces of our case. During a break, I told him how well he was doing.

"Still feel like you lost this case in your deposition?" he smirked.

"No," I smiled. "I'm feeling better. *Much* better."

"If I do my job, Susan will feel like you did last week."

"I sure hope so," I said, feeling the anger and bitterness welling up inside.

When we resumed, the next subject was my fees and expenses.

Alan: Did anyone say at that meeting words to the effect that if the bank were hired, it wouldn't cost Mrs. Hopper any money?

Susan: There may have been regarding that.

She admitted no one at the bank had told Stephen and Laura that I wasn't paying any fees. So much for a fiduciary duty to them. Finally, Alan played his last card. He wanted to know how many mistakes Susan had made on the Max Hopper Estate.

Alan: Were any mistakes made on the bank's handling of the Hopper Estate?

EICHMAN: Objection, form.

Susan: Define mistakes.

Alan: Anything you would consider to be a mistake.

EICHMAN: Objection, form.

Susan: No.

Alan: Is there anything, knowing now what's happened, that if you had it to do all over again, you would do differently regarding the handling of the Hopper Estate?

Susan: On my -- from my perspective?

Alan: On the part of anyone at the bank, including yourself.

Susan: No.

I wasn't surprised. JPMorgan didn't believe they ever made mistakes. Not the largest bank in the world! They were perfect and always did "the right thing." How dare a mere mortal even ask that question.

Unfortunately, we had a long list of mistakes, such as the inventory that had been filed. A year later, the errors had been corrected, and it was refiled. A year later, more mistakes were fixed, and it was re-refiled again. Yet, there were still errors. If I had not let it go, I'm sure JPMorgan would still be filing inventories to this day. And they'd more than likely still be wrong.

Things were going so well that Lenny gave Alan thirty minutes of his time. Alan used it to devastating effect.

Alan: Were mistakes made in the original inventory the bank filed?
Susan: No. They—no.
Alan: Were mistakes made in the first amended inventory the bank filed?
Susan: No.

That sums up what it was like to deal with JPMorgan. Any mistakes they made had been on purpose!

For Susan, the ordeal mercifully ended with the final thrust of the blade. Alan took me back to his office and asked me the total.

"Ninety-five 'I don't recalls,'" I recounted.

"It feels like it should have been more," he said. "But we'll see how many she says at trial."

FIVE DAYS AFTER Susan Novak's deposition, I was browsing for dogs to adopt on Operation Kindness' Facebook page. Operation Kindness is the largest no-kill shelter in North Texas, and Max and I had both enthusiastically supported it. I enjoyed following the excellent work they did finding *furever* homes for rescued dogs and cats.

To my surprise, a picture of a particular dog caught my attention. Its head hung low, eyes sad and heartbroken. The text below the photo explained that she was pregnant in another shelter and would be euthanized if a foster home could not be found immediately. She touched my heart, and I contacted a friend who was familiar with the foster program to find out if they had found someone to foster this dog. She said no. I said if they couldn't find anyone, I would foster the mom and her puppies. My friend was thrilled and promised to be there to help in any way. A few days later, Millie entered my life. She was a pit bull mix.

Operation Kindness believed Millie was three or four years old. She had been found on a street in Hurst, Texas. They had tried to find her owner, but had no luck. She came to me with her *nine* four-day-old puppies! The puppies had been born on my birthday, which had to be some sort of sign. I got to name them so I borrowed from the video game *Angry Birds*: Hal, Chuck, Stella, Matilda, Jack, Jay, Jake, Bubbles, and Red.

Millie was a gentle and loving mother. She didn't mind me handling her puppies. And they were so tiny, they fit into the palm of my hand! With their little eyes shut, I couldn't help but love every one of them. I sat up nights with the sick ones, nursing them back to health. Little did I know the adventure that awaited me and would *furever* change our lives.

MILLIE QUICKLY TOOK to 9 Robledo Drive. She enjoyed exploring the house when she wasn't taking good care of her puppies. Because she was a street dog, she'd never dealt with stairs and didn't know what to make of them. But since she wanted to be with me every waking moment, she quickly figured it out.

One place Millie loved was the backyard, especially Max's short peach tree (for some reason, peach trees aren't very tall). By now, I had been harvesting ripe peaches yearly. This year, the crop was a few weeks early. The limbs were heavy with fruit, making it easy for me to collect God's creations and turn them into preserves. Millie and her puppies, as well as the peaches, took my mind off the case.

One morning, I spread my homemade peach jam on some toast. Walking outside with my toast in one hand and a cup of coffee in the other, I found a shady spot under the peach tree and leaned against it. Millie came up and lay next to me.

The bees and dragonflies buzzed around the flowers while Millie and I watched them do their jobs. As I took a bite from the thick crusty bread, I smiled. For one brief moment in my life, all was right with the world.

Unfortunately, the moment was brief. I had to get back to work and prepare for the next deposition. My other nemesis, Tom Cantrill, was the next bull to enter the arena. And I didn't plan to leave anything on the table.

Chapter Twenty-Six

"Acting like everyone who's been successful is bad, and because you're rich you're bad. I don't understand it."
—Jamie Dimon, Chairman & CEO
JPMorgan Chase Bank, N.A.

The elevator doors opened, and Alan and I stepped in. It was just us. "Every time I come here," Alan said, "I think about Jenkens & Gilchrist. But, you know, Eichman will probably fight to keep out any stuff about that."

His comment caught me off guard. I wasn't sure what he was talking about. When I had first hired Tom Cantrill in the '90s to draft my will, I had come to this same building and gotten off on the 37th floor. At that time, Cantrill had worked for Jenkens & Gilchrist. Did that firm have something to do with my case?

As the doors closed, I turned to ask him what he meant, but another person jumped in with us. I decided to ask him later. The elevator raced up to the 37th floor and came to a stop. We stepped into the lobby and I glanced at the Hunton & Williams sign, which had replaced the Jenkens & Gilchrist sign years earlier. In all these years, Cantrill had not moved from this floor.

The conference room was full of people, so I had no chance to ask Alan about his comment. Instead, I took my familiar place at the table, making a note to ask him after the deposition. It was time to get my game face on.

One of the protocols of every deposition is timing the victim's appearance. When the lawyers are all set in their places, the attorney taking the deposition checks with the court reporter and videographer. When they say they're ready, the defending lawyer brings in the victim, which minimizes the time they're forced to spend in the same room with their enemy. Today, Tom Cantrill was brought in, and as soon as the videographer gave the thumbs up, Alan started in.

He had Cantrill detail his qualifications. Cantrill said he was certified in estate planning and probate. That meant he was an expert in those fields. I thought about how they should go back and update those certifications in light of this case.

He said he'd been a lawyer since 1973. Alan never asked, but I guessed he was about sixty-eight years old.

Alan danced around for a few minutes before getting down to business, then asked Cantrill about his nasty comment about me calling him before Max's body was cold. Cantrill testified that he couldn't recall what we discussed.

Okay. I get it. Better to say that than discover I had a recording of it.

Alan pressed him about a possible conflict of interest since he had worked with me in the past. Cantrill testified he never believed he had a conflict of interest. And no one ever told Cantrill that I had opposed his hiring. He didn't even learn about my objections until this deposition, when he reviewed some documents.

Hearing this, the first name that came to mind was Susan Novak. This was another nail in her coffin, showing that all roads led to JPMorgan. Information went in but never came out.

I soon noticed that Cantrill responded to many of the questions that he didn't recall or didn't remember. It reminded me of Susan Novak's deposition. This went on until Alan struck gold.

Cantrill said he had been representing JPMorgan since the 1980s. When Alan pressed for how many times, Cantrill refused to speculate on a number. But Alan kept tugging on him so Cantrill finally agreed it was probably fewer than 10,000 times, but he declined to narrow it any further.

Wow! That was a significant number. Cantrill and JPMorgan were very tight.

Alan tried a different tack to pry the information loose.

Alan: When was the last time you had an active matter for the
          bank other than the Hopper estate?
Cantrill: I don't recall.
Alan: Was it prior—since 2010?

Cantrill: I don't recall.
Alan: Was it since 2015?
Cantrill: Same answer.

Cantrill had so many cases and clients, he couldn't remember them all—*or any.*

We had a break, then Cantrill testified how I'd required a lot of attention and sent plenty of emails. But he also agreed that I had a right to make inquiries into the bank's administration of the estate.

Alan moved onto the issue of dividing up my house. Cantrill admitted that the IA did not need the court's approval to make distributions in undivided interests. He agreed with the statement from his law partner, John Eichman, that the IA would have distributed the house in undivided interests but for Stolbach's theories. Yet Cantrill believed the right thing for JPMorgan to do as a fiduciary was to encourage the parties to resolve their issues by agreement. If they couldn't, only then should the IA distribute in undivided interests.

Before he said that, I had thought JPMorgan was the only bad guy here. But there it was. Cantrill saw the job of the IA as a mediator, a facilitator of settlements. In reality, the IA was a judge designed to rule fast and close the estate to minimize the fees. Too bad with all that experience, Cantrill didn't agree with that.

Finally, Cantrill said JPMorgan had decided, in 2011, what they would do with my home. *The bank* made the decision. I liked my chances now of making JPMorgan pay for what they had done to me. The deposition went on and on with "I don't recalls" and "I don't remembers." I wondered if his memory would clear up by trial. I heard that sometimes happens.

Alan wrapped up his questioning by covering all the millions Cantrill's firm had raked in. He concluded with this gem:

Alan: Do you get credit within the firm in some way for bringing this matter to the firm?
Cantrill: Well, my compensation is evaluated on—in several ways, hours worked, fees collected, so I suppose the answer to that is yes, I would have—as part of the work I did, so it would be part of what is reviewed in determining my compensation.

Of course. The firm valued partners who brought in more money. Who wouldn't? That's Business 101. No wonder he couldn't remember his clients or cases. He had too many of them. It was clear to me that Cantrill was a cash cow for any law firm. He'd be the last person you'd let go if times were tough. A lawyer like him would be the one who locked the doors when the firm shut down.

Alan had used five hours and fifteen minutes of his time before passing the witness. It was the heirs' turn.

Lenny Vitullo wasn't there, but had instead sent Taylor Horton. Yet Mr. Horton didn't ask any questions or say one word during the deposition. This was odd. Fortunately, there to save the day for the heirs was Matthew Muckleroy. He worked for Lenny's co-counsel, James Bell. Mr. Muckleroy ran for forty-five minutes. Finally, Eichman stopped him, saying that six hours was the longest Cantrill would sit for the deposition.

There was some discussion by Eichman that the heirs had failed to send a proper deposition notice. Muckleroy objected, and after reconsidering his position, Eichman gave in and allowed him an extra sixty seconds to ask the rest of his twenty pages of questions! I felt sorry for Muckleroy. I knew what it was like dealing with John "Darth Vader" Eichman.

When Muckleroy had used up his sixty seconds, he declared his firm would be seeking a second deposition for Cantrill from the judge. I shook my head—another waste of time and money.

At 5:56 p.m., Cantrill's deposition ended. Alan had Kerry walk me out to my car because he had to leave for some function. As a result, I couldn't ask him about the Jenkens & Gilchrist comment.

On the way home, I pondered it. Instead of wasting Alan's time and my money, I decided a better investment was to buy dinner for an old friend who might be able to solve the riddle. I selected the Woodlands American Grill down the street from me.

I arrived early and ordered an appetizer of grilled chicken flatbread because I knew my guest would be hungry. And I avoided alcohol since he was fighting an addiction. But he was late, so I ate all the flatbread. It was delicious. When he did finally show up, he appeared haggard.

"What happened?" I asked my disheveled guest.

"Traffic accident right in front of me," said Tarian.

"Were you hurt?"

"No. But the folks in front of me were. I thought about handing them my business card," he winked in an attempt at dark humor, "but decided that it would be a conflict of interest if I was a witness."

"I'm learning a lot about those," I said. A textbook on ethics could be written on my case alone.

The waitress brought him a tall glass of water and he decided to pontificate. "The idea behind conflicts of interest is that we owe a duty to our clients and nothing else. Imagine if I stood up in court and told the jury that the damages to the victim were a billion dollars. Then I took the stand and testified as a fact witness for that same victim. I could tell the jury how bad she'd been hurt, how she'd begged for mercy. My desire for a large judgment, which would add to my bank account, versus my duty to tell the truth, could be compromised. Wouldn't I be more likely to lie if it made me filthy rich?"

"I guess," I agreed.

"And how would it look to the public if I'm giving an opening statement and testifying too?"

I thought about that question. "But you can still testify in front of a jury about your attorneys' fees. Right?"

"Right. That's different because we've decided that we lawyers are so honest, we'd never lie about our fees. Besides, we would have to hire experts in every case, which would add to the costs of litigation. And it's already so expensive that the average human being can't afford to get to trial. So, to keep costs down and our bank accounts full, we wink at the opposing lawyers and judge, and testify that we are righteous men and women. And what we've charged is the God's honest truth."

"Okay," I nodded. "If you say so."

"I do say so. But you didn't invite me here to talk about my two favorite subjects, money and me. Did you?"

"No," I laughed. "I need to ask you about a comment my lawyer made. Something about Jenkens & Gilchrist and Hunton & Williams. He said the lawyers for Hunton & Williams might fight to keep out some information about Jenkens & Gilchrist. Do you know what he's talking about?"

"I do. But let's order first. I'm starving."

Tarian asked the waitress what she recommended, and she said the lobster stuffed with lump crabmeat. Then he asked what her favorite dish was, and she said the lobster stuffed with lump crabmeat. After telling her how good that sounded, he selected a T-bone steak with a baked potato and salad. I chose the fresh trout. When she left, I seized the moment.

"All right, Tarian, tell me what I need to know." I wanted him to get this story out before the food arrived, otherwise he'd tell it with a mouthful of steak and potato bits flying through the air.

"Okay," he said. "Once upon a time, there was this law firm, Jenkens & Gilchrist. It started in the early 1950s and had ties to the Dallas Cowboys. It was a small firm, but it grew over the years. Eventually, it became the largest law firm in Dallas.

"During the S&L disaster of the 1980s, Jenkens & Gilchrist paid $18 million to the FDIC to settle a potential lawsuit and a legal malpractice case. This shrunk their firm size, putting a big dent in their future. But lawyers are smart and resilient. By December 2000, Jenkens & Gilchrist had grown to 600 attorneys, with offices all over the U.S. Yet, despite their success, they hungered for more.

"Enter a tax attorney in Chicago. In 1998, he was unhappy with his annual compensation from his current law firm. He began looking for a new firm, one that valued what he brought to the table. Jenkens & Gilchrist was a firm looking to expand their footprint and their partners' wealth, and didn't have an office in Chicago. When they heard this tax attorney's pitch, they grew excited. The coins in their pockets buzzed with electricity. And what a pitch it was.

"This tax attorney had found a loophole in the tax laws. He figured out a way for any client to offset huge gains with equally huge losses, ones he was able to create. This allowed the client to pay little or no taxes. And the best part was that these 'created losses' didn't cause the client to lose real money. The only thing they lost was the tax bill.

"I know nonlawyers might not understand this, but it was like hitting a legal Spindletop. Or finding the Hope Diamond. Or even Neil Diamond. Truly, it was the motherlode of legal brainpower. Sorry, but it tends to bring a tear to my eye."

He feigned brushing a tear from his cheek. "But I digress. Okay, so the smart partners of Jenkens & Gilchrist listened to this brilliant scheme and had lots of questions. They wanted to know what would happen if the IRS came a-knockin'. The tax attorney confidently explained that Jenkens & Gilchrist, if they were smart enough to hire him, would issue a letter to the client at the time of the scheme's creation. This letter stated that Jenkens & Gilchrist believed this scheme was more likely than not to be legal under the tax laws. By having this letter in hand, the client would be immune from any IRS penalties if their deductions were denied. Thus, the client had nothing to lose.

"The smart partners of Jenkens & Gilchrist liked what they heard. Telling their clients that they had nothing to lose would be an easy sell. What's not to love about this scheme? But the smart partners of Jenkens & Gilchrist had another question: 'If the client can't lose, how do we gain?' The Holy Grail of legal acumen was on display.

"The tax attorney calmly explained that his firm was already taking a percentage of the client's tax savings. If he saved a client $20 million in taxes, his firm received $600,000. He was bringing in millions to his firm. The problem was money. The tax attorney believed he should make more of it. That's why he desperately needed to find a law firm with smart partners who understood the value he could bring to the conference room table.

"Well, the smart partners of Jenkens & Gilchrist debated all this. Not only would they have to agree that the scheme was legal, but they would have to pay this tax attorney more than the other partners. That was a sore subject. Every partner wanted to be paid more than the other partners. It's an alpha dog thing, you know, one dog pees on a rock and another dog comes over and splashes its pee on the same rock. Sort of double stamp no erasies.

"Then there were the not-so-smart lawyers in the firm. They didn't like the scheme. They claimed it didn't have any real business purpose, something required by the IRS. They claimed it might even be illegal. The debate went on and on for a few minutes until the lure of incredible wealth and riches won the day. Jenkens & Gilchrist hired the brilliant tax attorney and set up a Chicago office for him. And just like he promised, the money flowed like toner in an HP printer.

"It was giddy times at Jenkens & Gilchrist. The smart partners were making a killing. And clients flocked to the law firm like swallows of wine from the San Juan Capistrano vineyards. What a glorious time it was.

"But then, two years after that brilliant tax attorney came on board, a lawsuit was filed against Jenkens & Gilchrist. It seemed a few of their clients were being audited by the IRS. For some crazy reason, the IRS wasn't buying this tax avoidance scheme. The IRS approached Jenkens & Gilchrist and asked for its client list. The firm politely told the IRS to get bent. Their client list was attorney-client privileged. The poor IRS investigators walked away, scratching their heads in confusion.

"The smart partners at Jenkens & Gilchrist grew concerned. This was a disturbing turn of events. They decided this tax attorney had to go, and maybe directly out the 37th-floor window. Yet a surprise was in store. The man who had recruited this Chicago tax attorney rallied support among the smart partners of Jenkens & Gilchrist and challenged the law firm's current chairman for his job. Before this election even started, to everyone's surprise, the current chairman stepped aside and let this upstart have the plum job.

"What a coup it was! And the brilliant Chicago tax attorney was spared the chopping block. He could continue saving the clients of Jenkens & Gilchrist all that tax money. I just love a happy ending."

"And? What does that have to do with Hunton & Williams?" I asked.

Tarian held up a hand to indicate he wasn't finished. "The lawsuit brought by those few disgruntled clients of Jenkens & Gilchrist soon grew to over 1,400. That was a problem. A *big* problem. Something needed to be done.

"After a few years of lawsuits, the smart partners of Jenkens & Gilchrist realized all this litigation was costing time and money. It was bad for business. It consumed their lives. They had to find a way out of it. What they needed was a new scheme where other folks paid their angry clients while they chipped in very little. And wouldn't you know it, the smart partners of Jenkens & Gilchrist figured a way out of this mess. In January 2005, Jenkens & Gilchrist agreed to settle with the plaintiffs for about $81 million. However, the smart partners of Jenkens & Gilchrist would only pay $5.25 million—mere pocket change for a firm like this."

"Who else paid?" I asked.

"Oh, the insurers and other defendants, such as the Chicago tax attorney. But believe me, this brilliant settlement was *the* reason why the partners of Jenkens & Gilchrist were so smart."

I shook my head. "So justice never prevailed."

"Wait!" he said. "There's more. Another storm was brewing. The new upstart chairman was up for reelection. Many lawyers at the firm were unhappy with him and the way things were going. He faced a formidable opponent. A challenge like this at any law firm is rare. It splits up the firm. Many firms dissolve after a fight like this. But it happened anyway.

"The two candidates campaigned hard. Partner against partner. Friend against friend. Rolex against Rolex. It was brutal. After a thoroughly bruising battle, the upstart beat back the challenger and won a second term. But no sooner had the confetti hit the floor than the shit hit the fan. The firm was badly divided. The chairman might have won the election, but the partners who didn't vote for him knew they'd be screwed in the yearly compensation battles. Dozens of attorneys were getting ready to defect to other law firms. In minutes, Jenkens & Gilchrist would be a shell of its former self.

"To stop them from jumping ship, one of the firm's senior partners, a brave man, talked to all the attorneys and asked them if they would stay if someone else were chairman. This was treason, going behind the victor's back and trying to undo a fair and square election. Yet this brave man pushed on."

"Did it work?" I asked, now fully absorbed in this long and winding tale.

"This brave, smart partner, who had been talking to the partners behind the chairman's back, picked up the phone two days after the vote, and called the chairman. Exhausted from the near-death match, the chairman was taking a much-needed vacation, but was happy to talk to this brave, smart partner, a man he ruled over.

"After some small talk, this brave, smart partner bluntly told the chairman that lawyers in the firm were leaving. The organization would be downsizing. Instead of the firm being a stretch limousine, it would now be a Volkswagen Beetle. Calmly and professionally, he told the chairman that the end had come, that he needed to resign to save the firm. And do you know the name of the smart partner who made that call?"

"How would I know that?" I was suddenly confused.

"Because he was none other than your most favorite lawyer, Tom Cantrill."

"Are you serious?" I gasped.

Tarian grinned like a Cheshire cat. "I am. The very next day, as the losing partners packed up their stuff to quit, the reelected chairman formally resigned, and a new chairman was selected, a man who had not run for the job. Who do you suppose this was?"

"I don't know," I said, holding my breath.

"The smart partner of Jenkens & Gilchrist, who had just climbed to the top without firing a shot, was none other than Tom Cantrill."

I slapped the table hard. "Are you kidding me?!"

"I'm not," Tarian said. "Tom Cantrill was now chairman of the formerly highly prestigious law firm of Jenkens & Gilchrist. Thus, he was smart. Very smart. Of course, waiting on the other side of victory was the Justice Department. But their special agents and lawyers were not as smart as the smart partners of Jenkens & Gilchrist. If they had been, they would've been working for Jenkens & Gilchrist and pulling down all that cash. But the special agents and lawyers at the Justice Department had two things on their side: persistence and facts. In the hands of dedicated people, those can be powerful weapons.

"As time ticked by, Jenkens & Gilchrist fought both the IRS and the Justice Department. Things looked bad. Despite the capable leadership of Chairman Tom Cantrill, lawyers began slipping out to other firms. With not enough new lawyers coming in, the firm's numbers dwindled. Jenkens & Gilchrist was a sinking ship.

"In March of 2007, the remaining smart partners of Jenkens & Gilchrist agreed to a non-prosecution deal with the U.S. Attorneys' Office. They also agreed to pay the IRS a $76 million penalty. It turned out all those letters generated by that brilliant Chicago tax attorney were worthless. They created nothing but abusive tax shelters with no real business purpose. In short, they were a complete fraud. And as a result, over $7 billion in tax revenue had been sucked out from the government's coffers."

"Whatever happened to that tax attorney?" I asked.

"It was reported that he had raked in $95 million in fees while paying only $8,000 in taxes himself. Sadly, he was indicted with other lawyers and accountants. A jury of common folk convicted him, and a judge sentenced the formerly brilliant attorney to fifteen years in prison and forfeiture of over $164 million."

"He had to give back $164 million?"

"Yes. I told you, being a lawyer pays. And think of all the smart partners of Jenkens & Gilchrist who got to keep their money. What a great country."

"But what happened to Jenkens & Gilchrist?"

"As part of the agreement with the Justice Department, the smart partners of Jenkens & Gilchrist agreed to close their doors permanently. On Saturday, March 31, 2007, they closed the main office in Dallas for good. Jenkens & Gilchrist was no more."

"How come Tom Cantrill is still on the same floor as when I hired him to prepare my will?"

"Ah, because the former partners of Jenkens & Gilchrist were still smart. Two days after closing their doors forever, they flung them open again as part of a new firm, one expanding into Dallas. Can you guess that name?"

"Hunton & Williams," I moaned.

"Bingo! Now, they are the smart partners of Hunton & Williams. Pretty slick. You see, lawyers aren't such bad businesspeople after all. And I don't know if Tom Cantrill even had to change his office. All's well that ends well."

The food arrived just as Tarian finished his story. It was perfect timing. Unfortunately, I'd lost my appetite.

Chapter Twenty-Seven

*"The goal of cross-selling is to better and more completely
serve customers' needs and help them realize their goals
in ways that save them time, money, and aggravation."*
—Jamie Dimon, Chairman & CEO
JPMorgan Chase Bank, N. A.
Letter to the Shareholders 2010 Annual Report

The deposition carousel continued. Betty was the next victim. She underwent a six-hour grilling.

Lenny Vitullo was back in the captain's seat, ready to inflict damage. After slicking back his jet-black hair, he wasted no time going hard after her. He questioned her about hidden assets and executed wills that were still missing (ones that would only give his clients less money). He interrogated her about my boyfriend, Jack Hooper. Lenny wanted to know when we visited each other and what we did. Betty answered most of the questions with a yes or no. Sometimes she used the Novak/Cantrill tactic of "I don't recall."

Soon into the show, Lenny hit a speed bump when he quizzed Betty about what she had done for American Airlines.

Lenny: And what was your position at American Airlines?

Betty: My last position was manager of passenger services at the Dallas/Fort Worth Airport.

Lenny: What is a manager of passenger services at the Dallas/Fort Worth Airport?

Betty: I was responsible for the daily operations of the passenger service part of the operation, the agents, the gate agents, the security checkpoints, the catering.

Lenny: Okay. My gosh. That's a tremendous responsibility. How long did you do that?

Betty: I believe I did that for about six years. Prior to that, I was manager of passenger services at Kennedy Airport, JFK.

Betty was no wallflower. She had thirty years of seniority at American Airlines. But Lenny was undeterred. He inquired about her two brothers, the clear implication that estate assets may have been funneled to them for hiding and safekeeping. For some reason, Lenny ignored her sisters.

In the end, Betty testified that she knew of no missing wills, hidden assets, or wrongdoing. But Lenny hadn't become the Han Solo of lawyers by being a slouch. He had brought his A-game. He carefully reviewed his stack of prepared questions for the next line of attack. Satisfied with a selection, he ran his fingers through his gelled hair, rubbed his hands together, and probed Max's sex life.

Lenny: Okay. Did you ever have a romantic relationship with Max Hopper?

Betty: No.

Lenny: Okay. And how would you describe your relationship with Max Hopper the year before Jo Hopper was married to him?

Betty: He was Jo's friend, he was Jo's boss. I knew him through Jo. He was my friend.

Lenny: Okay. All right. Did you and Jo Hopper ever discuss a book called "How to Marry a Millionaire"?

Betty: No.

Lenny: Did you and Jo Hopper ever discuss any type of relationship that you wanted to have with Max Hopper that may have been romantic in nature?

Betty: No.

Lenny: Did you and Jo Hopper ever have a friendly wager or a bet as to who would marry Max Hopper?

Betty: No.

For Lenny, it was a dry hole. So much for that angle. Yet the drilling continued. Here's a great snapshot of the shenanigans that go on in depositions.

Lenny: Okay. And did you review any documents in preparation for your deposition today?

Betty: Yes.

Lenny: And what were those documents?

ALAN: I instruct you not to answer.

Lenny: Pardon me?

ALAN: I instruct you not to answer that question.

Lenny: On what basis, counsel?

ALAN: Work product and attorney-client communication.

Lenny: You reviewed documents, correct?

Betty: I refuse to answer.

ALAN: You can tell him that you reviewed documents.

Betty: I did review documents.

Lenny: You reviewed documents in preparation for your deposition here today, correct?

Betty: Correct.

Lenny: Do you remember what those documents were, correct?

Betty: Yes.

Lenny: You're capable of identifying for us the documents you reviewed in preparation for your deposition, correct?

Betty: Yes.

Lenny: These documents that you reviewed in preparation for your deposition, they were given to you by your lawyer, correct?

Betty: Yes.

Lenny: Okay. And this is a lawyer that you don't know how he's being paid, correct?

Betty: Correct.

Lenny: All right. And you're capable of identifying the documents you reviewed in preparation for your deposition today, but you choose not to, based on the advice of Mr. Loewinsohn, correct?

Betty: Correct.

Lenny: Alan, why is that work product?

ALAN: Because it is. Case law says so.

Lenny: Do you have a case reference for me, because I have always—

ALAN: I'm good but not that good—

Lenny: Okay.

ALAN: —In terms of my memory.

Lenny: I thought you asked my client those questions.

ALAN: I did, and they chose to answer them, and there was no objection.

Ouch! Score a point for Alan.

Betty's deposition ended and Todd Baird was up to bat. Alan began.

Baird said he was the Managing Director of Investments at JPMorgan. He testified that he'd continued to ask me how Susan Novak and the Max Hopper Estate was going. He broke through JPMorgan's supposedly impenetrable Chinese Wall and told Susan to move faster. It didn't work.

Baird said this was his first deposition, but we could all see he was incredibly well-prepared. Eichman, who represented him, had done his job. In almost five hours of answering questions, Baird succeeded in giving us absolutely nothing. He won the gold medal, breaking the record for the most "I don't recalls" or "I don't remembers" in a single deposition—158. (The silver medal went to Susan Novak with 140. And Cantrill snagged the bronze with 139. Compare this to my two-day deposition where I said "I don't recall" five times.)

Another tactic Baird used to great effect was asking for the question to be repeated. This wasted valuable time, forcing Alan to reread each question. And it gave Baird time to think of an answer. He was smart. He used the phrase, "You know," 199 times. These words are typically fillers, allowing people time and space to compose their answers. It doesn't mean they're lying, just that they need more time.

Like Lenny, Alan was not easily put off the scent. He dug for information about cross-selling. He tried this way and that. I couldn't believe it but this Todd Baird fellow was unbreakable.

Baird spewed brilliant answers about how his and JPMorgan's mission in life was to help clients with their goals and objectives. All he wanted to do was help people. He was like the Red Cross, FEMA, and UNICEF all rolled into one. He wasn't in it for the money, just the satisfaction of a job well done.

Alan ripped out the email where JPMorgan employees virtually high-fived each other after landing the Max Hopper Estate, slapping it down in front of him. I figured that memo was the kitchen utensil needed to turn this guy into a bloomin' onion. Here's how it went:

Alan:	Why would it have been appropriate to describe it as "a terrific win for the bank" at the time?
Baird:	Well, because I think there was a real opportunity to help the families with their goals and objectives and trying to meet what the families were trying to do.

I'm not a lawyer, but Baird's deposition should be studied in law schools. This "goals and objectives" drivel was his go-to answer for anything touching on cross-selling or celebrating the bagging of a new client.

Throughout the deposition, Alan went back to this issue, trying to shake him off his game. We hoped for something like, "Look, we're like suppositories. We try to insert as many JPMorgan services as possible into each client so they'll crap out a steady stream of cash flow for us. We're no different than Wells Fargo. We just make it look like it's the client's idea." Unfortunately, Baird refused to go there. The man was a sheer wall of granite. Frankly, I had to tip my hat to Eichman. He wasn't Darth Vader for nothing.

One interesting tidbit we learned was that before taking a job at JPMorgan, Baird had worked for American Airlines Sabre Group for five years. He didn't know Max Hopper, though.

I also had to give it to Alan. He tried one last time to pry this oyster open, desperately hoping for a pearl we could use at trial.

Alan:	Did you have any communications, oral or written, with Ms. Novak about the fact that Mrs. Hopper was closing her accounts in 2011?
Baird:	I do not recall.
Alan:	Would there be any reason for you to be having communications with Ms. Novak on that topic if there was a Chinese Wall?
EICHMAN:	Objection, form.
Baird:	There may be—there may be reasons to communicate with her.
Alan:	Okay. And what would be the reasons?
Baird:	You know, I remember that she was—she was complaining. Jo was complaining about Susan, Susan was complaining that Jo was contacting her a lot, and so there was—there was—you know, I felt like I was caught

	in the middle and spent some time talking, you know, trying to—trying to—trying to figure out what was going on to make sure that everything was being done properly.
Alan:	And what were Mrs. Hopper's complaints about Susan Novak?
Baird:	That she wasn't very responsive.
Alan:	And Ms. Novak complained to you that Mrs. Hopper was contacting her a lot, correct?
Baird:	Correct.

We pounded and pounded and got nothing but sand from this guy. Alan finally gave up and passed the witness.

Lenny, who was tied up with Chewbacca in another galaxy, left Muckleroy of James Bell's office to have a go at Baird. He didn't get much either, except the allegation that I was high-maintenance.

Baird did add that JPMorgan lost money on the Max Hopper Estate. With the volume of clients that lawyers like Cantrill, Stolbach, and Round referred to JPMorgan, I couldn't understand how he could make that claim.

When the deposition was over, I was thrilled to see Baird walk out the door. He had managed to say "goals and objectives" 48 times. Sometimes, you just have to tip your cap and move on.

A few days later, the infamous Gary Stolbach sat in the victim's chair. Like Eichman and Baird, Stolbach's lawyer, Ronald Reneker, had thoroughly prepared him. So far, Stolbach was the best I'd seen at wasting time while avoiding answering any questions.

Stolbach began with his background. He had thirty-five years of experience in estate planning and probate matters. His firm Glast, Phillips & Murray had between 50 and 55 lawyers. While employed by the heirs, they had used 13 of them to work on this estate. That didn't include the four paralegals he said they loaded onto it. I could just imagine the size of their monthly bills.

A small tidbit we picked up had to do with Stanley Johanson. I had thought they hired him to produce an expert opinion. He had written an eight-page document titled "Expert Witness Report." Due to restrictions on presenting expert witnesses in probate hearings, they designated Johanson as their co-counsel in the matter. Since he hadn't withdrawn from the case, I guess he was still an attorney of record. Thus, he had lost the El Paso appeal so hopefully we could tag Johanson with a major jury loss in his chosen field.

Alan shifted gears and asked Stolbach about the heirs. I imaginarily clapped my hands as I sat there looking at him. This would be good.

Stolbach testified that Stephen and Laura were mad at the costs versus the results. Because of some friction there, the heirs and Stolbach's law firm had agreed to suspend the statute of limitations, giving the heirs more time to sue them. Due to the heirs' disappointment, Stolbach admitted that Glast, Phillips & Murray had notified their malpractice insurance carrier about a possible claim. He thickened the plot when he took a swing at the heirs.

Stolbach made it very clear that the heirs approved every position he took. Then, he admitted that the court of appeals had ruled against his clients but claimed he hadn't been given a fair chance. Stolbach said that the court of appeals had their hands tied because some of the appellate issues were moot due to the heirs' conveyance of the Robledo home to Quagmire, LLC.

What a clever move! The blame had been shifted to Stephen and Laura. Thanks to that ill-fated property transfer, the court of appeals could not rule on all the legal issues. This allowed Stolbach to say nobody knew what might have happened. The conveyance had likely saved Glast, Phillips & Murray from a malpractice suit and its own quagmire. Or maybe not.

Alan continued peppering Stolbach's head with questions before shifting to the body. He tried to get Stolbach to admit he was tight with JPMorgan, but Stolbach was crafty.

Alan moved into the area of working for JPMorgan.

Alan: Did you or your firm ever represent the bank in any
            capacity?
EICHMAN: Objection; form.
Stolbach: I expect that we did, yes.
Alan: Okay. And when did you, approximately?
Stolbach: Oh, I think from time to time over many years, we've—
            different lawyers with the firm have been asked to do
            work for JPMorgan.

Alan:	Okay. Well, first of all, have you ever represented the bank in any capacity?
Stolbach:	Yes.

Of course. These lawyers flipped back and forth between representing the bank, working for them on an estate, and sending them clients. But just when we thought we'd caught the lightning bug in a bottle, it disappeared with this testimony.

Alan:	And then what just happened in the interim two minutes that caused you to now change your sworn testimony and say you haven't represented the bank?
Stolbach:	I gave it further thought.
Alan:	What did you think about? What did you draw upon to cause you to change that testimony within a matter of two minutes?
Stolbach:	I'll explain it to you. When you first asked the question about whether I represented JPMorgan, my instinct was, yes, over the years, I would have definitely represented JPMorgan because I know people over there and I just have a—and I do work for different banks, and I would have thought that I did represent JPMorgan and any of its predecessor banks, so that's why I answered in the affirmative. Then when you asked me to recall specific representations and the most recent ones, none came to mind, so I can't recall.
Alan:	Well, so which is it, Mr. Stolbach? You're telling the jury under oath you've never represented the bank or are you telling the jury under oath you can't recall whether or not you represented the bank?
Stolbach:	I think I'm answering your question, but let me answer it again. My sense of it would have been that I would have represented the bank, but I cannot recall specific representations of the bank.
Alan:	Who at your firm can you tell the jury in fact has represented the bank?
EICHMAN:	Objection; form.

Stolbach:	I can't give you specific examples, except that I would have thought that, you know, with eight estate lawyers, that we would have had representations of JPMorgan.
Alan:	Are you able to remember other banks you've represented?
Stolbach:	Yes.
Alan:	Is there some reason you remember them but you can't remember whether or not you represented this very, very large bank?
Stolbach:	Well, the size of the bank doesn't really—the size of the bank reflects itself on whether I'm going to remember.
Alan:	You're telling the jury that the fact that you may or may not have represented one of the largest banks in the world wouldn't cause you to maybe remember them as a client?
Stolbach:	Apparently.

Stolbach went on to list the names of people he knew at JPMorgan before Alan sprung the trap.

Alan:	Isn't the truth, sir, you worked with Ms. Novak on the Galland, G-A-L-L-A-N-D, Estate?
Stolbach:	Yes.
Alan:	Just something you completely forgot?
Stolbach:	That's right.
Alan:	What was the Galland Estate?
Stolbach:	It was the administration of a decedent's estate. The decedent was named Galland.
Alan:	And whom were you representing in that matter, sir?
Stolbach:	JPMorgan.
Alan:	And whom were you working with at JPMorgan on that matter?
Stolbach:	I believe it was Susan Novak.
Alan:	And when were you working representing JPMorgan where Ms. Novak was the principal person at the bank on behalf of that estate? When was that representation?
Stolbach:	I'm going to be doing a little guessing. I just don't recall the exact time. But maybe 2012, maybe 2010. I don't really recall.

Just four years ago and he'd already forgotten.

During the deposition, Stolbach's attorney objected and fought over almost every question. Alan had his hands full with Reneker because Stolbach refused to provide information, claiming it was attorney-client privileged.

Eichman fiercely objected, too. Despite Alan's and Eichman's repeated promise to go into court to make Stolbach answer the questions, nothing ever happened. They just let it go. I sure hoped Alan knew what he was doing.

DURING THE HOT month of June, Max's tree started producing peaches. They were delicious. At least something worked in my life. Millie didn't like peaches, but she loved hanging out under that tree. It gave her a much-needed break from tending to her puppies.

At the end of June, the puppies were old enough to go back to Operation Kindness. They had all survived and were spread out to various foster parents before being adopted by loving families.

As for Millie, my time as a foster parent was up. I was required to return her to Operation Kindness. She seemed to know it was coming. The day I brought her back, she was very needy. We hung out all day together. When it was time, I took her for one final walk.

At the building, they unhooked her leash. Millie looked up sorrowfully at me before heading to her future—whatever that was. I could barely drive home through the river of tears. It hurt big time.

Waiting for me at my desk was both a voice message and an email from my financial advisor in San Francisco. Eichman had just sent him a massive subpoena for all documents known to man. It was another mountain I'd have to climb to get to trial.

After working for hours, I went to bed, but it was hard. I tossed and turned, thinking about Millie. We had grown so close. When the tears returned, I clicked on the light and dressed, going downstairs to sit under Max's peach tree by the moonlight. It was quiet and still. I just sat there, breathing deeply and thinking.

And crying.

I couldn't get Millie out of my mind. I looked at my watch. It was three in the morning. Operation Kindness didn't open until eight. I had five hours to get Millie back. But would I be too late?

Chapter Twenty-Eight

So who owns who? Which way can it be?
Do I own you? Or you own me?
Whoever owns who, it matters not.
Together we two, are all that we got.
—*Are You My Hound?* By Jack Hooper

I drove up to the office of Operation Kindness, but it wasn't open yet. Hoping Millie was still inside, I sat in my car and nursed a Starbucks.

I watched as an employee opened the door and went inside. Lights snapped on. Soon, another employee showed up. Then two more. When my cell phone displayed 8 a.m., I hustled in to the lobby.

"Oh," the girl said. "You're here bright and early. How can I help you?"

"I want to adopt a dog," I replied. "Her name is Millie."

The girl looked at a list. "The pit bull mix?"

"Yes," I said, my voice cracking. "I've been fostering her."

"Okay, let me see if she's still here."

My heart sank. "I brought her in yesterday afternoon," I said as she turned to leave. "Would she already be—*gone*?"

The girl smiled. "I was off yesterday. Let me check."

I fidgeted as I watched the girl disappear. I paced back and forth. When she was gone for more than five minutes, I was beside myself. This was getting bad.

She eventually appeared down the hall, but she was standing there talking to someone. She nodded, then shook her head. My anxiety increased. I wanted to charge back there and get some answers. Finally, the girl turned toward me and walked to the counter.

She smiled. "It seems that Millie is available! Could I have you fill out some papers?"

"Of course," I said, barely able to catch my breath.

"And there will be an adoption fee," she added.

I nodded, trying not to laugh inside. My latest legal bill was $139,000. *What're a few more dollars between me and man's best friend?*

The paperwork took fifteen excruciatingly long minutes. When we were finished and the money collected, Millie was led out on a leash. She was thrilled to see me. I dropped to my knees and hugged her hard. But not for too long. I needed to get her outside and loaded in my Volkswagen Beetle before they decided there had been an error. I wasn't taking any chances.

As soon as we hit the house, Millie and I ran to the backyard. We celebrated by having breakfast under the peach tree, she with her expensive dog food and me with my mug of oatmeal and a thick slab of toast with peach jam smeared all over it.

After she finished her kibble, I gave her a rawhide chew. With the chew firmly in her mouth and my hand draped over her, all was right with the world. For one moment, yes indeed, all was perfect in my life.

But just as quickly, the moment was gone, and it was back to work.

FIRST ON MY list of things to do was organizing the mountain of paper that my financial advisor had produced under the subpoena. By going through each document, I was able to tell Alan which ones would be responsive to JPMorgan's request. We (mostly me) worked for five days, fourteen hours a day, to whittle down the tens of thousands of documents to 400. We tendered them by the subpoena's deadline, subject to Alan's various objections.

Before I could take a breath, Alan called to talk about Susan Novak. In early June 2016, we had filed a motion to obtain a second deposition from Susan after she'd refused to answer ten separate questions. It had been contentious. In response to Alan's motion, Eichman fired off a stinging thirty-eight-page response with attachments.

Thirty-eight pages!

It took me all day just to write one page. How long would it take lawyers for JPMorgan charging $650 an hour to put together a coherent thirty-eight-page document?

Each filing, briefing, and motion were pages and pages, sometimes in the hundreds. For each filing, a lawyer had to research it, a lawyer had to draft it, and a lawyer had to proofread it. Once it was faxed or emailed, the other side had to spend hours reading it, assessing it, and discussing it before filing a response. The cycle never stopped.

"So, Jo," Alan said, "we've looked at their response and set that against what we need to get from Susan. We think the juice is not worth the squeeze."

"What does that mean?" I asked.

"It means we might win the motion and get everything we want. But the likely outcome is that we can only ask a few carefully worded questions of her. She will certainly have prepared answers for them since she'll know the questions in advance. Strategy-wise, we already have a nice, freshly squeezed glass of orange juice from her deposition. Why waste our resources fighting this?"

"I guess Susan doesn't want to answer more questions. Is that it?"

"Yep. And Eichman decided to put a ton of resources into protecting her."

"This is the same woman who decides which lawyer or law firm gets to represent future estates and bill all that money?"

Alan chuckled. "Now you truly get it."

"Yeah, I get it." *We just spent at least $15,000 filing a motion and reviewing Eichman's response for nothing.* I guess Eichman could have dropped the ball and not filed an answer, but what were the odds of that happening?

"And another thing," Alan said. "We just received a document about Susan Novak's boss."

"You mean Wendy Bessette?"

"That *was* Susan's boss. It's now Debra Round."

I let out a brief scream. "The one whose husband steered Stephen and Laura to JPMorgan?"

"Yep. It appears she's moved up. So has Wendy Bessette."

I shook my head. "I guess the cream rises to the top. They wouldn't be promoted unless they were doing exactly what Jamie Dimon wanted and making the bank money."

I hung up the phone, gritting my teeth. The world did not work the way I'd thought it did. Not even close. It was like a giant lake of money in the mountains. The money flowed down thousands of different streams. To do business and survive in this world, you had to understand where each one flowed and who dipped their pail into which stream. Max had understood this game. But keeping up with it was too much for me.

Later that day, Alan withdrew our motion, and that was that. Susan Novak would not have to answer any more questions until trial.

A FEW DAYS later, I found some spare time. First on my list was reviewing yet another lawsuit involving JPMorgan Chase as a trustee. It had all started with the STS Trust case. That had led me down a rabbit hole to the Patricia Burns Clark Dailey Trust lawsuit. Documents in that case had led to the MOSH Trust case. Then the MOSH file pointed to the Johnny Fisher lawsuit. I fired up the computer and decided now was the time to review it. With Millie's rawhide chew long gone, she seemed content to nap a few feet away. As the sun streamed through my window, I took a deep breath and inhaled the publicly-filed court documents. Here was the story, according to the plaintiff.

In 1987, the Fort Worth Osteopathic Hospital decided to self-insure. They put $4 million into a trust and made Texas American Bank the trustee. If anyone sued the hospital for malpractice, the $4 million would cover the attorneys' fees and any settlements. If the claim exceeded that, a $25 million excess liability policy would step in and make it right. JPMorgan eventually acquired Texas American Bank and became the trustee for the hospital.

In 1999, a young man needed cervical disk surgery. His name was Johnny Fisher. Due to complications from the surgery, Johnny died a few weeks later. An autopsy showed that both the surgeon and the hospital might be liable. In 2001, the Estate of Johnny Fisher filed suit against the surgeon and the hospital.

Upon responding to the lawsuit, the hospital assured the Estate of Johnny Fisher that if they succeeded, there was at least $4 million in the trust plus the $25 million insurance policy to pay their claim. The estate settled with the surgeon and then discovered the hospital had filed bankruptcy. The estate's lawyer, EL Atkins, obtained the bankruptcy filings and was shocked to learn that the trust had only $20,000. Somehow, the trust account had been drained!

Eventually, the estate obtained a $975,000 judgment against the hospital, but they still needed to be paid. Attorney Atkins filed suit against JPMorgan Chase in state court for breach of fiduciary duty, bad faith, and several other claims. The lawsuit alleged that JPMorgan, acting as trustee, had allowed the trust to be drained to pay the hospital's general operating expenses, in total violation of the trust agreement. Once again, where JPMorgan was supposed to be the hero and prevent this conduct, the plaintiff alleged they had been anything but.

With a lawsuit slapped on their desk, JPMorgan fired up their usual litigation tactics. Despite having branches and buildings all over Texas, the bank claimed they were really from Ohio and not a resident of Texas like Johnny Fisher had been. This allowed the bank to go to federal court on diversity grounds, since the parties on either side were from different states, with the plaintiff from Texas and the defendant (supposedly) from Ohio.

Yet attorney Atkins wasn't stupid. He'd seen this tactic before. When he sued JPMorgan, he also sued four local employees of the hospital. And they most definitely were residents of Texas. This should've easily stopped the removal tactic (meaning the transfer of a civil action from state to federal court) in its tracks, since there were Texas residents on both sides of the lawsuit. But it didn't.

During the removal hearing in federal bankruptcy court, Judge D. Michael Lynn queried JPMorgan's attorney, Jeffrey G. Hamilton, with Jackson Walker LLP.

Judge Lynn: Why are you uncomfortable not being there [state court], as opposed to comfortable being here [federal court]? Why are you not comfortable there?

Hamilton: I think that we get a better hearing in federal court. There is certainly some merit to the conventional wisdom that parties sometimes get a better hearing in federal court. And, again, we are certainly comfortable being in front of this Court."

That infamous light bulb went off in my head again. I had seen this same federal removal tactic in the STS Trust and the Burns Clark Dailey Trust litigation. I called Tarian and he told me this tactic delayed the case for maybe a year. It also ran up the costs for the other side. He explained that there were almost no plaintiff's attorneys on the federal bench so defendants had a better chance of having their cases dismissed by federal judges than by state judges. No wonder defendants were more comfortable in federal court.

On the Fisher case, federal judge Jane Boyle looked at this removal issue and sent the case back to state court. Of course, JPMorgan's tactic took over a year and gobs of money from the plaintiff. Since Judge Boyle refused to grant Fisher's motions for attorneys' fees and punish JPMorgan with sanctions, the bank suffered no consequences for the move and the Fisher Estate had to eat the litigation costs.

Yet, like Freddy Krueger, Chucky, and vampires, JPMorgan's removal tactic would not die. That's because JPMorgan filed for a rehearing. This wasted more time and money. Again, Judge Jane Boyle eventually denied JPMorgan.

Back in state court, JPMorgan objected to every discovery request. When the estate served a deposition notice, JPMorgan responded with a 57-page motion to quash it. Then the bank filed a 410-page motion for summary judgment causing attorney Atkins to file a 483-page response (including exhibits). Most novels aren't that long.

Once again, I noticed the appearance of Susan Kravik as in-house legal counsel to JPMorgan. She was everywhere.

In 2014, *fifteen years* after Johnny Fisher's death, the case finally settled, as evidenced by the filing of an Agreed Order of Dismissal with Prejudice signed by all parties.

Another day, another NDA.

I wondered if Jamie Dimon thought his bank had done the right thing in this matter.

THE SUMMER OF depositions finished up with one final blitz of experts. The only way I survived was by concentrating on the word "October" written on my desk. Four months away, and I would finally have my day in court.

At the depo-pallooza, Lenny Vitullo testified for the heirs that every penny they had spent was justified, and every penny JPMorgan and I had forked over was wasted. To bolster his claims, Lenny added Jerry Jones to his team as an attorney-fees expert. When I learned that, it made complete sense. Mr. Jones was the owner of the Dallas Cowboys football team and a wildly successful businessman. Surely, no one on the planet knew more about paying outrageous attorneys' fees than him.

Max had watched a lot of football. So did Jack. Living in Dallas, Mr. Jones was all over TV. For once, I was genuinely excited about a deposition. I wanted to see *the* Jerry Jones in person, even if he was on the other side. I brought my autograph book just in case he wanted to sign it. After all, he was an A-list celebrity, at least here in Texas. So, it's no surprise that I was sorely disappointed when he didn't appear. Instead, a lawyer from Ikard, Golden and *Jones,* P.C. in Austin, Texas, took his place. Apparently, there was more than one Texan named Jerry Jones.

Oops!

JPMorgan had their stable of experts, too. They designated Mark Sales, Michael Bourland, Lois Ann Stanton, and John Eichman to testify about attorneys' fees, mental anguish, and fiduciary duty. The only difference between their testimony and Lenny's was that they claimed JPMorgan had spent righteously, even though JPMorgan's costs for three expert witnesses exceeded $500,000. Of course, they also said the heirs and I had not spent wisely.

We were not to be outdone. Alan and our expert followed the same script as the others, testifying that my fees were completely justified and everyone else's were not.

I watched all this in wonder. Such bright lawyers with polar opposite opinions. How was this possible? How was this legal? It was time for a visit to the wise old oracle of Dallas.

We met at Pho Bidden, which had been renamed Kung Pho. "It's still great food," Tarian said sheepishly. "If they could just get the name right, they'd take off."

"Their loss is our gain," I joked, scanning the mostly empty restaurant.

After we ordered, I got down to business. "How do expert witnesses work? Each one has the exact opposite opinion as the other one. They can't all be right. So how does this happen?"

"Whoa, tigress. That's a mouthful," Tarian said, smoothing back what was left of his hair. "Let's start at the beginning. First, you would agree that we put the best and brightest legal minds on the U.S. Supreme Court. Right?"

"Sure. They wouldn't be there otherwise." I was confused at this change of subject.

"Exactly. So, let me read this." He pulled a notepad from his pocket. "Remember when I read this, that Scott is a Black man."

"Okay," I nodded. "Scott is a Black man. Got it."

"Here goes." He cleared his throat. "'We are satisfied, upon a careful examination of all the cases decided in the state courts of Missouri referred to, that it is now firmly settled by the decisions of the highest court in the state, that Scott and his family upon their return were not free, but were, by the laws of Missouri, the property of the defendant; and that the Circuit Court of the United States had no jurisdiction, when, by the laws of the State, the plaintiff was a slave, and not a citizen.' What do you think about that statement from the Supreme Court?"

"When was that?" I asked.

"Eighteen fifty-seven. Dred Scott sued for his freedom because he was in a free state. Seven of the nine Supreme Court Justices—our best and brightest—denied him that freedom. Dred Scott was a slave because, under the Constitution, Black people could never become citizens. That's what the justices said. Shocking, isn't it?"

"Horrific," I replied.

"Here's another one. A man, seven-eighths White and one-eighth Black, took a seat in a railcar reserved for Whites. He was arrested and convicted of sitting in the wrong car. It went to the Supreme Court. Here's what seven out of eight justices wrote:

"We cannot say that a law which authorizes or even requires the separation of the two races in public conveyances is unreasonable, or more obnoxious to the fourteenth amendment than the acts of Congress requiring separate schools for colored children in the District of Columbia, the constitutionality of which does not seem to have been questioned, or the corresponding acts of state legislatures...

We consider the underlying fallacy of the plaintiff's argument to consist in the assumption that the enforced separation of the two races stamps the colored race with a badge of inferiority... It is true that the question of the proportion of colored blood necessary to constitute a colored person, as distinguished from a white person, is one upon which there is a difference of opinion in the different states; some holding that any visible admixture of black blood stamps the person as belonging to the colored race; others, that it depends upon the preponderance of blood; and still others, that the predominance of white blood must only be in the proportion of three-fourths. But these are questions to be determined under the laws of each state, and are not properly put in issue in this case."

"Even more outrageous. Right?"

I was dumbfounded. "A Supreme Court justice wrote that?"

"No. Not *a* justice, but seven of them. This case allowed the separate but equal concept to become the law of the land. Black people could be separated from White people, with their own restrooms, water fountains, and railcars. And even today, this case, *Plessy vs. Ferguson*, has never been explicitly overruled by the Supreme Court. So this is what the best and the brightest have done to us—slaves have no rights because they can never be citizens, and Black people can be separated from Whites. It never stops."

"But what does the Supreme Court have to do with my case?" I asked.

"If the best and brightest go to the Supreme Court and turn out that kind of crap, what do you think the best and brightest local lawyers do? They become experts. Do you think they're any better than a Supreme Court justice?"

"I don't know. But I guess a Supreme Court justice has a lot of power. Do the lawyers who become expert witnesses do it for power?"

"No! They do it for money. Pay me $20,000, and I'll say Gwyneth Paltrow and Brad Pitt are the ugliest people on the planet. For $50,000, I'll say Willie Wonka's Oompa Loompas are real. And for $100,000, I'll say the Oompa Loompas are the love children of Gwyneth Paltrow and Brad Pitt from when they lived at Chernobyl. After all, it's my opinion."

I sighed.

"Remember the probate expert, Mr. Johanson?" Tarian asked. "You've been bitching about him from Day One. Have you forgotten Stanley?"

"No. It's just that we've been getting hit with a blizzard of paperwork. My lawyer calls it 'oceans of motions.' I've been buried and can't think straight."

Tarian reached over and covered my hand. "That's because the trial is on the horizon. Deadlines are rapidly approaching. The lawyers are just now taking a hard look at their case and realizing how many questions they forgot to ask. This is where the big mistakes are made. They're handling dozens of other cases while trying to ensure they don't leave anything out in this one. It's maddening because 95% of all cases settle, so the feeling of laziness sets in. 'Why should I work so hard on this case when it will just settle?'

"That's where good lawyers pounce and expose all the evidence you forgot to disclose or supplement. Like when you failed to designate a particular exhibit. Or a certain expert witness. Or maybe update your attorneys' fees. In the fog of litigation, your entire case could go down in flames."

"Thanks for the pep talk. I'll keep that in mind. I just don't see why JPMorgan keeps hurting clients like Stephen and Laura and me."

Tarian looked around like someone might be listening. "Remember what I told you about the men who took your family's land? Why did they do it?"

"Because they could!" I exclaimed, much too loud.

"Exactly. Because they could. That's why JPMorgan via Eichman is hurting you. Because they can. And please don't forget about *Bleak House*. Those lawyers kept fighting until there was nothing left."

"I feel pretty confident JPMorgan will always have something left."

"I wasn't talking about JPMorgan. I was talking about you and your bank account."

That stopped me in my tracks. Financially, October couldn't get here fast enough.

AFTER A DOSE of Tarian reality, I returned to my desk and continued sorting documents. Buried under reams of paper in my inbox were my notes from Cantrill's deposition. During that deposition, Eichman claimed the heirs and I were on the same team and should be counted as one plaintiff for Cantrill's deposition. Thus a six-hour limit applied instead of a twelve-hour limit. Alan had used up five hours fifteen minutes. When the heirs' attorney took over and used up the remaining forty-five minutes, Eichman terminated the deposition. The heirs' attorney strenuously objected and filed a Motion to Compel Continuation of the Deposition of Tom Cantrill. He wrote:

"Mr. Eichman's assertion that Mrs. Hopper and the Heirs are on the same 'side' flies in the face of Texas law and six years of litigation. The Heirs have been antagonistic to Mrs. Hopper (personally, legally, or in both contexts) for nearly six years. Beginning with Max Hopper's sudden death in 2010, distrust marred the relationship between the Heirs and Mrs. Hopper. This uneasy relationship is precisely what prompted the Heirs to insist Max Hopper's estate be administered by a neutral, independent third party. That is what the Heirs believed the Bank to be when they engaged its services as independent administrator in 2010."

Ouch to JPMorgan and me.

In August, I received a new interrogatory from Lenny Vitullo. He wanted to know about every share of stock or stock option Max had and if there were any more. I leaned back and laughed. Six and a half years after Max died, and this was the first time anyone had ever asked that simple question. JPMorgan and Susan Novak had failed to ask it even though they had been charged with identifying and collecting all the assets.

Lenny's interrogatory was followed by a demand from JPMorgan that I produce copies of my passport. To minimize my mental anguish damages, they wanted to see where I had been during the last six years. They also wanted all photos from any trip outside of Texas or vacations I'd been on. I had over 90,000 pictures on my hard drive, mostly of quilts, flowers, and bugs. After Alan objected, I had to produce only those photos that showed my face. It took a full week to find those.

As we prepared for trial, JPMorgan filed a motion to designate Glast, Phillips & Murray, and Gary Stolbach as partly responsible for the damages to the heirs and me. This would allow the jury to fill in a percentage for their misconduct. For example, if Stolbach and his firm were found 40% responsible and JPMorgan was found 60% responsible, the bank's damage amount could be reduced by 40%. That assumed JPMorgan lost, of course.

To further bludgeon me into submission, JPMorgan filed a motion for summary judgment on my attorneys' fees and mental anguish claims. This made Alan and his firm work especially hard. A motion for summary judgment basically says the facts are undisputed and the law is clear. Thus, there is no need for a jury to decide the issue. Eichman's motion created a massive level of anxiety. If we lost, the case would effectively be over.

We filed our own motion for summary judgment to declare the contract unambiguous and that I owed nothing to JPMorgan relating to the estate's attorneys' fees or other outside professionals. I couldn't understand why we hadn't filed it in 2011 and get a ruling then. It would have saved a ton of money.

Once we received Eichman's response to our motion, Alan and I met to discuss the evolving theories put forth by JPMorgan as to why I owed attorneys' fees for administering the estate. I put together a timeline of relevant events:

1. In 2010, Kal Grant told me I would not pay one cent to administer the estate.
2. The agreement I signed in 2010 with JPMorgan stated "Attorney fees, as well as charges by other outside professionals, are an expense of the estate and are in addition to our Estate Settlement fees."
3. In June 2011, I received copies of Hunton & Williams legal bills showing allocation percentages of the estate's attorneys' fees to me. This was the first time I knew JPMorgan planned to charge me.
4. Tom Cantrill stated in his deposition that Exhibit 7 - Hopper Heirs' Bank Agreement did not apply to me. Instead, JPMorgan would be going to court for a judgment allocating a percentage of the estate's attorneys' fees to me.
5. John Eichman, in response to our summary judgment motion, agreed Exhibit 7 is unambiguous when it states that I don't owe the fees. However, I had "waived" that issue in June 2011 when I emailed Cantrill regarding a math error he'd made on one of the bills.

According to JPMorgan, my simple act of pointing out a math error in a legal invoice made me liable for the attorneys' fees. When you go up against Jamie Dimon and JPMorgan, this is what you get.

Once we finished discussing that issue, Alan moved on to another subject. "We talked with our jury consultant, and he has a good suggestion."

After the heirs beat me to Stanley Johanson, I was determined to beat them and JPMorgan to the best experts in the other areas. Trey Cox was our expert on attorneys' fees. He had literally written the book on the subject: *How to Recover Attorneys' Fees in Texas*. For a hefty price, Trey would testify for me. And Robert Hirschhorn, a jury consultant, was also added to my stable of thoroughbreds.

Robert had successfully worked on all the top cases in the country. Cases like the *State of Florida v. William Kennedy Smith*, the *State of Texas v. U.S. Senator Kay Bailey Hutchison*, and the *State of Texas v. Robert Durst*. When lawyers opened up their legal dictionaries and saw the words "expert jury consultant," a photo of Robert Hirschhorn stared back at them. Now, he worked for me.

"What's Robert's suggestion?" I asked, ready to say yes.

"He wants to hold a mock jury trial. It will cost around $27,000. Are you game for that?"

"Sure," I replied. *In for a penny, in for a million.*

"Good," Alan said. "But he doesn't want you there. He finds it goes better when the jurors don't see your reactions to various themes we are trying out. And he doesn't want you thinking about their responses when you testify at trial. If you insist on being there, you're welcome, of course."

"No, I'll stay home. You can fill me in later." I had too much to do, anyway.

Alan and Robert put the mock jury trial together very quickly. While it was happening, I sifted through the stack of documents on my desk. Among the 2,000 documents, I spotted an order signed by Judge Thompson. The trial was scheduled for October 17, 2016, at 9:30 a.m. However, she had ordered another mediation. So I would have to shell out for another worthless day of nothing. I talked to Alan about getting out of it, but we decided just to go.

While I sat in the mediation, I read an article by USLegalWills.com. It claimed 63% of Americans don't have a will. Another 9% had wills that were out of date. I wish Max had read something like this. Maybe things would have been different.

Or maybe not.

As expected, we failed to settle in mediation. When I arrived home afterwards, Millie came up to my leg, demanding attention. I got down on the floor and rolled around with her. She didn't know about lawsuits or legal bills. All she cared about was me and having my attention.

Even though it was late, I decided she needed a good walk. I needed one too. My doctor had warned me to watch my health. If I got sick and died, no one would be left to make sure JPMorgan paid for all the damage they had caused. I was determined to stay alive if only to make them pay. At least it was motivation to break a sweat. How could that be bad?

DAYS LATER, MY cell phone rang. "I have the results of the mock jury," Alan said. "Do you want to discuss it?"

"Sure," I replied.

Alan explained they'd assembled thirty-six juror participants. This created six juries of six. Alan played his role. Jim Flegle played Eichman. Other attorneys from their office played Lenny and James Bell. Alan had videotaped me as if I was on the stand, answering both direct and cross-examination questions. Robert wanted the mock jury to see me and my responses.

"The good news," Alan said, "was that all the jurors found for you. Several jurors wondered if we were being paid on contingency versus by the hour. We told them by the hour. They wanted to see the canceled checks. So, we need you to collect every check you paid to an attorney or expert witness or anyone else. We need to supplement our discovery."

I shuddered. Six and half years of checks! That was a ton of work. "Sure," I said. "What else?"

"The jurors didn't like or understand the dynamics of the three-cornered hat."

"What is that?" I asked, mystified by his terminology.

"That's when you're firing a gun at JPMorgan to your right and the heirs to your left. JPMorgan is shooting at you to their left and the heirs to their right. The heirs are shooting at you on their right and JPMorgan on their left. If everyone fired their guns, you'd all be dead. That's what JPMorgan is counting on. If everyone dies, no one wins. They'll let you shoot out each other's hearts while they finish off the survivor."

"So what are you saying?"

"We settle with Stephen and Laura." Alan let that hang there.

"You've got to be kidding!" I yelled into the phone.

"Robert fully agrees with this strategy. He was there. And the heirs would have to pay for the attorneys' fees they caused you to spend."

"Oh, Alan," I cried, "they'll never sign an agreement. They couldn't make decisions before. Why would they be able to now?"

"Jo, come on. Let me try. We have tight deadlines. We must make it happen quickly, or it won't happen at all."

I hung my head and sighed. "Oh, all right. But don't waste too much money chasing them."

I felt sick as I tried rationalizing this new development. It was true that if JPMorgan had done their job, we would have been done quickly no matter what Stephen and Laura did. JPMorgan was supposed to be the expert, the adult in the room. If this held them accountable, I guess it was for the best. I just hoped the heirs saw the same wisdom.

But what were the odds?

Several hours after Alan's call, my computer dinged. I pulled up the email from Kerry, Alan's associate lawyer. Judge Thompson's courtroom was located in an old civil courts building that was undergoing extensive renovation. All the courts in that building had been moved to other buildings around Dallas. Judge Thompson's courtroom had moved to the Renaissance Tower, an office building several blocks from the courthouse downtown. We had been attending hearings there.

Kerry told me the judge's temporary courtroom was being remodeled to add a jury deliberation room and other spaces. Since the government was handling the remodeling work, it would likely take several years. Thus, Kerry had the unfortunate task of telling me that the trial in October would be moved. To when? She didn't know.

She was so sorry, but I'd have to wait to get my day in court.

I fell out of the chair onto the floor and cried, pounding the carpet with my fists. Millie came running, concerned that I was being harmed. I ignored her. All I could do was wail. This justice system was a total joke. No wonder people killed themselves. There was no end to it.

I looked around the room, wondering how hard it would be to use one of Jack's guns to kill myself.

.

Chapter Twenty-Nine

"Chase Private Client started as a gleam in our eye back in 2010. Chase Private Client branches are dedicated to serving our affluent clients' investment needs."

—Jamie Dimon, Chairman & CEO
JPMorgan Chase Bank, N.A.
Letter to the Shareholders 2014 Annual Report

As I was pondering ending my life, Jack walked in. He had just returned from Nashville. I told him how upset I was and he comforted me. I knew I needed help, but if I saw a professional, I'd have to disclose it to the other side. God only knows what they would do with my private thoughts and fears. I decided to self-medicate with Jack and Millie, and not necessarily in that order.

The next morning, I was barely awake when Alan called. "Jo, we've finally reached an agreement with the heirs. I want to go over it with you. I'm here with Jim and Kerry. Are you ready?"

"Yes," I said groggily.

"I know you're disappointed with the trial moving to January. But that's just three more months. We can accomplish a lot during that time. At least we can join forces with the heirs and make JPMorgan pay for what they've done to all of you."

I said nothing.

"The deal I've cut is a hi-lo arrangement. The most the heirs will pay you is $1.5 million. They're capped at that figure. The minimum they must pay is $300,000. Do you understand?"

"So, we're still going against the heirs. Right?"

"Yes, although we'll be jointly attacking JPMorgan. But since the most we can gain is an extra $1.2 million, and the fact that whatever we recover from Stephen and Laura will be deducted from any award from JPMorgan, essentially, we have joined forces."

"And all that back and forth over the wine, golf clubs, furnishings, and my home, they'll probably pay $150,000 each?"

"Yes," Alan replied confidently.

"I don't know, Alan."

"Well, everyone at this table likes this deal. Robert Hirschhorn likes this deal. Everything the heirs did was the fault of JPMorgan. The probate should've been completed by the end of 2010."

I remained silent.

"Jo, JPMorgan was the expert here. They assured you of that fact before you hired them. They were supposed to fix your brakes. Just because you and the heirs were arguing with each other inside the car doesn't relieve them of the liability when your brakes failed and you slammed into the back of that semi. All three of you were hurt. They owe you for the damage."

I listened for a while about the agreement but tuned most of it out. At some point, I finished the call and pulled down all my homemade signs that read October 17, 2016, replacing them with January 9, 2017. Then, I took Millie on a long walk and tried to convince myself that Alan, Jim, Kerry, and Robert knew what they were doing. I was betting the remainder of my life savings on them.

AFTER A FEW days of moping around, I slapped myself out of it. Tarian helped. He loved the strategy of the agreement. But he would've taken it further.

"Too many questions for the jury are bad," he said. "Anytime you're pointing fingers at each other, JPMorgan is smiling. I would've settled for $300,000 or some other number and be done with it. But I like the tag-team effect that allows you and the heirs your own time for opening statements and arguments. You'll understand that advantage at trial."

As for the trial date, Tarian offered this. "It was going to move, anyway. With all the motions filed, there was no way a judge could get to it in time unless she removed all the other cases from her docket. And that was never going to happen. Just sit down at your desk and get back to work. And check your email. I sent you something to cheer you up."

I grabbed a Starbucks, making it a double shot, and came back home, where I read his email. It was an article in the *Guardian* that detailed how JPMorgan had just made some changes to their private banking department. To have a private banker handle your affairs, JPMorgan raised the minimum you had to have on deposit from $5 million to $10 million. The article said $9.5 million was no longer enough. You'd better scrounge up an additional $500,000. It read:

> "JPMorgan's move was partly aimed at convincing clients to shift any assets they might be stubbornly holding at other banks, bringing them up above the $10M threshold... A sign of just how ruthless they have become is that JPMorgan's new rule even applies to the corporate lawyers with whom its investment bankers work closely on big deals. Until now, access to private banking programs have been among the perks offered to lawyers at firms like Skadden, Arps, Slate, Meagher & Flom; now, the word is that they, too, will be shut out from this special treatment."

When you cut your own attorneys out from exclusive deals, you know the world is changing.

Right next to the *Guardian* article was one from the *Wall Street Journal* titled "JPMorgan Culls Wealthy Herd." It added this:

> "In addition to the layoffs that have already taken place, J.P. Morgan's private bank late last year began putting more of its employees on performance-improvement plans, with the threat of layoffs for those who don't meet certain goals, according to people familiar with the matter."

In the last ten years, private banking departments have taken off. The idea was to provide first-class service to the rich. Besides sitting in an expensive chair in front of an even more expensive desk while a well-dressed banker doles out cash to you, some private banks walk your dog, snag you tickets to major events, invite you to hear VIPs speak, and have separate areas for the rich to avoid mingling with the working class. It's all so ridiculous.

Max and I had never used a private banker, and I didn't need one now. I had my financial advisor in San Francisco. For my banking needs, I just used the drive-thru when depositing checks or getting cash. Private banking sounded like those separate but equal facilities Tarian had mentioned. This article simply renewed my desire to see them punished.

With caffeine coursing through my blood, I got back to the thick stack of documents Eichman had sent us. He was certainly living up to his reputation. On many days, he filed multiple motions. The mountain of paperwork increased exponentially, not by the day but by the hour.

Some of the more interesting documents he filed claimed Max's estate was valued at $21 million. This was inaccurate because the estate didn't include my separate property. And the amount was highly inflated, resulting in more JPMorgan fees.

That same document stated JPMorgan was looking to collect $382,837 in expenses from me, which included legal fees. They also wanted an additional $103,475 for administration expenses. Good luck with that. Also, in the same filing, they blamed Professor Stanley Johanson for some of this mess, but they refused to list him as a responsible third party as they did with Stolbach and Glast Philips. That was interesting.

In another document, JPMorgan said that they had been wrongly sued under their corporate capacity. Instead, Eichman claimed they should have been sued solely in their capacity as the Independent Administrator for the Max Hopper Estate. When I talked to Alan, he told me not to worry about it. "They're just throwing stuff against the wall and hoping it sticks. It won't."

I told Alan it was like playing that Whack-A-Mole game. Whack one mole and another one popped up. No matter how many we beat down, more appeared.

Tarian added a different twist. "It's what we call the scorched-earth strategy. Challenge everything, including any i that's not dotted and any staple that's not in the right place. Our government used it in Vietnam when we sprayed Agent Orange over the jungle, killing everything. Just call this tactic Agent Eichman. It's what he does. It's why he's one of the top lawyers in Texas, if not the country. He's willing to burn everything to the ground if necessary. Not many lawyers can stomach that kind of destruction. Kinda makes me jealous."

"So, you used to do that?" I asked, incredulous.

"Sometimes, if I needed to break my opponent's will through brute force and gobs of money. Thank God our legal system encourages that strategy and punishes judges who try to stop it. It's a great time to be alive—with a bar card."

I went back to my work and found this email exchange on my computer.

Sent: *Friday, September 30, 2016 7:08 PM*
From: *John Eichman*
To: *Alan Loewinsohn, Kerry Schonwald, Anthony "Lenny" Vitullo,
Taylor Horton, Grayson Linyard*

I received these papers today. They are not exhibit lists. When are you going to serve true exhibit lists with descriptions of the exhibits?

    John C. Eichman

A few minutes later…

From: *Alan Loewinsohn*
To: *John Eichman, Kerry Schonwald, Anthony "Lenny" Vitullo, Taylor
Horton, Grayson Linyard*

John, I beg to differ. Mine are exhibit lists. I am not aware of any requirement that there be a description beyond the bates number if it exists. The scheduling order refers to "A list of all trial exhibits [with bates numbers as applicable]." So to what do you refer to support your rather snide accusation?

    Alan Loewinsohn

A few more minutes later…

From: *Taylor Horton*
To: *John Eichman, Alan Loewinsohn, Kerry Schonwald, Anthony
"Lenny" Vitullo, Taylor Horton, Grayson Linyard*

John, I agree with Alan. I understand Hunton & Williams' litigation strategy has recently been to inundate opposing counsel and the Court with a deluge of legally and factually insupportable motions, but this email takes the cake. Read the scheduling order's requirements before bothering me with yet another baseless communication on a Friday night.

    Taylor

On and on it went.

Tucked inside JPMorgan's filings was a motion asking the court to keep my experts on attorneys' fees from testifying at trial. It also sought to exclude the heirs' experts. The motion was long and detailed. I estimated it would cost me more than $25,000 for Alan to read, respond, and argue it.

Finally, on October 4, 2016, Judge Thompson held arguments on all the motions for summary judgment. Six lawyers from the various parties appeared, ensuring this would be an expensive day.

Before they started, thick binders had been put together for the judge. Each one had taken weeks to assemble. The lawyers tried stacking everything on the bench, but there wasn't enough room. The judge explained that due to the move, she had limited space to work. She mentioned carrying documents home each night to spread out on her kitchen table. It was the only place she had room to look at everything. How she would tote binders this size to her car, I had no idea.

Once the bell rang, the lawyers argued for hours, with Alan and Eichman going at it hard. It was like two heavyweights in the ring. Occasionally, Lenny proved his worth and threw some hard shots at Eichman.

I watched the back and forth, amazed as time raced by. Before I knew it, lunch had arrived. The judge announced that she had an afternoon docket and ordered everyone back the following day to finish the arguments.

For me, it was a critical time. I didn't sleep well. I had a lot on the line. If I won my motion, JPMorgan would stop trying to collect attorneys' fees from me. I prayed hard that I would win.

SIX DAYS AFTER the arguments, Alan sent me an email. The judge was overwhelmed with all the paperwork in the case. She was moving the trial to May 2017. Alan had begged her to consider March instead. I was devastated, remembering the judge in the STS Trust case saying to JPMorgan's lawyer, "This is just delay, delay, delay… it's stall, stall, stall."

Eichman's scorched-earth tactics had worked. By waiting close to the trial to fire his bullets, he had forced the judge's hand. JPMorgan had gotten what they paid for. I pictured CEO Jamie Dimon in his Park Avenue suite, smiling and rubbing his hands together with glee.

Thankfully, over the next few weeks, Alan finagled the trial back to February 13, 2017. But he cautioned it was hanging by a thread.

As I continued sorting through the mounds of paperwork, I noticed a recent account summary from JPMorgan. The estate account was down to $100. Yet, somehow, JPMorgan had been able to pay Hunton & Williams' $95,000 invoice. How did they do that?

I contacted Alan, concerned that they were somehow accessing my money. He did some investigating and couldn't understand how JPMorgan was paying their lawyers. It was a mystery. We would have to wait several more months before learning the shocking truth.

NOVEMBER ARRIVED, AND with it, a new trial date: March 22, 2017. However, this would work only if the other case set for that time slot settled. Before I knew it, January was upon us. Another year gone and I was no closer to the end. A mild depression had settled in. I saw no way out.

Alan learned that March was still available and that May was the backup date. The main problem was the length of our trial. The judge could borrow a courtroom for a week, but not for the six weeks we needed. With construction happening on the old civil courts building, there weren't any courtrooms available.

"Why don't *you* start looking for courtrooms?" Tarian told me. "Wear out some shoe leather. Look at the criminal courts building. They have extra courtrooms over there. Also, check out the truancy courts. Look up every government building and see if there is an extra courtroom."

It was a great idea! I did just that. It gave me a way to be productive. I went to every courtroom I could find. It took weeks. I compiled a list and sent it to Alan. He forwarded it to the judge. At the bare minimum, it showed how desperate we were to get to trial.

Unfortunately, none of the possible courtrooms panned out. There were all kinds of reasons: no jury deliberation room, jurors could not easily get to the court, or "it's not big enough." According to the lawyers, we needed a space to hold three tables, six lawyers, five litigants, a court reporter, bailiff, judge, six-person jury plus alternates, and the public.

By the time March arrived, that trial date was gone. Now, it was May.

"What about the Old Red Courthouse?" Tarian suggested.

Yet another good idea. I went to the ancient building and discovered a cavernous courtroom on the fourth floor. The space had been renovated in the style of the late 1800s when the courthouse was built. Even though it was a museum, anyone could rent it out for $650 per day.

I reported this to Alan. He got Lenny to agree to pay half the cost. It was a great solution!

Until the judge said no. I never learned why.

I kept at it, going to SMU and checking out their law school. Again, there was always a reason why it wouldn't work.

"Do you have any other solutions?" I asked Tarian. "I'm desperate."

"Yeah. File a writ of mandamus."

"What's that?"

"It's a request to a court of appeals that they order the judge to hold the trial on a certain date."

I thought about that. "Will it work?"

"Just the threat of it will move the wheels of justice. Imagine what the press would do with a story like that. 'Jo Hopper, a sad and lonely widow, is literally begging the court of appeals to order her case to trial. Seven long years after her husband died, she's not sure she can hang on long enough to see it through. This tragic scene is yet another example of the legal system's inability to dispense justice promptly. Justin Davis, reporting from the civil courts building. Sheila, back to you.'"

"Wow!" I laughed. "That would be something."

"Just ask your lawyer about a writ of mandamus."

I did. Twenty-four hours later, we had a firm date for August 28, 2017. No matter what, the judge said we would cram everyone and everything into the space that was now her courtroom in the Renaissance Tower. How that would happen, I had no idea.

I just knew the moment was coming: JPMorgan Chase would have to face the widow they had screwed.

PART THREE
A Tree Falls in the Forest

Chapter Thirty

She seemed so helpless, such easy prey.
It's too late now to back away.
Deeper and deeper, away from the truth,
Bound up in lies, they can't get loose.
Yet the day finally comes, when the jury sees,
And brings the monster to its knees.
                    —*She Sits Alone* by Jack Hooper

The alarm exploded and set my pulse racing. I reached over, hitting the off button to stop the disruption. Instead of getting up, I remained there with my head on the pillow, staring at the dark ceiling.

The endless punishment by JPMorgan had not stopped. Instead of admitting they'd screwed up, writing an apology, and settling, they forced me to carry on, spending myself toward bankruptcy.

Here I was, August 28, 2017, about to begin a new chapter of my life—or what was left of it. What a hard summer it had been. JPMorgan's lawyers, Hunton & Williams, had continued the deluge of motions. This was JPMorgan's final attempt to break me. With every check I wrote to my lawyers, I told myself JPMorgan would have to bring more than that. I was probably kidding myself.

Poor Judge Thompson. She was caught in the middle, forced to listen to all the nonsense and then spend hours and hours at home reading each filing. On one particular day, she issued sixteen orders. One of the orders stated that the contract I'd signed with JPMorgan was unambiguous, and I did not owe attorneys' fees incurred on behalf of the estate. That was a huge victory for me and another in a long string of wins.

The workload of our case, combined with all the other cases assigned to her court, had to weigh heavily on the judge. Then in July, she explained her dilemma of going forward with our trial. The Renaissance Tower courtroom Judge Thompson occupied was set to undergo extensive remodeling. It was not adequate to handle jury trials. And this was the temporary courtroom in which she held court while the central courthouse downtown was being renovated. What a complete mess!

She explained there was a fixed deadline when the construction would start. This meant we had fourteen business days for our trial. It would've been fifteen, but Labor Day would take up one of them. "One day past the deadline, and the contractors will be busting down sheetrock while we sit in the courtroom. If that happens, there's no other place to go. There's no other place we *will* go."

Alan spent time talking with Lenny. They wondered if it was worth the risk to start a trial that might not finish. It would give an incredible edge to JPMorgan and Eichman to see our cards spread out over the table during an aborted trial. They could plug any holes in the retrial.

We continued the conversations on what to do. There I was, pushing Alan to get this case to trial. At seventy, I didn't know how much life I had left. We had already prepped for trial twice in August 2016 and this past month, August 2017. I was almost certain I lacked the money to prep a third time if there was a delay or mistrial. Really, I had no choice but to throw my entire body weight into getting this case to trial.

Alan listened to me and agreed to push for the trial to start. But he explained the nasty part of it was the hard stop at fourteen days. This played right into JPMorgan's hands. Their break-and-bury strategy, as I called it, could be continued indefinitely. All they had to do was keep paying Eichman to file motion after motion. Once at trial, JPMorgan could switch from break-and-bury to the object-and-obstruct strategy. Alan knew Eichman would work hard to waste every minute in court. If Eichman could have me spend fourteen days of trial expenses and run out the clock to the remodelers, I'd have to pay for additional pretrial work and a whole new trial. From the estate's inventory of my assets, Eichman surely understood my financial limitations.

As the trial start date approached, Eichman filed a motion containing "limines." This legal concept prevents irrelevant prejudicial information from getting before the jury. If granted, it would stop Alan, Lenny, or James Bell from talking about certain subjects. They could still approach the judge and rediscuss them if needed.

When I received a copy of JPMorgan's motion in limine, I saw that it contained twenty different topics. I carefully reviewed them. The first one that hit me was No. 2: "Any reference to the IA's payment of attorneys' fees out of the Estate as stealing or taking from the Heirs." This was directed at the heirs because they kept saying in filings and hearings that JPMorgan/ IA had stolen money from the estate account. Of course, JPMorgan didn't want us saying they had stolen or taken money from the heirs or me. If this was suppressed, the jury would have to make the connection themselves. Would that even be possible?

Another one on this list prevented us from talking about their screwups on the estate's inventory. JPMorgan knew they had filed and amended the inventory three times in three years. And Hunton & Williams had been paid for each screwup. To me, this was an example of self-dealing. What incentive did Hunton & Williams ever have to get it right? The fact that neither the IA nor Hunton & Williams seriously coordinated the inventory with us was proof enough for me. Tom Cantrill even wrote, "The inventory continues to be a work in progress even though it has been filed." Again, if they could avoid having the jury hear about that, it was one less brick we'd have to throw at them.

As I read on, I made a shortlist of the bad ones.

- No mention of any other lawsuit JPMorgan had dealt with. (This would shut out the litigation involving the STS Trust, Burns Clark Dailey Trust, MOSH Trust and Estate of Fisher. If a criminal faced a stolen vehicle charge, no sense in letting the jury know he'd been accused of stealing ten other cars.)
- Any characterizations of JPMorgan's actions as "criminal" in nature. (Just asking for that was a crime.)
- No reference to the reasons Jenkens & Gilchrist stopped practicing law or any claims or disputes involving Jenkens & Gilchrist. (This matched what Tarian had told me when Cantrill, Eichman, and the other partners had shut down Jenkens & Gilchrist and reopened the next day in the same space, as Hunton & Williams.)
- No reference to JPMorgan's alleged role in the 2008 financial crisis or allegations that JPMorgan was responsible for it. (This made me wonder what JPMorgan's role actually *was* in the crisis.)

After the judge ruled on the limine motions, Alan explained that he, Lenny and James Bell would have to prepare a long list of all the topics they could not discuss. Alan planned to have Kerry sit next to him at trial and continually review the list. It was vital Alan did not mention any of those subjects without first talking to the judge. It might result in striking some testimony or a mistrial.

Kerry said she would also be watching Eichman. If he violated our motion in limine rulings, we could ask that the witness's testimony be stricken, or worse, that JPMorgan's defenses be eliminated.

Through this process, I learned that a motion in limine is like a minefield. Each lawyer plants as many mines as the judge will allow. Then, they wait for the opposing lawyer to accidentally step on one. If he blows off a leg, it's the client who feels the pain.

Despite all this, I had some good news. Neither the heirs nor JPMorgan had any evidence of me hiding assets or an executed will. And they had found nothing to show that Max had stolen $2 million from his ex-wife.

One of the final preparations for trial was the Joint Pretrial Report. It listed each party's claims, witnesses, and intended exhibits. It was 218 pages. Good grief!

Robert Hirschhorn, our jury consultant, suggested that we pay the jurors an extra $240 a day split three ways. Robert's idea was due to the financial burden on the people who were selected to sit for a three-week trial. Alan talked with Lenny, and he agreed to it. So did Eichman. What a nice thing to do—until the judge shot it down. Dallas County refused to allow jurors more than the legislated $40 a day. I did a quick calculation. Each juror would make $5 per hour. For a three-week trial, there was no way a single mother could support her kids on that. It was awful. No wonder no one wants to be called for jury duty!

I took in a deep breath and exhaled slowly. The darkness of my bedroom overwhelmed me. I had been lying there for a few minutes after the alarm sounded. I took one last breath and prepared to swing my legs to the floor. Before I could, Millie bumped my shoulder. She was jumping on the side of my bed, needing to go outside to do her business. Then, she would come back inside and sink her teeth into some canine vittles. I also needed to get some coffee in me so I could head to court. Seven years, seven months, and three days after my husband died, and almost six years since I filed the lawsuit, we were finally going to trial.

I hoped.

AUGUST IN TEXAS is super hot. This day was no exception. I parked my VW Beetle in the underground garage. Jury selection was being held in an auxiliary courtroom in the downtown district courthouse. Not only was it available for this one day, but it was easier for the county to assemble and organize the large panel we needed. Plus, it had a cafeteria big enough to serve the potential jurors.

As I walked by myself through the underground tunnel, Grayson Linyard, the lawyer assisting John Eichman, came alongside me. He smiled, and I smiled back. It was ironic. His job was to defend the actions taken by JPMorgan and Hunton & Williams, and mine was to defeat Hunton & Williams and punish JPMorgan with a large verdict. Like every battle, one of us would win, and the other would lose. Who would it be?

We made it to the courthouse lobby where Susan Novak and John Eichman stood. When Linyard saw them, he split off and joined them. I hopped on the elevator and looked around, noticing the pearls on a woman next to me. They were gorgeous. I commented on them, and she smiled. When I got to court, I discovered it was Judge Thompson. Without her robe, I hadn't recognized her. If I had, I would not have spoken to her, realizing that it would likely be a breach of etiquette.

I arrived at the courtroom at 8:45 a.m. Alan and Kerry were there along with Michael, Alan's son. Michael was assisting Alan by running all kinds of errands. Then there was Robert Hirschhorn studying his notes. Robert would be the star of this phase.

I glanced over at the heirs' table. Stephen and Laura occupied two seats next to Lenny and James Bell. Bell had Kelley Cash, a lawyer in his office, helping out. Lenny had Taylor Horton as his right-hand man. Stephen's wife, Barbara, sat with them. It was August 28, 2017, the first time I had seen Barbara since the *Wrath Boom in the Bathroom*.

Between Lenny's four lawyers and my three, we had a lot of firepower. And we needed it, because JPMorgan had Eichman and Linyard as its principal warriors. Surprisingly, though, JPMorgan did not have a jury expert.

While the lawyers argued about more limine issues, Robert took me aside. "Okay, Jo, here's the game plan. We have a panel of sixty potential jurors coming. A probate case requires only six jurors plus two alternates in case we lose a juror. The goal is for us to strike jurors who don't like our lawyers, the case, or you. Eichman will be trying to strike jurors who hate banks. Whoever is left will be our jury. In the end, it's a pool of jurors that don't scare either side."

"Alan said we get strikes," I said. "How many?"

"For cause, it's unlimited. Otherwise, we get three for-any-reason strikes."

"What's 'for cause'?" I asked.

"If someone said they could not be fair toward widows. Or they work for JPMorgan and could never find against the bank. Our job is to identify jurors we don't like and try to get them struck for cause instead of using one of our precious for-any-reason strikes."

"It's a real game, then?"

"Yes," he admitted. "One with devastating consequences for either side. Most lawyers don't get jury selection right. They'll start the trial forty points down and try to catch up later. It's sad."

"That's why we have you. To avoid that problem."

"You've got that right."

He went on to explain they had negotiated questionnaires for each juror to fill out. It would be our attorneys' job to review those quickly.

Before I knew it, the bailiff was calling, "All rise!" Row after row of men and women filled the benches. Since our chairs were on the opposite side of the counsel tables, we stood facing them. I studied each one as they made their way through the benches. They represented a complete cross-section of our city. Six of these good people held my future in their hands.

The judge started with some opening remarks. She noted that two potential jurors had not shown up. This caused us to start with fifty-eight. When she finished, she gave them one hour to fill out the questionnaire.

We sat there doing nothing, waiting for them to finish. After they turned in the forms, Judge Thompson said the case would take fourteen business days, so three weeks. A chorus of groans snaked through the panel. Several shook their heads in frustration. When the judge asked if anyone had any hardships or exemptions, the game began.

One by one the jurors were questioned about their hardship situation. If we liked a juror, Eichman tried to get that juror excused. We did the same to him.

Astonishingly, the wife of Mark Enoch, who had handled the appeal for the heirs, was on the panel. She was excused.

We worked on the hardship cases until lunch. Then we took a break, but it was not a relaxing one. Robert and my lawyers studied every aspect of those questionnaires, discussing strategy as they barely touched their food.

When we started back up, twenty-five hardship cases were granted. It was 2:50 p.m. before Alan began his *voir dire*. He questioned the jurors about issues that concerned us. When he was done, the jurors took a break. Then, Lenny did the heirs' *voir dire*. By the time Eichman started his, it was 5:05 p.m.

I sat there watching all this. The jurors were visibly angry at the late hour. I didn't blame them. It seemed too much time had been wasted in arguments at the bench. It was very frustrating.

After Eichman was through, another round of hardship cases began. Juror after juror was paraded before the judge. Alan, Lenny, and Eichman all questioned them. So many people wanted off this jury that we wondered if we would even have enough to pick from. It was exhausting for everyone.

With the panel out in the hall, Eichman argued over some jurors Alan wanted to let go. Then, Eichman argued over the jurors he wanted to keep. The judge sided with Eichman. He was on a winning streak until Alan and Lenny begged the judge to reconsider one juror. She changed her mind.

It was fascinating watching these men argue. After almost twelve hours, their minds were still sharp and fresh. Neither side gave an inch. Yet, I felt the clear winner had been Eichman. He was going to make us use our three strikes on jurors we found objectionable. He played the game well and was comfortable with this process. No wonder they had saved money on a jury expert. They already had one—John Eichman.

By the time the dust settled, another eighteen hardship excuses had been granted. We had started with fifty-eight potential jurors and were left with fifteen. Robert explained that because the judge had allowed only three strikes spread between Alan and Lenny, there would be six strikes total. "Since we have fifteen people left, once both sides use the six strikes, we'll have nine potential jurors. We only need eight. That's the closest I've cut it in a long time. We almost busted this panel."

"What would've happened if we did that?" I asked.

"We start all over again tomorrow and lose a precious day of our allotted fourteen."

I shuddered at the thought.

"Fifteen minutes," Judge Thompson warned. "I'll be taking your strikes in fifteen minutes."

Our team went to a private room and spread out a jury chart with rows and columns of information. Thick red Xs covered most of them.

"These are the strikes JPMorgan will make," Robert said confidently. "And here are our strikes." He circled six names. "This is our jury. And these two are the alternates."

Everyone fell silent as we took in the moment. Six of these eight people would decide my fate. And the heirs'.

And JPMorgan's.

I swallowed hard. The trial I'd been longing for had arrived.

We reconvened in court and officially submitted our strikes. Since I had one of the country's premier jury consultants, Lenny agreed to allow us to make all three strikes. When the judge had Eichman's strikes, she brought in the remaining jurors and read out the lucky names. It was just as Robert had predicted. The eight jurors stood up and walked to the jury box. One girl began crying. She had tried hard to get released due to a hardship but had been unsuccessful.

The judge swore in the jury and read some warnings before letting them go. After a few more arguments from the lawyers about a few motions, she released us too. At 8:25 p.m., thoroughly exhausted, I walked to my car. I felt like I'd been in a long war. How I'd last three weeks, I had no idea. But of one thing I was sure: I'd be back in court in twelve hours. Opening statements were scheduled, and I wouldn't miss that for the world!

Chapter Thirty-One

Who are these scoundrels who steal golden years?
With promises boundless to a widow in tears.
No heart. No soul. No compassion inside.
No respect for the law that's there as a guide.
They learn the law to discover its limit.
Use it against you while hiding within it.
　　—Scoundrels Steal Retirement Years by Jack Hooper

"Today, I'm putting you on the stand," Alan informed me. It was eight in the morning. He and I sat in a private room just outside the courtroom. "Each lawyer has one hour for an opening statement. That will take three hours. After lunch, I'll put you on the stand, and we'll knock out a half day. Tomorrow, I'll finish up and let Lenny ask you some questions. On Thursday, Eichman will cross-examine you. That should take a day. By Friday, your job will be over. You can sit there and watch the rest of the trial in comfort. How does that sound?"

"Sounds good," I replied calmly, my heart slamming against my chest. As much as I told myself I was ready, I didn't want to do it. I just wanted this over with. I tried to focus on Friday. That would be my reward.

We took our places in the cramped courtroom. It had been reconfigured to fit three parties and their lawyers. On the left wall, facing the bench, was the jury box. Attached to the judge's bench was the witness chair. It was barely six feet from the jury. Right in front of the witness chair was the court reporter's area.

The plaintiff's table was directly in front of the court reporter. It had two chairs—one for Alan and the other for Kerry. I sat behind them in a chair up against the bar separating the lawyers from the gallery.

To the right of the plaintiff's table was the defendant's table. It had three chairs—one for John Eichman and one for Grayson Linyard. (Note: If I were a lawyer, I'd want a name like Grayson Linyard. It sounds so distinguished.) But they had also crammed in a chair for Susan Novak. Behind them was Robert Gilbreath, an appellate attorney. I asked Alan about him and he said Gilbreath's job was to advise JPMorgan on preserving error. If the bank lost at trial, I assumed JPMorgan would want to crush me on appeal. That's when Gilbreath would take over.

Besides Gilbreath, Susan Kravik, JPMorgan's in-house legal counsel, sat in the back of the gallery with her computer. I assumed she would watch the trial and, most likely, generate daily updates on her laptop for JPMorgan's executives in New York. So, if Ms. Kravik saw things headed south, JPMorgan could approach Alan and settle the case. If it looked like a winner, the bank would offer nothing.

Stephen and Laura sat at a long table perpendicular to the defendant's table, with their backs against the towering wall of glass windows twenty-four stories off the ground. Lenny and James Bell occupied two seats next to them. Kelley Cash, a lawyer from Bell's office, was crammed over there too, along with Taylor Horton, Lenny's assisting lawyer.

To make matters more crowded, each party had racks brought in to store the volumes of exhibits, evidence, strategy, motions, and rulings. These racks sat anywhere there was room in the courtroom, sometimes obscuring the view from the gallery. If that wasn't enough, heaps of boxes sat in spectators' benches and towered in the rear. If a fire broke out, we'd all die.

As I looked around at all of us packed in like sardines, I had to silently thank Stephen and Laura and Lenny Vitullo. We would not be here if they hadn't agreed to take the distant T-boned table. From where they sat, seeing the witness stand was impossible. Lenny had to move near the spectator benches if he wanted a clear view. Someone had to take the short straw and the heirs volunteered. It showed me they wanted the trial as badly as I did. I hoped we'd both give JPMorgan pause before taking another estate through their unique version of probate hell.

The jury arrived, but as soon as the bailiff signaled they were ready to enter, Eichman had more issues to discuss at the bench. He wanted to designate Susan Novak as the corporate rep. Alan and Lenny objected, then wanted more information about this move. Up to this point, Wendy

Bessette had been the designated corporate rep. We even took her deposition in that capacity.

Alan quickly surmised that this would be a considerable advantage to Susan because of "the rule."

"The rule" was a requirement that any witnesses testifying at trial had to wait outside the courtroom. They were not allowed to watch the proceedings or discuss testimony except with their lawyer. This prevents a witness from tailoring their testimony to fit with another witness or anything else that's been raised during the proceedings. But being designated a corporate rep meant Susan could remain in the courtroom. She sat right beside Grayson, the farthest position from the jury. Lenny and Alan claimed this was a bait and switch. It was also another good move on Eichman's part, because the judge allowed it.

Alan appeared upset but later explained that he was okay with the move. He planned to use this corporate rep stuff against Susan. I sure hoped so.

Just when I thought the trial would finally start, Eichman objected to James Bell's PowerPoint presentation. Bell was slated to give the heirs' opening statement. As such, he had sent his PowerPoint deck to Eichman the night before. Eichman objected to the late hour he had received it: 11:32 p.m. This violated some agreement or ruling, so Eichman claimed Bell shouldn't be allowed to use it. The arguments went on and on until Eichman lost. Then, he changed tactics.

He objected to some of the items in the PowerPoint deck, particularly pages of deposition testimony. The purpose of an opening statement is to tell the jury what a lawyer believes the evidence will show them. Eichman claimed Bell was going a step beyond that and showing them the *actual* evidence. Not only was that improper, Eichman claimed, but a mistrial would be required if the evidence failed to be admitted. Eichman wondered who would pay for that. After hearing what the judge had to say, Bell decided to strike the text using a black marker. The presentation was a little messy but Bell plowed ahead. Nothing was going to stop him from giving his opening statement.

The next issue had to do with more limine issues. Alan and Eichman got into it, with lots of arm-waving and arguments by Eichman. Eventually, I tuned out the scene. It seemed the trial would never begin.

At some point during all this, a distraught juror sent out a note. She was pregnant and in her third trimester. A trial would be hard on her pregnancy, she claimed. Plus, she had high blood pressure. To top that off, she had a one-year-old at home. Eichman wanted her removed so we could start eating into the alternates. Alan tried hard to keep her and save the trial. After bringing her out for a talk, the judge agreed not to hold court when she had a doctor's appointment. Despite that, I could tell the juror was angry and upset. I sympathized with her.

The judge was just about to call the jury out when another juror had a problem. He had to be in Corsicana, Texas for a jury trial. The judge brought him out and we learned that he had been shot two years earlier. The police had arrested a man who was going to trial and this man was the main witness.

Judge Thompson appeared upset that we were just now hearing about this. There was a lot of discussion. The judge expressed hope that the juror's case might settle with a plea bargain. Either way, she promised to call the court in Corsicana to see if there was a way to postpone it.

Alan came back to the counsel table upset. "We haven't even started, and we're about to lose our two alternates," he whispered to me. "This is very bad. We're not going to make it three weeks with no alternates."

"At least we won't have to worry about the remodelers," I whispered back, trying to lighten the mood. He tossed me a courtesy smile and turned back around.

When everything was ready, I looked at my legal pad. Just below a list of prayers was the number thirteen. That meant thirteen days left to complete this trial. I didn't know how long a trial usually took, but I prayed it wasn't longer than thirteen days. As I finished praying, the jury was finally seated. It was 10:47 a.m. Half a day was almost gone.

They took their seats in the jury box, pinned on their juror badges, and listened to the judge's instructions. As soon as she finished, Alan rose to his feet, made his way to the podium, and began our opening statement.

Finally!

"INTESTATE. INDEPENDENT. INCOMPETENT." Alan hit the jury with those three words. He said this was an intestate estate that JPMorgan claimed to be able to handle. He said JPMorgan had promised they'd be independent. But in the end, they were completely incompetent.

Once he had that out of the way, he carefully detailed a roadmap of the journey the jurors were about to take. With JPMorgan behind the wheel, it should have been a leisurely drive along the coast. Instead, it had detoured into the jungle, where scary monsters stripped the heirs and me of our assets.

Alan referred to Steve and Laura either as Max's children or Jo's stepchildren. He said the bank had promised me that I wouldn't pay one cent for this administration. And he pounded in my favorite argument that it wasn't JPMorgan's job to wait for or force some kind of agreement on the parties. The bank wasn't supposed to be in the middle. They were supposed to divide the assets and release them.

"Still, today, Jo has not had all the assets returned to her, as they are still holding some of her money."

I watched several jurors nod. They were getting into this. Alan's presentation was clear, smooth, and uninterrupted. I was excited when he moved into the heart of the case.

"And when it came to Jo's house, all the bank had to do was fill out this three-page preprinted form. That's it.

"When it came to the wine, the putters, the art, the household furnishings for each of these categories, all the bank had to do was fill out a two-page printed form. And when did the bank fill out the two-page printed form to release Jo's interest in the wine and putters? 2010? No. 2011? No. 2012? No. The answer is not until 2013, over three years after Max died.

"And when did the bank fill out the two-page preprinted form to release Jo her interest in the art, the home furnishings, and jewelry? 2010? No. 2011? No. 2012? No. 2013? No. 2014? No, not until February 2015, over five years after Max died."

Alan's smooth style delivered a first-class opening statement. Before I knew it, he was finished. It was 12:15 p.m., and the judge released everyone for lunch.

"How'd I do?" Alan asked.

"Outstanding," I replied. "Any reasonable person could follow that logic."

"Good. Now, all we have to do is lay down the cards in the right order."

We were in the conference room of one of Alan's friends who had an office in the building. By using the freight elevator, we could be there right after the judge let us go. Corner Bakery brought lunch for us, and I had the same thing every day: a ham and cheese sandwich on pretzel bread with chips and a cookie that I shared with Jack. He had not attended the jury selection but was back for this.

As I munched on my sandwich, I asked Alan, "Do you still think I'll testify today?"

"No," he replied. "We've just wasted a half-day. We'll be lucky to get the opening statements done."

"Do you have to fight him on each issue?"

"Unfortunately, I do. This isn't some ego trip. We can't allow Eichman to pick our case apart or let jurors go. Give him an inch, and he'll take a million—*dollars*, that is."

I nodded and said nothing more. Alan spent the rest of lunch with Kerry, going over more legal issues. They were always working.

When we got back to court, Lenny approached Alan. "I want your opening statement," he said bluntly. "You laid out the keys to beating JPMorgan. Can I have it?"

Alan shook his head. "Our clients are suing each other, so no. But if you want it that bad, you can pay the court reporter to type it up."

Lenny did just that. It appeared that he planned on using it as a guide for his presentation. Alan said there weren't many lawyers who were smart enough to not only recognize a better mousetrap but to buy it. Most lawyers would have pridefully stuck to their contraption and missed the rat.

Judge Thompson took the bench and, right away, Eichman had objections. He knew the rules inside and out, using them to point out additional problems with Bell's displays. The judge agreed, forcing Bell to make more changes on the fly. It looked thoroughly messed up.

Another issue was that Stephen and Laura now claimed mental anguish damages. Eichman objected and was overruled. The problems kept coming.

A man came in to watch the trial as a guest of Bell. He talked with Judge Thompson and sat with the heirs. His name was Judge John Creuzot. As it turned out, Judge Creuzot was running for the district attorney's office of Dallas County. Eichman objected, for some reason, and Judge Creuzot was ordered to leave.

At 2:02 p.m., James Bell started his opening statement. His main point was that JPMorgan owed a duty to Bell's clients. He launched into the trip I took to New York on JPMorgan's dime and that the heirs didn't get the same treatment or even know about the trip. Bell stabbed at me a few more times before moving on to JPMorgan.

Eichman jumped up and objected. The judge reprimanded Bell for using an exhibit he had not disclosed. Undeterred, Bell crossed the same line again. This time, the judge reprimanded him longer. But he seemed unruffled. He told the jury the heirs had damages of $9 million. That was a massive increase from their depositions and court filings.

When Bell mentioned that JPMorgan had committed theft, Eichman exploded. Bell made another trip to the bench. This time, there was a break. With the jury gone, Judge Thompson ripped into Bell. She couldn't believe he was violating the motion in limine over and over again. It got heated at the bench, with more loud talking and waving of arms. Eichman stood between Alan and Bell and I heard the word "mistrial" from him. It was hard to know what was going on with the judge and attorneys. Everyone seemed very animated. The judge looked serious and appeared to be leaning toward a mistrial due to Bell's repeated violations. She took a ten-minute break to consider the situation.

During this break, I got up and joined Jack in the gallery, where I saw Barbara. I took Jack over to introduce him to Barbara since she had been so interested in him at the depositions. I hadn't spoken to her since the April 2016 *Overload in the Ladies' Commode*. After I introduced him, Barbara gestured to a young woman and said to Jack, "This is my daughter."

I was stunned. It had been almost seven years since I'd seen my granddaughter. Without thinking, I grabbed and pulled her in tight, crying hard. My crying turned into uncontrollable sobbing. The stress of the moment took over. I knew I couldn't stay in the courtroom in this condition, so I ran to the hall, where I cried and dropped to the floor. She came out after me, found me weeping, and reached down to touch me. "I thought you didn't love me anymore." That set me off again.

For the next five minutes, we hugged and cried. I couldn't utter a word. It was deep and emotional. JPMorgan had taken so much from me that I could never get back. Finally, I was able to tell her I loved her so much I had to let her go. I didn't want her caught in the middle between her parents and me. Jack came out and said we needed to return to the courtroom.

The judge appeared concerned. "Are you okay, Mrs. Hopper?" she asked.

"Yes," I replied, still crying.

As I wiped my eyes and retook my seat, I realized that my grand-daughter had been in the courtroom the whole time, but I hadn't noticed. I had been too focused on Alan. With a deep breath, I got to my feet as the jury came back, and James Bell continued his opening statement.

Instead of granting a mistrial, the judge instructed the jury to dis-regard any evidence from Mr. Bell. Alan whispered to me that Bell was worried the judge's instruction had damaged his credibility with the jury. I wondered how it might impact my case.

For some insane reason, Bell kept tempting fate. Three more times, Judge Thompson chastised him in front of the jury. He kept saying JPMorgan had a "secret agreement" with me, so Alan and Eichman objected. I could see a mistrial coming. But just when I thought Bell would say something like, "Jamie Dimon is the devil incarnate," he stopped and sat down.

The judge gave Eichman some time to set up. Alan had a podium on our table that he used for his opening statement. He agreed to let Eichman, Lenny, and Bell use it. Because it was directly over Alan's chair, Alan moved to the gallery and objected from there. I remained seated behind our table. It was a unique arrangement.

While Eichman prepared himself, I considered Bell's opening state-ment. It was full of excitement but somewhat disjointed due to all the deletions and changes he'd made at the last minute. Still, he had slogged through it and at least made some good points.

Eichman's AV guy wanted to hook into our AV, but Alan said no. Because the courtroom had no electronics except battery-operated microphones, the parties had agreed to hire Alan's AV guy to hook up everything. Alan had paid more to have the court reporter's transcript sent directly to a monitor on his table. We'd also brought in a large flatscreen. Eichman wanted to hook into that because he had a large white Elmo screen (an Elmo is a document camera used for making projections). It was located all the way across the courtroom by the heirs. I thought it was a mistake for Eichman to use his Elmo, but I wasn't getting paid $650 an hour.

At 3:30 p.m., John Eichman began his opening statement. He wasted no time scorching the earth. His first target was poor Max. Eichman stated that Max didn't have a will, then left behind a bad family relationship.

He said after selecting JPMorgan as the IA, the heirs and I hadn't agreed on anything. Then he talked about wills in Texas.

> "And there's an old saying among estate planning lawyers in Texas, that really no one in Texas dies without a will. Really everybody has a will. You either have one that you wrote, or a lawyer wrote for you, or the state of Texas in its statutes provides your will essentially, by state law. It says who gets what."

Eichman torched us for what seemed like forever before moving on to his team. He presented Susan Novak as the most experienced person at JPMorgan: "A diplomat, a people person." He also listed all the accolades Tom Cantrill had racked up. He claimed both Novak and Cantrill were the dream team for this estate.

Eichman laid the blame on us for not making better decisions to resolve matters. He hit Gary Stolbach, saying the heirs claimed Stolbach had committed malpractice. The more he talked, the sicker I became. He was creating steak out of nothing-burgers. I could see a few of the jurors buying into this crap.

Eichman didn't take his foot off the gas. He aired our dirty laundry—embarrassing arguments the kids and I'd had. It was horrifying sitting there listening to it.

One of his best moves was taking boilerplate language from Judge Miller's order and making it sound like the judge had stated the Estate of Max Hopper needed JPMorgan because JPMorgan was the best in the world. It was a clever but dastardly trick. And all of it was legal.

Eichman's central theme was that JPMorgan had been caught in the middle. Despite everything JPMorgan had to put up with, he presented a chart that showed how, in ten months of being hired, JPMorgan had distributed 85% of the assets. That came to almost $17 million! "How could that be bad?" he asked.

I wanted to close my ears. Eichman's words were hurting our case. And he didn't stop.

"JPMorgan did not miss any assets or lose any assets. These people are trying to make nothing into something."

He smartly admitted there had been some bumps along the way. "But no actions by JPMorgan caused any actual harm to the family members or their interests."

Eichman circled back to me, telling the jury I had sent 1,000 emails to Susan Novak, wasting 1,200 hours of her time. He wrapped up everything by saying we were here due to bad decisions of the heirs and me spending millions of dollars on attorneys. By the time he sat down, it felt like a flamethrower had just incinerated our case. No wonder JPMorgan didn't want to settle. If I had heard that presentation, I would've been torching me, too.

Judge Thompson let the jury go for the night. Then, she reminded us of our deadline. "Twelve days until the remodelers."

Before we left, James Bell wanted a piece of Eichman. He moved to disqualify Eichman under the Texas Disciplinary Rules of Professional Conduct—the legal rule book for lawyers getting and keeping their bar card. Bell said Eichman was a material fact witness and listed as an expert witness on attorneys' fees. Bell pointed out that Eichman would be bolstering his partner, Tom Cantrill. Hearing this was music to my ears. I had wondered about a possible conflict of interest from the very beginning. How could a person be part of the case, a fact witness, and a lawyer all in the same trial?

Bell said that JPMorgan would be suing Hunton & Williams if Eichman lost this case. Thus, JPMorgan would need someone to blame—and pay.

Judge Thompson said she'd take it under advisement. Then, we adjourned for the day.

Jack and I went home and I called Tarian, explaining what Bell had done to almost cause a mistrial and his motion to disqualify Eichman.

"Regarding Bell's mistakes," Tarian said, "there are four reasons why lawyers do or don't do something like that: inexperience, stupidity, laziness, or on purpose. When a guy like Bell makes it to this level, always bet it's on purpose. Successful lawyers get close to the speedway wall. To gain that extra edge over the competition, they'll risk crashing. It's a high-risk, high-reward strategy."

"What about disqualifying Eichman?" I asked.

"That won't go anywhere. It should've been done years ago. Besides, it would cause a mistrial, and you don't want that."

"No, I don't." I told him I was scheduled to take the stand in the morning. "Any advice?"

He cleared his throat. "There are two things in life a man must do himself: die and testify. No one can help you. Sorry."

"Gosh, thanks for the pep talk," I said. "Who needs enemies when I have friends like you?"

"You're welcome. My ex-wives seemed to enjoy my humble wisdom."

I chuckled.

"Okay, Jo," Tarian said, "how's this: just tell your story in your own voice, and you'll be fine."

"See, I knew you had it in you to talk nice," I teased.

"Gosh, thanks for the pep talk," Tarian shot back. "Who needs enemas when I have turds like you?"

Chapter Thirty-Two

"In all cases, we carefully tried to get the balance right while treating customers fairly."

—Jamie Dimon, Chairman & CEO
JPMorgan Chase Bank, N.A.
Letter to the Shareholders 2015 Annual Report

Riding up the elevator to the 24th floor to testify, my anxiety was palpable. Eighteen months earlier, I had testified in two depositions for over twelve hours. I hoped that experience would help now.

This scene would be much different than sitting in Alan's conference room, having Lenny Vitullo ask me questions. I would be in open court with at least thirty to forty people staring at and assessing me. A bailiff, court reporter, and judge would be within a few feet of me. I prayed for help in calming my nerves.

Thankfully, it worked. By the time I arrived at 8 a.m., I felt ready—or as prepared as one can be in a situation like this. *Just tell your story*, I reminded myself of Tarian's advice. *And don't foul Eichman as he's going for a slam dunk. Let him get his two points and no more.* Alan had used basketball analogies to prep me before the depositions.

When I arrived, everyone was ready. But of course, we didn't start on time. With the jury in their room, another lawyer stood before Judge Thompson on a different case. I immediately recognized him. He was a lawyer I had met with when looking to replace Jim Jennings. He had listened to my story and said he'd call me after talking with his financial partner. He had never called back. I guessed he and his partner didn't think I had a winning case.

To kill time, I envisioned myself sitting in the witness box. Looking out at the world, it wasn't so frightening. Paul Malouf, Alan's AV pro, had done a first-class job. The jury box had electronic screens mounted to the back of its wall so the jurors could look there instead of the larger screens in the courtroom. He had also hooked up a monitor on the witness stand, so instead of looking at the large monitor behind Alan, a witness could look right in front of them.

Paul would be in the courtroom every day. He sat at a foldout table in the gallery, directly behind Alan. From there, he ran our entire electronics system.

Before we could start, the pregnant juror who wanted to be excused brought a note from her doctor. She refused to give up. There was much discussion about the note. When it looked like the judge was leaning toward dismissing her, Alan relented, and she was released. That bumped up one of the two alternates.

Then, the juror with the case in Corsicana told us he'd received a subpoena. He had to be in Corsicana tomorrow for witness preparation. The judge called the court coordinator in Corsicana to discuss our juror's situation. We learned that the defendant had been in jail for almost two years. They would have to either put him on trial or release him. The coordinator suggested talking to the prosecutor.

While all that was going on, I observed that Lenny and James Bell were barely speaking to each other. I assumed Lenny was upset at the censored and disjointed opening statement. And Lenny was now interested in everything Alan did. He was hanging around Alan during breaks and had paid the court reporter for a written version of Alan's opening statement, cradling the manuscript like it was the latest *Harry Potter* book.

At 10 a.m., with the jury finally in their seats, Alan rose and said, "The plaintiff calls Jo Hopper."

I took the stand and settled in for what I knew would be a difficult couple of days. I was wearing a light gray outfit and looked down at my arm, trying to figure out where the spotlight shining on my sleeve was coming from. I looked up and realized the harsh light was reflecting off my silver hair, which made me remember how Dad used to scare us by holding a flashlight under his chin. I leaned forward in the witness chair, hoping to put the overhead light behind me and perhaps cast a more "heavenly glow" instead of the sheen that the jury was seeing.

The calmness I'd felt earlier had vanished. I was nervous. I clutched a single strand of pearls Max had given me.

Alan started with a few softball questions. "Tell me about your upbringing. Tell me about Max's upbringing. How did you and Max meet?" They were simple questions, and I soon fell into a comfortable rhythm.

I talked about my illness and how we thought I'd die first. I explained how Max and I had made our money and invested it in startups. As we moved into the hiring of JPMorgan, Alan pulled a fast one and got the judge to overrule Eichman on a key piece of evidence: the email where Debra Round and the higher-ups at JPMorgan celebrated landing the Estate of Max Hopper. Eichman lost a second time when I talked about how John Round, Debra's husband, represented the heirs. That had to sting.

Throughout my testimony, I went soft on Stephen and Laura. I turned everything back on JPMorgan. They were the experts here. The professionals. They should have known better.

Eichman lost a third time when Alan was allowed to explore all the screwups during the temporary administration. I felt this testimony caused severe damage to JPMorgan's case because Susan's mistakes and lack of action were on full display.

I noticed when I started my testimony that Susan sat up straighter, fully attentive. But with each screw-up we described, she seemed to slump deeper down into her seat, perhaps exhibiting some embarrassment?

During a break, Eichman complained about Alan using the most grumpy-looking photos possible to show Cantrill and the other JPMorgan employees. Alan laughed, saying they shouldn't have posed like that. The judge overruled Eichman's objection.

Jack and I talked in the hall. He was pumped. "You're doing great. You must be scoring some points."

"I sure hope so," I told him.

I retook the stand and continued stacking brick after brick of JPMorgan's incompetence. Before I knew it, lunch had arrived.

As a treat for the jurors, the three parties had decided to pay for their lunch. We had a restaurant deliver it each day. It was the least we could do.

When I returned to the courtroom, Laura approached me with a serious expression. "Jo, we have learned so much about this case."

I wanted to tell her, "All you had to do was review the 28,000 documents like I did." But I just smiled and said nothing.

As the judge took the bench, she informed us that the juror who'd been shot would be needed for the criminal trial. However, the prosecutor agreed to do the prep over the phone and put him on the stand for one day only. We would recess for that day.

Just as we were about to start up again, another juror had an issue. She said she had a prepaid vacation coming up. The judge studied the documents, listened to her, and said she was sorry but that she could not be released. She should've brought that up during jury selection.

I climbed back into the witness box and resumed my testimony. I talked about the error-riddled inventory and how JPMorgan had farmed it out to Cantrill. This had allowed Hunton & Williams to suck more money from the estate. To me, it was like an apartment complex hiring a maintenance worker. Instead of fixing the toilet, the maintenance man opens up the Yellow Pages and calls a plumber to fix it. It appeared to me that JPMorgan looked for every chance to have Cantrill do the work they were being paid to do.

One annoying aspect of my testimony was Eichman. He objected early and often, even making multiple requests for a mistrial. He also claimed he'd been prejudiced during jury selection now that the pregnant juror had been excused. I wondered what the jury thought about him.

Alan had me wrap up my first day explaining how JPMorgan didn't know how to exercise stock options for a set cash price. I glanced at Susan as she slumped down even further.

I was thrilled when I was able to testify about how much money Cantrill had billed the estate, and I kept going. Then I was able to raise something we'd recently learned. I explained that when the bank ran out of money in the Max Hopper Estate to pay Hunton & Williams' monthly invoices, they borrowed money from JPMorgan—*themselves*—and saddled the estate with the debt. John Pierpont Morgan would've been proud of that move. Now, the bank was seeking repayment of this self-loan from Stephen and Laura. The second those words left my lips, the jurors frowned. I wished I could tell them that JPMorgan did this very thing to other beneficiaries in Texas, drained trusts for legal fees and borrowed from themselves, but all that was excluded.

By the time I was done, it felt like I'd run a marathon. Thank goodness I'd be finished with Alan and Lenny by the end of tomorrow. I knew Eichman would hammer me all day Friday. At least I'd have the weekend to recuperate. I couldn't wait.

As we packed up our things, I pulled off a piece of paper from my legal pad and, in unfamiliar handwriting, saw the phrase, "Eleven days 'til the remodelers!" I had no idea who'd written it.

THURSDAY MORNING, EICHMAN started the day off with… surprise… more objections. Alan fought hard. Lenny had some strong arguments against Eichman too, but he often remained silent, letting Alan do most of the work. When Lenny did speak, good things came from his mouth.

My testimony began with the subject of how Stephen and Laura complained about me behind my back. Not once had Susan given me a heads-up. Instead, she'd allowed their fears to go unchecked.

When I discussed Susan's gaslighting and my ruined relationship with Max's children and their kids, whom I considered my grandchildren, my voice cracked as I held back tears. But court administrators know emotions run high in trials. That's why boxes of tissue are everywhere.

After I regained my composure, I felt strengthened. I testified about how JPMorgan missed the date to exercise the Jamcracker options. I detailed everything Susan had done behind my back and how devastating it felt.

Eichman objected but added in a new feature: the speaking objection. It went something like this: "Your Honor, we object to this question because, as you know, JPMorgan would never do such a thing. We didn't lose any money from the estate. That fact is well-established. We did everything right." His objections allowed him to plant doubt with the jury. It was a brilliant move, especially since neither Alan, Lenny, nor Bell objected to this tactic.

I was sure Eichman also used the speaking objection to accomplish another goal: wasting time. It was a solid strategy, one I could have admired if I hadn't been its victim. His objections often caused Alan to withdraw his questions or ask them differently. Rarely did Alan wait to see how the judge ruled. I assumed that was some type of trial strategy.

Eventually, though, Alan utilized the same speaking objection tactic himself. He spewed a lot of extraneous but valuable information at the jury. What's good for the goose is good for the plaintiff's attorney.

When the day ended, Alan still had me on direct. I was hoping I'd be done by the weekend, but it wasn't looking good.

"Ten more days 'til the remodelers!" I spotted on my legal pad. I looked at Alan and saw nothing but worry on his face. This was maddening.

MY LIFE SEEMED like that movie *Groundhog Day*. Wake up. Crawl out of bed. Eat breakfast. Get dressed. Drive to the parking garage. Ride the elevator to the 24th floor. Take the stand. Testify. Repeat.

Today was Friday, the day I should've been off the stand and sitting next to Alan. Instead, I saw no end in sight. There were three reasons for this.

First, Alan had a massive amount of evidence to admit using me on the stand. Because the case had gone on for six years, I had a lot of explaining to do. Between Alan and me, we'd grossly underestimated the time it would take to accomplish that.

The second reason was that we were continually starting late. If it wasn't an issue with a juror, someone was late getting to court. One time, a juror had a flat tire. These delays added up.

The third reason was Eichman's objections. Each morning, there was a fresh round. And during my testimony, his objections never stopped. His motions for mistrial were numerous. And the speaking objections were an effective time killer, since Lenny and Alan had both joined Eichman in using this strategy. Being on the stand felt like running in Jello. I worked hard but didn't get far.

The main issue on Friday was how I had hired Alan's firm. I wanted to tell the jury that Alan's firm had sued JPMorgan for $681 million on the STS Trust case. It had gone to trial and settled after a couple of witnesses had testified. It was such an important case that the media had covered it. Unfortunately, Eichman successfully blocked me from saying any of that, because it was part of the motion in limine. Chalk up another win for Team JPMorgan.

I did receive one piece of good news. In conversation during breaks, the judge ruled out many more of the private arguments the heirs and I'd had while Max was alive. Most of them were embarrassing. Lenny was the one who saved me. He argued that despite the relevance, the prejudicial effect substantially outweighed the probative value of the evidence, and thus it was inadmissible. Apparently, there was a rule for that—403. The judge agreed, and Eichman was sunk on that issue.

At one point during my testimony on the stand, my mind shut off for what seemed like an eternity, though in reality it was perhaps 30 to 45 seconds. Somehow, I was able to say aloud to the courtroom, "I have lost my mind." Then, something in my brain clicked back into place, and everything worked again. It was like the Wi-Fi had gone out, reset, and come back on.

Strange.

Perhaps it was the stress or the physical demand that testifying was taking on me. Tarian had warned me. He had suggested long before trial that I get a personal trainer and work out as if I was entering an Ironman Triathlon. I had worked out but not as hard as I should have. Now I saw the wisdom of his advice.

In the afternoon, we admitted all the checks I had paid to my lawyers. Eichman exploded with objections. Yet the judge allowed it. Thank you, mock trial jurors!

During a break near the end of the day, I thanked Barbara for not bringing their children to court. I was grateful they were spared hearing about the problems between their parents and me.

Before I knew it, the day was over. I flipped over a sheet of my legal pad and saw: "Nine days 'til the remodelers!" At least I had the long Labor Day weekend to recharge my batteries.

"MILLIE, COME HERE," I called. She sauntered over to me. It was early September and still hot, so I could only sit under Max's peach tree in the morning.

It was a gorgeous Sunday morning. I had made a little plate of oatmeal and crusted bread with a dish of peach jam. It was nice, being far away from all that drama—the courtroom, witness stand, and Eichman.

Sitting against the tree, I felt calm and at peace. Later on, I'd feed the four blue-winged teal ducks: Huey, Dewey, Luisa, and Daisy. They lived in a pond a hundred yards from my house. Every afternoon they would arrive for duck food and water. They were adorable. But for now, it was just me, Millie, Max's peach tree, and that delicious peach jam. With Jack running errands, I had the whole place to myself. I took a deep breath and exhaled. I intended to take plenty of me-time.

But in the deep crevices of my mind sat the specter of more testimony and, eventually, Eichman's cross-examination. If I thought about it too much, it might destroy me. So I put it out of my mind and stroked Millie. Then, I finished my breakfast and went back to bed.

THE ALARM RANG again. It was Tuesday morning. Something wasn't right. This time, I didn't lie there for a few moments but jumped out of bed and raced to the toilet. I had extreme diarrhea. I tried to leave the bathroom to dress but couldn't. I was in big trouble.

From the bathroom, I called Alan and explained the situation. I had already taken an over-the-counter medication to control it. "I need to see if this is going to stop," I told him. "I'll call my internist to find out if I can get in to see her."

"You do that," he said. "We'll run videos or do something else. Don't worry, we'll manage."

Jack drove me to Baylor Hospital, where I saw my doctor. She checked me out and said to stay on the Imodium. When I mentioned losing my mind on the stand, she said it was probably the vagus nerve. "Normally, a person would pass out," she told me. "You were lucky to be seated. It could've been bad."

If that happened, my estate would be handling matters.

I went home and took Imodium all day. The diarrhea subsided. I wondered how the other witnesses would handle the pressure of the stand.

WEDNESDAY MORNING, ALAN gave me a brief recap of what had happened on Tuesday while I was at the doctor's office. Eichman had added seventeen new exhibits to his list. Alan was outraged. Eichman should've asked the court for leave to add them, but he did it anyway. Judge Thompson allowed it, saying she'd give Alan and Lenny the same leeway.

Alan told the judge there had been a lot of objections and conferences. Judge Thompson replied that she didn't think it had been unreasonable. "I'm going to allow everybody adequate time," she said.

According to Alan, they argued all morning. Eichman worked hard to prevent any mention of the Chinese Wall fiasco. That issue affected the bank way beyond my case. Eichman was very aggressive about it. Yet the judge overruled him. The Chinese Wall could be discussed.

The lawyers argued for hours over other issues until Judge Thompson chided them. "You're running out of time to get this trial in," she scolded.

The jury stayed in their room all morning until 1:30 p.m. When they came out, the judge told them my testimony had to be interrupted to view some videos. They watched an hour of Todd Baird's video, "Private Banker at JPMorgan." He was the gold medal winner in "I don't remember" and "I just want to help families with their goals and objectives." Alan said Baird's testimony was impactful. I had no idea how.

The jury also saw ninety minutes of Gary Stolbach's deposition testimony. That was followed by thirty-three minutes of Kal Grant's. She was the one who'd promised I wouldn't pay a cent. Overall, Alan felt they had used the day as best they could without wasting time.

"Do you still feel like we'll finish the trial on time?" I asked.

"Yes. We'll get it in. Don't you worry." He was so calm and reassuring, I believed him.

Before I could testify again, Alan played another twenty-five minutes of Kal Grant's testimony. Then, he put me back on the stand, skillfully cleaning up a lot of loose ends.

To close out my direct examination, Alan covered the mental anguish damages. We addressed Jack's presence in my life and introduced him to the jury. Eichman objected, pointing out that I had presented no evidence of any medical treatment or medication for my mental anguish. He wanted that portion of my testimony stricken. This wasted a lot of time before the judge overruled him. When Alan finally passed me, I was exhausted and ready to go home, but it was only lunchtime.

When we returned from lunch, I went to talk with Stephen and Laura. To my surprise, they were no longer speaking to me. Neither was Barbara. I guess they'd heard too much bad stuff. Now, they appeared to want nothing to do with me.

As I left the courtroom for one last bathroom break before returning to the stand, I looked back at Max's children. He would be saddened. They were passive and uninformed of the evidence in this case. They had not put in the work as I had. It was difficult for me to believe they were his children.

As for James Bell, the rift between him and Lenny appeared to be complete. It seemed they were no longer speaking to each other, and Bell was merely sitting there. Lenny had grabbed the wheel and was driving the bus.

LUNCH WAS A nice break. Alan was finished, and it was Lenny's turn. When I retook the stand, he started with leading questions, most of them softballs. "JPMorgan treated you badly, isn't that true?"

"Yes, sir."

His questions required short answers.

Of course, Eichman objected to Lenny leading me as well as the questions in general. Yet, for some reason, Eichman allowed me to ramble on. My answers grew longer and longer as Lenny and I worked together. It was easy.

After two hours, Lenny was out of relevant questions to ask. I'd hoped that he would be able to run me to the end of the day, but he couldn't. When I heard him say, "Pass the witness," I swallowed hard. It was Eichman's turn. I assumed it would be bad.

I had no idea just how bad.

Chapter Thirty-Three

"The toughest are people mistakes, when you put the wrong person in a job. Sometimes you're too slow to move them out."

—Jamie Dimon, Chairman & CEO
JPMorgan Chase Bank, N.A.

It was 3 p.m. on Wednesday. For six days, the trial had been my life. Testifying for more than three days had made it even more intense.

I sat there uncomfortably with nothing else to do, watching the general of the opposing army position his notes on the podium. Squirming in my seat, I tried hard to focus on 5 p.m., when I could go home and regroup after a good night's sleep. But first, I'd have to endure two hours of Eichman's cross. I told myself I was ready. I hoped I was right.

Eichman began, and I was immediately taken aback. After being in litigation for six years, I'd learned some trial tactics, one of which was to start with agreeable questions to grab the low-hanging fruit from adverse witnesses. This is necessary because once the examiner pulls out the flamethrower, the witness is unlikely to agree with anything the lawyer says from that point on. That's why I assumed Eichman would raise topics like when I obtained appraisals or fired my previous attorneys. Easy stuff. It would be like two boxers dancing around half-heartedly, throwing an occasional jab into the air. Instead, he moved in close and hit me in the face. It was both stunning and painful.

In seconds, Eichman exposed the fact that even though the heirs and I were suing each other, we were all ganging up against JPMorgan. He pointed out that during Lenny's entire cross-examination, not once had he asked me about one of those claims. In the first minutes of his cross-examination, Eichman racked up gobs of points.

I thought he'd stay on that for a while, but he switched to my home on Robledo. Using a gorgeous photo of the property, he made it clear to the jury that this was a rich person's house. He also made it clear that it was three stories high and over 8,000 square feet.

I didn't want to look at the jurors because I sensed several of them shifting in their chairs. Suddenly, the courtroom was hot. I'm not a person who sweats much, but I felt tiny beads of perspiration forming on my forehead and upper lip.

Eichman knew what he was doing. He drilled down into the rare coins stored at the house and the spacious wine cellar with over a thousand bottles. These jurors were working-class individuals. That information had to make them uneasy.

Brick by brick, Eichman methodically tore down our wall of truth. No fact was too small to be overturned or clarified. He pointed out that JPMorgan had not brought in a moving van and stripped my house clean, an image we had somewhat created.

After an hour of this, I wanted to be sick—again. But he stopped for nothing and no one. Next up were my mental anguish damages. Eichman lit the flamethrower and deliberately went through every photo, trip, and good time I'd had in the last seven years. One devastating example was a photo of me sleeping on a train headed from London to Paris. What could I say? It had been a nice trip.

He drilled me on my boyfriend Jack Hooper, whose name was so close to mine that people thought we were married. When he shared how I had stayed with Jack at my lawyer's house in Hawaii, I could feel my case slipping away.

Once Eichman had squeezed every drop of credible evidence from the rag of mental anguish, he switched tactics. Using a cunning trick, he produced a transcript from the current trial to impeach me. Alan objected because it wasn't certified. The judge shut Eichman down, but not before he hit me with some hard questions.

Eichman went over the other lawsuits involving the heirs and me and all the money spent on attorneys' fees. He created the impression that we were all crazy, litigious fools. Based on my answers, his image was believable.

At times, I tried to hit back. I managed to slip in darts about how JPMorgan had poisoned the heirs against me. I straightened up and defended Max for not executing a written will. Just when I thought it was time for a break, Eichman pulled out every embarrassing incident involving the heirs and me—any argument or harsh words we had ever engaged in.

He showed hateful emails from Stephen and Laura and my responses to them. With each one, it felt like I was on a conveyor belt, slowly heading to a spinning saw blade. I tried to keep my answers short, giving him a point or two, but it was hard. Very hard.

Eichman displayed the insurance policy Max had left me. It had paid out $1.1 million. I was no longer a poor widow, I was a rich widow suing to become richer. It would be hard to feel sorry for someone like me.

There was not one tiny molecule of pain Eichman withheld. He burned everything. Each element of our case was charred. When the clock read 5 p.m. and Eichman said, "Pass the witness," I thought I might faint.

Alan hustled over to help me as the judge dismissed us. He could see I needed it. As we walked to my car, I tried to clear the fog from my mind. "That was a rough two hours," I said.

Alan's eyes snapped to me. "Two hours? What are you talking about?"

"I started at three. It's five now. Isn't that two hours?"

"Are you okay, Jo?" he asked, unable to hide the concern in his voice. I rubbed my head. "I think so. Why?"

"Eichman cross-examined you from three to five *yesterday*. This morning, you started again and testified for eight hours. Today is Thursday."

"T-that's not p-possible," I stammered, searching my mind for crucial details.

"You're done testifying. You just need to get home and get some sleep," he said calmly, glancing over at Jack. "We'll talk tomorrow."

I handed the keys to Jack and he drove home. I was in no shape to do anything.

IT WAS FRIDAY morning. Thank God I arrived back in court with a fully functioning brain. For some reason, my mind had been so focused on Eichman's cross-examination that I hadn't processed anything else. Six straight years of litigation and five days of testimony will do that to a person.

Two jurors were late so we couldn't start until nine. When they arrived, I took my seat behind Alan and waited for the trial to resume. I can't describe the sheer joy when Alan stood up and said, "We call

Susan Novak to the stand." Not only would I not have to answer any more questions, but now Susan would have to endure what lay ahead.

Good luck with that.

Alan employed the low-hanging-fruit tactic. He got her to agree to a wide variety of issues, many of which were vital in rehabilitating me.

From the very first question, it looked like Susan was shocked to be testifying. Alan had told me that standard trial tactics meant calling Stephen and Laura next before calling Susan. Some lawyers might call the experts before they brought Susan to the stand. "And some lawyers might not even call Susan," he'd said, "although they would be the inexperienced ones. We have too much good stuff not to call her."

Once Alan had plucked all the free goodies, he moved into the hard stuff. As he did, Susan shifted away from the microphone and began mumbling. No one, including Eichman, could hear her.

The judge admonished her several times to speak up. She didn't. At one point, Paul Malouf, our AV expert, repositioned her mic, trying to improve matters. It didn't.

While Paul tinkered, I invited Stephen and Laura to sit in the gallery behind me so they could watch Susan testify. They still weren't treating me any better but came over anyway, sitting on either side of Jack.

James Bell was another issue. The heirs seemed to be closer to him than they were to Lenny. After Bell's opening statement, I thought he was toast. Surely the heirs and Lenny would cast him aside. But Stephen and Laura seemed to favor him over Lenny. Now that I was off the stand, I could watch all the interactions, making notes on my pad.

Once the sound was better, the cross-examination continued. Susan began futzing with her necklace, then mumbling again. The judge issued new admonishments, but they had no effect. If she was the best JPMorgan had to offer, they were in trouble.

Alan's style was completely different than Eichman's scorched-earth approach. Alan used a surgical blade to slice a witness. The cut was so quick and the blade so sharp that the witness barely felt it. Before long, there were little blood trails all over the witness stand. This silent assassin method seemed to resonate with the jury.

An excellent example of Alan's style dealt with gaslighting. Alan displayed emails on the large courtroom screen of the heirs complaining about something. Then, he showed Susan's response directing some blame at me. When the heirs blamed me outright in other emails, she either agreed or failed to correct their wrong assumptions.

After I took a trip to Paris using my lifetime pass on American Airlines, Stephen and Laura were certain I had stolen miles from Max's massive frequent flyer account. Susan had the American Airlines Advantage statements and password to Max's account but didn't set the heirs straight. And she certainly didn't send those complaints to me so I could deal with them. It was Gaslighting 101.

Just like in her deposition, Alan asked Susan if she remembered the twenty-six-minute call I'd had with her when she called to inform me that Tom Cantrill would be the estate's lawyer. Despite my yelling and screaming, she couldn't recall it. Alan removed his reading glasses, rubbed his eyes, and let her answer hang in the air over the jury. It was extremely effective.

With each question, Susan slumped down in the witness chair and mumbled more. Cut by cut, her credibility dripped out and pooled on the floor.

Regarding the offer I'd sent her on three different occasions to buy everything from the heirs at the full appraised value, which was highly inflated, and thus resolve this entire nightmare—she'd never passed it on to Stephen and Laura. Her only response was, "I don't remember" and "I don't recall," the same responses she'd given in her deposition.

As Alan moved to a big conclusion, he asked Susan if I was a beneficiary of the estate. She said I was. Then, Alan showed how she had testified under oath in her deposition that I was not a beneficiary. Susan looked away from the jury. Obviously, she had not done any homework, like something as simple as reading the transcript of her own deposition.

Throughout her testimony, Eichman objected like crazy. To me, it emphasized to the jury that Alan was scoring points. It was like yelling out, "This is hurting my case so badly that I'm going to talk loudly and hope to distract you." I couldn't believe that would work.

Near the end of the day, Alan read a statement that said holding onto our personal property and not releasing it had caused additional expenses that could've been avoided. He asked Susan if she disagreed with that statement. Of course, she disagreed. But then Alan pulled the rug out from under her when he displayed the email containing the statement. It had been written and sent to her by Tom Cantrill. Susan had just disagreed with JPMorgan's expert probate lawyer. It was devastating.

During a later break, I ran into Ms. Kravik, JPMorgan's in-house counsel. She spent each day clacking away on her laptop. I assumed she was taking notes of the trial and generating reports to her superiors. For the first time, her face appeared somber.

One surprise Susan Novak managed to slip into the trial was a brand-new lawsuit awaiting me. After all they'd put me through, JPMorgan planned on suing me after the trial. When she said that, I watched two jurors lean back and cross their arms.

Alan got in some other body blows before finishing off his cross with a bang.

Alan: Okay. Ms. Novak, I have one last question for you. Is there anything, knowing what has happened, if you had it all to do over again that you would do differently, regarding the handling of the Hopper estate?

Susan: Well, what immediately comes to mind is I would manage expectations differently.

Alan: Is that it?

Susan: I would've explained the process differently and that everyone knew how hard I was working but specifically, right now off the top of my head.

Alan: That's it?

Susan: Right now.

Alan: Well actually, I asked you that same question a year ago, when you were under oath, closer in time to the events of the last six years, and I asked you if there was anything you would have done differently and do you remember what your answer was?

Susan: No.

Alan: That was your answer, wasn't it? "No, there's nothing I would have done differently," right?

Susan: I don't recall but, if that's—

Alan: Let's refresh your recollection and we'll be able to end then...

Susan's face appeared on the screen. She was in the deposition testifying. The video played.

Alan: Is there anything, knowing now what's happened, that if
         you had it to do all over again, you would do differently
         regarding the handing of the Hopper estate?

Susan: On my—from my perspective?

Alan: On the part of anyone at the bank, including yourself.

Susan: No.

Alan waited for what seemed like an eternity before he said, "Thank you for your time, Ms. Novak." And that was that.

James Bell was up next to cross Susan, but there wasn't enough time. The judge adjourned court until Monday.

When Alan said he'd walk me to my car, we lingered back, allowing everyone else to go ahead, including Jack.

The courthouse was empty as we strolled down the halls, our footsteps echoing off the marble walls. Once we reached the garage and no one was around us, I told Alan about Ms. Kravik's expression. He smiled. "When she makes her report to the folks upstairs, we'll be getting a settlement offer next week."

"You really think so?" I asked.

"Yes. Trust me, the executives at JPMorgan aren't stupid enough to allow this nightmare to go to a jury verdict. We'll have it settled soon, maybe on Monday."

"That would be wonderful," I said, "and you never told me how I did on the stand, especially after Eichman's cross."

"You did fine. Attacking a widow is never good. I don't care who you are."

"I didn't think I did well."

"That's because when you're under fire, everything seems different. I was very pleased with your testimony."

I mused over that for a moment. "If we settle, we won't have to worry about losing another juror or running up against the remodelers. Right?"

"That's right," Alan said, grabbing my arm and stopping me, "because I want to tell you the truth right now so you can digest it over the weekend. If we don't settle next week, we will most assuredly not beat the construction deadline or keep six jurors in the box."

"What are you saying?" I asked, the blood draining from my face.

Alan lowered his voice. "This trial is running so long we have almost zero chance of getting it to a verdict. I just hope JPMorgan doesn't realize that and settles next week. Then, we don't have to worry about it."

"Well, now I'm worried about it," I moaned, my voice shaking.

"I'm sorry, but I want you to be prepared for a mistrial. If so, we'll have to retry this again next year."

Suddenly, I was lightheaded. Before I knew it, Alan had me to my VW Beetle and into the passenger's seat. As Jack pulled away from the courthouse, I couldn't hold back any longer. I began to cry.

Chapter Thirty-Four

"We know every company makes mistakes. But if you don't acknowledge mistakes, it's unlikely you can fix them."
—Jamie Dimon, Chairman & CEO
JPMorgan Chase Bank, N.A.
Letter to the Shareholders 2011 Annual Report

The weekend was a blur. Millie, my precious dog, fell ill. I'd been up with her all night, barely getting two hours of sleep. On Monday, I was exhausted, and we hadn't even started.

"Four jurors are running late," Alan whispered to me when he returned from the judge's chambers. "They're all getting tired. We're running out of time."

"I hope JPMorgan makes an offer today," I whispered back. "Then, we can all go back to bed."

Alan offered a half-hearted grin.

Once we had all the jurors, Susan trudged to the witness stand and took her seat. She looked as tired as I felt.

James Bell stood there for a moment, sorting out his questions on the podium. I assumed we'd see a repeat of his censored and disjointed opening statement.

I was wrong.

What emerged from Bell was a movie star lawyer, something like Matthew McConaughey. He was different than both Eichman and Alan but highly effective. The second he began gutting Susan, the jurors leaned forward, interested in everything he had to say.

His first attack dealt with a $384,000 estimated tax payment JPMorgan had mistakenly sent to the IRS. The money was not lost but couldn't be immediately retrieved. Instead of informing Stephen and Laura about their sloppy mistake, Bell showed Susan's emails from various JPMorgan employees discussing how to hide it from the heirs or spin it as no big deal. Caught red-handed, Susan did the right thing and admitted she should have told the heirs.

Surely an offer would be forthcoming at any moment.

Bell moved on to show that under the written contract, JPMorgan's administration fee was based on asset values listed in the estate's tax return. Yet 2010 was a unique year in which the IRS estate tax was eliminated, so JPMorgan did not have to file an estate tax return in 2010. Susan admitted they hadn't filed one. Then, Bell sprung his trap. Without a tax return, there could be no administration fee. Susan tried to slough it off, but he had her cold. It was some of Bell's best work. Within twenty minutes, he destroyed what little of Susan my lawyer had left behind. Frankly, I was amazed. This guy was a real pro.

He peppered Susan with more wrongdoing, but she didn't answer the questions. On several occasions, the judge instructed her to answer, and each time the judge's voice sounded sterner. The jury appeared frustrated.

Eichman continued with speaking objections until Bell finally objected. Judge Thompson instructed each lawyer to give only their objection. If she needed the argument behind it, she'd ask for it.

Bell continued his theatrics, especially when Susan claimed the heirs had not lost a single dollar. Showing JPMorgan's written administration agreement on the screen next to the tax return that wasn't filed, it was clear the heirs owed no fee to JPMorgan. Thus, Stephen and Laura had lost at least $230,000—the amount JPMorgan had taken from the estate account to pay themselves. I wanted to stand up and clap, but of course, I couldn't. Instead, my soul smiled because I felt that admission guaranteed the heirs a victory. How much more they could obtain, we'd just have to see.

As Bell neared the end of his cross-examination, Susan switched back to, "I don't know," "I don't recall," or "I don't remember." It was at this very moment that the trial tactic of having Susan sit in the court- room backfired. Bell put his hands on his hips and told her she was the corporate representative for JPMorgan. The bank could've had anyone sitting there, but they chose her. "And now, you're telling this jury you don't even know basic facts about how JPMorgan works? Whose job it is to perform a particular function?"

It was powerful.

Bell passed the witness and we took a break. Alan asked my opinion of Bell's cross-examination. "I thought he did a marvelous job despite eighteen objections from Eichman. I counted them." Alan agreed.

I walked to the restroom and noticed Stephen snapping at Laura for not listening to something. They both seemed on edge. I guessed they could sense the witness stand creeping closer and closer. At any moment, it would be their turn. That had to be stressful.

After the break, Eichman took Susan back through all the events of the Max Hopper Estate administration. She appeared calmer on the stand. Remarkably, her memory improved, because she didn't forget anything with Eichman questioning her. It was a Festivus miracle!

With a bit of sparkle in her eyes, Susan recounted how a meeting in December 2010 with Stephen had surprised her. She claimed Stephen had yelled at her. I found that hard to believe since Stephen's demeanor is much like Mr. Spock's on *Star Trek*. Laura, I would've believed. But not Stephen.

Susan provided plenty of examples of how mean and cruel we were. For me, I had sent her seventeen documents in one day. She left out the part about how they were all scanned documents she had requested.

Susan continued by claiming she was the one who'd obtained a higher offer on the coins. That was news to me because I remembered doing it. A quick check of her emails reflected that she knew this. Of course, why she was trying to sell the coins instead of simply issuing a piece of paper that stated the three of us now owned them as joint tenants, I'll never understand. But this is the position in which I found myself.

At the tail end of the testimony, Eichman laid out how poorly I thought of her. That was true. I did. I was shocked he'd be exploring that fact. Then, he clarified. Susan testified that she was amazed I wanted to be her friend. Eichman displayed fake surprise when he asked her to explain. She claimed that despite my harsh feelings for her, she had been receiving connect requests over and over from me on LinkedIn.

I had done no such thing. My blood boiled.

When Eichman put the connection requests on the screen showing my name, I wanted to stand up and scream. I had not done that. They were either fake, or my computer had been hacked. The whole thing was outrageous and undermined my credibility.

Eichman ended his direct examination just after 5 p.m. The judge told us that Wednesday would not be an off day because the victim-juror's case had been moved. Also, the contractors could not start until next Tuesday. That bought us two extra days. Alan was somewhat relieved.

"I still don't think we'll make it," he said when we were alone in the elevator.

"Did Eichman bring you a settlement offer?" I asked.

"No. But after Susan's performance today, look for it tomorrow. The executives will read Kravik's report and send instructions back to get rid of this dog."

"What if they don't?"

Alan shook his head. "It's bad news. There aren't enough days left. Just think positively."

THE NEXT MORNING, another juror was late. We didn't start Day Eleven until 11 a.m. Alan tried not to look worried, but I could tell he was. I know I felt anxious.

Alan began his second cross-examination of Susan Novak. When he delved into my prior attorney, Jim Jennings, Susan called him a bully. Alan asked her for a definition of a bully. After hearing it, he read from a dictionary: "A bully is defined as a person who uses strength or power to harm or intimidate those who are weaker. Are you truly testifying that the nation's largest bank with a net worth of 200 billion dollars, 81,000 employees, and represented by a law firm of over 700 lawyers was weaker than Jim Jennings, a lawyer in Dallas with a firm of, at most, four lawyers? Is that truly your testimony?"

She stared at Eichman for help, but none came. As Tarian had taught me, no one can testify for you. Finally, Susan stiffened her back, stuck out her jaw, and said, "Yes." She was claiming that JPMorgan was weaker than Jim Jennings!

I had to give her credit, she was determined to stay on the Titanic even as the frigid water reached her knees.

The next subject Alan explored was legal bills from Eichman's firm. I did not realize Alan had found some interesting entries. Before I sued JPMorgan, the invoices clearly showed that Cantrill and Eich-man were busy drafting a lawsuit against me. If I hadn't beaten them to the courthouse, they'd be spinning the evidence first instead of me. It would've been a severe disadvantage.

The fact that JPMorgan looked to sue me first and planned to sue me again after the trial showed its true face. JPMorgan isn't friendly or benevolent. Rather than right a wrong, that bank will rip you to pieces—whatever it takes to hold onto your money.

The mystery of my LinkedIn invitation to Susan was solved. When you join LinkedIn, they devour your contact list and send out invitations without you ever knowing about it. Alan asked Susan if she knew how LinkedIn worked, and she admitted she didn't. I was glad Alan got the information out there to the jury, just in case they didn't know this was how she would have received those "invitations."

Alan finished up with the subject of Susan's suffering while working on this estate. She had testified to that fact, saying it had been very stressful. Her comment was all an apex predator like Alan needed. He asked Susan if she had lost any money working on the estate. Or personally paid any legal fees. Or been accused of theft. Or been told someone would sell her house to a stranger while she was living in it. If Susan had suffered while getting paid to do her job, imagine what I had felt like while paying to be tortured. In truth, her discomfort was nothing compared to the terrible stress I'd suffered. Alan's questions not only amplified my mental anguish damages, but were a powerful climax to this case.

Susan looked anxious to leave the stand, but James Bell popped up to beat on her again. He said he only had twenty minutes of questions, but then he took two hours. The main point of attack was why JPMorgan refused to step down as Independent Administrator. Bell claimed it was because they wanted to drain the estate's account. As he led Susan through the withdrawals, she was forced to admit $3 million had been taken to pay the attorneys. Then, Bell got her to admit that if JPMorgan had stepped down, the estate's account would have $3.285 million in it, and the heirs would have received all of it. His line of questioning made JPMorgan appear greedy. Bell was definitely on fire.

When he finally passed her and Eichman said he had no further questions, Susan stepped down looking like a refugee fleeing a war-torn country. I knew the feeling.

Alan kept the trial moving by immediately calling Trey Cox, our expert on attorneys' fees. This guy was one of the country's top experts.

He'd even written the definitive book—*How to Recover Attorneys' Fees in Texas*—for attorneys in Texas to use in court. The jury appeared to love him.

Trey explained how he had reviewed 85,366 pages of discovery, another 15,000 pages comprising 600 different pleadings, 5,426 pages of transcripts for 29 depositions, and 113 hours and eight minutes of videotaped depositions. He testified that there had been 48 hearings, which produced another 1,327 pages of transcripts. When he stacked up all the paperwork in this case, it was 65 feet high and stretched to the top of Big Tex, an icon at the State Fair of Texas. The jurors nodded and smiled as Alan put a picture of Big Tex on the screen.

Alan asked a few questions, letting Trey do all the work. Trey explained that the fees had to be *reasonable* and *necessary* for a jury to award attorneys' fees to me. Eichman had preadmitted an exhibit with a colorful diagram of the phrase "pigs get fat and hogs get slaughtered." Eichman intended to cross Trey with it, showing my lawyers had been overbilling me, and thus JPMorgan couldn't be expected to pay *unreasonable* attorneys' fees. Alan pulled out Eichman's exhibit and had Trey use it to explain that attorneys who overbilled their clients would get fat or slaughtered. Just like that, Alan had stolen Eichman's thunder. Good move, Alan.

JPMorgan's expert on attorneys' fees was Mark Sales. Eichman had Sales in the courtroom to listen to Trey's testimony. This was an exception to the rule and a good move on Eichman's part. Presumably, Sales would be testifying that he had listened to Trey's load of bull and that Trey knew nothing. Again, to beat Eichman to the punch, Alan had Trey point out Sales in the audience. Then, Trey proceeded to rip Sales up one side and down the other. It was easy to do since all experts had filed reports before the trial.

I looked back and Sales' face was red. No doubt he would soon return the favor.

Trey finished up the day describing all the attorneys I had hired. He made each one seem like the best in their field or near the top. He even went through Alan's long list of accomplishments, explaining to the jury that although it was embarrassing to Alan, this was required to prove attorneys' fees. Before I knew it, another day was in the books.

Alan and I had developed the habit of walking together to the parking garage. This gave us some time to talk privately. I turned to him and asked, "All this talk about attorneys' fees makes me wonder—what's my daily burn rate?"

"For this trial, it's about $35,000 a day."

I closed my eyes and exhaled. "Okay," I said, a little dizzy. "Do you feel more confident that the trial will end on time?"

"Truthfully, no. Four days until the remodelers and another day with no offer from JPMorgan. I can't believe they're that stupid."

"Maybe they are, Alan. They get fined by the government all the time. We'll just have to slap a big one on them."

He nodded, and we parted ways.

Wednesday's testimony began late once again. This time, it was the judge's dental problems. Because of an appointment she'd had, we started at 10 a.m. These delays were crushing us.

Trey Cox retook the stand and regained that "lovin' feeling" with the jury. He laid out a simple case that every dollar I'd spent in attorneys' fees was utterly righteous. Then, he calmly said he'd charged me $70,000 at $700 an hour, another reasonable and necessary fee that JPMorgan needed to reimburse. When Alan passed him, Lenny said he had no questions. Now it was Eichman's turn.

He started in on Trey, arguing about different theories of attorneys' fees. Trey said Texas adhered to one theory and Eichman claimed he was wrong, it was some other theory. All this talk about theories took the trial deep into the weeds.

Trey was a real pro, though. He bobbed and weaved as Eichman threw punch after punch. Trey was able to slip in some helpful words about all the mental anguish I'd suffered.

Eichman tried a final attack on Trey by claiming my attorneys' invoices were so heavily redacted there was no way for an expert like Trey, much less a juror, to decipher what task had been performed. As such, it was impossible to determine if the fees were reasonable or necessary.

I had to admit I followed Eichman's point. It was obvious that redacted legal bills made it hard to analyze. Yet Trey had been there before. He fired back with thoughtful, intelligent answers, forcing Eichman to give up.

When Trey left, it was like a rockstar leaving the stage. He mingled with the SMU law students and lawyers who'd come to watch him testify. His testimony had been great theater.

Once Trey left, Alan stood up and said, "You honor, the plaintiff rests."

The judge adjourned for the day, and Alan and I walked out to the garage. This time, I didn't mention the dwindling days or lack of an offer from JPMorgan. Instead, I said that Trey Cox had done a great job.

"Yes, he did," Alan nodded, deep in thought. "I don't know if I told you, but Trey's wife is a lawyer who works for JPMorgan."

"Are you kidding me?" I blurted out.

"Nope," Alan replied. "I bet they'll have some interesting conversations tonight."

"Why didn't it come up in trial?"

"I didn't bring it up because I didn't want to show a connection with the evil giant. Eichman didn't because how do you explain that Trey's wife is a great lawyer who JPMorgan is happy to employ, but her husband's an idiot? He couldn't risk the jury wondering about it."

"That's strange," I said.

"Yes, very. This whole trial is."

That was an understatement.

Jack drove me home, and I immediately called Tarian for some advice. I explained what had happened so far and how we had not received an offer. Tarian tried to fill in the blanks.

"Analyze this from all sides," he instructed. "What would Eichman and Cantrill be saying about settling?"

"That they did nothing wrong, and there was no reason to pay."

"Right. They'd also say they are knocking out your attorneys' fees. And with all the happy photos they showed of you on vacation, your mental anguish damages are minimal, if not zero."

"So, Eichman is telling JPMorgan not to pay me anything?" I asked.

"Right again. We've discussed this before. But now there are other players involved. JPMorgan has its people watching the evidence. Susan Kravik may be sending back scathing reports. So, analyze it from the standpoint of the bank's executives."

I thought for a few seconds. "Alan says they have super-smart people, so I guess they'd see the risk and potential liability and make a good offer."

"On the surface, you're right," Tarian said. "But since the law firm that may have assisted in creating this mess has a large malpractice policy, they've covered much of that risk. If JPMorgan loses, they'll likely turn to Hunton & Williams with their hand out and demand some satisfaction. And remember, Susan Novak said JPMorgan approved everything she did in this case. That seems to let Hunton & Williams off the hook."

"So, you don't think there will be an offer?"

"And pay that widow-bitch a penny? Absolutely not! If your team is waiting for an offer, you'll be in the ground before that happens. Which is another reason for them to wait you out, especially with all your health issues."

Now that was blunt.

"What about Stephen and Laura?" I asked.

"They might get an offer, but I doubt it. Still, JPMorgan did drain the estate's account. And that testimony about how the bank had no contractual right to charge them an administration fee might just draw out an offer. I don't know. It could go either way."

"Okay, thanks," I said, hanging up.

I dialed the number of my veterinarian. Millie still wasn't better. I hoped the vet had the results of the blood tests so we could figure out what was wrong with her. The vet answered and delivered the bad news: "Millie has lymphoma." Memories flooded back.

My second Scottie, Rion, had died of lymphoma in 2005. Then, I'd had lymphoma in 2007. Even though I was still alive, it's a death sentence for dogs.

I dropped to my knees and cried. It was yet another terrible setback I'd have to overcome. I just couldn't take it anymore.

Chapter Thirty-Five

"Our litigation system is increasingly arbitrary, capricious, wasteful and slow."

—Jamie Dimon, Chairman & CEO
JPMorgan Chase Bank, N.A.
Letter to the Shareholders 2017 Annual Report

Day Thirteen. Thursday. Each morning I woke up thinking I couldn't take one more day. The depression. My dog Millie. Jack was the only anchor in my life. Without him, I don't know how I would have endured it all.

After forcing myself to get out of bed, I pushed myself to the bathroom, more robot than human. Somehow, I kept moving forward. And the next thing I knew, I was in court again.

Alan continued to worry me. He whispered that we needed to have the verdict in by Monday evening or we were finished. It was going to be tight.

As usual, there was a delay. Three jurors were late. That made no difference because the attorneys spent an hour at the bench. Eichman argued for a directed verdict, claiming Alan had not proved our case. The judge denied his motion, and the bench conferences continued.

Eichman usually positioned himself in the center of the bench. Lenny would try to muscle in from the right with Alan on the left. James Bell lingered around looking for an opening, but Eichman was tall with a long wingspan. He used his arms effectively, waving and pushing the attorneys to the side. Sometimes, it appeared as if he was the only attorney up there.

After the bench conference, I noticed Lenny pacing around, nervous and talking to himself. His case was about to start.

For contingency-fee lawyers like Lenny, a lawsuit is a business venture. It's a partnership with a client. The client provides the claim, and the lawyer covers the expenses and handles all the labor. Lenny had probably spent a ton of money on depositions and staff time. I wondered if he felt pressure to bring in some significant revenue for his firm. He needed to hit a home run or his firm might take a loss.

Before we started back, I lowered my head and prayed for Millie. I asked God to take care of her. I needed her.

I thought we were about to start when another issue popped up. An emergency guardianship call came in for the judge. She talked on the phone as we all watched the day slide by.

When everyone was ready, we learned of yet another problem. A juror sent out a note. Her grandmother was near death, having suffered a stroke in Kansas City. The three parties agreed to release her. When Judge Thompson brought her out, she was torn about leaving. Still, it was more important for her to be there for her grandmother than stay here in this quagmire.

As Alan returned to the counsel table, he wrung his hands together. "No more alternates," he said. "If we lose one more juror, we try this again next year." I tried not to think about that prospect.

Lenny Vitullo called Laura to the stand. From a seat far away from the jury, it took a while for her to pick a path through the tables and chairs and get to the stand. Finally, she took her place.

Lenny led Laura through her childhood. She discussed Max's divorce, my entry onto the scene, and our relationship. She didn't say we were best friends, but she didn't blowtorch me, either. She detailed her educational background, a career in real estate, and eventual ascension to mayor from years on the city council in a suburb outside Kansas City. One of her mayoral career centerpieces was the sale and development of a golf course owned by the city. It was impressive. The jury responded to her with great interest.

Of course, Eichman tossed out lots of objections. Tarian had told me that those objections were a good sign because he was building a case for appeal. That might mean Eichman knew he was screwed at the trial level.

Lenny did an excellent job, allowing Laura to explain how not only had JPMorgan taken all the money from the estate account, but they intended to send Stephen and her a bill for between $900,000 and $1.5

million after the trial. She stated that at one point early on, JPMorgan wanted a release signed by her if they agreed to step down as Independent Administrator. She never signed it, but in her mind, a release meant JPMorgan wanted to be relieved of liability for something. The question hung in the air: Why was JPMorgan worried about being liable for something? It was a nice shot.

Laura complained about Tom Cantrill being the estate's lawyer because he'd done my will. That was a major conflict for her and me as well. Too bad we hadn't worked together to get him tossed.

Lenny led Laura through Susan's gaslighting against me. Laura said she had believed I was messing everything up when it was JPMorgan's job to do those things. By the time Lenny had finished, Laura had laid out a credible case for her and Stephen. I was impressed with her demeanor.

When Lenny finished his direct examination, to my surprise, Alan asked no questions and passed her to Eichman. That's when I gripped the table and waited for Laura to go off the rails.

Eichman started in on her, and for some reason, he allowed her to talk forever. He could've objected and cut her off, but mostly he didn't. As such, she slipped in all kinds of comments. Sure, he eventually had her answer stricken from the record, but the jury still heard it. This was beginning to get good. Like her deposition performance, could I have misjudged Laura?

One of Eichman's early weapons was the long, nasty emails and letters from Gary Stolbach. Eichman detailed each one. Just when I thought he would score big points, Laura gave it right back. She was feisty and combative but in a way that suited someone who had been completely screwed by a large bank. Laura's constant theme was how she knew so much more now than she had then. And she smartly blamed JPMorgan with almost every answer.

Eichman: What you want this jury to believe ma'am, is that the Bank should have ignored what Mr. Stolbach was saying, ignored your lawyer's arguments about the law, and made the distribution. That's the position that you have now, in front of this jury.

Laura: It would have been less expensive than $4 million in attorneys' fees, Mr. Eichman so, yes, I am saying that you knew this was a mess. This was not going anywhere positive and at that time, the Independent Administrator, as the fiduciary—my attorney was not the fiduciary; neither was Jo's attorney. You all were the fiduciary. You had the responsibility to put our interests first. All of ours, equally.

Eichman didn't give up.

Eichman: That was your lawyer Stolbach saying that stuff; right?
Laura: Yes, all of this seemed very silly, but none of this prevented you, Mr. Eichman, from doing what the Bank had been saying for a solid year, prior to all of this which is, we can do this. We can do this if you don't like it. We can do this if you don't want it. This can still happen because we're the Independent Administrator, we're your fiduciary and we're responsible for making decisions that are in the best interest of all parties. But you didn't do that because suddenly, you became very concerned that somebody was going to sue you.

Eichman showed her an email I'd sent, begging Laura to come to her senses. I'd stated that all the money Max and I had earned would now go to the lawyers. Using that email, Eichman asked Laura to admit I'd told her this litigation would break us all.

It went off the rails, but not against Laura.

Laura: This is what happened with JPMorgan as our Independent Administrator, yes. This is it, right here.
Eichman: Yes, ma'am, and the lawyers that were happy to feed your emotions with nonsense, that's Gary Stolbach, wasn't it, ma'am?
Laura: Sir, I believe that because JPMorgan was not administering this estate properly, attorneys got involved; they didn't need to be involved. This never should have needed attorneys in the first place. The fact that attorneys had to get involved, in this administration, goes to show how poorly this administration was being run.
Eichman: Ma'am, in June of 2011, the Bank said we're going to distribute in undivided interests and your man, Stolbach, came in and said in July, no way, no how, right?

Laura: You could have done it anyway. You sold my Gartner options; I didn't want that. You said you had the authority to do that because you were the Independent Administrator. You had the same authority, at this time, when you saw the legal bills coming in, when your firm was billing us, you had the opportunity at that point, to say you know what, this is in nobody's best interest and so we're going to make decisions that are in the best interest of the Estate. But you didn't do that.

It was both stunning and powerful to see Laura take on this legal giant. I could almost feel us winning our case right there.

We took a break. Alan and I were thrilled with how things were going. Alan and Lenny practically high-fived each other in the back.

After the break, the judge unwrapped a peppermint from a bowl on her bench as we started back. When Eichman was about to begin, he remembered he wanted a peppermint. Then, James Bell wanted one too. Soon, Eichman was passing the bowl around. Everyone in the courtroom, including the jurors, laughed. It was a brief moment of levity, showing that despite the anger, the lawyers and litigants were just people.

The next subject Eichman covered was all the money Stephen and Laura had paid to their attorneys. Eichman wanted to show that the heirs had authorized that money to be taken from the estate's account, and that's why there was no money left.

It was a good attack. If I'd been on the stand, I would've admitted it, let Eichman score a point or two, and move on. Not Laura. She refused to let Eichman score anything. To a shark like Eichman, she was just another struggling fish in the water. So, he pounced, pulling out an email to embarrass her. It didn't go well.

Eichman: Let's go above and see what you said in response to Susan's email. Susan sent you an email January 9, 2012: "As before, please confirm your approval of this invoice from Glast, Phillips." And you said to Susan on January 9, 2012—read that email, ma'am.

Laura: "Let the funding of Corvettes continue." Is that what you're referring to?

Eichman: Yes. "Smiley face, Laura," right?

Laura:	Again, we are being sued. We have no choice in this. We're being sued, Mr. Eichman.
Eichman:	Yes, ma'am.
Laura:	We're defending ourselves, and what this referred to, we found out that one of our attorneys didn't just have one Corvette, he had multiple Corvettes.
Eichman:	Was that—
Laura:	That's what that was referring to so, tongue-in-cheek, let the funding—that didn't mean I was happy about it. It meant what else am I going to do and yeah, let the funding of the Corvettes continue. That was a tongue-in-cheek response.
Eichman:	Okay. And that was Mr. Enoch, that wasn't Mr. Stolbach. That was his law partner that had the Corvettes?
Laura:	Correct. How do you know that?

Yeah, how did Eichman know that? That last question from Laura hung in the air. Did he collect Corvettes, too? Was he in an auto club with Enoch? Did all these lawyers hang out at bench and bar conferences or CLE getaways and talk about all the money they'd scored off their clients while holding snifters of brandy? There were so many places a juror's mind could wander. Once again, Laura racked up unexpected points.

Eichman cleared his throat and quickly moved on. He needed to point the finger at all the heirs' lawyers. It was their fault, not JPMorgan's.

Eichman:	Oh, by the way, you not only hired Stolbach, you hired that guy Stanley Johanson, from the University of Texas, right?
Laura:	One of the top lawyers in Texas, yes, expert.
Eichman:	Yeah.
Laura:	Who happened to agree with the position that our attorney was taking, as did you.
Eichman:	Well—
Laura:	You're leaving that out, that your firm also flip-flopped and then was agreeing with our position.

Again, Laura turned around what had started as a sure win for Eichman. He decided to wrap up with a guaranteed win. Or at least he hoped so. He asked Laura if she would've been better off simply giving her interest in Robledo back to me in 2010. Laura refused to answer. After fighting with Eichman, she finally gave in.

> Laura: Yes. In hindsight, did I know that I was going to be sued, or you were going to sue me, or that this was going to turn into a seven-year lawsuit? No, I didn't know that. And Mr. Eichman, you could have made all this not happen.

I put a hand to my mouth to stop from yelling out, "You go, girl!"

Laura continued, pointing out errors in Eichman's dates. She was at the top of her game, turning all the blame back to JPMorgan, where it rightly belonged.

When Lenny got her back, he made sure Laura explained how she'd never seen the offer I'd made to buy everything at highly inflated prices. I watched the jurors. Their eyes widened.

> Lenny: And had Susan Novak sent this offer that Jo Hopper was making to you and your brother, what would you have done?
> Laura: This is all we ever wanted.

That was the whole case right there—the offer Susan never sent them.

When Laura finished, I wanted to hug her, but, of course, I couldn't.

The judge announced that it was the court reporter Jackie Galindo's birthday. I heard a discussion of how we had two more days to finish this trial. We were cutting it really close. If the jury didn't deliberate long, we could do it. But that was a big *if*.

FRIDAY, DAY FOURTEEN. A first: everyone was on time! Yet the judge had another meeting at the bench.

First, she wanted to discuss the jury charge. This entailed deciding which factual questions they needed to ask the jury. The jury charge must be drafted in advance so the lawyers can reference it and explain the proper answers to the jury. Not getting the right questions asked of the jury could be fatal to one's case.

Many of the trials that were reversed on appeal were due to improper jury charges. That was why Alan had brought in Robert Dubose with Alexander Dubose Jefferson LLP. Mr. Dubose and his partners were some of the best appellate lawyers in Texas. If I won a verdict, it would be Mr. Dubose who would go up against JPMorgan's lawyers on appeal.

The next issue was a doozy. Alan and Lenny had discovered that JPMorgan had stopped adding to their attorneys' fees after June 30, 2017. This was a smart move by Eichman. It made their fees appear way lower than mine. If only he'd gotten away with it.

After Alan demanded answers, Eichman admitted to the judge that they had received a separate $415,000 bill to defend JPMorgan in their corporate capacity. Instead of making the heirs or me pay for that, JPMorgan had decided to eat it. Just before Alan exploded at this revelation, his highlighter exploded. Alan's hands were covered in yellow ink. This was not a good look. He'd have to go before the jury with *unclean* hands. (Okay, legal pun intended.)

Once he regained his composure, Alan exposed how Eichman and Cantrill had four different accounts to which they billed money. He claimed it was a shell game. It was like bringing your car in for service and getting a $20,000 bill. You're outraged and study the bill closely. It showed replacing the battery was $135. Fixing the air conditioning was another $200. Replacing the oil was only $65. Those looked reasonable. The rest—$19,000—was lumped into bodywork and painting. To Alan, that was the problem. Who knew if they actually charged $1,000 to replace the oil, $2,000 for the battery, and $5,000 for the A/C work? They could make the fees look however they wanted while arguing to the jury that ours were out of whack. Eichman adamantly denied this.

After listening to Eichman go on, Alan demanded production of all the bills from June 30 to today. He wanted those bills to cross-examine Mark Sales and Eichman. From Sales' report, he knew that Sales claimed none of my attorneys' fees were reasonable or necessary. Eichman resisted, but the game was up. He couldn't tell the jury my lawyers charged too much when they had withheld the total amount. As I listened to all this, I realized that either JPMorgan or Hunton & Williams would be eating a lot of attorneys' fees. If they had done nothing wrong, why would they do that?

The judge appeared very concerned but didn't have any immediate answers. She left it for the parties to sort out before she ruled. And that was the end of the bench conference.

Now it was Stephen's turn to take the stand. He said he didn't spend a lot of time with Max because his father worked so hard. He explained why he'd wanted an Independent Administrator: to preserve his relationship with his sister and me. He also understood that JPMorgan would be fair, honest, competent, professional, and a good communicator.

Stephen said he knew there was a flat fee in the contract but didn't focus on each sentence. He hadn't known there would be additional legal charges to the estate.

Lenny led Stephen through all the lawyers they'd hired and fired. With a bit of humor, Lenny asked Stephen, "And I'm still your lawyer, right?"

"Yes," Stephen replied sheepishly.

Lenny went one step further. "You're not firing me, are you?"

"No," Stephen answered with a grin, though later, after the trial, this line of questioning would become a sad reality.

To emphasize how much money we were talking about, Lenny put up a figure representing the attorneys' fees Hunton & Williams had billed to the estate. It was $3.9 million through June 30, 2017. That didn't include July, August, September, or the trial days. Their daily burn rate had to be as high as mine, if not higher.

Again, Lenny homed in on JPMorgan's tax mistake and cover-up. After that, he explored the gaslighting issues with Calamity Jane and how Stephen thought she was deceptive when, in fact, she had done a lot of work. Stephen called JPMorgan deceptive and said that it

> "... added kerosene to the fire... it really made us very distrustful of Jo Hopper. It made us feel like she was hiding something and, man, things got really ugly at that point."

Lenny was doing great as the hours ticked off. Seeing the time on the courtroom clock, Lenny appeared to cut short Stephen's testimony and passed the witness.

Eichman began his cross by catching Stephen in some mistakes and incorrect testimony. But Stephen was well-versed with his deposition testimony and dodged many of the bullets.

Eichman got him to admit he feared for his physical safety around me. Then, Eichman led him down a hit parade on me. Stephen had to agree to his prior statements. One said I had created the illusion of being helpful, but that wasn't the real me. Stephen also perceived malice and ill will from me. The lesson to Stephen was always to watch what you put in emails and say out loud.

Stephen was not very emotional but instead was more clinical. He asked Eichman for permission to go beyond the question to explain more fully. Eichman refused to let him drift or add to the question, unlike Laura, who just took it without asking. Laura's bull-in-the-china-shop technique made her much more effective.

Continuing the attack on me, Eichman put Stephen's "shame on you, Jo" email up on the screen. Eichman read it out loud. When he finished reading, Lenny demanded his rights of optional completeness—a rule that allows a party to read words that the other party left out. Lenny stood up and let it rip.

> "...as we pointed out before, all evidence of fighting between us is a plus for the Bank. The Bank will try slyly to use it as proof of supposedly why their misconduct and absurd fees are appropriate and reasonable when they are, in fact, not so."

It was another powerful moment. Thank you, Lenny.

Eichman finished his cross-examination, and Alan asked no questions. That's when Lenny rested.

Even though Stephen and Laura had both testified to the attorneys' fees they'd incurred, Lenny called no experts to say his were reasonable and necessary. I wondered how that would work since both JPMorgan and I had to do it.

Once again, the day ended, and Alan and I walked to my car. I told him excitedly, "It's Friday. Lenny rested. We can have closing arguments on Monday and a jury verdict that night. Right?"

"No, that's not right," Alan replied somberly. "Eichman still has to put on his case."

My jaw dropped. I'd forgotten about JPMorgan. They were suing all of us for attorneys' fees. Not only did they have to prove their case, but they were also entitled to a defense.

"How long with that take?" I asked.

"Long enough to see the carpenters tearing down walls or less than six jurors in the box."

I was devastated. We weren't going to make it.

The last thing I heard was someone shouting to Alan, "Have a nice weekend!"

Chapter Thirty-Six

"The devil is in the details."

—JPMorgan Chase Bank, N.A.
Our Business Principles website

Day Fifteen. Monday. The trial was entering its fourth week. Eichman had so many witnesses to call that there was no way we'd finish before the construction began.

At this point, my depression was intense. Not only would I have to write a gargantuan check to Alan's firm for this trial, but a retrial would be in my future. That meant at least twelve more months of legal invoices.

The anxiety before an invoice arrived was excruciating. The hesitation and fear of opening each one. The anger after seeing the amount due. The depression when thinking about the total figure, and finally, the acceptance as I called my financial advisor and sold more stock to raise the cash to pay it. Then, I had twenty-nine more days before another bill arrived.

Thoughts of a retrial haunted me. I didn't have the funds to sustain another year of billings and another trial. Of course, I couldn't let my attorneys know my financial situation was critical.

The weekend had been as stressful as any day in trial. I met several times with Alan and the team. When they were done with me, I talked to the veterinarian who was handling Millie's lymphoma. He explained that as quickly as the lymphoma had appeared, it was all gone. I was so numb from the trial that I wasn't as grateful as I should have been for God healing Millie. After all, my prayers had been answered. Maybe God had one more gift in store for me.

I spent whatever time I had left with Jack, and I tried to relax under the peach tree with Millie but found little comfort. All too soon, the alarm rang, and I refused to get out of bed. But I did, and somehow, I made it to court.

What a grind. How a federal criminal defendant made it through a three-month-long trial or a trial lawyer kept their marriage intact, I had no idea.

As I sat in my chair behind Alan, I watched the judge following a construction worker around the courtroom. Tomorrow they would be tearing down walls. I prayed for another miracle.

Somewhat on time, the trial resumed. Eichman stood up and called Tom Cantrill to the stand. By this time, I had fully settled into my role as a spectator. All I needed to do was take notes.

As fate would have it, Cantrill's microphone stopped working just as he began to speak. After changing out the batteries, Cantrill relaxed and took his time, detailing his stellar forty-four years as a lawyer and all the world-class experience he possessed in probate law.

He was a member of several elite probate law organizations, one of which had an extensive nomination process. He mentioned Jenkens & Gilchrist but stayed away from his role as managing partner or how it had shuttered two days before morphing into Hunton & Williams.

Eichman and Cantrill worked well together. They were smooth and easy to follow.

Cantrill explained how he'd had an attorney-client relationship with Max and me, but it ended after a few years. Thus, he was conflict-free. Cantrill did say he had verbally notified Stephen, Laura, or their lawyer John Round about his prior work with Max and me. That should provide cover for the jury to find he'd done nothing wrong. Yet after hearing about Cantrill's deep experience and qualifications, I couldn't help but wonder why he hadn't put such a conflict notice in writing.

Cantrill did remember receiving a call from me as Max was dying but didn't have "... an independent recollection of the telephone conversation." He was sure he didn't make any rude or insensitive remarks.

I burned inside. I'll never forget his "the body isn't even cold yet" comment just when I needed expert legal help and maybe (God forbid) some compassion.

Regarding Susan Novak, Cantrill said he'd worked with her before, and she was very experienced, very capable. They were sticking together. As Benjamin Franklin told his fellow rebels after signing the Declaration of Independence, "We must all hang together, or we shall all hang separately." It was a good strategy.

Cantrill described attorneys John Round and Mike Graham as colleagues and members in one of those earlier mentioned elite probate law organizations. He saw Round and his wife Debra around town at various functions, as well as Mike Graham, my previous attorney, whom he knew and had worked alongside. It all sounded like one cozy country club for lawyers who pass clients back and forth.

Cantrill testified that there was no reason to disclose to any of the Hoppers that John Round was married to a JPMorgan trust officer. "It just wasn't relevant," he said. A juror grimaced.

Eichman and Cantrill worked slowly and deliberately with their legal trowels to plug and plaster over the holes in their case. Cantrill easily explained away the tax return fiasco. Then, he testified about preparing the inventory because the lawyers always prepare that document.

He also testified that he had nothing to do with helping me try to buy out the heirs' interest in Robledo. But he did admit trying to help determine who would own each bottle of wine, mainly because it didn't make sense if three people owned a piece of each bottle. He was offering the jurors a plausible explanation for everything.

He testified in a gentle, fatherly manner, which seemed to sit well with the jury. As he went through all the issues that had come up, Eichman's dam was no longer leaky. Alan and Lenny would have to open up those holes again if we were to have a chance.

During a lunch break, the judge said she could not order the disclosure of Hunton & Williams's bills for the work they'd done for JPMorgan in their corporate capacity. But she could order specific bills for the estate administration be produced if JPMorgan had not previously provided them. And she did allow Alan to tell the jury about the bills that weren't disclosed and argue to the jury that they could infer why. Alan was excited about that. "To a jury, evidence hidden from the other side is often better than the real thing," he said, chuckling.

To my surprise, Cantrill laid off a lot of the estate responsibility on Susan Novak. He said Susan had a wealth of people at JPMorgan to help her. His work was restricted to any legal issues that came up.

Using another trial tactic, Eichman cleverly took some of the wind out of Alan's sails. He knew Alan would hit Cantrill on the fact that it wasn't Cantrill's job to cause trades. Cantrill had even written a memo to the parties, stating, "… it is not the responsibility or obligation of the Administrator to cause trades to happen (for example, the Administrator can deed the home to the parties subject to Jo's homestead right)." Did he wish now that would've happened?

But Cantrill's memo continued. "I intend to be as helpful as I can be in facilitating agreements as to the division of these assets." Eichman made sure he presented that memo to the jury instead of waiting for Alan to do it. In the trial lawyer toolbox, they call it inoculation. It's always better than rehabilitation. Score one for Eichman.

As Cantrill talked about taxes, he made a crucial mistake. He said, "Most of the property in Mr. Hopper's Estate was community property, fifty percent to Mrs. Hopper, fifty percent to Mr. Hopper."

With his years of experience, Cantrill surely knew that there was never any community property in Max's estate. There had to be a marriage to have community property. The moment Max died, the marriage ended. And I didn't own anything in Max's estate except a few slivers of separate property. At the instant of his death, my previous community property became my separate property, and the estate contained Max's *previous* community property plus his separate property.

As I've said repeatedly, I believe this fundamental mistake—not fully understanding property classification within the context of probate law—was the cornerstone of Cantrill buying into Stolbach's unorthodox probate theory and, thus, wasting all this time and money. I made a note for Alan, who I was sure had caught that, too.

Cantrill claimed the estate was challenging, with unique assets like limited partnerships and hedge fund investments. He said those assets required skill and knowledge to determine how they should be properly managed. I slid a quick note to Alan. "It wasn't his job to manage. It was his job to divide and return my assets!!!" Alan grinned and nodded.

Cantrill played up how we had made so many demands on Susan. He was correct, mainly because we demanded she divide the assets. I was so mad, I wanted to get back on the stand.

Well, not that mad.

Cantrill appeared to consistently defend Susan. He would hang with Susan and his longtime client JPMorgan and hope it all worked out. He did admit he had never seen my offer to buy the personal property from the heirs, at least not until this litigation. As for his deal-making role, he said, "We were trying to get the parties to make an offer on Robledo and settle it among the parties. We thought that was—we being the Independent Administrator and myself as their counsel—the logical way Robledo ought to be resolved." Cantrill used the word "we" many times, which led me to believe he and Susan had jointly run this disaster instead of just Susan.

Eichman had him play up the problems with Calamity Jane, making it look like I'd tried to hide assets or evidence. He also left a tremendous amount of blame at Gary Stolbach's feet. JPMorgan needed this testimony to allow the jury to divide blame between Stolbach and the bank if the jury was so inclined. That could reduce any recovery against JPMorgan.

Near the end of his direct examination, Cantrill slipped in a nice dig at Jim Jennings when he said he'd made a call to Jennings before I filed suit. He testified that Jennings had said, "'Mrs. Hopper is a wealthy lady and if she wants to fight, she'll send my children through college, the grandchildren through college' or something to that effect." I sighed.

Cantrill's testimony could be summed up like this: Everything he and Susan did was proper and just, and all the problems were caused by me, Stephen and Laura, and Stolbach. Nothing to see here. Move along.

When Eichman passed Cantrill, it was 3 p.m. Lenny had two hours to cross before our trial supposedly ended.

Lenny started in and found it tough to pry answers from Cantrill. He had to work hard and arm-wrestle for everything. Finally, Cantrill admitted he'd been representing JPMorgan for forty years. Cantrill also said his firm had been paid $4 million from JPMorgan as both the Independent Administrator for the Hopper Estate and its corporate capacity. But that figure was only as of June 30, 2017. He had no idea how much his firm had been paid to prepare for trial and during the trial.

Cantrill said Hunton & Williams had so many matters with JPMorgan that they didn't need to sign new fee agreements for each one. They had a master agreement and opened a new file number whenever necessary. That showed how vital JPMorgan was to Hunton & Williams' bottom line.

Cantrill was crafty, dodging dangerous blows from Lenny. But he also played lawyerball with semantics. That tactic appeared to alienate the jury.

Lenny ended the day by pointing out that there was no written loan agreement for the money JPMorgan had loaned to the estate to pay Hunton & Williams once the estate's funds were exhausted. Cantrill said the bank simply handed it over. Yet Cantrill represented both JPMorgan in their corporate capacity and as the Independent Administrator. The lines between Cantrill's loyalties quickly became blurred. His firm brought in millions while leaving the estate's bank account with $100. It was a powerful cross-examination; Lenny at his best.

As the day ended, the judge announced she had delayed construction through the rest of the week. What a relief! But make no mistake, the case would finish Friday evening.

On the way out, Alan shook his head. "I don't think we'll get there. Eichman has too many witnesses."

"You don't think we'd get this far only to suffer a mistrial?" I asked him with shock.

"Jo, you practice law as long as I have, you see all kinds of things. Any judge can do anything at any time."

I'd certainly seen that with Judge Miller. So, I gritted my teeth and prayed.

THE NEXT MORNING, Lenny was right back at Cantrill. He asked him how much money he'd taken from the estate. Cantrill said his firm had never *taken* any money from the estate. Instead, the IA *released* the funds from the estate to pay his firm's billings. Again, more lawyerball.

Lenny showed that Hunton & Williams had received over 70% of the estate's cash from the time I sued them. He also got Cantrill to say that there was a chance his bonus could be tied to the revenue he brought in. That was excellent work by Lenny.

Lenny asked Cantrill which hat he was wearing when he answered all these questions. Was he the lawyer for JPMorgan corporate? Or was he the lawyer for JPMorgan as an Independent Administrator? Several jurors looked at each other and smirked as his convoluted answer came out.

I guessed Lenny's main thrust was to show the blurry lines of conflict involving JPMorgan, Cantrill, and Hunton & Williams. Effectively, Cantrill represented JPMorgan, a creditor against an estate JPMorgan also managed as the Independent Administrator. Unfortunately for Cantrill, by representing the estate, he owed a fiduciary duty to the heirs. How did that work when JPMorgan was a creditor? Again, it opened up a gaping hole in Eichman's case.

For some reason, Cantrill refused to admit to even the most straight-forward facts. Here was a typical exchange:

Lenny: And then when you had to address this issue with the Honorable Brenda Hull Thompson about whether or not Jo Hopper has to pay these fees, you were wrong about the law, were you not, sir?

Cantrill: Judge Thompson ruled that we didn't, excuse me, that the IA didn't have a right to recover fees against Mrs. Hopper.

Lenny: And so you were wrong. Is that correct, sir? You were wrong on that issue?

Cantrill: That was Judge Thompson's ruling.

Lenny: Judge Thompson said you were wrong, correct?

Cantrill: That's what I just said.

As Lenny wound up his cross-examination, he dealt with the Gary Stolbach issue. Lenny showed that Cantrill was moving to sue the heirs and me before I sued them. Thus, JPMorgan was headed to litigation anyway. They were just using Stolbach as a scapegoat for their terrible behavior.

To conclude, Lenny pointed out Ms. Kravik at the back of the court-room. When Cantrill said Ms. Kravik was the corporate rep for JPMorgan, Lenny pounced. He pointed at Susan Novak, who was sitting next to Grayson Linyard. "I thought Susan Novak was the corporate rep?"

For the first time, Cantrill seemed flustered. His words were being twisted. At that moment, Lenny passed the witness. He had scored many more points than he should have, thanks to Cantrill fouling him.

Cantrill watched Alan approach the podium. Now, it was our turn to cross-examine Cantrill. *Good luck, buddy.*

Alan pointed to the letter Cantrill had written, in which he said I had property that didn't belong to me. He refused to admit that he accused me of theft, but the letter's intent was clear. Of course, it turned out I'd paid for the property months earlier. Susan showed the payment was in her files.

Alan maintained tighter control of Cantrill than Lenny had. Alan turned to the judge over and over, and she said, "The witness is instructed to answer the question." Early on, the judge said, "Mr. Cantrill, I don't want to prolong this, but I'll ask you to answer the questions, and I'm going to grant the Motion to Strike." I felt that Cantrill's combative posture was losing jurors, and he didn't seem to realize it.

Alan showed how Cantrill had participated in some of the gaslighting. Regarding the theft accusation letter, Cantrill had issued an apology but sent a letter to Stolbach casting me in a bad light. Cantrill had to know his letter would get back to Stephen and Laura through the discovery process. They would read it and continue their burning anger against me. It kept the litigation going, along with the money draining out of the estate.

Regarding my CPA, Calamity Jane, Cantrill admitted he had threatened her with legal action and filed suit against her for withholding documents. Alan got Cantrill to admit the bank didn't want to meet with my CPA if Jim Jennings was there. But then Alan put up deposition testimony from Susan Novak, who said she had been willing to meet with Calamity Jane if Jennings was present. This suggested Cantrill didn't want a resolution, just more litigation.

As the day wore on, the reality show continued. Alan asked a question, and Cantrill denied or avoided it. Then, Alan produced a document or video testimony showing the opposite. This went on and on until Cantrill, before he answered a question, stated he was certain Alan had something ready to show that proved he was wrong. Cantrill saw ghosts, never sure if Alan had the goods or not. I loved every minute of it.

Alan focused on the bank's failure to release my home to the heirs and me right after being appointed IA.

Alan: Could the Bank have released the Robledo interest in August 2010?

Cantrill: It could have.

Alan: But it failed to do so, correct? Right?

Cantrill: It chose not to do so, yes.

Alan: Well, it failed to do what it could have done. You'd agree with that?

Cantrill: It did not do it.

Like Lenny, Alan cinched the millions in attorneys' fees to Hunton & Williams like a noose around Cantrill's neck. Cantrill was supposed to be the smart guy in all this, but he appeared to be wrong on the law time and time again. It had to be embarrassing to someone of his stature.

Alan neared the end by having Cantrill admit that the right thing to do would have been to distribute the property in undivided interests. Then, Alan showed Cantrill's video deposition testimony contradicting himself, saying the right thing to do was encouraging an agreement and, only if one was not possible, distribute in undivided interests. It was thrilling to see Cantrill admit a key component of our case: JPMorgan's failure to give us the property. Instead, they held onto it.

During a final salvo, Alan focused on Stolbach's threats to file suit against the bank if Cantrill didn't do what Stolbach wanted. Alan chided Cantrill for failing to make a simple call to Gary Stolbach and tell him that if he filed suit, he would end up draining the estate bank account and hurting his own clients. Cantrill scoffed at that idea as completely ridiculous and a waste of time. Alan wondered aloud if one quick phone call could have avoided all this destruction. Cantrill was having none of it. He held firm that calling Stolbach would have been a waste of time. Alan finished up like this:

Alan: How much time would you have billed to call Gary Stolbach, approximately? One hour?

Cantrill: Probably, less.

Alan: Okay. And you bill at what rate?

Cantrill: At that timeframe?

Alan: Yes, sir.

Cantrill: Um, probably $625, $650, something like that.

Alan: Okay. So that would have been less than $625, correct?

Cantrill: Yes, sir.

Alan: And how much has Hunton & Williams billed, collectively, in matters two and four in this litigation?

Cantrill: Again, there's no matter four but you're asking—I think—

Alan: Mr. Cantrill?

Cantrill: —the number is around between four and four-and-a-half million dollars.

Alan: No further questions. Thank you for your time, sir.

Eichman jumped up and asked questions that tried to rehabilitate Cantrill. And he did plug some gaping holes. But there were too many, even for a skilled litigator like Eichman.

When Cantrill stepped down from the witness stand, he looked like he'd aged ten years. He tried holding his head upright while maintaining the same assuredness when he first took the stand, but Alan and Lenny had punctured him badly. He had turned into a deflating basketball, leaking air all the way out of the courtroom.

I had no idea if Cantrill drank alcohol, but I imagined him driving home in a coma, pouring a double shot of scotch, and calling in sick tomorrow.

I felt so sorry for him, I almost felt like driving over the bottle of scotch.

Almost.

Chapter Thirty-Seven

"Never take unfair advantage of anyone through manipulation, concealment, abuse of privileged or confidential information, misrepresentation of material facts or any other unfair dealings or practices."

—JPMorgan Chase & Co
2020 Code of Conduct
2.3 Ethical Business Practices

In my opinion, JPMorgan's case had problems—at least up to this point. As witnesses, neither Susan Novak nor Tom Cantrill had advanced their cause one iota. Sure, they had gotten in a few good licks. But with the Lenny and Alan duo, the two had left the stand a shell of their former selves.

Now, a parade of experts was coming. Eichman needed to regain the momentum, or his case was dead on arrival.

Lois Stanton was first. She'd been sitting in the courtroom for five days, listening to the testimony. It was her job to testify about the usual standards of care for estates and fiduciaries. Specifically, she would tell the jurors that JPMorgan's actions as the IA were proper and righteous. But first, she shared her background.

Stanton was a lawyer who had previously worked for banks, supervising estate officers like Susan Novak. Currently, she worked for a law firm that practiced estate planning and administration. The jurors could see she was highly qualified. This was a bad omen.

As Stanton talked, she added to her credibility. She said she was the chairman of a commission that reviewed all the applications for lawyers wanting to become board certified in trusts and estates. She even taught something called Trust School to administrators for banks. And when asked to be an expert in this case, she had carefully considered whether to become involved. All this painted a very credible picture of an honest expert witness.

To head off issues on cross-examination, Eichman had Stanton discuss what she'd been paid to testify. Her low billable rate—30% less than the other attorneys in the courtroom—was another boost to her credibility. Yet despite this low hourly rate, she'd been able to bill JPMorgan $115,000... so far.

Stanton went on to say that she'd been an expert for banks as well as people suing banks. Like our expert Trey Cox, Stanton said she'd done all the work required: interviewing witnesses, reviewing pleadings and motions, and reading transcripts.

As expected, Stanton toed the company line. She testified:

- This was a complex estate with complex assets. Thus, the time it took to do all that administration work was normal.
- The unfiled federal tax return was not relevant.
- Having outside legal counsel like Hunton & Williams spend lots of time was consistent with an estate like this.
- Not disclosing conflicts was proper by JPMorgan because they weren't conflicts.
- Wendy Bessette properly supervised Susan Novak and the administration of the estate. Susan also did her job well.
- Everything JPMorgan did was proper and customary in the banking world and for fiduciaries.

By now, I understood how expert witnesses worked. At first, I'd wondered how they could be so polar opposite. Then Tarian had explained how it's all about the money. I assumed a cannibalistic criminal defendant could find an expert to testify that if you ran out of food, it was standard industry practice to eat your neighbor. In my humble opinion, everything in the justice system is driven by money.

Every. Damn. Thing.

Stanton went on, and she was impressive. Her testimony hurt our case. Then, she seemed to make her first mistake. She talked about how it was impossible to distribute a putter by giving the bottom half to one side and the top half to the other. Because of this, she said, it was common to work out agreements with parties about which putter they would receive. She doubled down and said it was okay to hold property for a while to ensure everything was completed before the IA made distributions. I knew Alan would soon pick that apart.

Eichman transitioned into her experience in dealing with difficulties between heirs. Alan objected. Fortunately, the judge excluded that evidence because it wasn't in her report.

Stanton scored some valuable points when she testified that if JPMorgan had resigned, it would have been tough to find another entity to jump into our hornet's nest. And if we found one, the estate would still have to pay the new IA. That weighed in favor of letting JPMorgan stay on as the IA.

During a break, Lenny and Alan convinced the judge to strike portions of Stanton's testimony relating to two topics. It wasn't so much that we could un-ring the bell. The jurors had heard the information and had it in their minds, but it sure looked bad when the judge told them to disregard that testimony. It had to create some doubt in Stanton's otherwise stellar performance.

Stanton closed out her direct examination by saying some things could have been done differently, but overall, the administration met industry standards. She said JPMorgan acted in good faith by paying millions of dollars to Hunton & Williams from the estate's account to defend themselves. That was her expert opinion.

Alan jumped up and dove right in. He got Stanton to admit that she hadn't sat in on Susan Novak's testimony nor mine. Thus, she had no idea how it would affect her opinions. It was a minor point, but Alan was just getting started. He elicited testimony that Stanton's firm had been paid at least $130 - $140,000 so far. She then readily admitted that her firm represented JPMorgan on two unrelated and ongoing cases. From these, her firm received fees from the bank. She also admitted to referring clients to JPMorgan. Once Alan had all that in the hopper, he sprung the trap.

Alan: Would you at least concede it might be a bit awkward if you were to come into this courtroom and tell this jury that JPMorgan Chase breached their fiduciary duties, at the same time your law firm, and you specifically, are representing that bank and receiving fees from them? Would you at least concede that might be at least a little bit awkward?

Stanton: No.

Alan: Okay. You understand that, as you said, the jury is the judge of credibility.

Stanton: That's correct.

Alan: Do you think it fair for the jury to take into account, in assessing your credibility, the fact that you are being paid for your testimony and that you and your firm currently represent JPMorgan?

Stanton: Yes.

With this admission, Alan pulled out his scalpel and began performing open-heart surgery. He went over Stanton's misstatements to the jury about my CPA. Then he listed all the errors committed by Susan Novak and forced Stanton to agree that they were, in fact, errors.

Initially, Stanton was very controlled, answering with a simple yes or no. She didn't foul or play lawyerball. But suddenly, her tone and demeanor appeared to change. She stopped answering Alan's questions. He had to re-ask them and continually have Judge Thompson strike her answers. We were scoring points.

Several times, Alan led Stanton to admit facts that were true but then showed Susan had said something different. Not only did he make Susan look bad, but Stanton didn't appear to know all the facts of the case—the same facts on which she'd based her opinion.

The absolute truth was that no human being on Earth, other than perhaps me, could know all the facts of this case. I'd read everything, every day, many times. And even I was sometimes surprised.

Alan did an excellent job tearing down Stanton's credibility, better than I expected. When he passed Stanton, Lenny was smart. Because Alan had done such a fantastic job tearing her opinions apart, Lenny had her testify that she was not offering an opinion on the heirs' fraud or breach of contract claims. When he got that admission, he shut up and sat down. Forty-five seconds of cross-examination, and that was it.

I looked over at Eichman. The gaping wounds in Stanton's opinion needed patching up. Was the gain of surgery worth the risk of giving Alan a chance to rip open the stitches? Eichman sighed, stood up, and said he was done. With that, Lois Stanton was excused.

I'D BEEN CLOSELY watching the jury. Their body language and facial expressions told me Eichman was losing big time. Sure enough, Eichman brought it to the judge's attention. I was surprised it hadn't happened before now.

He told Judge Thompson that a male juror was making overt facial expressions and mouthing the word "no" at one of Stanton's answers. After some discussion, the judge said she'd repeat some instructions before the next break. But now, Eichman's team was on alert. If it continued, it could turn all this work into a mistrial, which would be a disaster.

Eichman's next witness was Michael Bourland. Grayson Linyard handled the direct examination for JPMorgan.

Bourland is a Fort Worth attorney who practices in estates, trusts, estate administration, business tax, and family business succession. He has all the education, honors, and credentials as Stanton and Cantrill. Bourland's job in this case was to provide an opinion on the reasonableness of the attorneys' fees charged by Hunton & Williams regarding their work in the estate administration. It was a narrow opinion, not touching the attorneys' fees that occurred during litigation.

Bourland charged $650 an hour. Because the lawyers in Bourland's firm billed at a lower rate, he had them review the documents. They brought him important items, and he studied those.

Like Cantrill, Bourland said JPMorgan was the decision-maker. Cantrill was just an advisor. According to Tarian, this would be more relevant *after* the case was over and JPMorgan was looking to recoup some money.

Bourland was an older man, easygoing and fatherly. Linyard walked him through the proper questions, getting him to say that all fees Hunton & Williams charged were reasonable and necessary.

Lenny handled the cross. Because they both had attended Baylor University, this exchange happened:

Bourland: Don't go this *sick 'em* stuff with me when you gut me.
Lenny: I am going to do my best.
Bourland: To gut me.
Lenny: To gut you nicely.

[Laughter]

At times, it looked like a lovefest.

Lenny: So I've got to control you here, Mr. Bourland.

Bourland: Yes, I'm familiar with that.

Lenny: I gotta rein you in, right?

Bourland: I'm sure you will.

Lenny: I gotta ask you questions that I know the answers to. They teach you that at Baylor, don't they?

Bourland: Absolutely.

Lenny: Okay. So when I ask you these questions, I already know the answers to them, don't I, sir? If I'm a good Baylor lawyer.

Bourland: If you're a good Baylor lawyer.

Despite all this, Lenny methodically pulled Bourland's opinion apart. And Bourland was smart. He agreed with Lenny without fighting or making himself look worse. Using this tactic, Bourland appeared even more credible.

Lenny had Bourland admit that he'd spent just ten hours of his own time on this matter before issuing his report. Bourland even said that one of his colleagues began writing the report. He only edited and reviewed it. It was an effective cross-examination.

After listening to Lenny's excellent work and knowing that Bourland's report had nothing to do with me, Alan passed the witness. Linyard cleaned up a few details, and that was it for Mr. Bourland.

BOURLAND HAD BEEN better than Stanton, but I was happy so far. Now, it was Eichman's turn. The courtroom grew silent as he took the stand. Linyard handled the direct. I could hardly wait.

Eichman testified that he'd spent a total of thirty-five years with Jenkens & Gilchrist and Hunton & Williams. He said every fee Hunton & Williams had charged in connection with this litigation was reasonable and necessary.

A surprise moment happened when James Bell, who would handle the heirs' cross, interrupted Linyard's direct examination to take Eichman on *voir dire*. To everyone's surprise, Bell had discovered that JPMorgan was no longer seeking $940,000 from the heirs to repay the borrowed money. That was contrary to testimony earlier in the trial. Apparently,

JPMorgan was so worried about the verdict that they had dropped this claim mid-trial. That was an exciting development.

Linyard resumed his direct and had Eichman clarify all this. Eichman reiterated that JPMorgan was not seeking attorneys' fees or damages from the heirs. All the bank wanted was a declaration from the judge giving them the right to obtain reimbursement from the heirs. This sleight-of-hand was clever. It reminded me of a movie where a prisoner agreed to tell the warden something vital in exchange for an agreement not to kill him. The warden accepted the deal, and the prisoner spilled the beans. Then, the warden had a jailer put a rope around the prisoner's neck. The prisoner, confused, said, "You promised not to kill me!" The warden replied, "That's right, I did. I'm not going to kill you. He is." Any way you sliced it, JPMorgan was coming after the heirs for the $940,000 in attorneys' fees.

Linyard passed Eichman to Alan, who quickly had Eichman admit his firm had been paid $4.3 to $4.5 million. Eichman also agreed that today was the official sixth anniversary of my filing suit in this litigation.

Later in the cross, Eichman divulged that JPMorgan, not Hunton & Williams, had paid the expert witnesses. It appeared that JPMorgan was eating upward of $500,000 in expert witness fees. "Yummy!" I wrote on my tablet. "Pay expert witnesses and trial lawyers instead of being a first-class fiduciary to your clients. Great business strategy!"

Alan made a big deal of Eichman not providing the legal bills from August 1 to today, September 21. But Alan's cross was quick and concise, and then he handed Eichman off to Bell. And Bell didn't mess around. Over and over, he had the judge strike Eichman's nonresponsive answers. Still, on the whole, Eichman didn't sound too bad. I hoped it wasn't a missed opportunity.

THE END OF this nightmare was near. I could feel it. Day after draining day, JPMorgan's witness list shrunk. Incredibly, Eichman's final witness was upon us. It was Mark Sales, their expert on attorneys' fees, and another Baylor Law School grad. JPMorgan's presentation needed some fireworks. Perhaps Sales would put an exclamation mark at the end of the case and leave the jury with lots of warm fuzzies. Naturally, Sales was well-qualified.

He handled probate, wills, and estate litigation. He also took on fiduciary litigation work. With this experience, he'd seen and sent out more than a few litigation bills in his time. His area of expertise allowed him to testify that JPMorgan's attorneys' fees for litigation were reasonable and necessary and that my fees were not. Without waiting for Sales to open his mouth, I already knew his answers. All I had to do was see who paid him.

Sales said he charged $650 per hour. To date, he'd been paid $180,000. He said he had reviewed everything. To decipher these attorneys' fees, Sales used the Andersen factors that Trey Cox had used. "Andersen factors" meant the 1997 Texas Supreme Court opinion in the Arthur Andersen case that spelled out what needed to be proved to receive attorneys' fees in Texas. Sales claimed that all my attorneys' fees were unnecessary because JPMorgan had pushed us to work it out. We didn't have to go to court over this small amount. It was ridiculous litigation, according to him.

Eichman had Sales testify about what a fiduciary should do in a case like this. Alan objected. Lenny added, "He went from an attorney fee expert to a liability expert." There was a big powwow at the bench, and sure enough, the judge ruled that since this information had not been included in his report, Eichman had violated the motion in limine. She told the jury that the testimony was struck and to disregard it.

Sales said pretty much everything Trey Cox had testified to was incorrect. And Sales essentially said that Gary Stolbach had committed professional malpractice.

After he finished testifying on direct, both Lenny and Alan convinced the judge to again punish Eichman for violating the motion in limine and instruct the jury to disregard Mark Sales' testimony on two more topics. Alan was very excited. Sales looked beaten up, and they hadn't even started the cross.

After a break, it was Alan's turn. He showed that Sales' hourly rate was more than Alan's, yet Alan had more years and experience. Alan also had Sales admit that the $180,000 he'd charged so far didn't include all of September or his time in court. Surely, Sales' firm would do well from this case.

Alan ripped him to pieces when Sales admitted he'd reviewed other cases for Hunton & Williams, and it wasn't possible for him to come up with an opinion other than Hunton & Williams' fees were reasonable and necessary. This sounded ludicrous to me. As Alan showed, it appeared the fix was in from the beginning. Sales didn't appear independent or open-minded.

Alan nailed down Sales' position that none of this litigation was necessary, so none of the fees I paid were reasonable. Not one single hour. Not one red cent.

Sales had been composed under Eichman's gentle direct. But as Alan performed an intestinal resection and spilled his guts onto the floor, Sales grew angry. His face turned beet red as Alan continually objected that the witness was nonresponsive. Each time, the judge sustained Alan's objection. And each time, Alan followed with a motion to strike. Once that was granted, Alan had the judge instruct Sales to answer the question. This happened over and over. For reasons known only to Sales, his testimony turned nasty.

Alan forced him to admit the most decisive Andersen factor was the dollar amount involved and the results obtained. Then, Alan went through every motion, hearing, and appellate court ruling I'd won. There were twelve of them:

1. Motion to Sever filed with Judge Miller (Jim Jennings);
2. Motion to Stay filed with Judge Miller (Jim Jennings);
3. Preparing and defending against declaratory judgment action regarding partition of the homestead and related issues to the Court of Appeals (Jim Jennings);
4. Motion regarding payment of 50% of the Robledo insurance premiums to Judge Miller (Jim Jennings);
5. Motion for Summary Judgment that Jo Hopper did not owe any legal fees from the estate filed with Judge Thompson (Alan Loewinsohn);
6. Motion for Summary Judgment by JPMorgan that Jo Hopper could not present mental anguish damages filed with Judge Thompson (Alan Loewinsohn);
7. Motion for Summary Judgment precluding presenting prelitigation legal fees filed with Judge Thompson (Alan Loewinsohn);
8. Motion for Summary Judgment precluding recovering reimbursements filed with Judge Thompson (Alan Loewinsohn);
9. Motion for Summary Judgment regarding the timing of the Robledo distribution and that JPMorgan could not be held

liable as a matter of law and that we could not present to the jury the claim that JPMorgan had waited too long to distribute Robledo filed with Judge Thompson (Alan Loewinsohn).

10. Motion for Summary Judgment that Jo Hopper Could Not Recover Her Attorneys' Fees Because the Court of Appeals Proceeding had been Severed filed with Judge Thompson (Alan Loewinsohn);

11. Motion for Summary Judgment prohibiting Trey Cox from testifying in court filed with Judge Thompson (Alan Loewinsohn);

12. Plea to the Jurisdiction filed by JPMorgan filed with Judge Thompson (Alan Loewinsohn).

As he listened to each victory, I watch Sales' face turn redder. It got worse when he was instructed to answer the questions. Anybody watching this could see that it was a complete disaster for Eichman's case—his final witness!

After Sales admitted I'd won all twelve of those decisions, Alan asked him to restate his professional opinion that not one dollar I'd spent was reasonable and necessary. To his credit, Sales held firm and said since this litigation wasn't necessary, none of the fees were reasonable. He wasn't changing his mind on that point.

Alan removed his surgical gown and washed the blood off his hands, then passed the witness and turned the show over to heirs.

Lenny popped up, ready to inflict some punishment of his own. For some reason, I thought Lenny's demeanor burned with rage. He seemed to dislike this witness. Instead of surgery, Lenny picked up a blowtorch. Right off the bat, he got down in the mud with Sales, pointing out how many times the judge had instructed him to answer the question. Treating the witness like a child, Lenny wanted Sales to admit to the jury that the judge was in charge. It was great entertainment.

Up to this point, I thought I'd seen it all. But when Sales—a witness on the stand—objected to Lenny's line of questioning, even Alan appeared amused. Sales claimed that because he was a lawyer, Lenny shouldn't ask questions like that. The scene turned crazy and combative, with Sales telling Lenny he wanted to finish and expand his answers while Lenny cut him off. Lenny maintained control of Sales, but barely.

When Lenny was through, Mark Sales seemed like a burn victim. The judge had harangued him so often for not answering the questions that it seemed like his credibility had been completely shot. Eichman tried to rehabilitate, but that gave Alan another opportunity to remove three more feet of intestine. Alan had Sales admit that during his review of all the documents, he had studied the reputation and experience of each person billing even a single dollar to Hunton & Williams' fees. This was part of the Andersen factors.

Alan pulled out names of people who had billed 1.9 hours or so and asked about their reputation and experience. There was no way Sales could know every detail of some of these obscure folks. No one could. But Sales had committed himself.

Alan: Do you know what the reputation and experience is of A. E. Lafibra?

Sales: I don't know their reputation or experience except I know that they're employed by Hunton & Williams.

Alan: Okay. Well, being employed by Hunton & Williams doesn't tell us what their reputation and experience is, as a lawyer or a paralegal does it, sir?

Sales: It absolutely does.

Alan: Okay. Then I'll ask my question again. Tell the jury what the reputation and experience is of A. E. Lafibra.

Sales: I don't know the person per se. What I'm simply saying is that they have a standard of hiring there that is going to be an exceptional standard.

Alan pulled out several vague and remote employees. Sales happened to know a little bit about some of the names, but this line of questioning was brutal and embarrassing.

On another subject, Sales seemed to claim that the heirs had objected to a distribution of the property in undivided shares early on, and thus, the parties guaranteed litigation. That made the case my fault or the heirs', not JPMorgan's. Yet Sales was mistaken about this fact. The heirs had not formally objected to the distribution until the summer of 2011. Alan knew the jury had seen this fact repeatedly because it was a crucial component of our case.

Alan pounced, using this misstatement to show Sales didn't fully understand the record or testimony in this case. This information might render his opinion worthless. Mark Sales' dramatic time on the stand ended like this:

Alan: Mr. Sales, do you stake your credibility, to the jury, that there is evidence, in this record, between August of 2010 and I'll just go to April of 2011 where Dr. Hopper or Laura Wassmer objected to the Bank distributing Robledo, in undivided interests, as you just told this jury? Are you willing to stake your credibility on that?

Sales: Well, first of all, you don't need to argue with me about it. But I've already said that I believe that the lawsuit would have been filed, if you looked at the acrimony that was there.

Alan: That wasn't my question.

Sales: The Bank was trying to work things out and they were objecting. And you could point to a period of time, you know, if they'd done it, would somebody sue, but in this situation, they didn't like each other, and that's why this led to where we are today.

Alan: Motion to strike nonresponsive, Your Honor.

THE COURT: Sustained.

Alan: I promise this is going to be my last question, if I get an answer.

Sales: I don't believe you but go ahead.

Alan: Do you stake your credibility, sir, to this jury that there is evidence in this record that between August 2010 and May of 2011, there was an objection, from either Laura Wassmer or Dr. Hopper, to the distribution of Robledo, in undivided interests?

Sales: I do not know what is in the record. I haven't been here for a month of this trial, but I can tell you I reviewed a lot of the emails and I saw the exchanges that were going on. And they were not friendly to each other, believe me.

Alan: Thank you for your time, sir.

Sales sat there, apparently fuming. Eichman sat diagonally to him. This looked bad. Surely, Eichman couldn't end his case like this. Yet, did he dare see what other damage Alan or Lenny might inflict if he continued?

Looking at the cards in his hand, Eichman got to his feet, dismissed Sales and proudly rested his case. The testimony phase was over.

Incredibly, it was Friday afternoon. I'd learned that regardless of when we finished, the judge would hold off the construction. This was an answer to my prayers. Except now, we had an even bigger problem. That juror who had a prepaid trip to Canada that we'd all known about from the beginning was leaving Tuesday morning—just three days from now. She made it clear that if we didn't finish on Monday, she was gone, along with our case.

Both Alan and I were extremely nervous and upset. But we had to pull it together. We were scheduled to work all day Saturday and Sunday to prepare for closing arguments. My future was about to be placed in Alan's hands, followed by the jurors'. It was both an exhilarating and sickening feeling.

Ready or not, this case and six years of litigation were almost over. What would the jury do? And more importantly, would they finish before Tuesday morning?

Chapter Thirty-Eight

"We're going to do the right thing for the company and our customers, all things considered."
—Jamie Dimon, Chairman & CEO
JPMorgan Chase Bank, N.A.

Monday. The final day. It was here at long last.

I was physically and mentally spent. By the time I hit the bed on Sunday night, I hoped and prayed deep sleep would find me.

Monday morning, the courtroom filled up. From experience, I knew this was my last chance to run to the restroom. On the way out, I caught a glimpse of someone familiar. It didn't hit me until I pushed in the restroom door. It was Jamie Dimon himself! He must have flown in from New York to be the face of JPMorgan Chase. This case was about his people and policies. They had caused this mess. It made sense that he was here for closing arguments.

Just as I headed to the stall, out came Stephen's wife, Barbara. Memories of our previous restroom encounter still smoldered in my mind. Thankfully, she brushed past me and left without incident.

After finishing, I stood at the mirror, washing my hands and checking my dour expression. What a mental, physical, and financial marathon this had been. There was no way I'd last through another one. This was it, no matter what happened.

I reached for some towels as the door swung open. In walked Susan Novak. She glanced at me and smiled. Then, she chuckled, making me grit my teeth.

Susan had retired six months before the trial had started. I assumed she was being paid to be the corporate representative for JPMorgan

Chase. I envisioned she had retired with a lucrative package. She was enjoying her retirement years while I was still mired down in probate hell. This fact and her attitude on the stand lit a bonfire in my chest.

There she was, the cause of all this, yet she was happy and satisfied. I couldn't take it any longer. In a blind rage, I ripped off my pearl necklace and wrapped it around her neck. Two seconds later, I was standing behind Susan, forcing her to her knees. She clawed at me, gasping for air. I didn't care. Pulling the strands tighter, I cut off her air supply. I kept the pressure on as I dodged her flailing arms. Just a few more seconds and she'd be dead.

Suddenly, a strong hand gripped my right arm. Another clamped on my left. As I twisted around, I saw Jamie Dimon reaching over me, trying to break the string of pearls. He jerked his hand back, his Presidential Seal cufflink catching a strand and breaking it. Like bank fees, pearls sprayed everywhere. Susan's body, no longer held by the necklace, dropped to the floor.

Could she still be alive? Did I fail to finish the job?

"Get up," Jamie said roughly. "Now!"

I fought and struggled, but he was too strong. Jamie Dimon operated the most powerful bank in the world. *He* was the one who'd allowed this to happen. And not once had he or his organization apologized.

"Get up!" he commanded again. "What's wrong with you?"

I shook my head and saw Jack's face in front of me. His hands were on my shoulders.

"Jo, it's time to get up," he said. "It's Monday morning. You're having a bad dream."

"What?" I choked out.

"Yeah. You were talking out loud and grabbing at something with your hands." He gave me a crooked smile. "Whatever it was, I'm glad it wasn't me."

My heart raced. I tried to slow my breathing, but that would take time. "It was so real," I told him. "I thought I'd killed…her."

"Well, get up and get dressed," he said. "We'll kill them in court. You'll see. I've been right there watching this trial from the beginning. I can't imagine anything other than a win for you."

"I sure hope you're right," I said, taking a deep breath. "One thing's for sure, I don't need any coffee."

As I READIED myself, I thought about the past two days. Alan and his team had worked all weekend, honing and refining their closing arguments. I had listened to the various versions, giving them my opinions over empty pizza boxes and sandwich wrappers. It had been exhausting.

One interesting development occurred Saturday. Alan had received an invitation to a fundraising party for Judge Thompson's reelection campaign. I recalled we had been solicited by Judge Miller's reelection team. He was the trial judge who had granted my motion for summary judgment, which had led to my appellate court victory. Now, here we were, staring at Judge Thompson's invitation in the middle of a lengthy and important trial. It had come at a most inopportune time.

Alan and I kicked it around. Donate too little, and it could be fatal. Donate too much... well, that probably wasn't possible. Whatever we did, we had to get this right. I'd spent millions and wasn't going to lose over a few thousand dollars.

I didn't like this crazy justice system or giving money to the judiciary branch, but I felt FOND—Fear of Not Donating. In the end, we decided to donate the maximum—$5,000—to Judge Thompson's reelection campaign. I would not be outbid.

It turned out we overbid by a large margin. Lenny gave $5,000 too, but neither Hunton & Williams nor John Eichman gave anything. Tom Cantrill donated a total of $350, and their expert Mark Sales' firm Diamond McCarthy donated $500. The only other lawyer in this case who gave was Gary Stolbach's firm Glast, Phillips & Murray. That firm donated $1,000, with five of their lawyers donating a total of $1,875. For some reason, Stolbach donated nothing. Did he see something I didn't?

IT WAS 8 a.m. For the twenty-first day, I sat in the chair behind Alan's. He and the other lawyers stood before the judge, arguing over the jury charge and making objections to preserve error on appeal. With nothing to do, I made a list of things I would do when this was all over.

1. Sit with Millie under Max's peach tree and have breakfast. Then, we'll lay back on a blanket and take a long nap.
2. Travel to somewhere special with Jack. See exotic sights and eat unique foods.
3. Volunteer time at an animal rescue.

I doodled for what seemed like forever. Right before the bailiff brought the jury in, Lenny announced that JPMorgan had just nonsuited its claims against Stephen and Laura for repayment of $947,120. This was the money the estate, run by JPMorgan, had borrowed from JPMorgan to pay Cantrill's and Eichman's law firm.

I made a quick calculation. With the expert witness fees the bank had previously admitted to eating and the money Hunton & Williams had not charged the estate since July, plus the almost $1 million it had borrowed from itself, JPMorgan was easily writing off over $2 million, if not $3 million. Instead of paying us what they owed, Jamie Dimon was willing to roll the dice that these strategic write-offs would prevent a nightmare ending. We'd soon find out if he'd made the right call.

Typically, the judge reads the entire charge to the jury. Then, closing arguments take place. This jury charge was fifty-four pages long. It would take half a day for her to read every word. To save time, all of us agreed to waive the full reading. Instead, the judge read an initial portion before turning it over to Alan. Suddenly, I could see the finish line.

Alan rose and approached the jury. "Intestate, independent, incompetent. It's hard to believe that it's been a month since I stood before you in the opening statement and uttered those three words. And I told you that those three words were the key to understanding this case."

He then eased into Max's humble beginnings, like when he'd used an outhouse in his childhood. Alan also produced an ancient putter from Scotland, one of Max's favorites, and showed it to the jury. He wanted to personalize Max for the jurors. But he didn't stay there long. Instead, he shifted the focus to Susan Novak and JPMorgan, using the word "bully" over and over.

He detailed each instance of bullying, pouncing on Susan's terrible performance in depositions and at trial. He methodically showed the jury how we had proved our case.

Alan was in his element. He was prepared, comfortable, and confident. He left no stone unturned. This was scorched-earth litigation in return.

I looked over to see how Susan was faring. She didn't look comfortable *or* confident. Her stomach had to be churning.

Alan moved on, crediting my previous attorney Jim Jennings for predicting the future.

"Mr. Jennings wrote, 'As we've pointed out before, all evidence of fighting between us is a plus for the Bank. The Bank will try slyly to use it as proof of supposedly why their misconduct and absurd fees are appropriate and reasonable, when they are in fact, not.'"

We hoped that put a dent in the notion that we had caused our own mess.

Even though I'd heard a preview of Alan's argument, it didn't compare to seeing it in the courtroom. He was slinging golden nuggets all over the place.

Alan mentioned attorney John Round, who had represented Stephen and Laura and was married to a JPMorgan trust officer. "Even Debra Round's husband recognized the incompetence of the Bank," Alan said, holding up the email that Debra Round had written to her husband after Stephen had fired him. In the email, Debra mentioned that John had complained about JPMorgan's estate service and had said that he wouldn't refer any more clients. She started off the email to her husband with "Hello!"

"Hello! I talked with John Powers and Tom Martyn about the experience you had with the estate. Tom is the National Head of the Estate Group. He joined JPMorgan about six months ago. Tom is going to call you to discuss your experience. He wants to understand the situation better so he can fully address the issues so that the Estate Services Unit can provide a better standard of service to avoid these experiences going forward. I told him that you expressed that you were not comfortable referring estate business to JPMorgan based on your recent experience. Again, I am sorry that has happened but appreciate you sharing with us so we can improve."

I saw two jurors grin. Yeah, they got it.

Alan marched forward, spreading a dead-skunk stink on every witness the bank had put on the stand. He argued that their inconsistencies and lack of preparation were indicators of how JPMorgan had ripped me off.

Just when I thought he was wrapping up, he turned to a long list of broken promises made by JPMorgan. Eichman looked uneasy as Alan went through each item. This was followed by a list of statements from

Susan Novak and Tom Cantrill agreeing with some aspects of our case. It was powerful.

Alan used charts to show how much money the bank had removed from Max's estate to pay their handpicked law firm.

"We now know why the Bank didn't want to be removed, because they would lose access to Max's estate funds in the cookie jar. They would be prevented from being able to control the account... and potentially, his children's money, to pay their lawyer bills, and to pay their own fee... And the same month, in which Gary Stolbach is threatening to have the Bank removed, the Bank made sure to pay itself its $230,000 fee. And although Susan Novak, you heard, sometimes would take days or weeks to be able to have time to write an email to Jo Hopper, within hours of her taking that fee out, she has time to write her superiors, to make sure that they knew that she had paid the Bank's fee."

Alan's argument of greed was devastating to JPMorgan. I could see it in the jurors' demeanors.

And he had several more nuggets to sling. Playing off one of his keywords, "incompetent," Alan pointed this out:

"Susan Novak still can't explain to you why JPMorgan took five years to release that property, and neither can any other witness they called to testify. The only reasonable inference is they wanted to harm Jo Hopper. She had sued them. They wanted her to have to spend her savings and retirement funds on legal fees. They wanted her to have emotional anguish. They were going to show her what happened when you try to take on the nation's largest bank."

Finally, Alan came to the delicate issue of how much they should award in damages. He explained that for someone who had a net worth of one dollar, a penny might get their attention.

"But the problem is, this bank has 200 billion of these dollars as part of their net worth and 1 penny's worth, for the Bank, 1 percent is 2 billion dollars. That's the only kind of number that banks with 200 billion dollars even begin to pay attention to, as opposed to, we'll just write this off, we'll write your verdict off as a cost of doing business."

Alan paused, building up to a dramatic moment.

"Whatever number you pick has to be loud enough to be heard in the corporate offices at 270 Park Avenue, in New York City. And this number has to be especially large because this bank doesn't get it."

Alan made it easy for the jury. He wanted $5.5 million in attorneys' fees to reimburse me for what I'd spent, $10 million for mental anguish damages, and $2 billion for punitive damages.

When he sat down, it was 5:30 p.m. All the legal wrangling and the reading of a partial jury charge had taken up the entire day. We still had Lenny and Eichman's closings, followed by Lenny and Alan again. With one juror leaving in the morning, the situation was precarious.

Alan whispered to me that we might have to try this case again. There wasn't enough time for all the arguments and a jury verdict. I wanted to scream. Then, I wanted to panic, but I couldn't. I had to hold it together. I could see the light at the end of the tunnel. I only hoped it wasn't a train coming straight at me.

LENNY ROSE FOR his turn.

Lenny's style was that of a swashbuckler, very different from Alan's paternalistic, wise owl style. Knowing Lenny, this would be good.

With his sticky notes taped all over the podium, he took a deep breath, slicked back his hair, and started. "Disloyalty, dishonesty, and destructiveness. That's what Chase is about." He nodded his head before starting with carefully crafted snippets.

Deception: "These lawyers at Chase did everything in their power to hide the truth from you for 30 days."

Deprivation: "Does it make common sense for Max Hopper to work his entire life, to save millions of dollars, only to have JPMorgan Chase take his children's potential inheritance and give it to these lawyers?"

After waving his legal sword around for a few minutes, Lenny slowly detailed the evidence supporting his three claims: breach of fiduciary duty, fraud, and breach of contract.

The exhibits and evidence he showed the jurors made complete logical sense. There was no way they could fail to see what had happened here.

When it came to talking about Eichman, Alan had been clinical. But Lenny tackled the issue with aggressive emotion.

"You saw Mr. Eichman on the stand. He could barely look at you when the question was asked... how much has JPMorgan Chase, through the estate, paid you?"

He followed up this statement with an exhibit displaying the amount of $4.5 million. That was how much the estate had paid from Stephen and Laura's inheritance.

It was odd watching both Alan and Lenny disparage Eichman. I still didn't understand how Eichman could be both a key witness and the lead lawyer in the same case. Thank God the Texas bar rules allowed it. The cross-examination of him on the stand had only helped my case.

Lenny paused, reviewed his thirty or so sticky notes, and moved to JPMorgan's tax payment error. Then, he smoothly transitioned to the gaslighting that the heirs and I had experienced. I was happy to hear he'd included that element, because Alan had talked less about it.

During the middle of Lenny's argument, he stopped and read an agreed statement, telling the jury that JPMorgan was no longer seeking reimbursement of the legal-fee overpayment from the heirs. The jurors arched their eyebrows. His subtle message was clear: JPMorgan knows it's in trouble, so it's tossing cargo overboard.

James Bell called out the time left, which told Lenny he'd better wrap it up. Instantly, Lenny shifted to a loud, booming tone as he singled out Susan Kravik, inside legal counsel for JPMorgan. Ms. Kravik hadn't taken the stand during the trial.

"Well, she's hiding in this courtroom. You can't see her. She's been here for 30 days, and she's positioned pretty well behind that TV. But she's here... So you send her a message and you make her go all the way up to New York, and you make her answer for what they did. You punish them. Absolutely, you punish them."

Then, he got philosophical.

"Whatever your verdict is, it will stand for ages to come. Your children and your grandchildren and their children. No one can ever take away the verdict you render. It will be registered in the courtroom. It will be registered in the records. It will have a profound effect forever, for ages."

Lenny asked for $3,695,000 as damages for loss in value to the estate. Then, he echoed Alan's call for $2 billion in exemplary/punitive damages.

He finished just as his time expired. Between Alan's and Lenny's summations, the courtroom was abuzz.

WE TOOK A brief break. The judge wanted to get this to the jury fast. When Eichman started his closing argument, it was 6:45 p.m.

He announced he would be taking his entire one hour and fifteen minutes in one big blowout. He didn't have a choice. As a defendant, he didn't get a rebuttal. It was one of the considerable disadvantages in being a defendant—something I'd almost become.

Right off the bat, Eichman addressed a recent wound in his case.

> "Ladies and gentlemen, I want to thank you again, on behalf of JPMorgan Chase Bank and Susan Novak, who is very much in this courtroom and has been throughout this trial, and her assistant Henry Etier and Susan Kravik, who hasn't been hiding from anybody, who was introduced to you during jury selection about a month ago."

Smart move. He was trying to personalize the bank. He then struck a serious tone.

> "Now, you're going to be asked to make some decisions based on the evidence. The evidence is an important word in this courtroom. It's not lawyer argument. It's not lawyer spin. It's evidence."

Eichman also addressed the bank's size by saying the plaintiffs wanted the jurors to be prejudiced against JPMorgan Chase because of its $2.1 trillion in assets. It was a trick the plaintiffs were using, he claimed.

> "You really don't need to focus so much on the evidence. Just think about bigness."

He then began turning over his cards of evidence. The more I saw them, the worse I felt. He even mixed in some of the heirs' self-inflicted damage.

> "Probably the truest statement about this case that's ever been made was made by Laura on September 14, 2011… 'this could have all been so easy with a little compassion and empathy, and without all the lawyer crap.'"

Like Alan and Lenny, Eichman had his own wordplay. He focused on "choices."

Choices the heirs had made.

Choices I had made.

Choices Max had made.

We, and no one else, were to blame for our choices. Certainly not the bank.

At one point, he popped one of Lenny's balloons. Lenny had argued JPMorgan should've just resigned and walked away, leaving over $3 million in the account.

"If JPMorgan had resigned, there would have had to be another admin-istrator come in there unquestionably. And they would have charged money. A great deal just to get up to speed."

I stared at the clock, watching every minute of his closing argument. It was slow and painful. For me, this was one of the worst parts of litigation yet. I had watched our team score all these runs and enjoyed the euphoria. Then Eichman began scoring runs, and it was deeply depressing. A trial is no place for the faint of heart.

Eichman pointed to another weakness in our case: We lacked an estate expert to say JPMorgan had done anything wrong. Neither the heirs nor I had paid an estate expert to testify.

Eichman said,

"Susan Novak has been getting trashed, trashed for the last month, and she sat here for every minute of it. But no professional has come in here... and said that they fell short, that Susan Novak fell short of the standards that apply to corporate fiduciaries."

Point made.

Every lawyer knows they have good and bad aspects of their case. To deflect some of the more damaging moments JPMorgan had suffered during the trial, Eichman said,

"All you heard was a bunch of lawyers pulling stuff out of context a lot of times in emails and spinning it around."

Spin and taken out of context. That was our evidence, he argued.

Next, he picked up a bat and beat the stuffing out of the relationship I had with Stephen and Laura.

"You heard testimony that sometimes when Stephen and Laura or the families visited Dallas, Jo would stay in her room the entire weekend, and would only come out when Stephen and Laura and their families were gone...You saw and heard Stephen call Jo unsafe, and it wasn't just because Jo was pinching his cheeks...Before JPMorgan was even appointed, Jo Hopper wanted no relationship with him. This notion that JPMorgan came in and trashed this relationship is ridiculous."

Besides making me look bad, it was another huge point for Team JPMorgan.

Eichman left no stone unturned. He addressed the gaslighting issue head-on.

"The argument that Susan Novak had a fiduciary duty to tell Jo Hopper that the children were saying bad things about her, it's illogical. The children were already saying bad things to Jo Hopper to her face... Essentially, they're saying that I'm not responsible for all those nasty things I said and that JPMorgan made me write those emails and that JPMorgan made me record that phone call back there in December 2010. Remember that phone call? That one that lasted for an hour-and-a-half, and Jo Hopper didn't tell [them] that she was recording them. No, she didn't."

To contrast the animosity, Eichman pointed out how chummy I now was with the heirs. I was even sitting next to them at times. But he failed to mention we weren't speaking to each other. I'm sure he didn't know that.

"Probably the way it should have been all the way along. If they'd shown each other one ounce of that same compassion in 2011 that they've shown in these past four weeks, we wouldn't have been here for one day, let alone over four weeks, and they wouldn't have spent millions of dollars in attorneys' fees, and JPMorgan wouldn't have had to spend millions of dollars in attorneys' fees."

Eichman explained away the conflicts Cantrill, JPMorgan, and he might have. He said since no expert had come into court and testified it was an actual conflict, so they were in the clear. Of course, the premise of his statement was true. No expert had said there was a legal or ethical conflict. The jurors never heard this because we couldn't hire an expert for every single issue in court. We had to draw the line somewhere, both financially and to shorten the length of the trial.

Eichman said that even if JPMorgan screwed up, there was no harm.

"Jo Hopper complains about the fact that Susan and the bank didn't distribute the interest in the furniture and art until 2015. Well, all that time, Jo Hopper's sitting on that furniture... it's in her living room, in her bedroom. The art is hanging on the walls. No harm."

He said the same with JPMorgan's erroneous tax payment, the one the bank hid from us. Eichman showed documents that a refund was eventually received with interest, so there could be no harm.

As planned, Eichman laid a tremendous amount of blame on the heirs hiring Gary Stolbach. He said Gary had caused a lot of this mess, and Stephen and Laura had hired him, so JPMorgan couldn't be blamed for Gary's mistakes.

Eichman's last line of attack was on the attorneys' fees we were all asking for. He laid out detailed arguments why we were owed nothing. I had spent all that money on top lawyers, and still, it was pretty convincing.

As he wrapped up, Eichman went back to his theme of "choices."

Choices we'd made about Robledo. Instead of negotiating a buyout, we litigated.

Choices we'd made about the wine and golf clubs. Instead of splitting it all up, we litigated.

He said we had made those choices and we should suffer the consequences.

For his final plea to the jury, Eichman had this to say:

"Susan for years tried to do the right thing. She may not have always gotten it perfect... but she tried her best, and we ask you to really look at this thing on the whole picture. Don't look at just little incidents here and little incidents there. Look at the whole picture. We think that at the end of the day, you're going to come to the conclusion that JPMorgan, as a fiduciary, it did what it was supposed to do. That Susan Novak did her best. That Mrs. Hopper wasn't harmed by anything that Susan Novak or this bank did. And that Stephen and Laura, they weren't harmed by anything that this bank did."

With that, he was finished. When he sat down, Stephen, Laura, and I looked greedy, dirty, mean, and vindictive. It was a sobering portrait.

At some point during Eichman's argument, the building's air conditioning had shut down. It was September in Texas, so the room quickly grew uncomfortable. Alan leaned over. "A few more degrees and the judge will have to let the jury go. She won't risk their health."

I swallowed hard.

Lenny stood up and spoke for only a few minutes. He urged them to use their common sense.

"The Bank's highest duty was to protect Stephen and Laura, not their own butt. The way they protected themselves [pointing to Susan Novak] was by paying Hunton & Williams millions of dollars to defend a lawsuit."

Alan followed and finished the case off.

"The Bank has spent a half a million dollars to pay these witnesses to come testify here. A half a million dollars. Who has the ability to fight a party in a lawsuit that can afford to pay a half a million dollars to come in and give testimony to? Well, thankfully, this woman right here had the resources to do it. And she told you from that witness stand from the bottom of her heart, she did it not for herself because she wanted what was right and fair, but she did it for other people who didn't have the money to go fight some bank who can spend half a million dollars to bring people in to give paid testimony. We didn't need to bring you experts. Your ears, your eyes told you what was right, and I got the admissions from their witnesses to prove what was right."

Just before Alan sat down, I teared up when he mentioned Max.

"What would Max want me to tell you? Max would want me to tell you, when you go into that room, do what is fair. Max would tell me to tell you, when you go in that room, do what is right. And Max would tell me to tell you, when you go in that room, do what is just. His family deserves no more, but they deserve no less. Max would want me to tell you as my final remarks to you, it's time. It's time to tell the nation's largest bank this is not how we treat people. Whether they're living in East Texas with an outhouse or whether they're living on 9 Robledo Drive in Dallas, Texas. All Jo Hopper has ever wanted was justice."

Before I could blink, the jury was in their room deliberating.

At 8 p.m.

Without air conditioning.

"How long do you think it will take?" I asked Alan nervously.

"The jury charge is fifty-four pages. How long would it take for you to read a fifty-four-page book in a hot room? And keep in mind, this 'book' is full of legal mumbo jumbo. Plus, they have to answer forty-one questions. Oh, and it's not just forty-one questions because, with all the subparts, there are 120 blanks in those questions. They also have to select a foreperson. Even if they skipped reading the charge and debating anything, it would take them close to three hours just to fill in 120 blanks if they started right now. Realistically, they need two to three hours minimum, just to get their minds wrapped around this beast."

"So how do we win? That juror is leaving tomorrow morning, which starts in four hours!"

"Jo, please don't get your hopes up. Unless they believe it's a slam dunk for us, they'll need a full two days to render a verdict. And that assumes there are no holdouts."

As the jury deliberated, Alan paced and worried about a retrial. "JPMorgan will have a great advantage knowing all our cards. They will tighten up their witnesses, especially their experts. They might even settle with Stephen and Laura to eliminate the huge advantage we have of whipsawing them from both sides. Who knows?"

"From the moment the trial started to right now, the bank didn't make me an offer to go away," I said somberly. "Why do you think that is?"

"They didn't see the risk. The lawyers advising them are blinded because they are witnesses in the case. Or the bank's management is incompetent. Or, JPMorgan just likes doing this to widows and children of decedents. My money is on the latter."

"At least Susan Novak is still hanging around," I pointed out.

"They're probably paying her by the hour. She and Bessette, and maybe even Debra Round—they all have jobs and salaries thanks to you. The bank can't afford to let them go and hear what they have to say from the unemployment line."

"How long will they stay with the bank?"

Alan rubbed his jaw. "I'd say through the appeals, until the bank pays the judgment."

"Let's hope it's a big one."

Waiting for a jury is extremely nerve-wracking. The lawyers spend time second-guessing themselves while the litigants think about all the money they've spent and how much more it will take. I felt like I'd lived three lifetimes in this one trial. If you have a serious enemy, wish a lawsuit on them. I can't think of anything more devastating.

Trying to take my mind off the money I'd spent, I flipped to a fresh sheet on my legal pad and started writing this book. No matter what happened tonight, I would tell the world my story.

I wanted a chapter in my book highlighting JPMorgan's litigation tactics. With my case and the other four trust cases, (STS Trust, Burns Clark Dailey Trust, MOSH Trust, and the Estate of Johnny Fisher), I'd had a preview of how JPMorgan acted and reacted in lawsuits. The first move it seemed to make was trying to transfer the case to federal court. This costs its opponents a lot of money while sometimes delaying the case a year or more. JPMorgan didn't try it in my case because federal courts have no jurisdiction over probate matters. There was some law or caselaw that kept probate matters in state court.

The next JPMorgan tactic was to fight every discovery request. It was clever to use sworn affidavits stating it would cost JPMorgan lots of money and take a long time to produce everything in the request. This tactic caused its opponents to cower and cut the request. If the opponent stood up to the bank, the matter would be placed before a judge who might take the bait and cut the discovery request anyway. In the worst-case scenario, the opponent was forced to spend time and money to get the requested discovery. For sure, no judge would ever sanction this conduct. I decided to try to collect all these affidavits and post them on my website. Then the world could analyze the affidavits for consistency and veracity.

The third tactic was brilliant. JPMorgan took money from the trust or estate and paid their own lawyers to defend itself. Usually, the wording of the trust allowed the trustee to use the money to pay for lawyers. So even though JPMorgan was being accused of fraud, breach of fiduciary duty, and other malfeasance, it could grab the cash that was just sitting there. This infuriated JPMorgan's opponents, usually the beneficiaries. They were forced to watch the account balance drop with each legal invoice. It was like claiming JPMorgan stole your TV and going to court to recover it. But as you put on your case, JPMorgan takes pieces of the TV and sells them to pay its lawyers. By the time the case goes to the jury, the TV no longer exists.

The fourth tactic I experienced was the attempt by JPMorgan to sell assets of the trust or estate to raise more cash to pay its lawyers. This is an incredibly evil tactic, especially when there's a sentimental value in the asset. In the case of MOSH, JPMorgan tried to shut down the trust and sell everything off. Just the attempt shifts the leverage to JPMorgan, which may cause a settlement to happen quickly, or at least make the other side sweat profusely while spending time and money to stop it.

The final tactic uses a combination of money and resistance. When JPMorgan runs out of money in the trust or estate, it will borrow from itself and charge the balance to the beneficiaries. This scares the litigants into realizing that not only will the trust be empty of cash, but they will have to reach into their pockets and pay JPMorgan back. And when the opponents try to have JPMorgan removed as trustee, it resists, burning through more time and money. Believe me, when a plaintiff is looking at having to write a massive check to JPMorgan for suing it for some alleged misconduct, a settlement is right around the corner. But if the litigant can endure the stress, JPMorgan will usually waive the borrowed amount in a settlement. In my case, they waived it before jury argument. And at least one of the plaintiffs in the cases I researched got the judge to order JPMorgan to stop taking money from the trust to pay its own lawyers. That is an effective countermove to this tactic.

When all is said and done, these litigation tactics can bring anyone to their knees. Trust me, the hole it creates in your stomach, not to mention your bank account, is maddening. All this means that suing JPMorgan is a challenging prospect, and you'd better be ready to experience all this.

I let my pen drop as I thought, *Gosh, I wish I had not agreed to hire JPMorgan Chase Bank. I'll regret that decision for the rest of my life.*

"Jo, something's happening." It was Alan.

I glanced at the clock on the wall. It was midnight.

Alan stared at his smartphone. "We have a verdict," he announced, shocking everyone, including himself.

My heart dropped twenty stories. I was so numb I couldn't process that the jury had been in deliberations barely four hours. I was sure I hadn't breathed since the announcement.

Feeling lightheaded, I was about to learn my fate.

My life.

My future.

This was it.

Chapter Thirty-Nine

"Our people have done an extraordinary job, often under difficult circumstances. I hope you are as proud of them as I am."
—Jamie Dimon, Chairman & CEO
JPMorgan Chase Bank, N.A.
Letter to the Shareholders 2010 Annual Report

"All rise!" called out the bailiff. The jurors entered the courtroom, their heads down.

What does that mean?

Judge Thompson cleared her throat. "Have you reached a verdict?"

"Yes, Your Honor," the jury said in unison.

"All right," the judge said as the bailiff handed her the verdict. She started going through the questions and announcing the verdict. It happened so quickly I could barely see straight. My blood pressure was sky-high.

"Did JPMorgan fail to comply with one or more of the following duties?"

It was "Yes" to each duty listed.

- JPMorgan had failed to act toward me in the utmost good faith.
- JPMorgan failed to exercise the most scrupulous honesty.
- JPMorgan failed to place my interests above its own.
- JPMorgan failed by using the advantage of its position to gain benefit for itself at my expense.
- JPMorgan failed to fully and fairly disclose all material facts known to JPMorgan that might affect my rights.

The judge moved to the next question. "Do you find by clear and convincing evidence that the harm to Jo Hopper from JPMorgan's breach of fiduciary duty resulted from malice? Answer: Yes."

The definition of malice given to the jury was "a specific intent by JPMorgan to cause substantial injury or harm to Jo Hopper." I felt that whenever you act with malice, you're going to pay.

I knew that was a tremendous win for us. My eyes darted to Alan, but he was stone-faced. He had warned me about showing any emotion. "Look straight at the judge," he said before the jury returned. "Whatever their verdict, this isn't over. Jumping up and down could affect other rulings down the road and even cause the jurors to change their minds. If you want to get excited, do it at home."

The judge moved to the next question. This was the big one. The finish line. The pinnacle. In a few seconds, I'd learn my fate.

"What sum of money, if any, if paid now in cash, should be assessed against JPMorgan and awarded to Jo Hopper as exemplary damages, if any, for the conduct found in response to question number three? Answer: $2 billion."

My heart seemed to explode. I was sure everyone could hear it, but apparently not. The room was so quiet you could've heard a pin hit the floor. No one showed any emotion or hardly breathed. The judge kept going.

"Did JPMorgan fail to comply with the Fee Agreement with regard to Jo Hopper? Answer: Yes. Does JPMorgan as Independent Administrator hold money that in equity and good conscience belongs to Jo Hopper? Answer: Yes."

The judge moved into the additional damages questions and said the jury had awarded me $5,812,778.30 for attorneys' fees—precisely what we'd asked for. They also awarded me the $58,000 I had fronted for the estate. And they awarded $500,000 for mental anguish, 5% of what we'd requested. I guess Eichman had to win something.

All too soon, my part was over. Now it was time to see what Summer Santa had left under the tree for Stephen and Laura.

The judge read the answers, explaining that the jury found the same failures on JPMorgan's part as they had in my case, but said Gary Stolbach had caused 10% of the damages.

Again, they found JPMorgan acted with malice to the heirs. So no one was surprised when the jury awarded another $2 billion to Stephen and Laura.

I thought we were done, but there was more. JPMorgan was found by clear and convincing evidence to have committed *fraud* on Stephen and Laura. That was especially damaging for a bank. Another $2 billion was awarded for that misconduct.

The jury piled it on, finding JPMorgan had been *grossly negligent* toward the heirs and gave them $3,695,000 plus a third $2 billion in exemplary damages.

The jury ruled that JPMorgan also committed *conversion* against the estate, which means it took money without permission—a civil tort for theft. Again, the heirs received $3,695,000.

Finally, JPMorgan was declared not to have acted in good faith in defending the action to remove them as administrator, and the heirs were awarded an additional $3,695,000 for loss of potential inheritance.

Judge Thompson asked the lawyers if they wanted the jury polled. Mr. Eichman, wearing a grim expression, said JPMorgan Chase wanted a polling. Judge Thompson then turned to the jury. "Juror No. 1, is the verdict I read aloud your individual verdict?"

The juror's reply was "yes," so she continued asking the next juror the same question until all six had responded that yes, it was their personal verdict. It was a complete annihilation of the world's largest bank.

Judge Thompson calmly thanked the jury. She explained that they did not have to speak with anyone, but if they wanted to, they could wait by the elevators for us to come out. Then, she excused them.

The lawyers spoke with the judge for a few minutes. When she released us, it was 12:45 a.m.

Alan, Kerry, Jack, and I raced to the elevators to meet the jurors. The foreperson and three others were waiting for us.

Just as we started talking, Stephen and Laura joined us. We had been together for four weeks without being able to say a word. Now the dam had burst, and we just wanted to exchange information.

No other lawyers, including Lenny, Eichman, or James Bell, stopped to talk to the jurors. They had disappeared.

It seemed like we only spent a few minutes talking and laughing with the jurors. But when we finally broke free, it was 2:45 a.m.

Jack and I walked to my car, so thankful my prayers had been answered. The end of this nightmare was in sight—no retrial. Or, at least, that's what I thought.

THE NEXT MORNING, I rubbed my eyes, waking later than normal. But today there was a new reality. I could hardly believe it. A few hours earlier, in front of my very eyes, JPMorgan Chase had been hit with a verdict of over $8 billion in damages. And $2 billion of it was mine.

No sooner had my feet hit the floor than I saw a special person's name appear on my cell phone.

"Hello, Tarian," I greeted, unable to disguise the glee in my voice.

"Well, hello to you, Ms. Billionaire."

I had not called him last night, or rather, in the wee hours of this morning, so I was baffled as to how he'd found out. "Where did you hear about it?"

"James Bell put out a press release early this morning touting his work on the case."

"James Bell?"

"Yep. It's out there. The news services are picking it up."

"Listen," I said, "I just got out of bed. Can we meet later at our favorite restaurant? Is it still in business?"

"It is," Tarian replied. "Barely."

I glanced at my watch. It was eleven in the morning. "Okay, I'll see you there at two. That's about the earliest I can make it."

THREE HOURS DISAPPEARED on me. I had talked to Alan, who wanted to meet later in the day. Meanwhile, Lenny had put out his own press release. Sure enough, the news wires were lighting up.

JPMorgan Ordered to Pay More Than $4 Billion to Widow and Family
—Bloomberg News

Jury Slaps JPMorgan Chase with $6 Billion-plus Verdict in Sabre Creator's Estate
—Business Insider

JPMorgan's $5b Whack after Unfairly Denying a Widow
—The Sydney Morning Herald

Dallas Jury Orders JPMorgan Chase to Pay American Airlines Executive's Widow $4B in Punitive Damages
—Dallas Morning News

JPMorgan Fined Over $4 Billion for Excessive Fuckery with Cancer Patient Widow and Children
—Busy.org/news

The news media isn't always accurate.

Even though there had been "excessive fuckery," JPMorgan was not fined. It was a verdict. Also, I was awarded over $2 billion, and Stephen and Laura received over $6 billion. Finally, the total verdict was over $8 billion—the largest probate award ever and the ninth-largest verdict in U.S. history. It was a tremendous victory for Alan, Kerry, and Jim, and a complete repudiation of JPMorgan's conduct.

I made it on time to Kung Pho. As usual, Tarian was late. But when he finally showed up, we hugged.

"Congratulations," he said. "You just had a little boy."

I chuckled as we sat down. "Thanks. But why do you say that?"

"Because you did. Your new baby will need nurturing for years before he'll be able to take care of himself. Then there's private school, a lawyer for his DWI, college out of state, a wedding where doves are released from cakes, and later, financial help when he fails to send the IRS his quarterly payment. The motherly supervision of your new jury verdict won't end for a long time."

My happiness dissolved faster than a pyramid scheme. "Stop talking in riddles," I demanded. "The Texas Rules of Civil Procedure says in thirty days the judgment will be signed, and I'll be in the appellate court. Right?"

"I'm afraid you are either mistaken or misinformed."

"Then inform me." I was exasperated.

"It may take months before the judge signs a judgment. Then, JPMorgan has thirty days to file oceans of motions. The judge can take up to seventy-five days to overrule them. JPMorgan will have another thirty days to file a notice of appeal. The court's record, along with the transcript, must be sent to the appellate court. The court reporter might take a lifetime to type it up. I've seen court reporters put in jail until they finish the transcript. Then there are seas of pleas in the court of appeals. God willing, I'll be alive when it's all over. You probably won't."

I stared at him in disbelief. "So once again, Eichman will do everything he can to drag this out?"

"Eichman? Not likely."

"He'll suddenly turn nice?"

"No. You see, JPMorgan believes their people never do wrong. They never screw up. Thus, the bank will likely conclude this eight-billion-dollar fiasco must be a failure of legal counsel. They'll tell themselves that Hunton & Williams shit the bed as well as their briefs. Because of this, JPMorgan will need some fresh sheets and undies. They'll probably tap a large firm with more offices and lawyers than Eichman's firm. The bank will send some men in suits with briefcases to this new firm's office. Once there, these men will open their briefcases and dump out stacks of Benjamins. As the new lawyers scramble to count it all, JPMorgan will feel like they're doing something to make this problem go away."

I sighed heavily. "So, how many more months will I have to suffer receiving legal bills?"

"That's hard to say. This new law firm will put twenty to thirty lawyers, clerks, and paralegals on it. They'll slip on rubber gloves and pick apart every letter and word. If you have a dangling participle, a damaged colon, or a missed period, they'll know about it. Then, they'll file acres of papers complaining of everything from res judicata to Lasagna Bolognese. It doesn't matter if it has zero chance to succeed. They just need to drag it out."

"For how long?" I said, growing impatient.

"Until you die or go broke. And with your health issues, which they clearly know about, they can send men in suits over to make monthly cash dumps until you croak."

I gritted my teeth in anger. "Okay. I see how it's gonna work. I'll show them. I'm going to lose weight, get healthy, and live until I'm ninety just to spite them."

"Try a hundred just to be on the safe side. Remember *Bleak House*? That case took decades."

We sat there in silence while I seethed. I knew he was right. The judgment wouldn't be entered in thirty days. JPMorgan would see to that.

"What's going to happen to Eichman, Cantrill, and the rest of this bunch?"

"Anyone still employed with JPMorgan will stay that way. They must keep them on board in case there's a retrial."

Retrial. I shuddered at the word.

"And Cantrill, he has a long book of business. Mrs. Haberman may lose her husband next year and call Tom up. She'll need help with the estate. His law firm will want to tap that revenue. My guess is that his partners will ease him out the door while finding a way to keep its fingers in his clients' potential pies."

"And Eichman?"

"He was the losing general. After the Civil War, Robert E. Lee was relegated to living with a woman who offered him charity and a place to stay. If I had to look into a crystal ball and make a prediction, I'd say that once this case is finally over, JPMorgan will sit down with Hunton & Williams. The law firm won't want to lose all that business, and JPMorgan will want to be reimbursed for their losses. At some point, my guess is that JPMorgan will hook up a Black & Decker shop-vac hose to Hunton & Williams' malpractice carrier and flip on the switch. Once the money is transferred, I'm guessing Eichman's days at the firm will be over. He might find another firm that wants him. If not, it's gonna be tough. He's gotta be sixty or so. Starting over at that age... man, that gives me the willies. But who knows? I'm not a licensed channeler, although my dad was an unlicensed channel changer."

I ignored his joke as we ordered. While we waited for food, I regaled him with the closing arguments and told him about the air conditioning going out.

"It's a miracle you landed this verdict in time," he said.

"Yep. That juror was gone this morning. A mistrial would've been granted. What a nightmare that would've been. Of course, it was already a nightmare."

Tarian laughed. "Yeah, surviving stage four lymphoma was easier than dealing with JPMorgan."

My body tensed. "That's it! Alan was looking for something to add to our press release. Let me send that to him."

I texted Alan. (By that evening, every news agency that ran a story on the now $8 billion jury verdict picked up Tarian's slogan: Surviving stage four lymphoma cancer was easier than dealing with JPMorgan Chase.)

As usual, the food at Kung Pho was excellent. When the plates were taken away and the bill arrived, Tarian insisted on paying for it. "You're going to need every dollar you have to preserve this verdict."

"Okay. So, how do you see this playing out?" I asked, all ears.

"You have a lot of leverage. Once the trial court signs the judgment, the case will be kicked up to the appellate court. JPMorgan would love for the trial transcript never to be typed up."

"Why's that?"

"Because the public will have access to all the testimony, which leads me to my next point: JPMorgan will not want an appellate court to write and publish an opinion detailing their misconduct and the jury's findings. The press might read it and start looking for other bad deeds committed by the bank. These things tend to snowball once they get rolling. Just ask Wells Fargo."

"I hadn't thought about that."

"And the last thing they need is for all the lawyers out there to learn the jury ruled JPMorgan violated their fiduciary duties, committed fraud and conversion, acted with malice, failed to exercise the most scrupulous honesty, and held money that didn't belong to them. That would sure slow down referrals of rich clients from all those lawyers. And then there are the law students. Their professors will, no doubt, make this case special reading. Every future lawyer will learn how terrible JPMorgan behaved towards a widow and the heirs of a decedent. Believe me, that would eventually impact their bottom-line."

I nodded enthusiastically.

"Don't forget, Tom Cantrill, John Eichman, Hunton & Williams, and all the expert witnesses will be on the sidelines rooting for JPMorgan's firm to settle your case. The last thing they need is a lengthy appellate opinion spelling out what they said and did—or, in your case, didn't do. No lawyer wants to die with that cloud hanging over them. I mean, hell might not let us in. Then where would we be?"

I chuckled. "Tarian, you sure have a way with words. When is your book coming out?"

He pushed back his shaggy hair. "Soon or maybe later, but definitely before I die."

"How can you be sure you'll be alive?"

"Because I owe people money. As long as you're in debt, you have a better chance of staying alive. That's basic biology."

"Then I guess I'd better not settle."

"Stay the course, Jo. When they start knocking on your door, you'll know you've got 'em. Stand firm and empty their ATMs."

"I'm going to miss our lunches, Tarian."

"They don't have to stop," he said, smiling and batting his eyelashes. "I'm still looking for wife number five. I even have a T-shirt that says *Marry me and sue for free.*"

I laughed. "Do you have a will?"

"No, but I have stepchildren."

"Goodbye, Tarian."

"Goodbye, Jo," he said, hugging me. Just as I hit the door, he yelled out, "And make the bastards pay!"

I intended to do just that.

The End.

(Well, not really.)

Epilogue

A verdict that size drew plenty of attention from the news media. Alan Loewinsohn was bombarded with calls for interviews and quotes. I ended up on the front cover of *D Magazine*, which is Dallas's version of *People,* and *Food & Wine.* The reporter, Joseph Guinto, and photographer, Jill Broussard, came to Robledo. After snapping various shots, they decided Millie needed to be in one of them. A rescue pittie from the streets made it into *D Magazine.*

The celebration after the verdict was short-lived. Texas, like many states, has a cap on punitive damages. A plaintiff can plead cap-busting claims, and Lenny did that for Stephen and Laura but for various reasons, we did not. This meant I was looking at a number below $20 million. The heirs, on the other hand, had a chance at just under $100 million. About this, Tarian said, "Too bad Texas doesn't have a graduated scale for punitive damages depending on the size of the defendant. By the time your verdict is whittled down to a final judgment, it will be nothing more than a piece of lint on Jamie Dimon's custom suit. JPMorgan won't feel any pain from this. And without pain, nothing will ever change. It's like a tree falling in the forest that no one ever hears."

As I talked to Alan and my litigation team, it didn't take long to realize this lawsuit could take another $1 million for the posttrial and appellate work. Of course, Tarian had been right again. There was no way this lawsuit would be resolved quickly.

The first court action was James Bell withdrawing from the case. He had aptly defended the heirs against JPMorgan's claims and was done. After the judge released Bell, JPMorgan began the marathon attack on the jury verdict by filing motion after motion.

Because the case was being appealed, the court reporter had to begin the long grind of typing up every word of the court proceedings. No hearing was excluded. Plus, her day job required her to be in court. I learned being a court reporter is very demanding.

So, 2017 ENDED, and 2018 began. It was a new year for humanity. To me, it was nothing more than another year of futility.

On January 4, 2018, we had a hearing before Judge Thompson. At the back of the room were three ominous men dressed in dark suits. They looked mean and serious.

Lenny, always the Han Solo swashbuckler, walked over and introduced himself. Later, Alan talked to Lenny and found out one of these guys was Robert Sacks from Sullivan & Cromwell in Los Angeles. Sacks was an attorney/negotiator for JPMorgan. The second man was JPMorgan's national head of the trust department. The third was the national head of estates. To me, they were like a consigliere and two hitmen for JPMorgan. Whenever the world caved in on JPMorgan or Jamie Dimon, he picked up the phone and sent these three to figure out which tool was needed to extract JPMorgan from trouble.

One of the first moves JPMorgan made was to "supplement" Hunton & Williams with attorneys from Baker Botts. They did all the talking while Hunton & Williams' attorneys sat to the side, saying nothing.

For some reason, JPMorgan didn't want to fire Hunton & Williams. Tarian told me that firing them might start the statute of limitations on JPMorgan suing them. By keeping them on the team, the bank could wait to see the final tab before cutting them loose. "And besides, Baker

Botts will need Eichman and Cantrill if there's a retrial. No sense in having them on the wrong end of a legal gun."

"Are the lawyers at Baker Botts any better than Hunton & Williams?" I asked Tarian.

He coughed. "You know, I've won my share of hard cases. I'm pretty smart legally. But I'd have to hire a surgeon and have three more brains added to my head to be considered for a job at Baker Botts. They only hire the best and brightest from the top five or ten law schools. They don't scrape the cream. They scrape *molecules* from the cream."

"Well, so what? Alan has whipped JPMorgan before. And he got me a $2 billion verdict. We'll see how he stacks up against these guys."

"Jo, you're in for a treat. You have a ringside seat to King Kong versus Godzilla. They'll square off against each other in the octagon—albeit a very large one."

"Which one of those represents me?"

"I've always been partial to King Kong," Tarian winked. "He has an eye for the ladies and can be gentle when he needs to be. And Godzilla is a lizard who ate some superhot Terlingua chilies. His breath burns buildings to a cinder. Not real handy on a date. But hey, that's just me."

SIX MONTHS AFTER the jury verdict, I was no closer to getting a judgment signed. In early April 2018, we attended a hearing and received a shock. Lenny announced to the judge that JPMorgan had reached a settlement with Stephen and Laura and he would no longer be appearing in this case. Then he exited the courtroom.

The very next day, an angry Lenny returned to court, announcing that Stephen and Laura had fired him within one hour of leaving court yesterday. He also said they had hired legal malpractice lawyer James Pennington of the Law Offices of James E. Pennington PC, and they were attempting to prevent the settlement money from landing in Lenny's trust account. Instead, they wanted JPMorgan to send the money to either Pennington's or Jeffrey Levinger's account. Levinger was an appellate lawyer the heirs had hired right after our trial ended. I sat behind Alan taking this in as it was all laid bare in court with the public watching.

Apparently, Lenny was requesting a temporary restraining order (TRO) to send JPMorgan's settlement payment into the court's registry for safekeeping. John Malesovas, with the Malesovas Law Firm, also showed up. He was another lawyer the heirs had hired at the same time as Lenny. This was the first time he had appeared in the case. He stood next to Lenny and agreed with him.

I learned that in the ordinary course of settling a case, the money is sent to the winning lawyer's trust account. That lawyer then doles out the funds to any vendors before paying the parties. The remaining balance is transferred to the lawyer's operating account. In this case, Stephen and Laura were trying to send the money to another lawyer and bypass Lenny—the same guy who'd scored them a $6 billion verdict!

Judge Thompson set all this for a hearing in a few days. When I walked into court, I could hardly see the judge through a forest of lawyers. It was like an ABA convention. As I took my seat, I was reminded of both Max and Tarian. When Max was alive, he'd told me about Moore's Law: The number of transistors on a computer chip doubles every 18 months. Then there was Tarian's Law: The number of lawyers on a case doubles with every $1.8 million at stake. I took out my pad and made a list.

First, there was Lenny's new lawyer, Brian Lauten with Brian Lauten PC. As I said before, John Malesovas was there representing himself. Lauten and Malesovas pushed hard for a TRO and injunction.

Stephen and Laura were there with their lawyers, Anne Johnson and Andrew Guthrie, with Haynes and Boone, and James Pennington. The heirs also had their appellate lawyers Jeffrey Levinger and Carl Cecere. They argued for the whole affair to be sent to arbitration. Stephen and Laura claimed their fee agreements with Lenny required that. And by the way, Lenny had drafted the fee agreements and inserted the mandatory arbitration clause.

Crowding Judge Thompson's front shelf were JPMorgan's lawyers Van Beckwith and Jessica Pulliam with Baker Botts. Evan Young was also listed as another Baker Botts lawyer. Off to the side was the surprisingly new entry of Robert Tobey with Johnston Tobey Baruch. Tobey had just been hired by Block, Garden & McNeill. Their appearance would soon be explained.

To round out the group, Grayson Linyard from Hunton & Williams was there. And of course, Alan and I were there.

As Judge Thompson heard this latest development, she appeared annoyed. She even stated how much time resolving these issues would take from her court, considering she still had to rule on my case.

Lenny was visibly angry. His argument was that he didn't want the new attorneys for Stephen and Laura getting his 45% contingency fee. I waited to see if Lenny would say, "We want our money put into the registry of the court because we don't want Stephen's and Laura's attorneys touching it!" But he didn't.

JPMorgan's lawyers argued against placing the money in the court's registry because the judge would know the settlement amount. They claimed if she knew that amount, it might prejudice her when it came time to sign a judgment in my case. That comment from Baker Botts lifted my spirits. I felt the heirs must be getting such a large amount that Judge Thompson would be more inclined to grant me a sizable judgment, too. Otherwise, JPMorgan wouldn't be so stressed about her seeing the amount.

The judge, shaking her head several times, ordered the money, whatever the amount, placed in a special account at JPMorgan Chase Bank and treated like a deposit into the court's registry. For the time being, she kept this new case in her court while she decided if it should be sent to arbitration. Then she ordered an expedited discovery. This meant Stephen and Laura would be back in Dallas to sit for more depositions.

Boy, that sounded like fun.

While all this was going on, Block Garden & McNeill, a law firm that had handled the partition suit for Stephen and Laura, claimed it was owed 20% of Lenny's contingency fee. Lenny sued them for a declaratory judgment—a suit to have the court say he didn't owe them money—and they countersued. It was a complete quagmire.

I told Tarian about all this, and he said, "If there's ten tons of chum in the water, you shouldn't be surprised when dozens of sharks show up. I just wish I had an angle into all that cash."

Lenny and the heirs were now at war with each other. The public court filings and hearings gave us so much information, I couldn't believe it. I had a front-row seat to everything as Alan and I attended Stephen and Laura's depositions. Their attorneys tried to bar us from attending, but after a call to Judge Thompson, she ruled we could stay. I heard stuff my former stepchildren never intended for me to hear.

Let me warn you that when you sue a lawyer, it's brutal. Since your former lawyer no longer represents you, they're allowed to spill the beans on anything you told them in confidence. They can reveal every conversation and produce all the emails you exchanged with them. It's a nasty weapon.

Excerpts from Stephen and Laura's new depositions were filed as exhibits in court motions and briefs. Like the hearings before Judge Thompson, these exhibits became part of the record available to the public. I ordered copies from the various court clerks and perused them. It made for great reading.

During Laura's deposition, Lenny's lawyer, Brian Lauten, led her on a sentimental journey of her and Stephen's past legal counsel. Laura testified that:

- John Round was Stephen's lawyer, he was fired, and she didn't know if there was an unpaid balance.
- Lyle Pishny was her lawyer, he was fired, and Pishny claimed Laura still owed him money.
- Gary Stolbach and Mark Enoch with Glast, Phillip & Murray were her lawyers and she fired them. Stolbach and Enoch claimed to be owed $300,000 and Lenny sued them for malpractice. The suit resulted in a settlement of $990,000 paid to Lenny's trust account. Lenny received his contingency cut while Laura and Stephen got the balance. Also, the $300,000 the heirs allegedly owed to Glast, Phillip & Murray was erased with the settlement.
- James Bell was her lawyer and he was fired, too. Since he was paid a $200,000 flat fee upfront, Bell wasn't claiming any money.
- Lenny Vitullo was her lawyer and he was the seventh lawyer fired. Laura agreed that Lenny successfully defended her on a claim of $3 million by JPMorgan that the bank eventually dropped.

I leaned back and studied the transcript. It was fascinating.

Laura went on to say that before trial, JPMorgan had not offered a cent to settle her case. Then there was this exchange:

Brian: Okay. Have you ever apologized to Lenny for acting ungrateful for his hard work? Have you ever done that?

Laura: I've not felt the need to apologize to Lenny.

Brian: Have you ever apologized to Lenny for being ungrateful for how you've treated him? Have you ever done that?

Laura: I don't feel I owe Lenny an apology—an explanation or an apology for being ungrateful.

Brian: I'm talking about in the past. Have you ever written to Lenny and apologized for being ungrateful? Have you ever done that?

Laura: I don't consider myself ungrateful, no.

Then Lenny's lawyer pulled out an email from Laura to Lenny dated one year before the trial.

> Again, I apologize for coming across as ungrateful for all you are doing, and for taking my frustration with Jo out on you. I know that you, James, and the entire team are working hard for us. I'm scared and just needed some reassurance. As Steve mentioned, I think getting some additional response to our e-mails, to know if we are on the right track or not, would be helpful. I don't know if anything below would be helpful; just some notes I jotted down as I read through the declaratory judgment action. Please let me know if there's any additional information I can provide. Thanks again, Laura

But Brian Lauten wasn't through.

Brian: All right. Did—when you told him you apologized for your ungrateful behavior, did you—was it sincere at the time?

Laura: You know, it wasn't that sincere. It was I felt that if I did not suck up to Lenny at that moment, he was going to walk out of our case.

Then it was Stephen's turn. He testified that within a week or two after the trial and record verdict, he hired James Pennington, a malpractice lawyer, because he had questions about Lenny's performance at trial. A few days later, he hired Mr. Levinger for the appeal. Stephen didn't tell Lenny about these hires until two months after the trial. And he recorded his conversations with Lenny—six in all. The first recording was the very next day after the verdict and took place in Lenny's office with Laura present. Of course, Stephen didn't tell Lenny he was being recorded.

When asked why he did this, Stephen replied, "Because I knew that Mr. Vitullo would be putting his interest over mine and pushing for a quick settlement. And I knew that—or I didn't feel that—it would be in my best interest."

John Malesovas was Lenny's case investor. A case investor gives a lawyer cash to help finance a lengthy and expensive litigation in exchange for a percentage of a potential verdict. Malesovas questioned Stephen hard:

Malesovas: Were you happy with the settlement your appellate attorney, Mr. Levinger, negotiated with JPMorgan Chase?

Stephen: I was happy given what we had to work with.

Malesovas: You authorized Mr. Levinger to enter into that settlement, didn't you?

Stephen: Yes, I did.

Malesovas drilled down deeper and got Stephen to testify to all the things Lenny did that Stephen was happy or satisfied with:

- Lenny successfully prevented JPMorgan from clawing back the $2.5 million the bank had already given to Stephen before the lawsuit.
- Lenny successfully defended Jo Hopper's request for $1 million in attorneys' fees.
- Lenny successfully defended all claims from JPMorgan against Stephen, including one totaling $3 million, thus zeroing the bank out.
- Lenny sued and reached a settlement with Glast, Phillip & Murray. Stolbach's firm paid Stephen and Laura $990,000 while dropping the law firm's $300,000 outstanding invoice.
- Lenny obtained a jury verdict in the billions of dollars.
- And Stephen was happy with the verdict amount.

One thing Stephen appeared to be unhappy about was paying Lenny and Malesovas their 45% share of the total recovery. Stephen testified that he wanted to pay the lawyers something, but not the full 45%—whatever the arbitrator decided was fair.

Stephen grudgingly admitted that at times, he received valuable legal services from Lenny.

Malesovas: All right. And he provided you a valuable legal service from the time he appeared in the case until the time you terminated him on April 5th, correct?

Stephen: He provided some valuable services, yes.

Finally, Stephen said they terminated Lenny on April 5, 2018, right after they received the Rule 11 agreement from JPMorgan to settle the case.

Nice!

Judge Thompson eventually ordered a resolution using arbitration. Lenny and Malesovas appealed this ruling.

In December 2018, the arbitrator made his ruling, dividing up the money between the parties. The appeal was dropped. Unfortunately for Lenny, the fight raged on.

In April 2020, Lenny appealed a ruling against him by Block, Garden & McNeill. One month later, the matter was disposed of with an undisclosed settlement.

All this reminded me of Hemingway's *The Old Man and the Sea*. The story is about an aging Cuban who has gone 84 days without catching a fish. On Day 85, he leaves his home and sails a tiny wooden skiff over a vast ocean. Then, with some string and his bare hands, he catches a huge marlin. It takes three long days and every ounce of strength to pull in the massive fish. However, the fish is too big to fit into the skiff. He must lash it to the side. With such a massive catch, the old man will become rich.

Unfortunately, the fish leaves a trail of blood behind. As the old Cuban sails home, he's forced to fight off sharks, killing some of them. All the blood in the water attracts more sharks. By the time he reaches the dock, the old man learns that all he has left is a fish head and skeleton. He collapses into bed from total exhaustion.

I guess that's the life of a contingency fee lawyer.

BACK TO MY side of the litigation, I was stuck in quicksand. The legal bills continued to roll in like clockwork. All I had to do was sell more assets to pay them.

Finally, ten months after the verdict, the trial court signed the judgment awarding me just over $7 million. This event allowed JPMorgan to file acres of papers to contest the judgment just signed, delaying everything. I assumed this was part of their game plan.

It took thirteen months after the verdict before JPMorgan had to file their notice of appeal. Now the battle would shift to the Court of Appeals for the Fifth District of Texas in Dallas.

The court reporter, no doubt having severe hand cramps from typing up everything, needed extension after extension. On August 20, 2019, one month short of two years from the jury verdict, the transcript was filed in the appellate court. This started the clock on JPMorgan's appellate brief due date. However, they were able to receive extensions to November 20, 2019.

During this time, a beehive of Baker Botts lawyers must have been busy reading every hearing, deposition, ruling, and witness testimony. I don't think one person could read it all in one year. They had to have a dozen appellate lawyers going through all the legal documents.

On my side, I had Robert Dubose and company working on our appellate response. We'd see how Mr. Dubose stacked up against Baker Botts.

Before JPMorgan filed their appellate brief, they contacted us about reaching a mutual agreement. Up to this point, JPMorgan had stated to the jury and in post-verdict hearings to the judge that I was entitled to zero dollars and zero cents. But now, as they knocked on our door, Alan laughed. "I guess they've finished reading the transcript, and it's not looking too good."

Two months shy of the tenth anniversary of Max's death, the parties resolved the litigation to their mutual satisfaction. All parties signed the non-disclosure agreement and Motion to Dismiss with Prejudice. The Motion to Dismiss was filed with the court. Although the non-disclosure agreement prohibits me discussing the terms, it doesn't prohibit my discussing the case or writing this book. Hey, it pays to have a great lawyer!

I called Tarian and he was pleased it was over. We reminisced about meeting so long ago in Starbucks and exchanging gift cards. I couldn't imagine making it through this case without him.

As we finished the conversation, he offered one last nugget. "Jo, JPMorgan listed Gary Stolbach as a possible cause of yours and the heirs' damages. Yet they didn't add Stolbach and his law firm as parties to the lawsuit. If the bank had, they could've tapped Stolbach and company to help pay the judgment. Why didn't they?"

I thought for a moment. "Well, I guess because Stolbach was the lawyer JPMorgan hired to represent it on another estate it was administering. I can't imagine it would be smart letting word get out to those heirs about Stolbach's work in my case."

"Okay, what else?"

"Maybe he still refers rich clients to JPMorgan?"

Tarian sighed. "There's a time when every teacher must set his apprentice free. I can see we've reached that point." He hesitated, his voice heavy with emotion. "The stick is straight, yet in the water it appears to bend. Now you understand why. So long, Grasshopper."

And with that, Tarian hung up.

It was early December, 2019. With my case over, I loaded up the records—34 boxes—and sent them to storage. For no reason, I sat down one afternoon and added up the carnage. Based on the complaint I filed on September 21, 2011, the judges in this case had held 140 hearings in person or telephonically, including the trial. More than 240 motions had been filed. JPMorgan sure didn't understand the words "Independent Administrator."

My final cost for all the lawyers was more than $7.3 million. Think there's any justice in the justice system?

Think again.

And you'd better be prepared to go up against Godzilla to get a sliver of it.

AFTER ALL THIS and seeing what had happened to the beneficiaries of the STS Trust, Burns Clark Dailey Trust, Mosh Trust, and Estate of Johnny Fisher, I realized that having trusts was not a bed of roses. A trust allows a middleman (trustee) to come between money bequeathed and my intended beneficiary. And the trustee has absolutely no supervision. If the trustee injures you, your only choice is a costly lawsuit. This lawsuit allows the trustee to drain the assets—*your* assets—in order to pay their attorney. If you win, there might be nothing left. See *Bleak House*.

I immediately hired Mike Graham to rewrite my will. After explaining all this new information I'd found, I eliminated all the trusts and made them straight bequeaths. If my beneficiaries spend all their inheritance, well, too bad. At least they received 100% of it. There was no way I'd leave them with potentially costly and destructive lawsuits.

WITH THE LITIGATION over, I spent more time at home. At least once a week, depending on the weather, I took Millie out to the backyard, spread out a blanket, and napped under the peach tree. Both of us found some much-needed deep sleep.

Sometimes, I'd twitch and wake up Millie. Other days, she'd bark in her sleep, waking me up. We were quite a pair.

It was a warm Saturday morning. I sat under the peach tree cradling a bowl of thick oatmeal topped with raisins, yogurt, and honey in one hand and a slab of cranberry and pecan bread in the other. I was enjoying life.

Millie lounged on the blanket between my legs, soaking up the sun's rays. By happenstance, my eyes looked up and spotted a troubling sight. A stain was spreading up the tree. Startled, I called Matt, an arborist. He promised he'd come right over and check it out.

Four hours later, Matt stood next to the peach tree, inspecting the stain. Like the JPMorgan jury, it didn't take him long to render a verdict.

"It's a fungus. This tree must be taken down right away."

"Why?" I asked, distraught that the last vestige of Max would disappear.

"If it spreads to those," he said, pointing to two large oak trees, "you could lose them too."

"Oh no," I said, fighting back the tears.

"When a tree gets old, they're more vulnerable to disease and insects. I can tell this tree has seen its share of battles."

You don't know how right you are, I thought to myself.

At 5:00, just as the afternoon light was fading, the tree men arrived. Jose, the foreman, stopped his man with a chainsaw so I could talk to the tree. He didn't seem surprised at my request.

I went to the tree and hugged its six-inch-diameter trunk. Tears fell on the bark. "Max, your wonderful peach tree covered me with shade in the summer. The peaches got better each year. This tree was a comfort when I needed it. And a place to sleep when I couldn't find any.

"We won a $2 billion verdict against JPMorgan Chase. I'm sure it wasn't like you planned, but it worked out, though it was my fault for trusting that bank. God help other widows." I looked at Jack, who stood next to the tree men and knew well enough to let me be.

"Max, I still have some life left, so I'm finally letting go. It's time for me to move on. I hope to see you one day and tell you all about what happened."

I turned to walk to the patio but noticed something. "Oh, and Max, JPMorgan Chase never did reimburse me for the roof like Kal Grant promised, but the jury took care of it in their verdict."

I stood off to the side with tears streaming down my cheeks as the man with a chainsaw cut through the trunk in barely a few seconds. When the tree fell, another man caught it. Peach trees aren't very big.

As they disappeared, dragging Max's peach tree behind them, Jack put his arm around me. "I guess it's just you and me now," he said.

"And Millie too," I added, sobbing.

"And Millie too," Jack repeated. "Goodbye, litigation tree."

I put my arm around him and went inside. After the door was closed, I lingered there, staring back at the stump.

Max's tree had helped me through nine years of torture. Now that the case was over, he knew it was time to leave me in peace.

Goodbye, Max.

A WEEK LATER, Jack asked me what I wanted to do now.

"I'm going to finish my book about this nightmare, tell everyone what happened to me. Perhaps I can save one soul from going through this hell."

Jack nodded. "Good idea. It should be called *Rest in Peace. Robbed in Probate*. It might even make a great miniseries."

It just might.

> *You'll have a new motto and soon it will be,*
> *Posted in breakrooms for all you to see.*
> *Estate Departments seeking widows to screw.*
> *Just make damn sure she's not an I.T. Guru.*
> —*The Bank's Lesson* by Jack Hooper

> *"The Firm's legal expense was $1.1 billion… for the year ended December 31, 2020."*
> —JPMorgan Chase Bank, N.A.
> 2020 Annual Report

Suggested Reading

Note: All the material below is linked to on my website: www.RIPHopper.com.

For *D Magazine's* article on the case and verdict written by Joseph Guinto with photographs by Jill Broussard in the January 2018 edition, https://www.dmagazine.com/publications/d-magazine/2018/january/jo-hopper-jpmorgan-chase-lawsuit/.

During my litigation, I engaged Gerry Meyer. Even though he was removed due to possible conflict of interests, his blog, http://lawprofessors.typepad.com/trusts_estates_prof/, provided me invaluable insight and ammunition in the world of probate. I highly recommend checking out his blog.

Before you go to war yourself, I strongly suggest you check out Russell J. Fishkind's *Probate Wars of the Rich and Famous: An Insider's Guide to Estate Planning and Probate Litigation.* https://tinyurl.com/4rpzjbpb Mr. Fishkind lists six recurring fact patterns that will universally spark a probate fire. When I read his book, I knew what lay ahead because we had five out of the six fact patterns present. I wish Max and I had read this book before he died. At least I have the information now.

Another interesting article that was a big help to me was "Restoring Hope for Heirs Property Owners: The Uniform Partition of Heirs Property Act" by Thomas Mitchell and the American Bar Association, https://tinyurl.com/y44nw28r. It covers how poor people lose their property. And it's easily readable.

Continuing with the theme of frightening you, read "Dishonest Executors Can Devastate Your Estate" by Mitchells Solicitors, https://tinyurl.com/yxbyxvru. It's British, but you'll see how it applies across the pond.

To read about another JPMorgan lawsuit loss involving a 94-year-old widow, Beverley Schottenstein, see Nanny's War, https://cathyschotten stein.com/media/ written by Beverley's granddaughter Cathy Schottenstein. HBO Max has optioned the story for future development.

For a documentary on the legal system in Texas that will make you seriously sick (and it spills the names of lawyers, law firms, and judges), you must absolutely watch *The Patent Scam* (2017) by Austin Meyer. Right now, it's on Amazon Prime. Maybe one day we will have some reform. Or maybe not. Austin's movie strategy for dealing with a lawsuit and wrongdoing may be the only way we can defend ourselves. https://www.thepatentscam.com/austin-meyer

If you want to be frightened at how much power the courts and banks have over your life, read *A Breach of Trust* by Susan Hodges, https://tinyurl.com/y34qhcrb. It's a great read!

For a nice rundown of the sins from the original J.P. Morgan to today's corporate version, see *JP Morgan and Electric Power: 100 Years of Misconduct* by The Global Critical Media Literacy Project Writing Team on May 10, 2013. I had no idea J.P. Morgan, the man, had been involved in a war over the form of electricity we currently receive in our homes and businesses. He certainly understood how to use litigation costs to beat an opponent. https://gcml.org/jp-morgan-electric-power-100-years-misconduct/

Poems

Beast In the Forest
by Jack Hooper

MY PRAYER TO THE JURY

All of the city, and countryside,
All that you see, far and wide.
It changes hands at a rapid rate,
Sooner or later, through probate.
This great forest, the innocent pass through.
No way to know what's waiting for you.
A devastating loss. Then a jungle of beast.
Pretending to help, but wanting to eat.
A beast has no morals, no fear of sin.
Less leaves the woods than what goes in.
Regaining your senses, always too late.
Lies and deception, as you've taken the bait.
Those working hard, who play by the rules,
Find themselves being taken for fools.
It takes all you have left to expose the creature.
Then pray for help to render him weaker.
Without power, to punish or kill,
Just expose the monster to society's will.
That rarely happens. He's adapted too well.
He knows when to climb, and when to repel.
The animal's game in his place of birth.
Either you win, or he eats you first.
You think it rare, but it's what they do.
The forest is full and waiting for you.
All I hold dear, I have invested.
For you to hear, is all I've requested.
My duty fulfilled, I can do no more.
It's up to you to settle the score.
You decide, give me justice or don't.
I know for sure the monster won't.

Without a Will
by Jack Hooper

I lost my husband. He had no will.
The big bank said, there'd be no bill.
If I'd just sign, and hand things over,
I could rest in fields of clover.
Divide by two and get me out.
Professionalism, I should not doubt.
Not an heir, nor beneficiary.
Half-owner status I carry.
Nothing from him is left to me,
Except to live in our house for free.
Two years I gave them, all they ask.
I wound up doing the entire task.
My life's a crime scene, not to touch.
All this time, they haven't done much.
Then I find they've turned about,
From my home, they'd throw me out.
Now they say, it's complicated.
To the beneficiaries, they're dedicated.
Suddenly the law, they don't know.
An expensive trip to court we go.
Answers is what they would provide.
Such incompetence, they can't hide.
Can't add or divide. No skills to act.
All they know is how to subtract.
Probate judge, the law he don't know.
Reverses himself, guessing what's so.
My, how things got out of hand,
Where's the justice in this land?
Now in appeals, the mighty foe.
Only defense is judge didn't know.
All they've said and all they've done,
Conclusion you reach could only be one.
All you experts, the law should be clear.
One lone widow screams in your ear.
Do what you said. Give me my half.
To your defense, a jury will laugh.

Are You My Hound?
by Jack Hooper

Are you my hound, or am I your person.
Were we happier unfound? Has our life worsened?
We both had strife, each in deep need.
I in legal fight, you with puppies to feed.
Food and shelter the world provides, to you I advance.
Love and trust the world hides, you bestow with just a glance.
So who owns who? Which way can it be?
Do I own you? Or you own me?
Whoever owns who, it matters not.
Together we two, are all that we got.

My Baby
by Jack Hooper

My baby's a fighter, not easy to bluff.
They tried to take her, but they ain't got enough.
Can't break her spirit. Can't beat her down.
Too bad for them, she's back for another round.
What drives this woman to more than it's worth?
What keeps her going? What force on this earth?
The answer's so simple, the old people know.
It's all in our raising, long years ago.
When we followed the law, don't claim it's not fair.
Unorthodox thinking, no one would dare.
Courts can't find fair. They just ain't that smart.
Only the Lord knows what's in your heart.
So the rules are wrote down before things begin,
Not to be changed until it all ends.
What my gal learned from her farm girl raising,
It's not that complicated, but the simple she's praising.
What drives these people? No need for all this.
What life lesson? Is it love that they miss?
If they'd be honest, but so far they won't.
She cares about people, and they just don't.

The Bank's Lesson
by Jack Hooper

At last family gathered in court to find out,
Show Jo and the world what this was about.
Court takes a while to get to the truth.
This conflict started back in Jo's youth.
Untraceable assets from forty years ago?
If untraceable sir, how would she know?
The $5 million you want, and assets you seek,
Are a pretty high price for pinching a child's cheek.
Of the coins you can't find and have so much doubt,
The statute of limitations six times has run out!
Jo's lock box keys. Could those be the reasons?
We've spent eight million bucks and six football seasons.
Robbing widows is a game, it's how JP makes money.
But I want you to know to Jo it's not funny.
You'll have a new motto and soon it will be,
Posted in breakrooms for all you to see.
Estate Departments seeking widows to screw.
Just make damn sure she's not an IT guru.

Scoundrels Steal Retirement Years
by Jack Hooper

Who are these scoundrels who steal golden years?
With promises boundless to a widow in tears.
No heart. No soul. No compassion inside.
No respect for the law that's there as a guide.
What drives the wicked for more than they need?
How'd society produce such a poisonous breed?
A foul seed created this beast.
Without remorse, its young it eats.
They learn the law to discover its limit.
Use it against you while hiding within it.
Connivers of weak, making their rounds.
Once in a while they step out of bounds.
They take a bite, but to their surprise,
This one bites back. They've tears in their eyes.
"Son of bitch, I need to unhitch!
This widow's not funny. This ain't worth the money!"
Perhaps the courts will make them quit.
Or crossing the street, they'll get hit.
These scoundrels found dead in the road smashed flat.
Not even a skid mark in front of a pole cat.

She Sits Alone
by Jack Hooper

He would be great with a little fix.
She put her skills into the mix.
Forfeiting childbirth and career,
She took her place in the rear.
His family would be her own.
His position would be the throne.
Behind the scene, day and night,
She made everything turn out right.
He was smart but spots were blind.
She filled them all with grace and
    kind.
So hard to see what role she'd play.
No way to measure. No one to say.
Family and court underestimate,
How hard it is, her wealth to take.
Made-up laws. Confuse the issue.
Impose their will, made need for
    tissue.
Her end was planned and charity
    picked.
Put on delay, their butt she'd kick.
She backed off from suicide,
For a chance to tan their hide.
'Cause if she doesn't it won't end.
On more widows they will descend.
She sits alone three long years.
Reads their lies through her tears.
When greed and corruption brings
    them pain instead,
They double down. They wish her
    dead.
Who defeats such a mighty foe?
Who can tell? Who could know?

She sits alone making Tacky Bobs,
In the place of her first sobs.
While they drink her wine and plan
    to steal,
She sits alone, no time to heal.
When she was young, everyone
    knew,
The rule of law is what you do.
So when they came, and all agreed,
She felt quite sure they'll fill her
    need.
But their plan was to make her poor.
The truth was what she heard no
    more.
She sits alone and wonders why,
The law's so easy. Why not comply?
Divide by two, give half to me.
That's all you do. Can't you see?
Drive the wedge, divide and conquer,
With all the power of the monster.
She sits alone and takes their heat.
But they find no fault to aid her
    defeat.
She seemed so helpless, such easy
    prey.
It's too late now to back away.
Deeper and deeper, away from the
    truth.
Bound up in lies, they can't get loose.
Yet the day finally comes when the
    jury sees,
And brings the monster to its knees.

Discussion Questions

Book Clubs (General Questions)

1. What surprised you about this book?
2. Do you and your spouse have an executed will? Why or why not?
3. After reading this book, will you draft or update your will?
4. Do you know people who died and had an executed will and still had a lawsuit?
5. Do you live in a community property state? What does community property mean?
6. Have you ever been involved in a probate matter or lawsuit? How did it go?
7. When you receive a jury summons, do you try to get out of serving? Why? Should you?
8. Would you hire any of the lawyers in the book? If so, which ones?
9. Do you feel that the bank or Jamie Dimon, Chairman and CEO of JPMorgan Chase Bank, N.A., care about customers like Jo Hopper? If so, why did they treat her like that?
10. How do you feel about large jury verdicts? Without them, what incentive do companies have to follow the law?
11. Should there be a cap on jury verdicts? Why or why not?
12. How did you feel about the attorneys' hourly rates being charged? Could you afford those?
13. What did you learn from this book and Jo Hopper's experience that you didn't know before?
14. How do you think banks select outside lawyers to assist them in probate and trust matters? What criteria do they use?

Book Clubs (Detailed Questions)

1. List everything Jo Hopper did wrong. Have you done any of these things?
2. Did you understand the term "intestate"? Did you understand property division under intestate laws of Texas?
3. Are you part of a blended family? Describe your relationship with your step-family members.
4. In your state, how can you transfer property without going through probate? Cars? Houses? Bank accounts? Financial assets?
5. Do you think "loser pay" (i.e., the losing side in a lawsuit pays the attorney's fees for the winning side) is something we should add to our justice system? Do you think "loser pay" would affect the number of lawsuits filed? Would it keep poor people from suing?
6. In August of 2011, JPMorgan wanted Jo Hopper and the heirs to agree and sign a letter releasing JPMorgan of liability in exchange for JPMorgan releasing the property to the parties. They did not sign those documents. Should they have? Is it fair for JPMorgan to make such an offer?
7. If you saw a house for sale that had a someone living in it for the remainder of their life, how much discount would you need off the appraised value before buying it? Before making an offer, what information on the property or the person would you like to see? Would you want the person's medical records? Are you familiar with the term "viaticals"?
8. What did you think of the gaslighting storyline in the book? Have you seen the 1944 movie? Do you understand the concept of gaslighting? Have you personally experienced it?
9. What does "cool the mark" mean? Have you been a victim where someone "cooled" you?
10. Do you think lawyers run up legal bills to extend a case or break a person financially? If so, why do the judges allow it?
11. Did you understand the concept and purpose of a "Chinese Wall" at JPMorgan Chase? If not, can someone in your group explain it?

12. Are you aware the tort cap for punitive damages in Texas is $750,000 regardless of the size of the company? What is the cap in your state? Is it fair to have a cap on punitive damages? Should the cap be graduated like income tax (i.e., based on the value of the company) rather than one size fits all?

13. How did you feel when paid experts contradicted each other on the same topic? Should we make changes in the legal system regarding expert witnesses? Should a master database be created that lists every case an expert witness testifies in, along with their expert report, and make it available for the public or lawyers to read?

14. Would you have pursued the case as Jo Hopper did? Or would you have given up and allowed JPMorgan Chase Bank, N.A. to sell your home?

15. Do you think NDAs (Non-Disclosure Agreements) are proper in our society? Should they be voided? Should people or companies be able to cover up misdeeds with NDAs? Should people or companies be required to disclose how many NDAs they have signed and to whom they have given them?

16. Have you had any experience with private banking? Is it another way to separate the haves from the have nots? Does it feel discriminatory to you?

17. How many family members of decedents do you think JPMorgan Chase Bank, N.A. has used the same "Jo Hopper" tactics against? Do you know of any?

18. Do you know of anyone who worked at JPMorgan Chase Bank, N.A.? What was their experience with estates? With customers trying to remove money? With cross-selling?

19. Did you understand what "cross-selling" is? Is cross-selling by banks bad? Why or why not?

20. Before reading this book, if you were a current customer of JPMorgan Chase, N.A., are you going to remain a customer? If so, why?

About the Author

I'm still alive—fighting to protect widows from probate abuse. I can be reached at Jo@RIPHopper.com. Visit my website at www.RIPHopper.com.

"Death is not the end. There remains the litigation over the estate."

Ambrose Pierce (1842–1914)
American Writer and Journalist